SICILY

THE ROUGH GUIDE

Local Novel: Lampdusa - The Leopard.

History - John Julius Norridge (Duff Cooper son)

THE ROUGH GUIDES

OTHER AVAILABLE ROUGH GUIDES

PERU, MOROCCO, TUNISIA, KENYA, CHINA, FRANCE, GREECE, SPAIN, PORTUGAL, EASTERN EUROPE, SCANDINAVIA, YUGOSLAVIA, BRITTANY & NORMANDY, CRETE, MEXICO, NEW YORK, PARIS AND AMSTERDAM.

FORTHCOMING TITLES INCLUDE

ITALY, VENICE, GERMANY, HUNGARY, IRELAND, ISRAEL AND CALIFORNIA

ROUGH GUIDE CREDITS

Series Editor: Mark Ellingham
Editorial: Martin Dunford, John Fisher, Jack Holland
Production: Susanne Hillen
Typesetting: Greg Ward
Design: Andrew Oliver

Thanks for help in compiling this book to Clare Bayley, Graeme Jones, Paul Duncan, Peter Glencross, David Lodge, Anne-Marie Barrett, the Italian State Tourist Office; in Sicily we're grateful to Agata Scamporrino, Flavia Ruggeri and family, the Taormina AAST, Rosella Iacone and Ines de Natale; for eating above and beyond the call of duty, thanks to Joanna, Jean and Ken Brown and Matt Dunkley; for some sound production work, to Greg Ward and Susanne Hillen; for copy-editing to Alison Cowan; for help and encouragement to Mark Ellingham; for enduring every page, special thanks to Martin Dunford. And above all, for love, support and sharpening the pencils, a million thanks to Helen Lee and Josephine Morgan . . . and to Quincy.

First published 1989 by
Harrap-Columbus, 19–23 Ludgate Hill, London EC4M 7PD.

Typeset in Linotron Univers and Century Old Style.
Printed in the United Kingdom by Cox & Wyman Ltd. (Reading).

British Library of Congress Cataloguing in Publication Data
Andrews, Robert
  Sicily : the rough guide
  Italy. Sicily. Visitors' guides
  I. Title II. Brown, Jules

914.5'804928

ISBN 0–7471–0125–6

SICILY

THE ROUGH GUIDE

WRITTEN AND RESEARCHED BY

ROBERT ANDREWS AND JULES BROWN

Edited by Martin Dunford

HARRAP COLUMBUS · LONDON

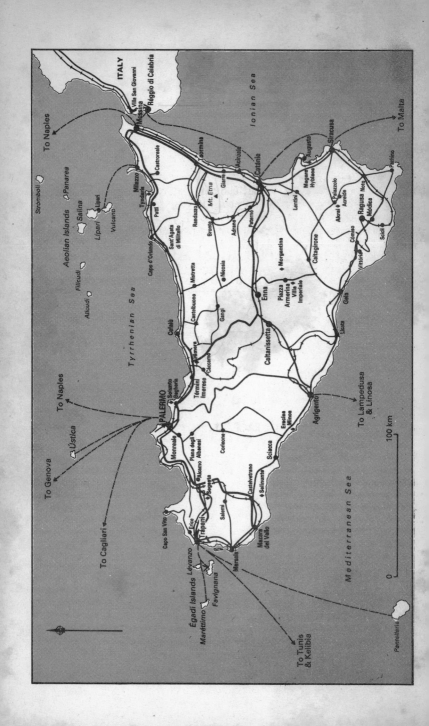

CONTENTS

Introduction vi

INTRODUCTION

*God first made the world
and then he made the Straits of Messina
to separate men from madmen*

Sicilian proverb

At the centre of the Mediterranean, but on the periphery of Europe, **Sicily** is a quite distinct entity from the rest of Italy. Although just three kilometres away across the water, it's much further away in appearance, feel and culture. A hybrid Sicilian language is still widely spoken, and many place-names are tinged with the Arabic that was once in wide use on the island; the food is noticeably different, spicier and with more emphasis on fish, fruit and vegetables; while the flora echoes the shift south – oranges, lemons, olives, almonds and palms are ubiquitous. The nature of day-to-day living is somehow different here, too, experienced outdoors with an exuberance that is almost tropical, and reflected in numerous traditional festivals and processions that take place around the island throughout the year.

There's certainly an immediately separate quality in the **people**, who see themselves as Sicilians first – and Italians a very firm second. The island's strategic importance meant it was held as a colony by some of the richest civilisations in the western world – from the Arabs to the Normans to the Spaniards – who looted Sicily mercilessly and made it the subject of countless foreign wars, leaving it with many fine monuments but little economic independence. Hundreds of years of oppression have bred insularity and resentment, as well as poverty, and the island was probably the most reluctantly unified Italian region in the last century, Sicilians almost instinctively suspicious of the intentions of Rome. Even today, relations with the mainland are often strained, for many here illustrated every time they look at a map to see the island being kicked – the perpetual football.

And Sicilians do have a point. There's much that hasn't changed since Unification, and **this century** has brought a whole host of new problems, with mass-emigration, both to the mainland and abroad, a high level of crime, and the continuing marginalisation of the island in the Italian political mainstream. Even modernisation has brought associated ills. Pockets of the island have been devastated by a tide of bleak construction and disfiguring industry, and although Sicily does now, at last, have some degree of autonomy, with its own parliament and president, little has really been done to tackle the island's more deep-rooted problems: poverty is still endemic, and there's an almost feudal attitude to business and commerce. Both EEC and central government aid continues to pour in, but much has been siphoned off by organised crime, which – in the west of the island at least, and in spite of the much-publicised Mafia trials – is as widespread as it ever was.

However, this is just the background, and the island's appeal for travellers is astonishingly wide-ranging. You'd do well to investigate the life – and monuments – of **Palermo**, one of Italy's most visually striking and energetic cities; and the second city of **Catania**, where you may well arrive, has its charms. But the chief pleasure is in the **landscape**: much of the island is mountainous, making for some of Italy's most dramatic scenery and providing one of its most beautiful rugged coastlines. The graceful cone of **Mount Etna**, Europe's largest volcano, dominates the east of the island, easily the most memorable of Sicily's natural sights; the northern **Monti Madonie** offer strenuous walking country; or there's the simple, isolated grandeur of the **interior** – the island's most sparsely populated, and most undiscovered, region. The **coast** is home to much of the island's life and action, with any number of resorts along its northern and eastern stretches, from lively sun-worshippers' haunts like **Taormina** and **Cefalù** to simple fishing villages fronted by long beaches – out of season, at least, amazingly uncrowded. And for real solitude, there are Sicily's **outlying islands**, where the sea is as clean as you'll find anywhere in the Mediterranean and you truly feel you're on the edge of Europe.

Sicily's diverse history has also left it with what is for many a surprising surfeit of **archaeological remains**. The island was an important power-base during the Hellenistic period and the island's Greek relics, especially, are superb: most spectacularly at **Agrigento**, **Selinunte**, **Siracusa** and a host of remoter sites dotted around the countryside which stand comparison with any of the ruins in Greece itself – and are for the most part a good deal less crowded. There are also well-preserved mosaics at **Piazza Armerina** which recall the lavish trappings of Sicily's Roman governors. In terms of later architecture, too, the island is remarkably varied, the **Arab** and **Norman** elements of its history vividly manifest, particularly on the west and north coasts, and **Baroque architecture** showing its face in the elegantly restrained cities of the south east: **Catania**, **Noto**, and **Módica** – planned new towns rebuilt after the mighty 17C earthquake.

When to go

Any of these places can be extremely uncomfortable to visit at the height of a Sicilian summer, when the dusty *sirocco* winds blow in from North Africa, and your choice of **when to go** should take this into consideration. In **July and August**, you'll roast – and probably in the company of tens of thousands of other tourists all jostling for space on the beaches and in the museums and archaeological sites. Hotel availability will be much reduced and prices will often be higher in response to the demand. If you want the heat but not the crowds, there's no reason why you shouldn't go in June or September, while swimming is possible right into November, the season starting again in April. **Spring** is the optimum time to come, though, and it arrives early: the almond blossom flowers in February and there are fresh strawberries in April, while Sicily is famous for the exuberance of its spring flowers. **Easter** is a major celebration, a good time to see some of the more traditional festivals, like the events at Trápani, Érice and Piana degli Albanesi, though again they'll all be over-subscribed with visitors. **Winter** is mild by northern European standards and is a nice time to be here, at least on the coast, where the skies stay clear and life continues to be lived very much outdoors. The interior on the other hand, especially around Enna, can get snowed under. You can ski south of Cefalù, at Piano Battáglia, or on Mount Etna, though elsewhere in the interior it simply rains.

Average daytime temperatures °C		
	Palermo	Taormina
January	10.3	11
February	10.4	10.6
March	13	13.1
April	16.2	16.2
May	18.7	20.1
June	23	24.1
July	25.3	27.1
August	25.1	27.1
September	23.2	23.7
October	19.9	20
November	16.8	16
December	12.6	12.6

PART ONE

THE
BASICS

GETTING THERE

Much the easiest way to get to Sicily is to fly, and prices for charter flights compare well with the long, overland rail option. Still, there are advantages to travelling by train, not least that you'll run the length of Italy and be able to stop off on the way.

BY PLANE

Direct flights take around 2½ hours from London either to Catania, in the east of the island, or Palermo in the west. The only **direct scheduled service** is with *British Island Airways*, roughly three times weekly in winter (Oct to May), five times weekly in summer (June to Sept), to either Catania or Palermo: the standard summer **excursion** return fare to each is £225 (winter £195), valid for one month; or there's a **PEX** summer return fare of £215 (£199 if you travel mid-week), for which you have to fix a return date and stay at least one Sunday night abroad: it's valid for a maximum of three months and 50% of the cost is non-refundable if you change/cancel your booking before you leave. PEX fares are cheaper still in winter, from £190 (£175 mid-week); and there are also special year-round one-way fares, cheapest the **Eurobudget** fare at £139.

The **other scheduled options** are less attractive and more expensive. *British Airways*

and *Alitalia* flights don't travel direct, and the best you can do is fly to Rome and change there for Sicily: current PEX fares are around £226 return to Rome, with the internal leg on to either Catania or Palermo around another £114 return; total journey time anything up to six hours, depending on how long you have to wait for your connecting internal flight. On the plus side, there's a youth/student discount of 25% off normal fares for anyone under 26, and scheduled services to Rome are very frequent throughout the year.

Direct **charter** flights are a better bargain, though you'd be advised to book some weeks in advance in peak season. *Pegasus Holidays, Island Sun* and *Pilgrim Air* (see *Packages,* p.6, for addresses) all offer daily summer departures from London, down to once or twice a week in the winter, and current high-season prices work out around £139–149 return to Catania or Palermo. You'll often get flights even cheaper than this by going to a specialist **agent** – last summer's bargains started at £89 return to Catania or Palermo. There are usually dozens of sources: look in the classified sections in the Sunday newspapers (*The Sunday Times* especially) and, if you live in London, *Time Out* magazine or the *Evening Standard*. Always worth a ring for specifically Sicilian charters are *Inter-Air, Rapid Air Travel Service, CTS Travel, Mundus Air Travel* and *Italflights* (for addresses see below), *Citalia* (see *Packages,* p.6), and the youth/student specialists *STA* and *London Student Travel*.

Some agents and operators can sell you an '**open-jaw**' return, flying to Catania and returning from Palermo, or vice versa – a good idea if you want to make your way across the island (or to Sicily from somewhere else in Italy), and generally no more expensive than a standard charter return. Consider a **package deal** (see below) too, which takes care of flights and accommodation for an all-in price.

It may also be worth looking at flights to **other destinations**: Naples is around seven hours by train and ferry from Messina; Lamézia (in Calabria: summer charters only) is just two hours from Messina; and even Malta (see p.309) is only five hours by ferry from Siracusa, seven from Catania.

AIRLINES AND AGENCIES

Alitalia, 205 Holland Park Avenue, London W11 (☎01-745 8200); 27 Piccadilly, London W1 (☎ 01-745 8286).

British Airways, 75 Regent Street, London W1 (☎01-897 4000).

British Island Airways, Island House, Church Road, Lowfield Heath, Crawley, West Sussex (☎0293-545 900).

CTS Travel, 33 Windmill Street, London W1 (☎01-636 5915/6).

Inter-Air, Liberty House, 222 Regent Street, London W1 (☎01-439 6633).

Italflights, 125 High Holborn, London WC1 (☎01-405 6771).

London Student Travel, 52 Grosvenor Gardens, London SW1 (☎01-730 3402).

Mundus Air Travel, 5 Peter Street, London W1 (☎01-437 2272/437 7387/8).

Rapid Air Travel Service, London House, 26–40 Kensington High Street, London W8 (☎01-937 6042).

STA Travel, 86 Old Brompton Road, London SW7 (☎01-581 8233).

BY TRAIN

It can be a real endurance test reaching Sicily by **train**: the 2672km journey from London to Messina – across the Channel, through France and down the length of Italy – is scheduled to take 42 hours, though long delays on the Italian stretch are not uncommon. You'll need to change trains at least once, too, depending on which of the three possible routes you take. It's well worth **reserving** a **seat** (currently £1.50 for each separate train, meaning £3 or £4.50 for the whole journey), if not a **couchette bed** (around £8 on each train) for at least part of the journey – and you should do both well in advance.

Ordinary **return fares**, on the fastest route (via Paris and Modane, avoiding Switzerland), are currently around £170 to Palermo, Messina or Siracusa; all tickets valid for two months. Under 26s can buy *BIJ* train tickets through *Eurotrain* or *Transalpino*, which give up to 50% discounts on

normal fares and allow as many stopovers as you like over a two-month period; fares are currently around £148 return to the main cities. Any of these tickets are available at offices in Victoria Station, London (from where all the trains depart), youth/student agents or direct from *Eurotrain* or *Transalpino* (addresses below). Under 26s travelling from **outside London** can also arrange *BIJ* add-on fares – eg £23.90 return from Manchester – or, alternatively, qualify for reduced price tickets if they join the train at the Channel ports.

Given these prices, under 26s might consider investing in an *InterRail* pass, which costs £145, is valid for one month's unlimited rail travel throughout Europe, and gives discounts on cross-Channel services – though it's not a lot of help once you've arrived, see *Getting Around*, p.10. It's available from British Rail stations and youth/student travel agencies, and you need to have been resident in Europe for at least six months to qualify for one.

RAIL TICKET OFFICES

British Rail European Travel Centre, Victoria Station, London SW1 (☎01-834 2345).

Eurotrain, 52 Grosvenor Gardens, London SW1 (☎ 01-730 8518).

Transalpino, 71–75 Buckingham Palace Road, London SW1 (☎01-834 9656).

BY COACH

Frankly, it's difficult to see why you would want to subject yourself to the rigours of getting to Sicily by **coach**, particularly since there isn't even a direct service from London. You have to use the *National Express Eurolines* (☎01-730 0202) service from London to Rome (£118 return, £108.50 for under 25s and students); and then take the daily *SAIS* bus from there to Messina/Catania/Siracusa (leaves 7.30am, a 12hr trip), or to Messina/Palermo (leaves 7.45am, 13hr). The *SAIS* terminal in Rome is at piazza della Repubblica 62 (☎06-475.4006), near the main Términi railway station, and a one-way ticket to Siracusa costs L65,000, L70,000 to Palermo, including lunch – L115,000 return. About the only advantage of this route is that you are guaranteed a seat all the way to Sicily.

BY CAR/HITCHING: THE FERRIES

There's no one fixed route to Sicily if you're travelling under your own steam. The best cross-Channel options for most drivers and hitchers will be the standard **ferry/hovercraft** links between Dover and Calais or Boulogne (with *Hoverspeed*, *P&O* or *Sealink*), Folkestone and Boulogne (*Sealink*), or Ramsgate and Dunkerque (*Sally Lines*); the longest haul – though a fairly comfortable ride – is the drive/hitch south through France and Italy. From the France-Italy border, with a bit of luck, it's possible to reach the Straits of Messina in a long day if you keep on the autostradas. The shortest crossing over the Straits is from Villa San Giovanni **by ferry**; or, fifteen minutes further south – at the end of the motorway – **ferries and hydrofoils** leave from Réggio di Calabria. Something to note is that driving in Italy is more expensive than just about anywhere else in Europe. On top of the inflated petrol prices (around 60p/L1300 for a litre), it'll cost around another £25 per car to use the toll motorways between the French border and Naples, after which it's free until you reach Sicily – both things that make the earlier sea-crossings from the Italian mainland (see below) financially more attractive.

CROSSING THE STRAITS OF MESSINA

Drivers buy their **tickets** at kiosks on the way onto the ferry; foot passengers (most of whom are locals) just walk on and can usually avoid the occasional roving ticket collector. All prices given below are for one-way tickets; returns cost exactly double.

VILLA SAN GIOVANNI-MESSINA: with *FS* **car-ferries**, around 25 crossings per day, a 35-minute journey; first departure 2.30am, last departure 10.40pm; L700 per person, cars from L12,700 (two passengers travel free): with *Caronte* **car-ferries**, crossings every 20 minutes (fewer throughout the night), a 35-minute journey; L500 per person, cars from L15,000.

RÉGGIO DI CALABRIA-MESSINA: with *FS* **car-ferries**, around 10 crossings per day; first departure 5.05am, last departure 9.55pm; L700 per person, cars from L12,700 (two passengers travel free): with *SNAV* **hydrofoil**, 13–18 departures daily except Sunday, a 20-minute journey; L4500 per person.

CROSSINGS FROM THE ITALIAN MAINLAND

There are a few options for those who want to cut the driving or train-journey time, using one of a number of earlier **ferry/hydrofoil crossings from the Italian mainland** to Sicily. These are:

GENOVA-PALERMO (with *Tirrenia* or *Grandi Traghetti*); 5 times weekly, journey 25hr, from L80,000 per person, cars from around L100,000.

LIVORNO-PALERMO (with *Grandi Traghetti*); 3 times weekly, journey 19hr, from L50,000 per person, cars from L94,000.

NAPLES-PALERMO (with *Tirrenia* or *SNAV*); 1 car-ferry daily, journey 10hr, from L48,000 per person, cars from L67,000. Hydrofoils run 3 times weekly, journey 5hr 20min.

NAPLES-CATANIA/SIRACUSA (with *Tirrenia*); 1 weekly, journey 15hr/19hr, from L44,000 per person. This service continues to Malta.

NAPLES-AEOLIAN ISLANDS/MILAZZO (with *Siremar* or *SNAV*); ferries 2–5 weekly, journey 7hr; hydrofoils daily in summer, journey 4–6hr.

CROSSING VIA CORSICA AND SARDINIA

If you have bags of time, you can even approach Sicily by travelling **via Corsica and Sardinia**. There are daily *Tirrenia* ferry services from Genova to northern Sardinia (Porto Torres; from L36,000 per person one-way), from where you can take the train to Cágliari for the weekly ferry-crossing to either Palermo or Trápani (from L26,000 per person one-way). Or, in summer, you could cross to Corsica first with *Corsica Ferries* (from La Spezia and Pisa; from L35,000 per person one-way), make the short crossing to Sardinia, and take the same ferry as above to Palermo.

FERRIES AND AGENCIES

Any travel agent can provide up-to-date schedules and make advance bookings (which in season, if you're driving, can be essential). Or contact the **ferry companies** direct: for the latest cross-Channel details ring the numbers below; for the Italian crossings, contact the companies or their agents and note that *Siremar* and *SNAV* only have offices in Italy.

Sally Lines, ☎01-409 2240.

Sealink, ☎01-834 8122.

P&O European Ferries, ☎01-734 4431.

Hoverspeed, ☎01-554 7061.

Grandi Traghetti, c/o *Associated Oceanic Agencies*, Eagle House, 109–110 Jermyn Street, London SW1 (☎01-930 5683).

Siremar, via Francesco Crispi 120, Palermo

(☎091-582.688); via dei Mille 57, Milazzo (☎090-928.6381).

SNAV, *Agenzia Demartour*, via Solferino 28–30, Rome (☎06-494.0777); Messina booking number ☎ 090-77.75.

Tirrenia Line, c/o *Serena Holidays*, 40–42 Kenway Road, London SW5 (☎01-373 6548).

Corsica Ferries, c/o *Serena Holidays*, see above.

PACKAGES

On the whole Sicily is not a cheap package destination, but it's always worth looking at **travel-plus-accommodation** package holidays, especially if you live some way from London. Many companies offer travel at rates as competitive as you could find on your own, and any travel agent can fill you in on all the latest offers. Most packages are to Taormina, the most chic resort, and to Cefalù, though you'll also see holidays in the Aeolian Islands, and special tours of the major historical sights, which take in overnight stops in several Sicilian towns.

It's obviously cheapest to go **out of season**, something we'd recommend anyway as the resorts and sights are much less crowded, and the weather is often warm enough to swim: in Cefalù, you could get something for as little as around £160 for a week's bed and breakfast accommodation; Taormina is more likely to cost

you from around £219 for the same. A week's coach tour of the island (with all meals) is going to be substantially more, from around £359. In **high season** (Easter, July and August), all these prices shoot up considerably, and you can expect to pay around £350–450 for a week's half-board in Taormina, though your travel agent might come up with good, last-minute deals. Some operators organise **specialist holidays** to Sicily, particularly walking tours, and art and archaeology holidays, but they don't come cheaply either: Accommodation, food, local transport and the services of a guide are nearly always included, and a week's half-board holiday can cost from £500 per person, full-board around £700.

If you want to hire a car in Sicily, it's well worth checking with tour operators before you leave as some **fly/drive deals** work out very cheaply; best prices seem to be with *Island Sun*. See p.12 for more car-hire details.

SPECIALIST OPERATORS

Aeolian Friends, 6 Palace Street, London SW1 (☎01-834 7651). For self-catering and other holidays in the Aeolian Islands; room reservations even on the smallest islands.

Alternative Travel Group, 1–3 George Street, Oxford OX1 2AZ (☎0865-251195/6). Costly walking holidays in the Monti Madonie.

Citalia, 50–51 Conduit Street, London W1 (☎01-434 3844/686 5533). Packages to Taormina, island tours, self-catering holidays.

Island Sun, Island House, Church Road, Lowfield Heath, Crawley, West Sussex RH11 0PQ (☎0293-547300). Packages to Taormina, Cefalù, Palermo, the Aeolians, Capo d'Orlando, art and archaeology tours, fly/drive holidays.

Pegasus Holidays, 24a Earls Court Gardens, London SW5 (☎01-370 0555). Packages to Taormina and self-catering holidays.

Pilgrim Air, 44 Goodge Street, London W1 (☎01-436 3911). Palermo, Cefalù, island tours.

Quo Vadis, 243 Euston Road, London NW1 (☎01-387 6122). For Cefalù and island tours.

FROM EIRE

There are **no direct flights** from Eire to Sicily and you'll have to fly **to London** and pick up one of the services from there. Daily flights from Dublin to London are available with the airlines – or, better, the agents – listed below. Current under-26/student fares are IR£68 return, and there's an APEX fare which costs around the same; everyone pays a £5 airport surcharge. A second option is to buy a *BIJ* **train** ticket: the Dublin-Palermo run costs £212 return, uses the Rosslare-Le Havre crossing, and takes a massive 64 hours; tickets are valid for two months.

ADDRESSES IN IRELAND

Aer Lingus, 42 Grafton Street, Dublin 2 (☎01-794 764), or at Dublin airport (☎ 01-370 011). *Dan-Air*, no Dublin office but reservations on ☎01-428 311/417/831.

Ryan Air, College Park House, Nassau Street, Dublin 2 (☎01-797 444 or ☎01-770 444). *USIT*, 7 Angelsea Street, Dublin 2 (☎01-778 117)

FROM AUSTRALIA AND NEW ZEALAND

Coming from **Australia**, you can **fly direct** from Melbourne or Sydney via Rome to Catania or Palermo, and the price right now is around Aus$2270 return. From **New Zealand**, the best you can do is to pick up a flight to Rome from Auckland – currently from NZ$1080 return – and take an internal flight from there. Alternatively, for both countries, you might do best to get whatever deal you can **to London** and then pick up a charter flight to Sicily from there.

The best agent in both Australia and New Zealand is the long-established *STA Worldwide* who have offices at 1a Lee Street, Sydney 2000, Australia (☎02-212 1255), and 64 High Street (PO Box 4156), Auckland, New Zealand (☎9-390 458); as well as in Melbourne, Canberra, Perth and Wellington.

RED TAPE AND VISAS

British and other EC citizens can enter Sicily, and stay as long as they like, on production only of a valid passport. The temporary *British Visitor's Passport* (£7.50), available over the counter at post offices, is valid for one year. Citizens of Eire, Australia and New Zealand need only a valid passport, too, but are limited to stays of three months. All other nationals should consult the relevant embassies about visa requirements.

Legally, you're required to register with the police within three days of entering Italy, though if you're staying at a hotel this will be done for you. Following the recent scares about terrorism, some policemen have become more punctilious about this, though most would still be amazed at any attempt to register yourself down at the local police station while on holiday. If you're going to be living here for a while, you may as well do it; see p.28 for more details.

ITALIAN EMBASSIES AND CONSULATES

UK: 38 Eaton Place, London SW1 (☎01-235 9371); 6 Melville Crescent, Edinburgh 3 (☎031-226 3169); 79 Oxford Street, Manchester (☎061-228 7041).

EIRE: 12 Fitzwilliam Square, Dublin 2 (☎01-762 401).

AUSTRALIA: 6169 Macquarie St, Sydney 2000, NSW (☎02-278 442); 34 Anderson St, Yarra, Melbourne, Victoria (☎03-267 5744).

NEW ZEALAND: 34 Grant Road, Wellington (☎04-735 339).

COSTS, MONEY AND BANKS

Sicily isn't cheap, certainly compared to the other Mediterranean holiday spots. But neither is it as expensive as the rest of mainland Italy, and you'll find that food and accommodation especially are good value.

COSTS

If you're watching your budget – camping, hitching a little, buying some of your own food in the shops and markets – you could get by on as little as £7–8 a day; a more realistic **average daily budget** is around £18 a day; while on £25–30 a day you could be living pretty comfortably. Most basic things are inexpensive compared with Britain: a pizza and a beer costs around £2.50 just about everywhere, a full meal with wine under £8; buses and trains are very cheap and distances small; and hotel rooms in the cities start at around £7–10 double. It's the snacks and drinks that add up: eating ice-creams and crisps, drinking soft drinks or coffee, all costs around the same price (if not more) as in Britain. And if you sit down to do any of this, it'll cost twice as much.

Of course, these prices are subject to where and when you go, and whether you're alone. You'll pay a lot more in summer for rooms and food in the big resorts – Taormina, Cefalù, Siracusa and Érice; and more all year round on most of the offshore islands, particularly the Aeolians. The interior, too, is not as cheap as you might expect – because it's little visited, there's no competition and rarely a choice of places to stay and eat. **Out of season** you'll be able to negotiate lower accommodation prices in nearly all the small hotels and *pensioni*. However, **single accommodation** can be hard to come by: what there is tends to fill quickly and you'll often have to pay most of the price of a double room. There are no **reductions** or discounts for students or young people in Sicily: it's the one place where your *ISIC* card is no use at all; under 18s and over 65s, on the other hand, get into museums and archaeological sites free everywhere.

MONEY AND BANKS

The Italian unit of **money** is the *Lira* (plural *Lire*), always abbreviated as L: the rate right now is around L2300 to the pound sterling. You get notes for L1000, L2000, L5000, L10,000, L50,000 and L100,000; and coins for L50, L100, L200 and L500. Smaller denomination coins still float around and you might get given them as change – though a lot of places will give you sweets instead.

The easiest and safest way to carry your money is as **travellers' cheques**, available for a small commission (1% of the amount ordered) from any British high-street bank and some building societies, whether or not you have an account. You'll usually – though not always – pay a small commission, too, when you **exchange money** using travellers' cheques, around £1 a time. Alternatively, most banks can issue current account holders with a **Eurocheque card** and chequebook, with which you can get cash from the majority of banks in Sicily; you'll pay a few pounds service charge a year but usually no commission on transactions; or the major **credit cards** – *Visa* and *American Express* – are accepted in most places in return for goods or cash; *Access (Mastercard)* comes a very poor second, at least as far as getting cash advances from banks is concerned. It's an idea to have at least some Italian money for when you first arrive, and you can buy *Lire* in advance from British banks, but are limited to taking in no more than L400,000 in cash (around £170).

The main **banks** you'll see in Sicily are the *Banco di Sicilia*, the *Cassa di Risparmio* and the *Banca Nazionale di Lavoro*. **Banking hours** vary slightly from town to town, but generally banks are open Monday to Friday, 8.30am–1.20pm and

3–4pm. Outside these times you can change travellers' cheques and cash at large hotels, the two airports and some main railway stations. In Taormina and Cefalù banks stay open later in the summer, sometimes on Saturday as well; check the town and city *Listings* sections in the text.

HEALTH AND INSURANCE

EC nationals can take advantage of Italy's health services under the same terms as the residents of the country. You'll need form E111, which in theory you can get by applying on form SA30 by post, one month in advance, to any DHSS office in Britain. In practice it can often be issued over the counter at a main DHSS office (not an Unemployment Benefit office).

HEALTH PROBLEMS

If you need treatment, go to a **doctor** (*médico*); every town and village has one. Take your E111 with you: this should enable you to get free treatment and prescriptions for medicines at the local rate – about 10% of the price of the medicine. If you're looking for repeat medication, take any empty bottles or capsules with you to the doctors – the brand-names often differ.

An Italian **chemist** (*farmacia*) is well-qualified to give you advice on minor ailments, and to dispense prescriptions, and there's generally one open all night in the bigger towns and cities. They work on a rota system, and you should find the address of the one currently open on any *farmacia* door. If you get taken **seriously ill**, or involved in an accident, hunt out the nearest hospital and go to the *Pronto Soccorso* (casualty) section, or phone ☎113 and ask for *ospedale* or *ambulanza*. Try to avoid going to the **dentist** (*dentista*) while you're in Sicily. These aren't covered by the *mutua* or health service, and for the smallest problem they'll make you pay through the teeth.

INSURANCE

It might be as well to take out ordinary **travel insurance** too – certainly if you're a non-EC citizen. Ask about policies at any bank or travel agency, or use a specialist, low-priced firm like *Endsleigh* (97 Southampton Row, London WC1; ☎01-436 4451), who offer two weeks basic cover for around £12. For medical treatment and drugs, keep all the bills and claim the money back later. If you have anything stolen (including money), register the loss immediately with the local police – without their report you won't be able to claim.

INFORMATION AND MAPS

Before you leave, it's well worth dropping in at the Italian State Tourist Office (*ENIT*) and picking up a selection of maps and brochures, though don't go mad – much of it can easily be picked up later in Sicily. Worth grabbing are any accommodation listings they may have for the area you're interested in, and a camping brochure (*Sicilia Campeggi*) – both often in short supply once you get there.
Italian State Tourist Offices abroad include:
UK: 1 Princes Street, London W1 (☎01-408 1254); open Monday–Friday 9am–2.30pm.
EIRE: 47 Merrion Square, Dublin 2 (☎01-766 397).
AUSTRALIA/NEW ZEALAND: c/o *Alitalia*, AGC House, 124 Phillip Street, Sydney, NSW.

TOURIST OFFICES

Most Sicilian towns, main railway stations and the two airports have a tourist office: either an **EPT** (*Ente Provinciale Turismo*), a provincial branch of the state organisation, or an **AAST** (*Azienda Autónoma di Soggiorno e Turismo*), a smaller local outfit. When there isn't either an EPT or AAST there will often be a **Pro Loco** office, which will have much the same kind of information. All of these vary in degrees of usefulness, and apart from the main cities and tourist areas the staff aren't likely to speak English. But you should always be able at least to get a free town plan and a local listings booklet in Italian, and some will book you a room, and sell places on guided tours. Likely summer **opening hours** are Monday–Friday 9am–1pm and 4–7pm, Saturday 9am–1pm, but check the text for more details. If the tourist office isn't open and all else fails, the local telephone office (see below) and most bars with phones carry a copy of the regional *Tuttocittà*, a listings and information magazine which details addresses and numbers of all the organisations you're likely to want to know about, as well as having indexed street maps for local towns and adverts for restaurants and shops.

MAPS

The best large-scale **road map** of Sicily is published by the *Touring Club Italiano* (Sicilia, 1:200,000; £5.75), available in Britain from *Stanford's* (12 Long Acre, London WC2; ☎01-836 1321) or *Robertson McCarta* (122 Kings Cross Road, London WC1; ☎01-278 8278). Otherwise, the *Automobile Club d'Italia* issue a good, free 1:275,000 road map, available from the State Tourist Office. For **hiking**, you'll need at least a scale 1:100,000 map (better 1:50,000), though there's not much around – check with *Stanford's* and *Robertson McCarta* or with the *Club Alpino Italiano*, via Foscolo 3, Milan. For specific towns and islands, the maps we've printed should be fine for most purposes, though the EPT/AAST often hand out reasonable town plans and regional maps.

GETTING AROUND

Distances aren't especially large in Sicily, but getting around by public transport is not always as easy as it should be. The rail system is slow, few buses run on Sunday and route information can be frustratingly difficult to extract, even from the bus and train stations themselves. Sicily's geography means that it's a push to get right across the island – say Siracusa to Trápani – in one day; though you'll be able to travel most of one of the coastlines easily enough. On the positive side, public transport prices are among the cheapest in Europe. Although general points are covered below, each chapter's *Travel Details* section has the full picture on transport schedules and frequencies. One thing to bear in mind is that travelling by train is not the best way to see all of the island. Some stations are miles away from their towns – Enna and Taormina are two notable examples (though there are usually bus connections) – while much of the west and centre of Sicily is only accessible by bus or car.

TRAINS

Operated by Italian State Railways, *Ferrovie dello Stato* (*FS*), **trains** connect all the major towns, but are more prevalent in the east of the island than the west. Rarely does a train leave on time, however, especially on the routes between the major cities (Messina-Palermo and Messina-Catania/Siracusa), where most of the trains have come from the mainland, and delays of three hours are not uncommon – though around an hour late is normal. There are four types of train: the major services are known as either a *Rápido* (the fastest Sicilian train) or an *Espresso*; *Diretto* trains stop at most stations, useful for fairly quick jaunts along the coasts; while a *Locale* stops everywhere – usually one to avoid. In summer it's often worth making a **seat reservation** on the main routes, something you'll be obliged to do anyway on many more expensive *Rápido* trains – check before you get on or you'll pay a whacking *supplemento* (around 30% of the ordinary fare) to the conductor. If you don't have time to buy a ticket you can simply board your train and pay the conductor, though again it'll cost around 30% more this way.

As well as the boards displayed at stations ('Departures' are *Partenze*, 'Arrivals' *Arrivi*, 'Delayed' *In Ritardo*) a **timetable** is useful, even if you use it only to discover exactly how late your train is. The main Sicilian routes (*Rápido* and *Espresso* trains only) are covered by *FS*'s little national pocket book, *Principali Treni*, issued twice yearly and free from most railway stations, but if you're travelling exclusively by train you'll need something more detailed: get the much weightier *Pozzorario: Sud Centro Italia* (L3800), also issued twice yearly, from station *tabacchi*, or pick up the free *FS* leaflets detailing individual train lines, from major railway stations. Pay attention to the timetable notes, which may specify the dates between which some services run (*Si effetua dal . . . al . . .*), or whether a service is seasonal (*periódico*).

Prices are very reasonable. Tickets are charged by the kilometre and the 300km loop from Siracusa to Caltanissetta, for example, costs around L15,000, though most of the journeys you'll make will be much shorter and cheaper. As for **rail passes**, *InterRail* gives free travel on the whole *FS* network (though you'll be liable for supplements on the fast trains), and there are two specific Italian passes available: a *Biglietto turistico libera circolazione* (travel-at-will ticket: 8 days, £56; 15 days, £67; 21 days, £79; 30 days £97), valid for free travel on all *FS* trains, including a *Rápido*; and a *Chilométrico* ticket, valid for up to five people at once, giving 3000km worth of free travel on a maximum of twenty separate journeys – cost £60. You can get both these tickets before you leave from *FS* agents in Britain (*Citalia*, 50–51 Conduit Street, London W1; ☎01-434 3844; and branches of *Thomas Cook*). In Sicily, you can only buy the travel-at-will ticket at Palermo or Messina railway stations. Other **reductions** on normal fares are for families

(minimum four people travelling, adults 30% discount, kids 65% discount), kids (50% discount for 4–12 year olds) and for Senior Citizens (reductions on production of a Senior Citizen's Rail Card); more information from the Italian State Tourist Office.

For details of Sicily's only **private railway**, the *Ferrovia Circumetnea* route around the base of Mount Etna, see p.160.

BUSES

The trains don't go everywhere and you'll have to use the **regional buses** (*autobus* or *pullman*) at some stage. Almost anywhere you want to go will have some kind of service, usually quicker and more reliable than the train (especially between the major towns and cities), but schedules can be sketchy and buses are more expensive than trains. An average journey, say Catania to Palermo, costs around L13,000. There are two main **companies**, *SAIS* and *AST*, which between them cover most of the island; other companies stick to local routes. Nearly everywhere, services are drastically reduced, or non-existent, on Sunday, something the timetables – and the drivers/conductors – don't necessarily make clear: always double check. Note, too, that lots of departures (on rural routes especially) are linked to school/market requirements – sometimes meaning a frighteningly early start, and occasionally no services during school holidays.

Bus terminals can be scattered all over the bigger towns, though often all the buses pull up in one particular piazza, or outside the local railway station – if you want the bus station ask for the *Autostazione*. **Timetables** are worth picking up at every opportunity, from the companies' offices, bus stations or on the bus. You buy **tickets** on the bus, though on longer hauls (and if you want to be sure of a place) try and buy them in advance from the companies' offices. On most routes it's usually possible to flag a bus down if you want a ride: the convention, when it stops, is to get on at the back, off at the front. If you want to get off, ask *posso scéndere?*, the next stop is *la próssima fermata*.

City buses are always cheap, usually a L500–700 flat fare, and worth mastering in the bigger towns and cities. Invariably you need a ticket *before* getting on. Buy them in *tabacchi*, or from the kiosks and vendors at bus terminals and stops, and then validate it in the machine at the back of the bus. Checks are frequently made by inspectors who block both exits as they get on, though if you're without a ticket the worst that will usually happen is that you'll get an earful of Sicilian and be made to buy one.

A few bus services are operated by *FS*, the State Railways, to substitute discontinued lines. These complement the other bus services and are detailed in the *Pozzorario* rail timetables, and in the text.

CARS, HITCHING, BIKES AND WALKING

Car travel across the island can be very quick if you use the often spectacular **motorways** or *autostrade*. Carried on great piers which stomp across the island, these link Messina-Catania (A18), Catania-Palermo (A19), Palermo-Trápani/ Mazara del Vallo (A29) and – though still incomplete – Messina-Palermo (A20). The Messina-Catania and Messina-Palermo motorways are toll roads: take a ticket as you come on and pay on exit, the amount due flashed up on a screen in front of you; Messina to Catania costs around L4500 for a medium-sized car. Elsewhere, roads are pretty good though you should take care whenever you strike off on the minor routes: in rural areas they can soon deteriorate into rough tracks.

For **documentation** you need a valid driving licence *plus* an Italian translation (available from the Italian State Tourist Office), and an international green card of insurance. It's *compulsory* to carry your car documents and passport while you're driving, and you'll be required to present them if you're stopped by the police – not an uncommon occurrence. **Rules of the road** are straightforward: drive on the right; at junctions, where there's any ambiguity, give precedence to vehicles coming from the right; observe the speed limits (50kph in built-up areas, 110kph on country roads and on motorways during the week, 130kph on motorways at weekends); and *don't* drink and drive. If you **break down**, dial ☎116 at the nearest phone and tell the operator where you are, the type of car and your registration number: the nearest office of the *Automobile Club d'Italia (ACI)*, an *AA/RAC* equivalent, will be informed and they'll send someone out to fix your car, though it's not a free service. If you need towing anywhere you can count on it costing a fairly substantial amount, and it might be worth joining

ACI to qualify for their discounted repairs scheme; write to *ACI*, via Marsala 8, 00185 Rome. Any *ACI* office in Sicily can tell you where to get **spare parts** for your particular car: see the city *Listings* sections for details.

Car hire in Sicily is fairly dear, currently around £170–180 per week for a *Fiat Panda* plus petrol, with unlimited mileage. All the major international firms are represented and addresses are detailed in the city listings. Two Italian firms with offices in Britain are *Maggiore* (through *Transhire*, Silver House, 31–35 Beak Street, London W1; ☎ 01-437 0951) and *Italy by Car* (through *Pilgrim Air*, see p.6 for address). Better, though, is to arrange it in conjunction with your flight/holiday – on which most travel agents or tour operators can provide details. Italy is one of the most expensive countries in Europe in which to buy **petrol**: it's currently around L1300/ litre (60p/litre or £3/gallon), but take your own car and you're entitled to **petrol coupons** (worth 15% off) and concessions on the motorway tolls; information from the Italian State Tourist Office.

Never leave anything visible in the car when you leave it, including the radio. If you're taking your own vehicle, consider installing a detachable car-radio, and always depress your aerial or you might find it snapped off. Most cities and ports have **garages** where you can leave your car, a safe enough option which costs from around L4000 a day. At least your car is unlikely to be stolen if it's got a right-hand drive and a foreign number-plate: they're too conspicuous to be of much use to thieves.

Hitch-hiking (*autostop*) is not widely practised in Sicily. Getting around exclusively like this would be impossible, though you should pick up lifts easily enough on the main roads, and on short hops. On motorways you have to stand at the slip-road; venturing onto the motorway itself risks a spot-fine. Hitching is not something that women should do on their own, particularly in the more out-of-the-way places: pairs are best and always ask where the car is headed before you commit yourself (*Dov'è diretto?*). If you want to get out, say *Mi fa scéndere?*.

A better way to get off the beaten track is by **bicycle**, especially on the offshore islands. However, on the Sicilian mainland, renting is virtually unheard of and although cycling the coastal routes is alright, heading inland and up into the mountains requires a decent machine and plenty of stamina: a mountain-bike would be a good bet, though you can expect to be a real curiosity in some rural places. An alternative is to tour by **motorbike**, though again you'll have to bring your own. **Mopeds** and **scooters** are easier to find: virtually everyone in Sicily – kids to grandmas – rides these, although the smaller models are not on for any kind of long-distance travel. For shooting around towns they're ideal, and hireable in Taormina, Cefalù and other holiday centres – check the text for details and expect to pay around L20–35,000 a day. Crash helmets are compulsory, though you'll see many Sicilian youths just riding with one slung over one arm.

However you get around on the roads, **watch the traffic**. Driving in Sicily is almost a competitive sport, and although the Sicilians aren't the world's worst drivers they don't win any safety prizes either. It's not as horrific as it first looks, and if you're driving, the secret is to make it very clear what you're going to do, using your horn as much as your indicators and brakes. **Pedestrians**, too, will find that far from being unable to step off the pavement – ever – you'll be able to cross quite easily by staring straight at the drivers and strolling boldly across. If in doubt, follow someone old and infirm, or put out your hand policeman-like, but *never* assume that you're safe on a pedestrian crossing – regarded by drivers as an invitation to play human skittles.

Walking – ie serious hiking – is rarely an option in Sicily. There are no long-distance paths and few marked routes. That said, there are mountain refuges around, on Etna and in the Madonie (see *Sleeping*), and we've detailed some hiking possibilities in the text; see p.88, p.93 and p.260.

PLANES, FERRIES AND HYDROFOILS

Hardly surprisingly, **flying** isn't a major form of transport within Sicily. Still, if you're short on time, taking a plane to the Pelágie Islands or Pantelleria is a distinct – and not particularly expensive – possibility. Flights are with *ATI*, the internal arm of *Alitalia*, and there are tempting **discounts** available: a third off the normal fare if you go on Saturday and return on Sunday; 50% off if you make a day-return-trip on Sunday.

As for **ferries** and **hydrofoils** you'll use them to get to all the offshore islands: the Aeolians, Égadi and Pelágie Islands, Pantelleria and Ústica – full details under the respective accounts. There's also a summer hydrofoil service which runs along the northern, Tyrrhenian coast, from Palermo to the Aeolian Islands and stopping at a couple of towns along the coast – see *Travel Details*, chapters 1 and 2. Further options are to use the **catamaran** service to Malta which connects Giardini-Naxos, Catania and Siracusa, or the ferry from Naples/Réggio di Calabria to Malta – a slower service which also connects Catania and Siracusa. For each, check under the relevant *Travel Details* section.

SLEEPING

On the whole, accommodation in Sicily is slightly cheaper than in the rest of Italy. There's a whole range of places in all price categories and on average you can easily pay under £15 a night for two, sometimes (in Palermo especially) as little as half that. If you're watching your budget, a (very) few youth hostels, some private rooms and many campsites are all possibilities – for more on which see below.

All types of accommodation are officially graded, their tariffs fixed by law. In tourist areas and big cities there's often a low-season and high-season price, but whatever it costs the price of hotels and campsites should be listed in the local accommodation booklets provided by the

EPT and AAST, and posted on the door of the room. If the prices don't correspond, demand to know why, and don't hesitate to report infractions to the EPT/AAST. Loopholes do exist, however: in summer especially, when there's more demand for accommodation than what's available, hotels are prone to add a breakfast charge to the price of the room, whether you eat breakfast or not. There's nothing you can do about it, just make sure you know exactly how much you're going to be paying before you accept the room.

> All hotel prices given in the text are for a double room without bath/shower, unless otherwise stated.

HOTELS

Hotel accommodation, while normally abundant in the main towns and tourist areas, tends to thin out in remoter areas, and especially inland. It's worthwhile phoning ahead to book if you're heading for a one-hotel town.

Cheapest hotel-type accommodation is a *locanda* – basic but on the whole clean and safe, and usually costing around L16–24,000 for a double room without bath/shower. If you want a hot shower you'll generally have to pay extra, though only around L2000 per person. You'll find *locande* in all the cities, some large towns and a few out-of-the-way places too. More common are regular hotels, either a *pensione* or *albergo* (plural *alberghi*), the distinction between which has become obsolete since *pensioni* – the smaller, family-run establishments – have been edged out of business by *alberghi*, though some establishments still retain the name. All come graded with from one to five stars. A double room without bath/shower in a 1* hotel costs from around L24,000; a 2* hotel from around L35,000; a 3* place from L45,000. Anything swankier usually commands international hotel prices (upwards of L80,000), though there are some bargains around – in Palermo for example – for a splurge. Three or more people sharing a room should expect to pay around 35% on top of the price of a double room. Quirks in the official grading system mean that you can sometimes pay around the same in a one- or two-star hotel as in a basic *locanda*, or that the same price elsewhere gets you a bathroom included: always ask to see the room before you take it (*posso vedere?*), and check if there's hot water available (*c'è acqua calda?*).

Note that if you're **travelling alone** hotels will often charge you for the price of a double room. Check in the local hotel listings book, which may explicitly state (in English and Italian) that you're only liable for the price of a single room: waving the book at the offending hotel-manager might have some effect. In the cheaper places you might be able to negotiate a lower rate if you're staying for any length of time (*c'è uno sconto per due/tre/quattro notti?*).

PRIVATE ROOMS, YOUTH HOSTELS AND CAMPSITES

Certain tourist resorts, especially around Taormina and on the Aeolian and Égadi Islands, also have cheapish **private rooms** in people's houses for rent. They're fairly rare, though, so don't count on them: ask in local tourist offices, check the text for details and watch for signs saying *cámere* (rooms).

Official *International Youth Hostel Federation* (*IYHF*) **youth hostels** are sparse too, having dwindled to just two, in Castroreale and on the island of Lípari. It's hardly worth joining just to use these (which, out of season, probably won't want to see membership cards anyway), though if you're planning to cross to the Italian mainland it's worthwhile: contact the *YHA* office/shop at 14 Southampton Street, London WC2 (☎01-836 8542); membership for under 21s costs £4, over 21s £7. There are a few unofficial hostels as well, in Siracusa, Érice and Alì (near Messina) – all detailed in the text alongside the official places: expect to pay around L8–10,000 per person for a dormitory bed.

Camping is popular, with approximately ninety officially-graded sites dotted around the island's coasts, on a few of the Aeolian Islands, on Favignana (Égadi Islands) and on Lampedusa. At the last count there were only a couple in Sicily's interior, around Mount Etna. Again, addresses, telephone numbers and rates are listed in accommodation booklets, as are their months of opening (few are open all year round), though bear in mind that these months (also detailed in the text) are flexible, and campsites generally open or close whenever they want, depending on business. If you want to be sure, it's always worth a phone call. Full details of all the campsites are contained in the book *Campeggi e Villagi Turistici in Italia* (L21,000), published by the *Touring Club Italiano*, Corso Italiano 10, Milan. Or simply get the listings booklet *Sicilia Campeggi*, which details all the Sicilian campsites, free from the State Tourist Office in London. Daily rates are around L3–5000 per person plus the same again for a tent, and L2–3000 for a vehicle.

By and large, **camping rough** is a non-starter in much of Sicily: it's frowned on in the tourist areas and on the offshore islands, and difficult in the interior where there are scant water supplies and little flat land. Some possibilities are detailed in the text; anywhere else you're likely to attract the unwelcome attention of the local police.

OTHER OPTIONS

In Sicily's hillier regions it's possible to stay in a staffed **mountain hut** (a *rifugio*) – particularly in the Madonie and Nébrodi ranges and on Mount Etna, where overnight fees are around L6000 per person. They're operated by the *Club Alpino Italiano*, via Foscolo 3, Milan, who can provide lists and further information; or ask at local tourist offices and check the text.

For longer-term stays, you can rent holiday **apartments** in both Taormina and Cefalù. Although it's horrendously expensive in the summer – anything up to L1 million a month even for a one-bedroomed place – there are real bargains to be had during the winter: if you're staying for a few weeks in either of these towns, ask in the tourist offices or a local estate agency (*agenzia immobiliare*). Other places for rent include rural cottages or farmhouses, operated by **Agriturist**, Corso Vittorio Emanuele 101, Rome: local tourist offices can usually tell you if there's anywhere suitable in the district and it'll cost from around L40,000 a night.

Finally, students on holiday can stay in the **students' hostel** in Catania: apply (in Italian) before you leave to the *Casa dello Studente*, Università di Catania (Segreteria Studenti), via A. di Sangiuliano 256, Catania (☎090-325.333).

FOOD AND DRINK

There's much to be said for coming to Sicily just for the eating and drinking. Often, even the most out-of-the-way village will boast somewhere you can get a good, solid lunch, while places like Catania and Palermo can keep a serious eater happy for days. Historically, the cuisine was held in high regard: in medieval times Sicilian chefs were much sought after in foreign courts, and accorded the same esteem as a French chef today. Contemporary cooking is still excellent, leaning heavily on locally-produced basic foodstuffs – olive oil, tomatoes, bread and wine – and whatever can be fished out of the sea. And it's not ruinously expensive either, certainly compared to prices in the rest of mainland Italy: a full meal with good local wine generally costs around L15,000 a head, though see below for more detailed prices.

FOOD

Sicilian **food** mixes Italian staples – pasta, tomato sauce and fresh vegetables – with local specialities and products of the traditional island industries: red chillies, tuna and swordfish, olives and capers all figure heavily. The mild winter climate and long summers mean that fruit and vegetables are less seasonal than in northern Europe, and are much bigger and more impressive than the scraggy offerings in British supermarkets: strawberries appear in April, oranges are available right through the winter, and even bananas are grown on a small scale. Unusual and unexpected foods and fruit are a bonus, too: prickly pears (originally imported from Mexico by the Spanish), artichokes, asparagus, medlars and persimmons are ubiquitous, while in the south and west of the island, the North African influence is evident in the Sicilian version of couscous, less meaty than the original. The lists below will help you find your way around supermarkets and menus, but don't be afraid to ask to look in the kitchen if you're not sure what you're ordering. Also, check our lists of specialities, some of which crop up in nearly every restaurant.

BASICS: BREAKFAST, SNACKS, MARKETS ... AND ICE CREAM

Most Sicilians start the day in a bar, their **breakfast** consisting of a milky coffee, a cappuccino, and the ubiquitous *cornetto* – a jam-, custard- or chocolate-filled croissant, which you usually help yourself to from the counter. Bigger bars or a patisserie (a *pasticceria*) will usually have a bit more choice; an *iris* is a pastry ball stuffed with sweet ricotta cheese, an *arancino* a deep-fried ball of rice with meat (*rosso*) or butter and cheese (*bianco*) filling, and *cannoli* are pastry tubes filled with sweet ricotta cheese and candied fruit. Breakfast in a hotel (*prima colazione*) will be a limp affair, usually worth avoiding.

At other times of the day, **sandwiches** (*panini*) can be pretty substantial, a bread stick or roll packed with any number of fillings. There are sandwich bars in the bigger towns, though often in small villages you can go into an *alimentari* (grocer's shop) and ask them to make you one from whatever they've got on hand: you'll pay around L1500–3000 each. Bars may also offer *tramezzini*, ready-made sliced white bread sandwiches with mixed fillings – lighter and less appetizing than your average *panino*. Toasted sandwiches (*toste*) are common too: in a sandwich bar you can get whatever you like put inside them; in bars which have a sandwich toaster you're more likely to be offered a variation on cheese with ham or tomato.

Apart from sandwiches, other prepared takeaway food is pretty thin on the ground. You'll get most of the things already mentioned, plus small pizzas, portions of prepared pasta, chips, even full hot meals, in a ***távola calda***, a sort of stand-up snack-bar that's at its best in the morning when everything is fresh. The bigger towns have them, often combined with normal bars, and there's always one in main railway stations. Otherwise, you'll have to make do with what you can get from a ***rosticceria***, something you'll find in every town on the island. The big speciality here is spit-roast chicken: half a chicken with chips will cost around L4000; anything else, like Sicilian hamburgers or hot-dogs, is worth steering clear of.

You'll get more adventurous snacks in **shops** and **markets** – good bread, fruit, pizza slices and picnic food, like cheese, salami, olives, tomatoes and salads. Some markets sell traditional takeaway food from stalls, usually things like boiled artichokes, cooked octopus, sea anemones and mussels, and *focacce* – oven-baked pastry snacks either topped with cheese and tomato, or filled with spinach, fried offal or meat. In the larger cities, you'll occasionally come across an old-fashioned *focacceria* – take-away establishments selling only bread-based snacks. For picnics, some tinned and bottled things are worth looking out for too: sweet peppers (*peperoni*), baby squid (*calamari*), seafood salad (*insalata di mare*) and preserved vegetables. Although you'll only find **supermarkets** in the larger towns, they're worth seeking out if you're on a budget for the 'two-for-the-price-of-one' offers on things like tinned fish and meat, biscuits and soft drinks. Island-wide store chains with food halls are *Standa* and *Upim*.

Sicilian **ice-cream** (*gelato*) is justifiably famous: a cone (*un cono*) is an indispensable accessory to the evening *passeggiata*. Most bars have a fairly good selection, but for real choice go to a **gelateria** where the range is a tribute to the Italian imagination and flair for display. You'll have to go by appearance rather than attempting to decipher their exotic names, many of which don't mean much even to Italians; you'll find it's often the basics – chocolate, lemon, strawberry and coffee – that are best. There's no trouble in locating the finest *gelateria* in town: it's the one that draws the crowds. Sitting down at a bar, on the other hand, is the place to sample a typical Sicilian *cassata*, no relation to the soapy ice-cream cake served in Italian restaurants in Britain: the real McCoy is very creamy, packed with candied fruit or marzipan and served with a wafer biscuit.

PIZZAS

The whole world knows about **pizza**, and outside its home of Naples, Sicily is the best place to eat it. Here, as elsewhere in Italy, your pizza comes flat and not deep-pan, and the choice of toppings is fairly limited – none of the pineapple and sweetcorn variations you find in Britain. It's also easier to find pizzas cooked in the traditional way, in wood-fired ovens (*forno a legna*), rather than squeaky-clean electric ones, so that the pizzas arrive blasted and bubbling on the surface, pock-marked, and with a distinctive charcoal taste. **Pizzerias**, which range from a stand-up counter to a fully-fledged sit-down restaurant, on the whole sell just pizzas and drinks, usually chips, sometimes salads; a basic cheese and tomato pizza costs around L2–3000, something a bit fancier between L4000 and L5000. To follow local custom you order your pizza with chips, ketchup an optional extra, cut it into slices and eat it with your hands, washing it down with a beer or Coke. You'll also get pizzas in larger towns and tourist areas in a hybrid pizzeria-ristorante, which serves meals too and is slightly more expensive. Check our list of pizzas for what you get on top of your dough.

MEALS: LUNCH AND DINNER

Full **meals** are much more elaborate affairs. These are generally served in a **trattoria** or a **ristorante**, though these days there's often a fine line between the two: traditionally, a trattoria is cheaper and more basic, offering good home-cooking (*cucina casalinga*), while a ristorante is more upmarket (tablecloths and waiters). The main differences you'll notice, though, are more to do with opening hours and the food on offer. In small towns and villages a trattoria is usually best at lunchtime and often only open then – there probably won't be a menu and the waiter will simply reel off a list of what's on that day. In large towns both will be open in the evening, though there'll be more choice in a ristorante, which will always have a menu. In either, a pasta course, meat or fish, fruit and a drink should cost around L15–20,000, though watch out for signs saying *pranzo turístico* or *pranzo completo* – a limited set menu including wine for as little as L10,000. **Other types of eating-place** include places that flaunt themselves as a trattoria-ristorante-pizzeria, usually found in tourist resorts – and which generally mean you pay a steep service charge for food you could get better

and cheaper elsewhere – and restaurant-bars called spaghetterias, which specialise in pasta dishes and are often the haunts of the local youth.

Traditionally, a **meal** (lunch is *pranzo*, dinner is *cena*) starts with an **antipasto** (literally 'before the meal'): you'll only find this in restaurants, at its best when you circle around a table and pick from a selection of cold dishes, main items including stuffed artichoke hearts, olives, salami, anchovies, seafood salad, aubergine in various guises, sardines and mixed rice. A plateful will cost around L5000, but if you're moving on to pasta and the main course, you'll need quite an appetite to tackle it. As far as the **menu** goes, it starts with soup or pasta, **il primo**, and moves on to **il secondo**, the meat or fish dish – generally served alone except for perhaps a wedge of lemon or tomato. Vegetables and salads (**il contorno**) are ordered and served separately and often there won't be much (if any) choice: potatoes will nearly always be chips, salads are simply green (*verde*) or mixed (*mista*), usually with tomato. If there's no menu, the verbal list of what's available can be a bit bewildering, but if you don't hear anything you recognise just ask for what you want: everywhere should have pasta with tomato sauce (*pomodoro*) or meat sauce (*al ragù*). Afterwards, you'll usually get a choice of fruit (*frutta*) while in a ristorante, you'll probably be offered other desserts (**dolci**) as well. Sicily is renowned for its sweets, an Arab legacy that you can't help but notice in every bar and bakery you pass, though most restaurants will only have fresh fruit salad (*macedonia*) and ice-cream (or *cassata*); sometimes there'll be *zuppa inglese* (trifle), *zabaglione* or *torta* (tart, cake) too.

If you're **budgeting** it's useful to know that you don't have to order a full meal in trattorias and most restaurants. Asking for just pasta and a salad, or the main course on its own won't outrage the waiter. Something to watch for is ordering fish, which will either be served whole (like bream or trout), or by weight, like swordfish and tuna – if you don't want the biggest one they've got, ask to see what you're going to eat and check on the price first.

VEGETARIANS – A FEW POINTERS

Some **vegetarians** might find their food principles stretched to the limit in Sicily. Fish and shellfish are abundant and excellent, while if you're a borderline case then the knowledge that all eggs and meat are free-range in Sicily might just push you over the edge. On the whole, though, it's not that difficult if you're committed. Most pasta sauces are based on tomatoes or dairy products and it's easy to pick a pizza that is meat- (and fish-) free. Most places, too, can be persuaded to cook you eggs in some shape or form, or provide you with a big mixed salad. The only real problem is one of comprehension: many people don't know what a vegetarian is. Saying you're vegetarian (*sono vegetraiano/a*) and asking if the dish has meat in it (*c'è carne dentro?*) is only half the battle: poultry and especially *prosciutto* are regarded by many waiters as barely meat at all. Better is to ask what the dish is made with (*com'è fatto?*) before you order, so that you can spot the offending 'non-meaty' meat.

Being a **vegan**, you'll be in for a hard time, though pizzas without cheese are a good stand-by, vegetable soup is usually just that and the fruit is excellent. However, you'll have absolutely no success in explaining to anyone why you're a vegan – an incomprehensibe moral concept to a Sicilian.

THE BILL ... AND TIPPING

At the **end of the meal**, ask for the bill (*il conto*). In many trattorias this doesn't amount to much more than an illegible scrap of paper, and if you want to be sure you're not being ripped off, ask to have a receipt (*una ricevuta*), something they're legally obliged to give you anyway. Nearly everywhere, you'll pay cover (*pane e coperto*), which amounts to L1–2000 per person; service (*servizio*) will be added as well in most restaurants, about another 10%. If service is included, you won't be expected to tip; otherwise leave 10%, though bear in mind that the smaller places – pizzerias and trattorias – won't necessarily expect this.

DRINK

Although Sicilian children are brought up on wine, there's not the same emphasis on dedicated **drinking** here as there is in Britain. You'll rarely see drunks in public, young people don't make a night out of getting wasted, and women especially are frowned upon if they're seen to be indulging. Nonetheless, there's a wide choice of alcoholic drinks available in Sicily, at low prices; soft drinks come in multifarious hues, thanks to the abundance of fresh fruit, and there's also

mineral water and crushed ice drinks: you'll certainly never be stuck if you want to slake your thirst.

WHAT TO DRINK

One of the most distinctive smells in a Sicilian street is the aroma of fresh **coffee**, usually wafting out of a bar (many trattorias and pizzerias don't serve hot drinks). It's always excellent: the basic choice is either small and black (an *espresso*, or just *caffè*), or white and frothy (a *cappuccino*), but there are other varieties, too. If you want your *espresso* watered down, ask for a *caffè lungo*; with a shot of alcohol – and you can ask for just about *anything* in your coffee – is *caffè corretto*; with a drop of milk is *caffè macchiato*. Although most places let you help yourself, some will lace your black coffee with sugar; if you don't want it, you can make sure by asking for coffee *senza zúcchero* – though the barman will think you're quite mad. Many places now also sell decaffeinated coffee (ask for *Hag*, even when it isn't); while in summer you'll probably want to have your coffee cold (*caffè freddo*). For a real treat, ask for *granita di caffè* – cold coffee with crushed ice and usually topped with cream.

If you don't like coffee, there's always **tea**. In summer, you can drink it iced (*tè freddo*) – excellent for taking the heat off. Hot tea (*tè caldo*) comes with lemon (*con limone*) unless you ask for milk (*con latte*). **Milk** itself is drunk hot as often as cold, or you can get it with a dash of coffee (*latte macchiato*), and sometimes in a variety of flavoured drinks (*frappe*) too.

Alternatively, there are various **soft drinks** (*analcóliche*) to choose from. A **spremuta** is a fresh fruit juice, squeezed at the bar, usually orange, lemon or grapefruit. You might need to add sugar to a lemon juice (. . . *di limone*), but orange juice (. . . *di arancia*) is usually sweet enough on its own, especially in the crimson-red variety, made from blood oranges. A **granita** (a crushed-ice drink) is a Sicilian speciality and comes in several flavours other than coffee. Otherwise, there's the usual range of fizzy drinks and concentrated juices; *Coke* is prevalent, but the homegrown Italian alternative, *Chinotto*, is less sweet – good with a slice of lemon. Tap **water** (*acqua normale*) is drinkable everywhere and you won't pay for it in a bar. But **mineral water** (*acqua minerale*) is the usual choice, either still (*senza gas* or *naturale*) or fizzy (*con gas*, *gassata* or *frizzante*) – about L500 a glass.

Beer (*birra*) is always a lager-type brew which usually comes in third-litre (*píccolo*) or two-thirds-litre (*grande*) bottles: commonest (and cheapest) are the Italian brands, *Peroni* and *Dreher*, and the Sicilian *Messina*, all of which are fine, if a bit weak. A small bottle of *Messina* beer costs about L1200 in a bar or restaurant; if this is what you want, ask for *birra nazionale*, otherwise you'll be given the more expensive imported beers. In most bars and bigger restaurants you also have a choice of draught lager (*birra alla spina*), measure for measure more expensive than the bottled variety, while in some bars you might find so-called 'dark beers' (*birra nera* or *birra rossa*), which have a slightly maltier taste, and in appearance resemble stout or bitter. These are the dearest of the draught beers, though not necessarily the strongest.

With just about every meal you'll be offered **wine** (*vino*), either red (*rosso*) or white (*bianco*), labelled or local. If you're unsure and want the local stuff, ask for *vino locale*: on the whole it's very good, often served straight from the barrel in jugs or old bottles and costing as little as L2–3000 a litre. Bottled wine is much more expensive, though still good value compared to Britain; expect to pay at least L7000 a bottle in a restaurant. A standard brand you see everywhere is *Corvo*; others to watch for are *Etna* (red and white), from vines grown on the slopes of the volcano, *Zucco* (a medium-sweet white from Carini), *Montevagno* or *Salemi* (a tangy wine from Sicily's far west), and *Cervasuolo* (red and white) from the area around Vittória. One peculiarity is that bars don't tend to serve wine **by the glass** – when they do, you'll pay around L1000.

Sicily produces good **dessert wines**, the most famous being *marsala*, sometimes sweetened and mixed with eggs, called *marsala all'uovo*; but if you're heading to the offshore islands, watch out for *malvasia* (from the Aeolians) and *moscato* (from Pantelleria). **Fortified wine** is fairly popular too: *Martini* (red or white) and *Cinzano* are nearly always available; *Cynar* (an artichoke-based sherry) and *Punt'e Mes* are other common aperitifs. If you ask for a *Campari-Soda* you'll get a ready-mixed version in a little bottle; a slice of lemon is a *spicchio di limone*; ice is *ghiaccio*..

All the usual **spirits** are on sale and known mostly by their generic names, except brandy which you should call *cognac* or ask for by name. The best Italian brandies are *Stock* and *Vécchia*

Romagna; for all other spirits, if you want the cheaper Italian stuff, again, ask for . . . *nazionale*. A generous shot costs around L1200. There's the standard selection of **liqueurs**, too, though at some stage try **amaro** (literally 'bitter'), an after-dinner drink served with (or instead of) coffee. It's supposed to aid digestion, and is often not bitter at all, but can taste remarkably medicinal. The favourite is *Averna* but there are dozens of different kinds. Look out, too, for a red liqueur called *Fuoco dell'Etna*, mostly sold on the east coast, whose effect – fittingly – is of a miniature volcanic explosion. Other strong drinks available, though not especially Sicilian, are *Grappa*, almost pure alcohol, made from distilling the grape husks left over from the manufacture of wine, and *Sambuca* – a sticky-sweet, aniseed liqueur, traditionally served with a coffee bean in it, and set on fire at the table, though only tourists are likely to experience this these days.

WHERE TO DRINK

Bars are less social centres than functional places, and all very similar to each other – bright, with a chrome counter, a *Gaggia* coffee machine and a picture of the local football team on the wall. You'll come here for **ordinary drinking**, a coffee in the morning, a quick beer, a cup of tea, but people don't generally while away the afternoon in bars, or spend all night drinking in them. Indeed, in many places (Palermo included), it's difficult to find an average bar open much after 9pm. Where it does fit into the general Mediterranean pattern is that there are no set licensing hours and children are allowed in; there's often a telephone and you can buy snacks and ice-cream as well as drinks. Whatever you're drinking, the procedure is the same. It's cheapest to drink standing up at the counter (there's often nowhere to sit anyway), in which case you pay first at the cash-desk (*la cassa*), present your receipt (*scontrino*) to the bar person and give your order. If you don't know how much a drink will cost, there's always a list of prices (the *listino prezzi*) behind the bar. When you present your receipt it's customary to leave an extra L50 or L100 on the counter – though no-one will object if you don't. If there's waiter service, just sit where you like: it's more expensive to sit down inside than stand up (the difference in price is shown on the price list as *tavola*) and it's up to twice the basic price if you sit at tables outside (*terrazza*).

For more **serious drinking**, most people go out and eat as well, at a pizzeria or restaurant, and spin the meal out accordingly if they want a few more beers. Otherwise, the other choice is a **birreria** (literally 'beer-shop'), where people go just to drink, though often they sell food too. These are where you'll find young people at night, listening to music or glued to rock-videos; they're often called 'pubs', although they bear little relation to their British namesakes. In tourist areas, bars and cafés (a *caffè*) are more like the real European thing, and they're open later, but they're much more expensive. Other places to get a drink are the **bar-pasticceria**, which sells wonderful cakes and pastries too, and a **távola calda** in a railway station always has a bar.

Basics and snacks

Aceto	Vinegar
Aglio	Garlic
Biscotti	Biscuits
Burro	Butter
Caramelle	Sweets
Cioccolato	Chocolate
Focaccia	Oven-baked snack
Formaggio	Cheese
Frittata	Omelette
Gelato	Ice-cream
Grissini	Bread sticks
Maionese	Mayonnaise
Mermellata	Jam
Olio	Oil
Olive	Olives
Pane	Bread
Pane integrale	Wholemeal bread
Panino	Bread roll/sandwich
Patatine	Crisps
Patatine fritte	Chips
Pepe	Pepper
Pizzetta	Small cheese and tomato pizza
Riso	Rice
Sale	Salt
Uova	Eggs
Yogurt	Yoghurt
Zúcchero	Sugar
Zuppa	Soup

Pizzas

Calzone	Folded pizza with cheese, ham and tomato.
Capricciosa	Literally 'capricious'; topped with whatever they've got in the kitchen, usually including baby artichoke, ham and egg.
Cardinale	Ham and olives.
Funghi	Mushroom; tinned, sliced button mushrooms unless it specifies fresh mushrooms, *funghi freschi.*
Frutta di mare	Sea food; usually mussels, prawns, squid and clams.
Margherita	Cheese and tomato.
Marinara	Tomato.
Napoli/Napolitana	Tomato, anchovy and olive oil.
Quattro formaggi	'Four cheeses', usually including mozzarella, fontina and gruyère.
Quattro stagioni	'Four seasons'; the toppings split into four separate sections, usually including ham, green pepper, onion, egg, etc.

Antipasti and starters

Antipasto misto	Mixed cold meats and cheese.
Caponata	Mixed aubergine, olives, tomatoes.
Caprese	Tomato and mozzarella cheese salad.
Insalata di mare	Seafood salad.
Insalata di riso	Rice salad.
Insalata russa	Russian salad; diced vegetables in mayonnaise.
Melanzane in parmigiana	Aubergine in tomato and parmesan cheese.
Peperonata	Green and red peppers stewed in olive oil.
Pomodori ripieni	Stuffed tomatoes.
Prosciutto	Ham.
Salame	Salami.

The first course (Il primo): soups, pasta . . .

Brodo	Clear broth.
Cannelloni	Large tubes of pasta, stuffed.
Farfalle	Literally 'butterfly'-shaped pasta.
Fettucine	Narrow pasta ribbons.
Gnocchi	Small potato and dough dumplings.
Lasagne	Lasagne.
Maccheroni	Tubular spaghetti.
Minestrina	Any light soup.
Minestrone	Thick vegetable soup.
Pasta al forno	Pasta baked with minced meat, eggs, tomato and cheese.
Pasta fagioli	Pasta soup with beans.
Pastina in brodo	Pasta pieces in clear broth.
Penne	Smaller version of rigatoni.
Ravioli	Ravioli.
Rigatoni	Large, grooved tubular pasta.
Risotto	Cooked rice dish, with sauce.
Spaghetti	Spaghetti.
Spaghettini	Thin spaghetti.
Stracciatella	Broth with egg.
Tagliatelle	Pasta ribbons, another word for fettucine.
Tortellini	Small rings of pasta, stuffed with meat or cheese.
Vermicelli	Very thin spaghetti (literally 'little worms').

. . . and the sauce (salsa)

Arrabiata	Spicy tomato sauce, with chillies.
Bolognese	Meat sauce.
Burro	Butter.
Carbonara	Cream, ham and beaten egg.
Funghi	Mushroom.
Matriciana	Cubed pork and tomato sauce.
Panna	Cream.
Parmigiano	Parmesan cheese.
Peperoncino	Olive oil, garlic and fresh chillies.
Pesto	Green basil and garlic sauce.
Pomodoro	Tomato sauce.
Ragù	Meat sauce.
Vóngole	Clam and tomato sauce.

The second course (Il secondo): meat (carne) . . .

Agnello	Lamb
Bistecca	Steak
Cervello	Brain
Cinghiale	Wild boar
Coniglio	Rabbit
Costolette	Chops
Cotolette	Cutlets
Fegatini	Chicken livers
Fegato	Liver
Involtini	Meat slices, rolled and stuffed
Lingua	Tongue
Maiale	Pork
Manzo	Beef
Mortadella	Salami-type cured meat
Ossobuco	Shin of veal
Pancetta	Bacon
Pollo	Chicken
Polpette	Meatballs
Rognoni	Kidneys
Salsiccia	Sausage
Saltimbocca	Veal with ham
Spezzatino	Stew
Tacchino	Turkey
Trippa	Tripe
Vitello	Veal

. . . and fish (pesce) and shellfish (crostacei)

Acciughe	Anchovies
Anguilla	Eel
Aragosta	Lobster
Baccalà	Dried salted cod
Calamari	Squid
Céfalo	Mullet
Cozze	Mussels
Dentice	Dentex
Gamberetti	Shrimps
Gámberi	Prawns
Granchio	Crab
Merluzzo	Cod
Ostriche	Oysters
Pescespada	Swordfish
Pólipo	Octopus
Sarde	Sardines
Sgombro	Mackerel
Sógliola	Sole
Tonno	Tuna
Triglie	Red mullet
Trota	Trout
Vóngole	Clams

Vegetables (contorni) and salad (insalata)

Asparagi	Asparagus	*Finocchio*	Fennel
Basílico	Basil	*Funghi*	Mushrooms
Bróccoli	Broccoli	*Insalata verde/*	Green salad/mixed
Cápperi	Capers	*mista*	salad
Carciofi	Artichokes	*Melanzane*	Aubergine
Carciofini	Artichoke hearts	*Orígano*	Oregano
Carotte	Carrots	*Patate*	Potatoes
Cavolfiori	Cauliflower	*Peperoni*	Peppers
Cávolo	Cabbage	*Piselli*	Peas
Cetriolo	Cucumber	*Pomodori*	Tomatoes
Cipolla	Onion	*Radicchio*	Chicory
Fagioli	Beans	*Spinaci*	Spinach
Fagiolini	Green beans	*Zucchini*	Courgettes

Sweets (dolci), fruit (frutta), cheeses (formaggi) and nuts (noce)

Amaretti	Macaroons	*Mozzarella*	Bland soft white cheese
Ananas	Pineapple		used on pizzas
Anguria/Coccómero	Water melon	*Néspole*	Medlars
Arance	Oranges	*Parmigiano*	Parmesan cheese
Banane	Bananas	*Pecorino*	Strong tasting hard sheep's
Cacchi	Persimmons		cheese
Ciliegie	Cherries	*Pere*	Pears
Fichi	Figs	*Pesche*	Peaches
Fichi d'India	Prickly pears	*Pignoli*	Pine nuts
Fontina	Northern Italian cheese	*Pistacchio*	Pistachio nut
	used in cooking	*Provolone*	Hard strong cheese
Frágole	Strawberries	*Ricotta*	Soft white cheese made
Gelato	Ice-cream		from ewe's milk
Gorgonzola	Soft blue-veined cheese	*Torta*	Cake, tart
Limone	Lemon	*Uva*	Grapes
Macedonia	Fruit salad	*Zabaglione*	Dessert made with eggs,
Mándorle	Almonds		sugar and marsala wine
Mele	Apples	*Zuppa Inglese*	Trifle
Melone	Melon		

Some terms and useful words

Affumicato	Smoked	*Grattuggiato*	Grated
Arrosto	Roast	*Alla griglia*	Grilled
Ben cotto	Well done	*Al Marsala*	Cooked with Marsala wine
Bollito/lesso	Boiled	*Milanese*	Fried in egg and breadcrumbs
Brasato	Cooked in wine	*Pizzaiola*	Cooked with tomato sauce
Cotto	Cooked (not raw)	*Ripieno*	Stuffed
Crudo	Raw	*Sangue*	Rare
Al dente	Firm, not overcooked	*Allo spiedo*	On the spit
Ferri	Grilled without oil	*Surgelati*	Frozen
Fritto	Fried	*Úmido*	Steamed/stewed

Specialities: a few dishes

Cassata	Ice-cream cake with candied fruit.
Cozze alla marinara	Mussels in wine and seafood soup.
Cozze pepata	Mussels in spicy tomato stock.
Fritto misto	A standard seafood dish; deep-fried prawns and calamari rings in batter.
Fritto di pesce	As above but also with other fried fish, like sardines and whitebait.
Involtini di pescespada	Slices of swordfish, stuffed, rolled and fried. Usually expensive.
Pasta con sarde	Macaroni with fresh sardines, fennel, raisins and pine kernels; a speciality of Palermo.
Penne all'arrabiata	Short tubular pasta with spicy tomato sauce made with chillies (*arrabiata* means angry).
Peperonata	Peppers (capsicum) sauted in olive oil until soft and sweet, either served as *antipasto* or as a vegetable.
Spaghetti alla Norma	Spaghetti with tomato sauce topped with fried aubergine; a speciality of Catania, named after one of Bellini's operas.
Stocca alla Messinese	Dried cod stewed with potatoes, olives, tomatoes, capers and celery; a speciality of Messina although there are other regional variations.
Uova in tegame	Eggs fried in olive oil served at the table in a little metal pan.
Zuppa di cozze/vongole	A big dish of mussels/clams in rich wine-based soup.
Zuppa di pesce	As above but usually with pieces of cod, squid and prawns, and served with fried bread. Often expensive, usually marvellous.

Drinks

Acqua minerale	Mineral water	*Succo*	Concentrated fruit juice with sugar
Aranciata	Orangeade		
Bicchiere	Glass	*Tè*	Tea
Birra	Beer	*Tónico*	Tonic water
Bottiglia	Bottle	*Vino*	Wine
Caffè	Coffee	*Rosso*	Red
Cioccolata calda	Hot chocolate	*Bianco*	White
Ghiaccio	Ice	*Rosato*	Rosé
Granita	Iced coffee- /fruit-drink	*Secco*	Dry
Latte	Milk	*Dolce*	Sweet
Limonata	Lemonade	*Litro*	Litre
Selz	Soda water	*Mezzo*	Half
Spremuta	Fresh fruit juice	*Quarto*	Quarter
Spumante	Sparkling wine	*Salute!*	Cheers!

POST, PHONES AND THE MEDIA

Post office opening hours are usually Monday–Saturday 8.20am–6.30pm; smaller towns won't have a service on a Saturday and everywhere the post offices close at noon on the last day of the month. If you want stamps, you can buy them in *tabacchi* too, as well as in some gift shops in the tourist resorts: to Britain, post cards are L550, letters L650. Letters can be sent poste restante to any Sicilian post office, by addressing them 'Fermo Posta' followed by the name of the town. When picking something up take your passport, and make sure they check under middle names and initials (and every other letter when all else fails) as filing is diabolical.

Public **telephones** come in various forms, usually with clear instructions printed on them (in English, too). For the most common type, you'll need L100 or L200 coins, or a token known as a *gettone* (L200), available from *SIP* offices (the state telephone company), *tabacchi*, bars and some news-stands – they're also in common use as currency. Other phones take L500 coins, handy for long-distance calls. **Phone cards** (*schede telefóniche*), too, are available for L2000, L5000 and L10,000 from *tabacchi* or news-stands; they'll soon be accepted in all phone booths. Bars too will often have a phone you can use, though these often take *gettoni* only: look for the yellow phone symbol. Alternatively you could find a *SIP* office (listed in the text in the larger towns) or a bar with a *cabina a scatti*, a sound-proofed and metred kiosk: ask to make the call and pay at the end. You can do the same at hotels, but they

normally charge 25% more. To make a **reversed charge** call, dial the international operator (☎176) and ask for a call *cárico a destinatario* (for England, say *Vorrei telefonare all'Inghilterra, cárico a destinatario*).

> For direct **international calls**, dial the country code (given below), the area code (minus its first 0), and finally the number.
> UK: 0044
> EIRE: 00353
> AUSTRALIA: 0061
> NEW ZEALAND: 0064

You'll find the main national **newspapers** on any news-stand: *La Repubblica* is middle-to-left with a lot of cultural coverage; *Il Corriere della Sera* is authoritative and rather right-wing; *L'Unità* is the Communist Party organ; and *Il Manifesto*, a more radical and readable left-wing daily. Sicily also has its own local papers, useful for transport timetables, concerts and film listings, etc. In Palermo the best is *L'Ora*, in Catania *La Sicilia*, in Messina *La Gazzetta del Sud*, while *Il Giornale della Sicilia* has separate editions printed all over the island. The most widely-read paper, though, is the pink *Gazzetta dello Sport*, essential reading for the serious sports fan. **English newspapers** can be found for around L2000 in Palermo, Catania, Messina, Taormina and Cefalù, at the railway station and the main piazza or Corso, usually a couple of days late.

If the opportunity arises, take a look at Italian **TV** to sample the pros and cons of deregulation in television. The three state-run channels, *RAI 1, 2* and *3*, controlled by the *DC, PSI* and local networks respectively, have got their backs against the wall in the face of the massive independent onslaught, led by the Euromogul Berlusconi. The output is generally pretty bland, with a heavy helping of American sitcoms and films, and ghastly Italian cabaret shows, though the *RAI* channels have less advertising and mix some good reporting in among the dross. The situation in **radio** is even more anarchic, with the FM waves crowded to the extent that you can pick up a new station just by walking down the corridor. Again, the *RAI* stations are generally more professional, though daytime listening is virtually undiluted non-stop dance music.

OPENIING HOURS AND HOLIDAYS

Basic hours for most shops and businesses in Sicily are Monday to Saturday from 8am/9am to around 1pm, and from around 4pm to 7pm/8pm, though some offices work to a more standard European 9am–5pm day. Everything, except bars and restaurants, closes on Sunday, though you might find fish shops in some coastal towns and pasticcerias open until Sunday lunchtime.

Other disrupting factors are **national holidays** and local **saint's days** (see below). Local religious holidays don't generally close down shops and businesses, but they do mean that accommodation space will be tight; check the *Festivals* section at the end of each chapter. However, everything, except bars and restaurants, will be closed on the following national holidays:

PUBLIC HOLIDAYS

1 January

6 January (Epiphany)

Good Friday

Easter Monday

25 April (Liberation Day)

1 May (Labour Day)

15 August (*Ferragosto*; Assumption of the Blessed Virgin Mary)

1 November (*Ogni Santi*, 'All Saints')

8 December (Immaculate Conception of the Blessed Virgin Mary)

25 December

26 December

CHURCHES, MUSEUMS, AND ARCHAEOLOGICAL SITES

The rules for visiting **churches** are much as they are all over the Mediterranean. Dress modestly, which usually means no shorts, and covered shoulders for women – and try to avoid wandering around during a service. Most churches open in the early morning, around 7–8am for Mass and close around noon, and open again at 4–5pm, closing at 7pm; more obscure ones will only open for early morning and evening services; some only open on Sunday and on religious holidays. One problem you'll face all over Sicily is that lots of churches, monasteries, convents and oratories are **closed for restoration** (*chiuso per restauro*): we've indicated in the text the more long-term closures, though you might be able to persuade a workman or priest/curator to show you around, even if there's scaffolding everywhere.

Museums generally open daily from 9am to 1pm, and again for a couple of hours in the afternoon on certain days: likely closing day is Monday, while they close slightly earlier on Sunday, usually 12.30pm. **Archaeological sites** are usually open from 9am until an hour before sunset, in practice until around 4pm in winter, 7pm in summer: again, sometimes closed on Monday. The **entrance fee** for museums and sites is usually L2000, although under 18s and over 60s get in free on production of documentary proof of their age. Some sites, churches and monasteries, and Palermo's oratories are nominally free to get in, though there'll be a custodian around to open things up and show you around. It's expected that you'll hand over a tip, say L1–2000 per person.

FESTIVALS AND ENTERTAINMENTS

Every day in Sicily is a Saint's Day, celebrated as an *onomástico* or name-day and, for the people called after that saint, ranking above a birthday in importance. The ones you'll notice are the feste, feast-days for saints that have a special role for a particular locality. These are still basically unchanged in the smaller towns and villages, though some have evolved into much larger affairs spread over two or three days, and others have been developed with an eye to tourism. But the ingredients are the same everywhere: people performing old songs and dances, a costumed procession, special food and sweets and noisy fireworks to finish with.

The local EPT/AAST can tell you about events in its area: you're likely to come across a *festa* at any time throughout the year (check the *Festivals* section at the end of each chapter for exact dates), though there are certain occasions which stand out. *Carnevale* (carnival or Mardi Gras time) is a floating festival, five days of celebration in the period just before Lent – which means in practice some time between the end of February and the end of March. Literally the term means 'farewell meat', referring to the last bout of indulgence before the abstinence of Lent, which lasts for forty days and ends with Easter. The best festivities are along the Ionian coast, at Taormina and especially at Acireale, although most Sicilian towns put on a little bit of a show. **Easter week** itself is celebrated all over the island, with slow-moving processions and ostentatious displays of penitence and mourning. Particularly dramatic events take place in the west of the island, at Trápani, Marsala and the Albanian village of Piana degli Albanesi, as well as at Enna in the interior. Other, more unconventional affairs take place at Prizzi, in the western interior, and San Fratello, on the Tyrrhenian coast. The biggest island-wide celebration is at **ferragosto**, the Feast of the Assumption on August 15, a mid-summer excuse for spectacular fireworks. This is a good time to be in Messina, when the procession of the enormous *Giganti* on August 14 is followed by the mad scramble of the *Vara* at *ferragosto* itself, ending with fireworks over the Straits late at night.

Of the various **pilgrimages** that take place throughout Sicily, the most interesting are in September, notably at Palermo on the fourth, and Gibilmanna and Tíndari on the Tyrrhenian coast on the eighth. Among the biggest and best-known of the **other popular festivals** are: the Epiphany celebrations in Piana degli Albanesi (Jan 6); the *Festa di Sant'Agata* in Catania (3–5 Feb); the *Sagra del Mandorlo in fiore* celebrating the almond blossom in Agrigento (1st or 2nd week of Feb); the *Festa di Santa Rosalia* in Palermo (11–15 July), and *Il Palio dei Normanni*, a medieval-costumed procession and jousting in Piazza Armerina (13–14 Aug).

MUSIC AND CINEMA

There's a fair selection of cultural things happening throughout the year aside from the festival events. Sicily's archaeological remains – particularly its Greek and Roman theatres – provide spectacular settings for **concerts**, usually classical, and there are regular events by local and visiting international orchestras in the theatres at Taormina, Segesta, Siracusa and Tíndari. The **opera** season runs from December to May and while the Teatro Mássimo in Palermo remains closed, the best place to see it is in Catania at the Teatro Bellini. Smaller theatres in all the main towns and cities also have music programmes, as well as the dramatic arts. There's no specific Sicilian **rock music** scene: radio and TV are dominated by mainstream Italian pop which is mostly bland Europop, slushy ballads or bad cover-versions of British and American hits. Increasingly, though, some of the big, international bands are coming to Sicily, and, especially during the summer, some of the more enterprising local councils – in Palermo, Messina and Catania – sponsor open-air concerts in public squares or parks.

There are **cinemas** in most towns, though all English language films are dubbed into Italian: the only exception is the *English Film Club* in Palermo; see p.66. An alternative in summer to the indoor movie-houses are the open-air film shows that take place in some towns and tourist resorts, detailed in the text. And Taormina hosts an important **international film festival** every year in July, with screenings in the Greek theatre.

THEATRES AND PUPPET THEATRES

Regular **theatre** is popular in Sicily: Palermo has twelve theatres, Catania a few less, and the summer sees open-air performances in many places, including some dramatic productions in the ancient theatres at Siracusa, Tíndari and Taormina. The biggest and most famous theatrical productions are the biennial classical dramas performed at Siracusa (May and June in even-numbered years), and the Pirandello week (July) performances at Agrigento. All theatre performances will, however, be in Italian , although it's well worth getting tickets to the Siracusa and Agrigento performances anyway. You should also try to spend at least one evening at a Sicilian **puppet theatre** (*teatro dei pupi*). A traditional entertainment, there are still some original theatres around in Palermo and elsewhere, as well as a few productions put on for tourists. Check the text for details of where to catch a performance, and see below for the full picture on who's doing what and why, once you get there.

PUPPET THEATRE: THE STORY

Popular in Sicily since the 14C, the stories portrayed by the puppets, or marionettes, are always the same – chivalric episodes from the lives of the Paladins, the twelve peers of Charlemagne's court. Basically, it's a tale of the clash between Christianity and Islam, and while the particular **story** unfolds in fairly incomprehensible Sicilian dialect, the **format** is straightforward and unchanged from theatre to theatre. A succession of stiff-legged knights is introduced, the main two Orlando (or Roland) and Rinaldo; they always stand on the left side of the stage and strut around as the puppeteer lists their exploits and achievements; the Saracens, with baggy trousers and shields marked with stars and crescents, stand on the right. There may be a love interest, too, perhaps a jousting tournament to decide who gets the hand of Charlemagne's daughter. But the main business of each performance is the succession of formal, staged **battles** between the Christian knights and the Saracen invaders. Cross-stage charges by Orlando and Rinaldo, accompanied by drums and shouts, lead to the inevitable clashes of sword and armour, the pile of Saracen dead mounting with each attack. There's often a distraction between bouts as Orlando fights a crocodile, or confonts other monsters and magicians sent to try him. But whatever the enemy, the engagements are always coloured by great splashes of artificial blood spurted from bodies as each victim tries to outdo the one before in groaning and shrieking. The climax will be the representation of some great historical battle, like Roncesvalles, culminating in betrayal and treachery for the boys who face an untimely and drawn-out death on the battlefield.

Most Sicilians know the stories and a performance in an original theatre is accompanied by a lot of vocal audience participation. If you want more enlightenment, you can see examples of the puppets, stage scenery, handbills and other paraphernalia at the Museo delle Marionette (p.58), or the Museo Etnográfico (p.61), both in Palermo.

POLICE AND THIEVES

Mention Sicily to most people and they think of the Mafia. But the association is one you'll forget as soon as you set foot on the island: Cosa Nostra is as invisible as it is ineradicable, and the violence that sporadically erupts is almost always an 'in-house' affair.

Of more immediate concern is **petty juvenile crime**, mainly in the cities and more prevalent here than elsewhere in Italy, barring Naples. Bag-snatchers, *scippatori*, will strike in crowded streets or markets, on foot or on scooters, disappearing before you've had time to react. As well as handbags, they whip wallets, tear off visible jewellery and, if they're really adroit, unstrap watches. You can minimise the risk of this happening by being discreet: don't flash anything of value, keep a firm hand on your camera, and carry shoulderbags, as you'll see many Sicilian women do, slung across your body. It's a good idea, too, to entrust money and credit cards to hotel-managers. On the whole it's common sense to avoid badly-lit areas at night, or deserted inner-city areas by day. Confronted with a robber, your best bet is to submit meekly: it's an excitable situation where panic can lead to violence – though very few tourists see anything of this.

THE POLICE

If the worst happens, you'll be forced to have some dealings with the **police**. In Sicily, as in the rest of Italy, they come in many forms. Most innocuous are the *Polizia Urbana* or town police, mainly concerned with directing the traffic and punishing parking offences. The *Guardia di Finanza*, often heavily armed and screaming ostentatiously through the cities, are interested in smuggling, tax evasion and other crimes of that ilk, and the *Poliza Stradale* patrol motorways. Most conspicuous are *the Carabinieri* and *Polizia Statale*; no one knows what distinguishes their roles, apart from the fact that the *Carabinieri* – the ones with the blue uniforms – are organised along military lines, and are a branch of the armed forces. They are also the butt of most of the jokes about the police, usually on the 'How many *Carabinieri* does it take to…?' level. Each of the two forces is meant to act as a check and counter-balance to the other: a fine theory, though it results in a lot of time-wasting and rivalry in practice. Hopefully, you won't need to get entangled with either, but **in the event of theft**, you'll need to report it at the headquarters of the *Polizia Statale*, the *Questura*; you'll find their address in the local *Tuttocittà* magazine, and we've included details in the various city listings. The *Questura* is also where you're supposed to go to obtain a *permesso di soggiorno* **if you're staying** for any length of time, or a **visa extension** if you require one.

In any brush with the authorities, your experience will very much depend on the individuals you're dealing with. Apart from **topless bathing** (permitted, but don't try anything more daring) and **camping rough**, don't expect a soft touch if you've been picked up for any offence, especially if it's **drugs**-related: it's not unheard of to be stopped and searched if you're young and carry a rucksack. Drugs are generally frowned upon by everyone above a certain age, and universal hysteria about *la droga*, fuelled by the epidemic of heroin addiction that is a serious problem all over Italy, means that any distinction between the 'hard' and 'soft' variety has become blurred. Theoretically everything is illegal over and above the possession of a few grams of cannabis or marijuana 'for personal use', though there's no agreed definition of what this means. In general the south of Italy is more intolerant than the north, and in any case, if found with suspicious substances you can be kept in gaol for as long as it takes for them to analyse the stuff, draw up reports and wait for the bureaucratic wheels to grind – which can be several weeks, and sometimes months. For the nearest **British consulate** (in Naples/Rome), see Palermo's *Listings* section (p.67), though bear in mind that they're unlikely to be very sympathetic, or do anything more than put you in touch with a lawyer.

EMERGENCIES

In an **emergency**, note the following national emergency telephone numbers.

☎112 for the police (*Carabinieri*).

☎113 for any emergency service (*Soccorso Pubblico di Emergenza*).

☎115 for the fire brigade (*Vigili del Fuoco*).

☎116 for road assistance (*Soccorso Stradale*).

SEXUAL HARASSMENT AND WOMEN IN SICILY

Italy has a reputation for **sexual harassment** of women that is well-known and well-founded. Generally it's worse the further south you travel and many women count Sicily as the nadir of their experiences in this respect. If you're travelling on your own, or with another woman, you can expect to be tooted and whistled at in towns every time you step outside the hotel door. You're also likely to attract unwelcome attention in bars, restaurants and on the beach. This persistent pestering is not usually made with any kind of violent intent, but it's annoying and frustrating nevertheless. There are a few things you can do to ward it off, though you'll never be able to stop the car-horns and wolf-whistles. Indifference is often the most effective policy, or try hurling a few well-chosen examples of the vernacular, like *lasciátemi in pace* ('leave me alone'), *sei fesso?* ('are you stupid?'), or – when all else has failed – *va fan culo* ('fuck off'). As a last resort, don't hesitate to approach a policeman. Obviously, travelling with a man cuts out much of the more intense hassle, though even this won't deter the more determined onslaughts.

Perhaps the best strategy of all for a woman alone in Sicily, where the sanctity of the family is still paramount, is to flaunt a wedding ring. As you might guess from the prominence of the Virgin Mary in all post-Norman churches in Sicily, women are certainly not absent from the Sicilian landscape, it's just that most of them are mothers. The gap between marriage and motherhood is usually very small, while unmarried women are carefully closeted indoors, their only escape the evening *passeggiata* – needless to say, well-chaperoned. Unlike the rest of Italy, in Sicily you won't even see women working in the countryside, another legacy of the Arabs.

Hardly surprising then, that women tourists, radiating freedom and independence, are assumed to be easy numbers, and that Sicilian women themselves have found it so hard to break the rigid rules governing their conduct.* The degree of freedom they enjoy varies from place to place: it's probably greatest in Messina, smallest in the rural interior. Catania is fairly progressive, but Palermo still labours in the Dark Ages. It's here, though, that you'll find most of the very low level of feminist activity on the island, at *ARCI-Donna* (via Dante 44; ☎091-588.994), a branch of the *Partito Comunista*, and *Unione di Donne Italiane* (via Siracusa 16; ☎091-329.604); these are the people you should contact for information on the present women's movement scene.

---

* The problems women face are closely linked to the problems of Sicilian men, specifically to the traditional adoration of the male-child that lingers on into adult life. After all, it is said that Jesus Christ himself was a Sicilian: he thought his father was God, his mother was a virgin, and he lived at home till he was thirty.

FINDING WORK

With an unemployment rate of 15–20%, higher than most other Italian regions, there are few opportunities to find work in Sicily.

However, all EC citizens are eligible to work, the two main **bureaucratic requirements** for both working and living in Sicily being a *libretto di lavoro* and *permesso di soggiorno*, respectively a work- and residence-permit, both available from the *Questura* (see *Police and Thieves* above). For the first you must have a letter from your prospective employers saying they are prepared to take you on, for the second (which is also necessary if you want to buy a car or have a bank account in Italy) you'll need a passport, passport-sized photos, and a lot of patience.

TEACHING

The obvious choice is to **teach English**, for which the demand has expanded enormously in recent years. You can do this in two ways: free-lance private lessons, or through a language school. **Private lessons** generally pay best, and you can charge up to L25,000 an hour, though there's scope for bargaining. Advertise in bars, shop windows and local newspapers, and, most importantly, get the news around by word-of-mouth that you're looking for work, emphasising your excellent background, qualifications and experience. An advantage of private teaching is that you can start at any time of the year (summer especially is a good time because there are schoolchildren and students who have to re-take exams in September); the main disadvantage is that it can take weeks to get off the ground, and you need enough money to support you until then. You'll find the best opportunities for this kind of work in the tourist resorts and the bigger towns and cities.

With **teaching in schools**, you start earning immediately. Teaching classes usually involves more hours per week, often in the evening, and for less per hour, though the amount you get depends on the school. Don't accept anything less than L10,000 an hour – the bigger schools should pay much more than this. For the less reputable places, you can get away without any qualifications and a bit of bluff, but you'll need to show a TEFL certificate for the more professional language schools. For these, it's best to apply in writing from Britain (look for the ads in the *Guardian* and *Times Educational Supplement* and contact the *Italian Cultural Institute* at 39 Belgrave Square, London SW1; ☎01-235 1461), preferably before the summer, though you can also find openings in September. If you're looking on the spot, sift through the 'yellow pages'

(*págine gialle*) and do the rounds on foot, asking to speak to the *direttore* or his/her secretary; don't bother to try in August when everything is closed. The best teaching jobs of all are with a university as a *lettore*, a job requiring fewer hours than the language schools and generally offering a fuller pay-packet. Universities need English-language teachers in most faculties and you should write to the individual faculties at the universities of Messina, Catania or Palermo (addressed to *Ufficio di Personale*). Strictly speaking, you could get by without any knowledge of Italian while teaching, but some definitely helps.

OTHER OPTIONS

If teaching's not up your street, there's the possibility of **courier work** in the summer, especially around the resorts of Cefalù and Taormina. These are the only places where you might find **bar/restaurant work** too – not the most lucrative of jobs, though you should make enough to keep you in Sicily over the summer. You'll have to ask around for both types of work, and some knowledge of Italian is essential. **Au pairing** is another option: contact *Au Pairs Italy*, 46 The Rise, Sevenoaks, Kent TN13 1RJ (☎0732-461522) for more information.

DIRECTORY

ADDRESSES Usually written as the street-name followed by the number – eg via Roma 69. *Interno* refers to the flat-number – eg *interno* 5 (often abbreviated as int.).

AIRPORT TAX None to pay.

BARGAINING Not really on in shops and restaurants, though you'll find you can get a 'special price' for some rooms and cheap hotels if you're staying a few days; and that things like boat/bike hire and guided tours (especially out of season) are negotiable. In markets, you'll be taken for an imbecile if you don't haggle for everything except food.

BEACHES You'll have to pay a few hundred lire for access to most of the better beaches (referred to as lidos), a few thousand to hire a sun-bed and shade and use the showers all day. Elsewhere, on the offshore islands and along the south coast, they're free though not always clean. During winter most beaches look like rubbish dumps, which is what they are: it's not worth anyone's while to clean them until the season starts at Easter.

BRING Photographic film . . . and wait until you get home to have them developed too, as it costs around twice as much in Sicily; an alarm clock for early morning buses; mosquito repellent and antiseptic cream; a water bottle for visiting hot, exposed archaeological sites; English tea-bags (Italian tea is very weak) and a torch if you're camping.

CAMPING GAZ Easy enough to buy for the small portable camping stoves, either from hardware stores (a *ferramenta*) or camping/sports shops. You can't carry canisters on aeroplanes.

CIGARETTES Everyone smokes *MS*, the cheapest brand – fairly strong and less expensive than in Britain. You buy cigarettes (and tobacco) in shops called *tabacchi*, which distinguish themselves by a sign outside with a T on it. Historically, tobacco and salt were both state monopolies, sold only in *tabacchi* – salt's no longer deemed so important, but cigarettes are still hard to track down anywhere else. You'll be able to buy sweets and stamps in a *tabacchi* too.

CONSULATES Nearest consulates are in Naples or Rome, see p.67.

CONTRACEPTION Condoms (*profilático*) available over the counter at all chemists and some supermarkets; the Pill (*la píllola*) on prescription only.

DISABLED TRAVELLERS Facilities aren't particularly geared towards disabled travellers, though people are helpful enough. Disabled drivers should contact *Radar*, 25 Mortimer Street, London W1 (☎01-637 5400) to obtain a badge enabling them to park more freely. A list of tour operators who specialise in holidays for the disabled is available from the Italian State Tourist Office, see p.9 for address.

ELECTRICITY The supply is 220V, though anything requiring 240V will work. Most plugs are two round pins: a travel plug is useful.

GAY LIFE There's not much of a gay scene in Sicily, no gay resorts and few specifically gay bars and clubs. In this respect, Sicily has much in common with the rest of the south of Italy, where attitudes towards homosexuality (male and female) are generally much less tolerant than in Rome or the industrial north. That said, there's no legally-sanctioned discrimination against gays and what gay groups there are in Italy work at getting the public to accept and understand homosexuality. Also, it's worth noting that physical contact between men is fairly common in Sicily, on the level of linking arms and kissing cheeks at greetings and farewells – though an overt display of anything remotely ambiguous is likely to be met by hostility. The only contact address in Sicily is the Palermo branch of *ARCI-Gay* (see p.67), part of the cultural wing of the Communist Party's youth section.

KIDS Children are revered in Sicily and will be made a fuss of in the street, welcomed and catered for in bars and restaurants. Hotels normally charge around 30% extra to put a bed or cot in your room, though kids pay less on trains (see *Getting Around*). The only hazards when travelling with children in Sicily in summer are the heat and sun.

LAUNDERETTES Coin-operated launderettes are very rare, though see the *Listings* section for Palermo. More common is a *lavanderia*, a service-wash laundry, but this will be expensive. Although you can usually get away with it, washing clothes in your hotel room can cause an international incident – simply because the room's plumbing often can't cope with all the water. It's better to ask if there's somewhere you can wash your clothes.

PUBLIC TOILETS Usually found in bars and restaurants and you'll generally be allowed to use them whether you're eating and drinking or not. Carry a supply of your own paper around and don't expect facilities to be spotless.

TAMPONS From chemists and supermarkets everywhere; slightly more expensive than in Britain.

TIME Sicily (and Italy) is always one hour ahead of Britain except for one week at the end of September when the time is the same.

VACCINATIONS None required. However, cholera and typhoid jabs are a wise precaution if you intend to continue to North Africa – in which case make sure you also have an up-to-date polio booster.

WAR CEMETERIES World War II saw several fiercely contested battles on Sicilian soil; information and a list of Allied cemeteries from the *Commonwealth War Graves Commission*, 2 Marlow Road, Maidenhead, Berkshire (☎0628-34221).

WATER Safe to drink everywhere, though bottled mineral water is always more pleasant.

PART TWO

THE
GUIDE

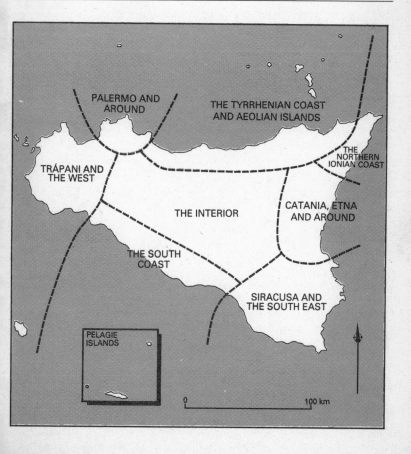

PALERMO AND
AROUND

THE TYRRHENIAN COAST
AND AEOLIAN ISLANDS

THE
NORTHERN
IONIAN COAST

TRÁPANI AND
THE WEST

THE INTERIOR

CATANIA, ETNA
AND AROUND

THE SOUTH
COAST

SIRACUSA AND
THE SOUTH EAST

PELAGIE
ISLANDS

0   100 km

CHAPTER ONE

PALERMO AND AROUND

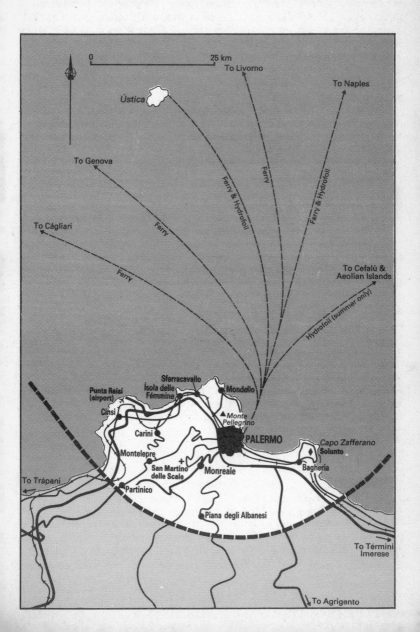

U nmistakably the capital of Sicily, **Palermo** is fast, brash, loud and exciting. Hub of the island since the 9C, it borrows heavily from the past for its present-day look, the city showing a typically Sicilian fusion of foreign art, architecture, culture and lifestyle. In the narrow streets of Palermo's old town elegant Baroque and Norman monuments exist cheek-by-jowl with Arabic cupolas, Byzantine street-markets swamp the medieval warrens, and the latest Milanese fashions sit in shops squeezed between Renaissance churches and Spanish palazzi. And ricocheting off every wall, the endless roar of traffic adds to the confusion. The city was recently nominated the noisiest in Italy, and there's pollution in the air, too – a pall of yellow smog hangs over Palermo, visible on bad days from the sea or from the mountains behind.

It may not be the healthiest place in the world, but it's certainly not dull, with the oppressive summer climate and frenetic street-scenes redolent of North Africa or the Near East. Indeed, there's little that's strictly European about Palermo, and its geographical isolation has forced the city to forge its own identity, distinct enough to demand that you devote a fair proportion of your stay in Sicily to the capital and its environs. Easily the most populous centre on the island, with around 700,000 inhabitants, a week wouldn't be too long here. In terms of sights, Palermo has some of the island's most intriguing; also some of its best food and markets, cheapest hotels, and easy access to one of Sicily's finest beaches, at **Mondello**. The other obvious quick retreat from Palermo's bustle is to the heights of **Monte Pellegrino**, the mountain which looms beyond the city to the north.

More substantial targets lie just outside the city's boundaries, most warranting a day-trip. If your enthusiasm has been fired by the city's great Norman heritage, you shouldn't miss the medieval cathedral of **Monreale** and its celebrated mosaics. The **Golfo di Carini**, the curving bay to the west of Palermo, sports a couple of low-key holiday resorts, all with beaches of varying attractiveness and local popularity. Or, heading east along the coast, you can spend an unhurried afternoon at **Bagheria** and its palazzi, and take in the nearby Roman site at **Solunto**. Further afield, around 25km south of Palermo, **Piana degli Albanesi** survives as an Albanian Orthodox enclave in a stridently Catholic island. Further out is the offshore island of **Ústica**, possible to visit in a day, though you're likely to want to stay much longer, given the natural attractions of this craggy, black, volcanic slab.

PALERMO

In its own wide bay underneath the limestone bulk of Monte Pellegrino, and fronting the broad and fertile *Conca d'Oro* ('Golden Shell') valley, **PALERMO** is stupendously sited. Originally a Phoenician colony, it was taken by the Carthaginians in the 5C BC and became an important Punic baulk against the Greek influence elsewhere on the island. Named Panormus (or 'All Harbour'), its mercantile attractions were obvious, and it remained in Carthaginian hands until 254 BC. Long considered a prize worth capturing, the city then fell to the Romans, despite a desperate counter-siege by

Hamilcar Barca, directed from the slopes of Monte Pellegrino. Yet Palermo's most glorious days were still to come: the **Arabs** captured the city in 831 AD and under them and, two centuries later, the **Normans**, Palermo flowered as Europe's greatest metropolis – famed for the wealth of its court, and unrivalled as a centre of learning.

This century, by way of contrast, has been one of social and economic decline. Allied bombs during **World War II** destroyed much of the port area, and turned parts of the medieval town into a ramshackle demolition site – a state of affairs that, 45 years on, has still not been resolved, and much of Palermo nowadays seems ominously poor and decaying. Unemployment is endemic, the old port largely idle, and **petty crime** commonplace. Palermo's underworld exists on many levels and, in a city that absorbs its villains with ease, you'd be well advised to take all due precautions – avoiding the market and back-street areas after dark, and not flashing around bulging wallets and cameras.

However, most areas are never anything less than perfectly safe in the daytime and nothing should put you off getting around the city. There are notable relics extant from the 9–12C, Palermo in its prime, but it's the rebuilding of the 16C and 17C that shaped the city as it appears today: essentially a straightforward street-grid confused by the memory of an Eastern past and gouged by World War II bombs. Traditionally Palermo has been a city of rich **churches**, endowed by the island's ruling families and wealthy monastic orders, and they're still an obvious draw for visitors, from the hybrid **Cattedrale** and the nearby mosaic-decorated **Cappella Palatina**, tucked inside the Royal Palace, to the glorious Norman foundations of **La Martorana** and **San Giovanni degli Eremeti**. And that's not counting the Baroque candidates, like **San Giuseppe dei Teatini** and **Santa Caterina**. Really, though, to see Palermo in terms of an architectural tour would be to ignore much: three significant **museums** – inspiring collections of art, archaeology and ethnography – some splendid markets, back-street puppet theatres, and a wealth of bars and restaurants.

The Mafia in Palermo

The **Mafia** problem, the most glaring symptom of decay in Palermo, is intimately connected with the welfare of the city. For years it has been openly acknowledged that a large part of the funds pouring in from Rome and the European Community, ostensibly to redevelop the city centre, are unaccounted for – channeled to dubious businessmen, or simply raked off by Mafia leaders. The subtle control exerted by the Mafia is traditionally referred to only obliquely, though it periodically erupts into the news. Mafia issues have had a higher profile than usual of late, following a series of high-security show trials in Palermitan law courts, and a recent spate of shootings in the city, one largely the result of the other, as vendettas and realignments convulse the old hierarchies of the underworld.

The problem is deeply rooted and unlikely to go away, despite the courageous efforts of various individuals. Prominent among these is Palermo's mayor, **Leoluca Orlandi**, who has attempted to combat corruption at municipal level by removing companies suspected of links with organised crime from the tenders list for new contracts. It's a brave stand, and one which gives him short odds on surviving close Mafia attention in the future. The problem has recently assumed new proportions as preparations for the 1990 World Cup soccer tournament get under way: several of the matches are to be held in Palermo, generating a stack of new business that Orlandi will be hard-pushed to keep out of the Mafia's hands.

Fortunately, the Mafia has little relevance for casual travellers, and the closest you'll get to it is through the screaming headlines of local newspapers. Follow the rules and you'll probably avoid having your bag snatched by Vespa-borne delinquents, many destined to be sucked into the lower ranks of the big Mafia families.

Arriving

All planes use the **airport** at Punta Raisi, 31km west of the city. From just outside, fairly regular buses (*Prestia & Comandè;* fifteen daily) run right into the centre, stopping behind the Politeama Garibaldi theatre on via I. La Lumia: first bus at 5.40am, last bus 9.30pm, journey time 45 minutes; buy your ticket (L3300) on the bus. Taxi fares for the same trip run to around L45,000 per car, so night-flight arrivals may have no option but to wait for the first bus of the day. (Palermo is *not* the island's main airport, Catania is; facilities are spartan, and the seats are fairly uncomfortable, though there is a bar.) For details of car-hire at the airport see *Listings*, p.67.

Trains all arrive at and leave from Stazione Centrale, in piazza Giulio Césare at the southern end of via Roma. Some (from Trápani/Álcamo) stop first in the north west of the city at Stazione Notarbartolo: sit tight and you'll end up at Stazione Centrale. Local, provincial and long-distance, island-wide **buses** operate from a variety of terminals all over the city, of which there are full details in *Listings*. Handily, though, the **main bus arrivals** are in the streets around the railway station: *SAIS* buses (from Rome, Catania, Enna, Messina, Siracusa and Cefalù) stop at via P. Balsamo 16, *Segesta* (from Rome and Trápani) at via P. Balsamo 26, and *Cuffaro* (from Agrigento) at via Lincoln 42. The other major termini for buses are piazza Marina, down by the old port, and piazza Lolli, off via Dante from piazza Castelnuovo – both mostly used by *AST* services to and from Palermo province.

Palermo is a grand place in which to arrive by sea, all **ferry** services – from Ústica, Genova, Livorno, Naples and Cágliari (in Sardinia) – docking at the Stazione Maríttima, just off via Francesco Crispi, from where it's a ten-minute walk (straight up via E. Amari) to piazza Castelnuovo and the modern city centre. There are also regular **hydrofoil** connections with Ústica and occasional summer hydrofoil services from Cefalù and the Aeolian Islands, again docking at the Stazione Maríttima. *Listings* has all the relevant ticket-office details.

Driving into the city is madness, something to avoid if you possibly can. Directional signs are confusing and the traffic unforgiving of first-time-around foreigners. Coming in on the A20 (from Cefalù), turn right at the first round-

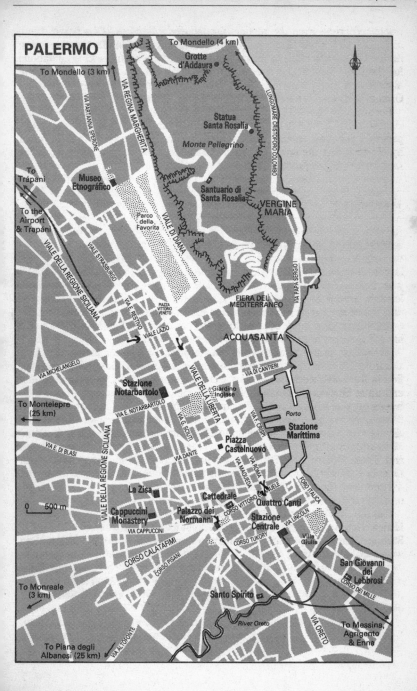

PALERMO

To Mondello (4 km)

To Mondello (3 km)

Grotte
d'Addaura

Statua
Santa Rosalia

Monte Pellegrino

To
Trápani

Museo
Etnográfico

To the
Airport
& Trapáni

Parco
della
Favorita

Santuario di
Santa Rosalia

VERGINE
MARIA

FIERA DEL
MEDITERRANEO

PIAZZA
VITTORIO
VENETO

ACQUASANTA

VIALE STRASBURGO

VIALE DELLA REGIONE SICILIANA

VIA MICHELANGELO

VIA E. RESTIVO

VIALE LAZIO

VIA DI CANTIERI

To Montelepre
(25 km)

Stazione
Notarbartolo

VIA E. NOTARBARTOLO

Giardino
Inglese

VIA G. SCIUTI

Porto

Stazione
Marittima

VIA E. DI BLASI

VIALE DELLA LIBERTA

VIA DANTE

VIA CRISPI

Piazza
Castelnuovo

VIA MAQUEDA

VIA ROMA

FORO ITALICA

0   500 m

La Zisa

Cattedrale

CORSO VITTORIO EMANUELE

Quattro Canti

VIALE DELLA REGIONE SICILIANA

Cappuccini
Monastery

Palazzo dei
Normanni

Stazione
Centrale

VIA LINCOLN

VIA CAPPUCCINI

Villa
Giulia

CORSO CALATAFIMI

CORSO TUKORY

San Giovanni
dei
Lebbrosi

To Monreale
(3 km)

CORSO PISANI

CORSO DEI MILLE

Santo Spirito

VIA ALTOFONTE

River Oreto

VIA ORETO

To Messina,
Agrigento
& Enna

To Piana degli
Albanesi (25 km)

LUNGOMARE CRISTOFORO COLOMBO

VIA PAPA SERGIO

VIALE DI DIANA

VIA REGINA MARGHERITA

VIA PARTANNA SPERONE

about and keep straight on to reach Stazione Centrale. Otherwise, follow anything that says *Centro* and aim/ask for piazza Castelnuovo – around which is the best place to dump your vehicle. Finding a **parking space** can be a real problem at any time, apart from the early morning or late evening, though you might get lucky if you drive around for long enough; if someone in a peaked cap shows you to a space, they're a contracted attendant to whom you give L1000. There are always **garages** scattered about town, a wise option if you have to leave your car in Palermo's old-town area overnight; there's a list of some of the most central ones on p.67. *Never* leave anything of value, including the radio, visible in the car, and retract your aerial if you can or someone will probably snap it off. **Leaving the city** by car you need via Oreto, behind Stazione Centrale, for the Palermo-Catania (A20) and Palermo-Messina (A19) motorways; Corso Vittorio Emanuele (westbound) for Monreale; and viale della Libertà (northbound) for the airport and Trápani.

Orientation: some pointers

Much of the old medieval street system survives in Palermo, particularly in the area just north of the railway station, which makes losing your way a distinct possibility if you don't take note of the major landmarks and thoroughfares – though our maps should be sufficient for most purposes.

On the ground the **medieval town** isn't as difficult to negotiate as it looks. It's quartered by two distinctive straight roads: the **Corso Vittorio Emanuele**, which runs from the old harbour, La Cala, south west to both royal palace and cathedral; and, crossing it, **via Maqueda**, which starts just to the west of the railway station and runs north west – both streets dating from the city reconstruction of the 16C. The crossroads is known as the **Quattro Canti**, the centre (if anywhere is) of the medieval town area. Parallel to via Maqueda, and running north from piazza Giulio Césare, **via Roma** was a much later addition, the two parallel streets now carrying most of central Palermo's traffic. In between, and on either side of these streets, you'll find nearly all the major sights, churches and buildings. And if you keep surfacing from the labyrinthine alleys onto the main streets, you shouldn't go too far wrong.

Further north everything becomes much clearer, most of the **modern city** being a frustrated grid-plan of large proportions. Beyond Corso Vittorio Emanuele, via Maqueda (and its continuation, via Ruggero Séttimo) and via Roma strike off for the double squares of **piazza Ruggero Séttimo** and **piazza Castelnuovo** – a hefty 25 to 30 minutes' walk if you've come from the railway station. East of here, down at the water, is the Stazione Maríttima, while further north still, Palermo assumes a more European mantle: **viale della Libertà** is the central spine of a staid, gridded network of shops, apartments and office blocks, which runs right the way to the southern end of the **Parco della Favorita**.

Information and getting around

You'll be able to pick up **information** and free **maps** from small offices at most points of arrival: at the **airport** (Mon–Sat 8am–8pm; ☎091-591.698), **Stazione Centrale** (opposite the main snack bar, Mon–Fri 8am–8pm, Sat 8am–2pm; ☎091-616.5914) and **Stazione Maríttima** (Mon–Sat 9am–1.30pm; ☎091-586.830).

You face a fairly lengthy walk, though, if you want to use Palermo's main **EPT** (Mon–Fri 8am–8pm, Sat 8am–2pm; ☎091-586.122/583.847) – on the ground floor at piazza Castelnuovo 34, hidden behind the trees across from the bandstand. Few of the staff speak English, but if you haven't already got one you can get a big free map of the city and province from here (also including maps of Ústica, Mondello and Cefalù); and a booklet in English (*Palermo Hotels*) containing full accommodation lists (and prices), local bus details and some handy addresses. There's another central EPT office in **piazza Sepolcro** (Mon–Sat 8am–2pm; ☎091-616.1361), below the church of San Cataldo off via Maqueda.

For more complete **city listings** and a rundown of **what's on where**, pick up a copy of *Un Mese a Palermo*, a free arts and entertainment guide issued monthly and available from the EPT offices. It's in Italian but fairly easy to decipher. There's an afternoon daily paper too, *L'Ora*, available from newsstands all over the city, which details forthcoming events and also includes transport timetables.

Getting around the city

While Palermo is very much a city in which to **walk** when you can, you'll find getting around exclusively on foot exhausting and impractical, certainly for the peripheral sights. The **city buses** (run by *AMAT*) are easy to use, covering every corner of Palermo and stretching out to Monreale, Mondello and beyond. There's a flat fare of L600 and you buy **tickets** from *AMAT*'s glass kiosks (outside Stazione Centrale or at the southern end of viale della Libertà), in *tabacchi*, or wherever else you see the sign *Vendita Biglietti AMAT*: validate one in the machine at the back of the bus each time you ride. If you intend to hop about a bit there's a **discount** if you buy twenty tickets at once (L10,000). **Fare dodging** – seemingly commonplace – is theoretically punished by spot-fines from roving gangs of inspectors who board buses at random. More likely, especially if you're a tourist, you'll just be made to buy a ticket: it's not unusual on rush-hour buses that *every* person aboard has to cough up.

As far as **routes** go, the box below details some of the most useful ones. One thing to watch out for is that some buses have the same number as others but run on different routes: these buses are distinguished either by the colour of the bus-number (usually black but sometimes red), or by a stripe (or bar) through the number. We show them written as #42 (red), or #∄.

CENTRAL CITY BUSES

From the ranks outside Stazione Centrale
#5 to piazza Marina/Corso Vittorio Emanuele.
#14, #15, #16 and #19 to piazza Ruggero Séttimo/piazza Castelnuovo.
#14 and #15 to Parco della Favorita/Mondello; and #6 in summer direct to Mondello.
#9 or #27 to piazza dell'Indipendenza (for Palazzo dei Normanni).

From via Lincoln
#39 to Stazione Maríttima.

From Corso Vittorio Emanuele
#5, #8, #23 run along the Corso.
#3 to Mondello (from Quattro Canti/via Maqueda).

From via Roma
#41 and #43 to via Príncipe di Belmonte.
#2 to Giardino Inglese.

Elsewhere, the text details numbers and routes where relevant. Buses run up until around 11pm, when **night-services** take over on all the main routes – generally once an hour, even out as far as Mondello. You'll find main **city bus ranks** outside the railway station, in piazza Castelnuovo/piazza Ruggero Séttimo, along Corso Vittorio Emanuele and along the southern stretch of viale della Libertà.

Other forms of city transport are few and far between. Don't be afraid of hailing a **taxi** (ranks outside the station and in other main squares), a safe way to get around at night. They're cheap, L500 on the clock, L2000 for the first kilometre and L900 for each kilometre after that: just make sure the meter is switched on, or for long distances (back from Mondello, say) agree on a price beforehand. Taking a horse-drawn carriage, a *carrozza*, would be a rather swanky way to see the city. They lurk outside Stazione Centrale: get a group together and, again, agree on a price before setting off. Don't consider getting around the city **under your own steam**: hiring a car just to see congested Palermo would be extremely misguided, there's nowhere to rent a bike or scooter, and in any case one short afternoon driving here could take years off your life.

Finding a place to stay

Palermo is the easiest Sicilian city in which to find good, cheap **accommodation**. Prices here are the lowest on the island, though in high season (July and August), and especially around the time of Palermo's annual festival (July 11–15), you'd be wise not to leave it too late in the day if you want the better rooms; before noon is best, or ring ahead and reserve. Otherwise, just turn up and check out the options.

Hostels and camping

There's no *IYHF* hostel but there's been talk of a city-run **youth hostel** in Palermo for years: it even appears in the EPT accommodation listings. But it has yet to open. When it does it will be out at SFERRACAVALLO (see p.74), thirteen kilometres north west of the city, reachable on bus #28 from the Politeama theatre; check with the EPT for the latest details. Also at Sferracavallo are the two nearest **campsites** to the city: *Trinacria* (☎091-530.590), on via Barcarello, open all year and with four-bedded **cabins** for rent (L45,000); and the cheaper *Ulivo* (☎091-584.392), May to October only, on via Pegaso. Other sites within range are stretched along the Golfo di Carini, to the west of the city; see p.74–75.

Don't even think of **sleeping rough** in the centre of the city: if the thieves don't get you, the police will. Even hanging around Stazione Centrale is rife with risk. Best bet, if you're desperate, is to head for the open spaces of Monte Pellegrino (see p.70), and don't sleep out alone.

Hotels: *alberghi, pensioni* and *locande*

Nearly all the reasonable budget **hotel accommodation** in Palermo is to be found on and around the southern ends of via Maqueda and via Roma, roughly in the area between Stazione Centrale and Corso Vittorio Emanuele. Here, there are often several separate places in the same block, usually cheaper the higher the floor. Beyond the Corso the streets begin to widen out and the hotels get more expensive, though there are some notable exceptions. Our lists below are divided by price and listed alphabetically.

Something to note is that although there are a couple of cheapish places in and around La Kalsa (see p.59), it's largely an area to avoid at night. Also, women might feel safer if they stay in hotels on the main roads, rather than side-streets – though all the places listed are safe enough, unless otherwise stated.

Inexpensive: under L25,000

Locanda Calabrese, via Orologio 56 (☎091-587.095; L14,000); a right turn off via Maqueda at the Teatro Mássimo. Fairly handily sited, halfway between old and new Palermo, but on a rather dingy side-street.

Cortese, via Scarparelli 16 (☎091-331.722; L24,000); follow the signs from via Maqueda that point left down via dell'Università. This place is alright, but the area is not particularly salubrious, and rather intimidating at night.

Locanda Eden, via Maqueda 8 (☎091-237.455; L15,000). As cheap as you'll get, but not terribly inspiring; one of several places in this block. Inexpensive singles too, and showers for L2000.

Locanda d'Ignoti, via Roma 188 (☎091-331.282; L16,000). Again, dirt cheap, but a fairly grotty choice.

Locanda Marchese Maria, vicolo dei Mezzani 4 (☎091-321.909; L15,000); from the railway station, turn right down Corso Vittorio Emanuele at its junction with via Roma, and the entrance is just on the left down a narrow street, part of the Vucciria market. Welcoming, if on the noisy side; spartan but clean rooms, showers L2000 extra.

Milton, via Roma 188 (☎091-331.282; L20,000). Nice, clean rooms, a good bargain; showers L2000.

Locanda Sabatino, via Maqueda 165 (☎091-283.649; L16,000). Fine building, good rooms, and excellent location – just around the corner from La Martorana church.

Locanda Serena, via Roma 72 (☎091-281.731; L18,000). Very friendly, big rooms, free hot water and splendid views of central Palermo from its fifth-floor bathroom window. Recommended.

Pensione Sud, via Maqueda 8 (☎091-283.681; L24,000). Large rooms and handy for the railway station; showers included in the price.

Universo, piazzetta Chiesa Cocchieri 4 (☎091-616.5232; L18,000). Good value, right in the middle of the rundown via Alloro in La Kalsa, though the area's a bit freaky at night. Not advised for single women; showers L2000.

Moderate: L25,000–35,000

Alessandra, via Divisi 99 (☎091-616.7009; L32,000 with bath); at the corner with via Maqueda. Nice modern rooms in a well-maintained building; a safe choice for single women.

Castelnuovo, piazza Castelnuovo 50 (☎091-334.072; L30,000); under the Cambridge Academy. Best if most noisily sited of the cheaper hotels in the modern city.

Concordia, via Roma 72 (☎091-617.1514; L29,000). Rather indifferently run, but a reasonable enough price for its rooms.

Diana, via Roma 188 (☎091-329.959; L28,000). One of several in this block, a fair second choice after the *Milton*, see above.

Italia, via Roma 62 (☎091-616.5397; L27,000). Reputed to be friendly; shower included in the price.

Madonia, via Mariano Stabile 136 (☎091-333.672; L25,000). Cheaper than average along this main street in the modern city. There are several others along the street, though most are more expensive.

Odeon, via E. Amari 140 (☎091-332.778; L30,000 with bath); just to the side of the Politeama theatre. An attractively placed hotel, some rooms with balconies. A good choice if you've arrived by ferry or airport bus.

Olimpia, piazza Cassa Risparmio 18 (☎091-616.1276; L28,000 with bath); up via Roma from the railway station and on the right just before Corso Vittorio Emanuele. A pleasant hotel, cheaper than its two stars suggest, with small rooms overlooking the piazza; some cheaper double rooms without baths too.

Orientale, via Maqueda 26 (☎091-616.5727; L28,000). One of the most atmospheric hotels in the old town, an 18C palazzo with marble courtyard and columns, and one cavernous double room (no.7; L34,000, with bath) complete with long balcony overlooking via Maqueda. Recommended.

Paradiso, via Schiavuzzo 65 (☎091-617.2825; L29,000). Good location in piazza della Rivoluzione in La Kalsa, but again, caution advisable when you're coming back at night.

Petit, via Príncipe di Belmonte 84 (☎091-323.616; L34,000 with bath). Small, neat rooms in a traffic-free street; useful for arrivals at the Stazione Maríttima.

Pretoria, via Maqueda 124 (☎091-331.068; L28,000). Slightly cheaper than the *Orientale* but similarly endowed, housed in a restored palazzo. A popular hotel, showers included in the price.

Rizzico, via Mariano Stabile 139 (☎091-332.434; L25,000). Good cheap choice on this well-lit main street in the modern city; for other hotels on this street, see *Madonia* above.

Rosalia Conca d'Oro, via Santa Rosalia 7 (☎091-616.4543; L28,000). Conveniently close to Stazione Centrale, but popular and fills quickly.

Sicilia, via Divisi 99 (☎091-284.460; L35,000 with bath). One floor below the *Alessandra*, and with similar facilities; also some cheaper double rooms without bath. Good choice for women.

Vittoria, via Maqueda 8 (☎091-616.2437; L27,000). The best of the options in this block, but pricey for its old-town location.

Expensive: L35,000 upwards

Grande Albergo e delle Palme, via Roma 396 (☎091-583.933; L105,000 with bath). Easily the best hotel in central Palermo. It's a magnificent building where Richard Wagner stayed and finished composing *Parsifal* in 1882. It's also known as a meeting-place of the Mafia: Sicilian Mafia leaders met here in October 1957 to organise the operation of their heroin trade on an international basis.

Grande Albergo Sole, Corso Vittorio Emanuele 291 (☎091-581.811; L50,000, L80,000 with bath). Best of the medieval town's hotels and ideal for an extravagant end-of-holiday binge: bang next door to piazza Pretoria and close to the Cattedrale.

Le Terrazze, via Roma 188 (☎091-586.365; L39,000). Swankiest of the options in this large block, though just a bit over-priced.

Piccadilly, via Roma 72 (☎091-617.0376; L37,000). Another higher-class hotel in an otherwise cheapish block; again, expensive for what you get.

Terminus, piazza Giulio Césare 37 (☎091-616.2597; L37,000). Comfortable and convenient if you've just arrived after a long haul on the trains.

Villa Igiea Grand Hotel (☎090-543.744; L270,000) out at Acquasanta, three kilometres north of the city. A classic art nouveau building, originally a villa of the Florio family (the first people to put tuna fish into cans), designed by Ernesto Basile in 1900. Still sumptuous and for the seriously wealthy only.

The city

Historical Palermo sits compactly around one central crossroads, the **Quattro Canti**, which is at the core of four distinct quarters. The **Albergheria** and the **Capo** quarter, the latter beyond the cathedral, lie roughly west of via Maqueda; the **Vucciria** and old harbour of La Cala and **La Kalsa**, lie to the east, closest to the water. In the past there was little contact between the inhabitants of each quarter, which had their own dialects, trades, palaces and markets; even inter-marriage was frowned upon. Today these areas, together with the more modern stretch along **viale della Libertà**, hold all of Palermo's most enduring monuments and buildings. It's a fairly undisciplined mess, 16C and 17C town-planning conspiring with late 19C ambition and 20C bombs to lend an eclectic look to the city – tight alleys, stately piazzas, bomb-sites and contemporary office blocks mixed to distraction. But each quarter retains something of its medieval character in a web-like system of streets, where decaying buildings often mask gardens or chapels containing outstanding works of art, a world away from the din of the urban assault course outside.

Given that cars, let alone buses, can't get down many of the narrow streets in the old city centre, you'll often have no choice but to walk around most of what is detailed below, although for certain specific sights don't hesitate to jump on a bus. Certainly, you'll need some form of transport to reach Palermo's **outskirts**: it's no fun at all slogging up and down the long thoroughfares of the modern city.

Around the Quattro Canti

Heart of the old city – ten minutes' walk from the railway station – is the **Quattro Canti** or 'Four Corners', erected in 1611: not so much a piazza as a dingy Baroque crossroads that divides central Palermo into quadrants. You'll pass this junction many times, awash with traffic, newspaper vendors sitting under the ugly fountain water-spouts, and it's worth one stroll around to check the tiered statues – respectively a season, a king of Sicily and a patron of the city in each concave 'corner'. It's not a particularly promising starting-point, but within a few seconds' walk are some of Palermo's most opulent piazzas and buildings, including four of the city's most extraordinary churches.

On the south west corner (entrance on Corso Vittorio Emanuele), the early 17C **San Giuseppe dei Teatini** is the most harmonious of the city's Baroque churches. The misleadingly simple facade conceals a wealth of detail inside, from the tumbling angels holding the water-stoups on either side of the door to the lavish side-chapels. There's plenty of contrasting space, though, with 22 enormous columns supporting the dome, mostly restored after bomb damage in 1943. Outside, adjacent to the church, is the main building of the **Università**, a dull 19C restoration job replacing what was originally a convent adjoining San Giuseppe. There are generally plenty of students around here, and one good bar, in the little piazza across from the entrance.

Cross via Maqueda to **piazza Pretoria**, floodlit at night to highlight the nude figures of its great central fountain, a racy 16C Florentine design, since protected by railings to ward off excitable vandals. The piazza also holds the restored **Municipio**, now plaque-studded and pristine, and, towering above both square and fountain, the massive late 16C flank of the church of **Santa Caterina** (open at 10am for short visits, Sun only; enter from piazza Bellini), the antithesis of the quiet magnificence of San Giuseppe over the road. This is Sicilian Baroque at its most exuberant: every inch of the enormous interior is covered in wildly decorative, pustular relief-work, deep reds and yellows filling in between sculpted cherubs, Madonnas, lions and eagles. One marble panel (first chapel on the right) depicts Jonah about to be devoured by a rubbery-lipped whale, a Spanish galleon above constructed with wire and string rigging. An overwhelmingly theatrical design, it's difficult to argue with Vincent Cronin's image of a ' . . . frenzied mind . . . throwing out powerful and extravagant images before tumbling over the verge of madness'.

Piazza Bellini: the churches of San Cataldo and La Martorana

Just around the corner from the Pretoria fountain, **piazza Bellini** is largely a car park by day, with vehicles jammed together next to part of the city's old Roman wall and under two more wildly contrasting churches. The little Saracenic red golf-ball domes belong to **San Cataldo**, a squat 12C chapel on a palm-planted bank above the piazza. Other than the crenellations around the roof, it was never decorated, and in the 18C the chapel was even used as a post office: it still retains a good mosaic pavement in an otherwise bare and peaceful interior. (San Cataldo is usually locked: get the keys from the desk at the back of La Martorana.) The understatement of this little chapel is more than offset by the splendid interior of **La Martorana** opposite (daily 8.30am– 1pm & 3.30–7.30pm, closes 5.30pm in winter and Sun afternoons all year; free) – one of the finest surviving buildings of the medieval city. A Norman foundation, it was paid for in 1143 by George of Antioch, King Roger's admiral, from whom it received its original name, Santa Maria dell'Ammiraglio. After the Sicilian Vespers, the island's nobility met here to offer the Crown to Peter of Aragon, and under the Spanish the church was passed to a convent founded by Eloisa Martorana – hence its popular name.* It received a Baroque going-over and its curving northern facade in 1588, but happily this doesn't detract from the great power of the interior. Enter through the slim 12C campanile, an original structure which retains its ribbed arches and slender columns. Inside, on and around the columns supporting the main cupola, are a series of spectacular **mosaics**, Greek works commissioned by the admiral himself, who was of Greek descent. A gentle Christ dominates the dome, surrounded by angels, with the Apostles

---

* When Palermo's religious houses were at their late medieval height, many supported themselves by turning out remarkable sculpted confectionery – fruit and vegetables made out of coloured almond paste. La Martorana was once famous for the quality of its almond 'fruits', which were sold at the church doors, and today most Sicilian pasticcerias continue the tradition. It's always worth looking in cake-shop windows, which usually display not only fruit but also fish and shellfish made out of the same sickly almond mixture.

To Càgliari, Genova, Livorno,
Ustica & Naples
Hydrofoils to Ustica, Cefalù,
& Aeolian Islands.

100 m

Stazione Marittima

VIA FRANCESCO CRISPI

VIA FRANCESCO CRISPI

To La Favorita
& Mondello

Ucciardone
Prison

PIAZZA
UCCIARDONE

VIA DOMENICO SCINA

VIA E. AMARI

VIA PRINCIPE BELMONTE

VIA MARIANO STABILE

VIA ROMA

VIALE NOTARBARTOLO

VIA E. ALBANESE

VIA ARCHIMEDE

VIA CARINI

VIA MAZZINI

VIA DANTE

Teatro
Politeama

PIAZZA
RUGGERO
SETTIMO

VIA RUGGERO SET

VIA L. DA VINCI

VIA P. CALVI

VIA CATANIA

VIA SIRACUSA

VIALE DELLA LIBERTA

PIAZZA
MONTELEONE

EPT

VIA DI GIARDINO

Giardino
Inglese

PIAZZA
CRISPI

VIA MESSINA

VIA DANTE

VIALE DELLA LIBERTA

VIA XX SETTEMBRE

VIA PRINCIPE DI VILLAFRANCA

VIA CAVOUR

CENTRAL PALERMO

and the Madonna to the sides. The colours are still strong, a golden background enlivened by azure, grape red, light green and white, and in the morning especially, light streams through the high windows picking out the admirable craftsmanship. Heavy Baroque marble and frescoes by the entrance do their best to dampen the effect but even here there's some respite: on both sides of the steps, two more original mosaic panels (from the destroyed Norman portico) have been set in frames on the walls, a kneeling George of Antioch dedicating the church to the Virgin, and King Roger being crowned by Christ – the diamond-studded monarch contrasted with a larger, more simple and dignified Christ.

The Albergheria and the Palazzo dei Normanni

The district bounded by via Maqueda and Corso Vittorio Emanuele, just to the north west of Stazione Centrale – the **ALBERGHERIA** – can't have changed substantially for several hundred years. There are proud palazzi on via Maqueda itself, notably the 18C **Palazzo Santa Croce**, at the junction with via Bosco. But behind is a warren of tiny streets and tall, blackened and leaning buildings: it's atmospheric to wander in, and much of the central area is taken up by a street market which conceals several fine churches too. It's a poor neighbourhood, as a stroll down shored-up **via Ponticello**, a block before the university, proves – the bomb damage of World War II has never been made good. The road leads directly to the church of **Il Gesù** (or Casa Professa; daily 7–10.30am & 5–6.30pm), the first Jesuit foundation in Sicily, whose glorious Baroque swirl of inlaid marble and relief work – topped by a green and white patterned dome – took over a hundred years to complete. Via Ponticello leads down to **piazza Ballarò**, which, together with the adjacent **piazza del Cármine**, is the focus of a raucous daily fruit and veg **market**, along with some very cheap snack- and drinking-places. Above all the activity looms the bright majolica-tiled dome of the 17C church of the **Cármine**, a singular landmark amidst the dirty and rubbish-strewn alleys, with a spacious interior and adjoining cloister and convent.

Any of the long streets west of piazza del Cármine lead to via dei Benedettini, which marks the westernmost edge of the quarter. Over the busy road, behind iron gates, is the Albergheria's most peaceful haven, the deconsecrated church of **San Giovanni degli Eremeti** (Mon–Sat 9am–2pm, Tues/Wed/Fri 3–5pm, Sun 8.30am–1pm; free) – St John of the Hermits. Built in 1132, this is the most obviously Arabic of the city's Norman relics, its five ochre domes topping a small church that was built upon the remains of an earlier mosque (part of which, an adjacent empty hall, is still visible). It was especially favoured by its founder, Roger II, who granted the monks of San Giovanni 21 barrels of tuna fish a year, a prized commodity controlled by the Crown. A path leads up through citrus trees to the church, behind which lie some celebrated late-13C cloisters – perfect twin columns with slightly pointed arches, surrounding a wild garden. Immediately behind the church, on Corso Re Ruggero, the **Palazzo d'Orleans** is also set in its own garden: once home to the exiled Louis-Philippe of France in 1809, it's now the official residence of Sicily's President.

The Palazzo dei Normanni

Turn left out of San Giovanni and it's a few paces to the main road, where, if you turn right and veer left up the steps, you'll climb out of the clamorous traffic to gaze on the vast length of the **Palazzo dei Normanni** or Palazzo Reale (Mon & Fri–Sat 9am–12.30pm; free) – entrance on the left-hand side, behind Philip V's statue. A royal palace has always occupied the high ground here, above medieval Palermo. Originally built by the Saracens in the 9C, the palace was then enlarged considerably by the Normans, under whom it housed the most magnificent of medieval European courts. Sadly, there's little left from those times in the current structure. The long front was added by the Spanish in the 17C and most of the interior is now taken up by the Sicilian regional parliament (which explains the security guards and the limited opening hours).

To see anything of the interior you have to take a **tour**, which is free. Present yourself at the gate (for times, see above) and a guide steers you through the **Royal Apartments**, two flights up: pretty run-of-the-mill formal rooms except for the so-called *Sala di Ruggero*, one of the earliest parts of the palace and covered with lively 12C mosaics of hunting scenes. It's a brief visit, best done first, before you descend a floor to the beautiful **Cappella Palatina** (Mon–Sat 9am–1pm & 3–5pm, Sun 9–10am, 11–11.30am & 12.15–1pm, closed Wed afternoon; free), the undisputed artistic gem of central Palermo. The private royal chapel of Roger II, built between 1132 and 1143, its intimate interior is immediately overwhelming, with cupola, three apses and nave entirely covered in **mosaics** of outstanding quality. The oldest are those in the cupola and apses, probably completed in 1150 by Byzantine artists; those in the nave are from the hands of local craftsmen, finished twenty-odd years later and depicting Old and New Testament scenes. As at Monreale (p.71) and Cefalù (p.89), it's the powerful representation of Christ as Pantocrator which dominates the senses, bolstered here by other secondary images – Christ blessing, open book in hand, and Christ enthroned, between Peter (to whom the chapel is dedicated) and Paul. The colours are vivid, the style realistic, but even so it takes time to become accustomed to the half-light inside the chapel. However, unlike the bright pictures of La Martorana, the mosaics here give a single impression – an immediate feeling of the faith that inspired their creation and more than a hint of the mastery of the work.

Aside from the mosaics, the whole chapel is a delight. There's an Arabic ceiling with richly carved wooden stalactites, a patterned marble floor and a 12C Norman candlestick (by the pulpit), four metres high and contorted by manic carvings. Quite clearly, the chapel is stamped with a sense of Roger II's imperial standing. A dedicatory inscription around the cupola proclaims him to be ' . . . Roger, mighty ruling king . . . ' and in 1140, on Palm Sunday, it's recorded that Roger rode into the chapel on a white donkey before sitting in the royal throne at the back of the church – emphasising his role as Christ's representative on earth.

The Cattedrale and the Capo

From the Quattro Canti, the south western stretch of **Corso Vittorio Emanuele** is a busy street dotted with secondhand book shops and the wrecks of rundown 18C palazzi. Passing the peeling piazza Bologni, on the left, and the war-damaged shells of other churches and buildings, is no preparation for the huge bulk of the **Cattedrale** (daily 7am–noon & 4.30–6.30pm; free), set back in gardens on the right of the Corso. This is a more substantial Norman relic than the Royal Palace. Founded in 1185 by Palermo's English archbishop Gualtiero Offamiglio ('Walter of the Mill'), it was intended to be his power base in the city. Yet the Cattedrale wasn't finished for centuries, and in any case was quickly superseded by the glories of William II's foundation at Monreale (see p.71). The Cattedrale is an odd building in many ways, due to the less-than-subtle alterations of the late 18C which added the dome – completely out of character – and spoiled the fine lines of the tawny stone. Still, the triple-apsed eastern end (seen from a side-road off the Corso) and the lovely matching towers are all 12C originals; and despite the fussy Catalan-Gothic facade and arches, there's enough Norman carving and detail to give the exterior more than mere curiosity value. The same is not true, however, of the inside, which was modernised by Fuga, the Neapolitan architect responsible for the dome. It's grand enough, but cold and neo-classical, and the only items of interest are the fine portal and wooden doors (both 15C) and the royal **tombs**, Palermo's royal pantheon. As you enter, two crowded chapels to the left contain the mortal remains of some of Sicily's most famous monarchs: among others, Frederick II (left front) and his wife Constance (far right), Henry VI (right front) and Roger II (rear left) – Roger's tomb brought back shortly after he died from the cathedral at Cefalù, where he had requested he be laid.

Perhaps more rewarding than the rest of the over-blown interior is the **treasury** (*tesoro*; L1000), to the right of the choir: a sumptuous collection which includes a jewel- and pearl-encrusted skull cap and three simple, precious rings removed from the tomb of Constance of Aragon in the 18C. This was enterprising enough, but pales into insignificance beside the ingenuity required to extract a tooth from Santa Rosalia, also exhibited here in a reliquary.

Over the road, at the western end of the Cattedrale, stands the **Palazzo Arcivescovile**, the one-time archbishop's palace, entered through a 15C gateway. Inside, the Museo Diocesano, brings together art from the cathedral and from city churches destroyed during World War II: it's reported to be closed indefinitely, but check to see. You should be able to take a look in the courtyard, anyway, and a little way up via Bonello (left out of the palazzo) there's usually some activity in the **antique/junk market** in piazza Peranni.

Back on the Corso, the road runs up to the Royal Palace, on the northern side of which lies the **Porta Nuova**. Erected in 1535, it commemorates Charles V's Tunisian exploits, with suitably grim and turbanned figures adorning the western side. Through the gate, the long road, now Corso Calatafimi, heads south west to Monreale.

On foot, circle left around the apses of the Cattedrale and stroll up into the **CAPO** quarter, one of the oldest areas of Palermo and another tight web of rundown streets, unrelieved by space or greenery. There's not much to see, save a few surviving sculpted portals in the decaying palazzi, but it's an instructive tour if you've seen only grand buildings up to now. One alley, via Porta Carini, climbs past shambolic buildings and locked and battered churches to reach the decrepit Porta Carini itself, one of the city's medieval gates. There are a few scrappy market stalls in the streets hereabouts, the Capo quarter's western edge marked by via Papireto.

Better, from the Cattedrale, is to do a right at piazza Beati Paoli for the graceful **piazza del Monte**, tree-planted and with a couple of good bars. There's an atmosphere of faded splendour here, pell-mell on market days when the stalls spill over from the nearby goings-on down **via Sant'Agostino**. A lively market, mainly clothes but with food too, runs all the way down to via Maqueda, and, just around the corner, is the **chiesa di Sant'Agostino** (Mon–Sat 7am–noon & 4–6pm, Sun 7am–noon), built by the Chiaramonte and Scláfani families in the 13C. Above the main door (on via Raimondo) there's a gorgeous lattice-work rose window and, if you can get in through the adjacent side door, some calm 16C cloisters. Otherwise, turn the corner, and along via Sant'Agostino, behind the market stalls, the church sports a badly chipped, sculpted 15C doorway attributed to Domenico Gagini – just one of a whole dynasty of talented medieval sculptors who covered Sicily with their creations (see also the Galleria Nazionale, p.59).

Along via Maqueda and viale della Libertà: the modern city

North of the Quattro Canti, you leave most of the interesting medieval alleys behind, and the streets off to the left of via Maqueda gradually become wider and more nondescript as they broach the area around the late 19C **Teatro Mássimo**. Built in strictly neo-classical style by Giovanni Battista Basile, this is a monumental structure, all dome and columns, and supposedly the largest theatre in Italy, though it's impossible to judge since it remains closed indefinitely for restoration.

The theatre marks the dividing line between old and new Palermo. Beyond here there's little that's vital, though plenty that is grand and modern. Via Maqueda becomes **via Ruggero Séttimo**, which cuts through gridded shopping streets past the enclosed piazza Ungheria to the huge double square that characterises modern Palermo – made up of **piazza Castelnuovo** to the left (EPT at no.34) and **piazza Ruggero Séttimo** to the right. Far removed from the intimate piazzas of the medieval town, these spacious expanses double as car parks and bus ranks, while dominating the whole lot is Palermo's other massive theatre, the **Politeama Garibaldi**. This at least has the virtue of being open and, despite its peeling exterior, is worth a look for the city's **Galleria d'Arte Moderna** (Tues–Sat 9am–1pm, Tues & Thurs 4–8pm; L500); entrance on via Turati. There's some nice work inside, all 20C Sicilian stuff, best of which is the sculpture, including a small bronze study of an exhausted old horse (by Enrico Quattrociocchi), and Gerbino's sympathetic statuette of his greatcoated, heavily bearded father – though Michele Catti's autumnal scenes of Palermo are good, too. Watch out, as well, for the international touring exhibitions that often visit here.

Many of the city buses stop in between the two large piazzas. You might want to hop on one if you're heading any further north, along the wide **viale della Libertà**, as it's about a kilometre to the modern city's other attractions. At viale della Libertà 52, the **Fondazione Mormino** (Mon–Fri 9am–1pm & 3–5pm, Sat 9am–1pm; free) sponsors an archaeological and historical collection in the sumptuous *Banco di Sicilia* building. The exhibits are beautifully presented – a 6C BC bronze helmet, vases and coins – and there's also a fine set of old maps and prints, including a map of the Mediterranean made in the 17C by a cartographer in Wapping, London. From here, you're close to the **Giardino Inglese**, one of the city's few parks, though actually not much more than a palm-planted garden. For real expanses of parkland you'll have to take the bus a couple of kilometres further north to the Parco della Favorita (p.60).

A couple of blocks east of the Giardino Inglese is Palermo's notorious **Ucciardone** prison, connected by an underground passageway to the maximum-security bunker where the much-publicised maxi-trials of Mafia suspects were – and continue to be – held. The gloomy Bourbon prison has been called 'the best-informed centre in Italy for gossip and intelligence about the operations of organised crime throughout the world', not least because it's home to a good percentage of the biggest names in the underworld at any one time. It's reported that Mafia affairs are conducted here almost undisturbed, by bosses whose food is brought in from Palermo's best restaurants, and who collaborate with the warders to ensure that escapes don't happen – something which might increase security arrangements and hamper their activites.

Via Roma: the Vucciria and Museo Archeologico Nazionale

Running from the Stazione Centrale to piazza Ruggero Séttimo, **via Roma** is a fairly modern addition to the city: parallel with via Maqueda it offers a second chance for orientation if you get lost in the narrow alleys between the two. It's nothing like as interesting as via Maqueda in its lower reaches, its buildings mostly tall apartment blocks concealing hotels, and the only real diversion is **via Divisi**, off to the left: a narrow street whose pavements are chock-full of stacked bicycles from a series of bicycle shops. The rest of via Roma is all clothes shops and shoe shops, and there's nowhere to linger until you cross Corso Vittorio Emanuele. Just up from here is the church of **Sant'Antonio**, raised on a platform, to the side of which, steps lead down into the sprawling **market** of the **VUCCIRIA** quarter. Winding streets radiate out from a small enclosed piazza, wet from the ice and waste of the groaning fish stalls – swordfish heads stuck to the marble slabs and huge sides of tuna from which the fishmonger carves bloody steaks. There's a couple of excellent little restaurants tucked away in the alleys (best at lunchtime, see p.64), some very basic bars where the wine comes straight from the barrel, and all manner of food and junk on sale. This is also the place to buy great porcelain pasta bowls, espresso cups and coffee-makers. Other than early morning, when the action is at its most frenzied, lunchtime is a good time to wander around here, when the stallholders take a break for card-playing sessions conducted around packing cases, or simply fall asleep amongst their produce.

The northern limit of the market is marked by **San Domenico** (daily 7.30–11.30am, weekends also 5–6.30pm), a large church set back off via Roma and fronted by a statue-topped marble column. The fine 18C facade, with its double pillars and slim towers, is lit at night to great effect, while inside a series of tombs contains a horde of famous ex-Sicilians. Parliamentarians, poets and painters, they're of little interest to foreigners except to explain the finer points behind Palermitan street-naming. Outside, on the north side of the church at piazza San Domenico 1, you have to ring for entry to the small **Museo del Risorgimento** (Mon, Wed & Fri 9am–1pm; free), an historical collection pertaining to the 19C Italian anti-Bourbon revolt. More worthwhile, ring at via dei Bambinai 16 to get into the **Oratorio del Rosario di San Domenico**, behind the San Domenico church – one of many such small chapels in the old part of the city, many of which contain the best of Palermo's Baroque decoration. This 16C oratory, built and still maintained by the Knights of Malta, was adorned by the acknowledged master of the art of stucco sculpture, Giacomo Serpotta (see p.297), who lined the walls with allegorical figures. Born in Palermo in 1656, Serpotta devoted his entire life to decorating oratories like this, a tradition continued by his son, Procopio (some of whose work can also be seen, in the Oratorio di Santa Caterina behind the main post office). Here, the figures are of 'Justice', 'Strength' and suchlike, resembling fashionable society ladies, who often served as models, the whole thing crowned by an accomplished altarpiece by Van Dyck. It was finished in 1628, after the artist had fled Palermo for Genova to escape the plague.

Spacious **piazza San Domenico** has that rare thing in Palermo, a bar with outdoor tables, and it's a good place to sip a drink, close to the flower-sellers and with the sound of the Vucciria market in full swing behind you. Further up via Roma, on the left, is Palermo's main post office, the gargantuan **Palazzo delle Poste**. Built by the Fascists in 1933, it's a monstrous concrete block, with a wide swathe of steps running up to a colonnade of ten unfluted columns which run the length and height of the building itself. The empty pretension of the post office is put to shame by what hides behind it, around the corner in piazza Olivella. Here, the church of **Sant'Ignazio all'Olivella** displays an opulent Baroque touch in its great chandeliers and rich side-chapels; next door, the cloisters and surviving buildings of a 16C convent – once the property of the church – now house the city's excellent archaeological museum.

Museo Archeologico Nazionale

Open daily 9am–2pm, Tuesday & Friday 3–6pm, Sunday 9am–1pm; L2000.

If you've been touring the best of western Sicily's ancient sites (or are intending to do so), the archaeological museum at Palermo is a must, gathering together artefacts found at all the major Carthaginian, Greek and Roman settlements in a magnificent collection that culminates with items from the site at Selinunte. The exhibits are displayed on two main floors, together with a top floor of prehistoric bits and pieces and Greek vases that is closed indefinitely. For up-to-date information, pick up the free illustrated booklet, in English, on the way in.

The entrance to the **ground floor** is through the smaller of two cloisters, which displays anchors and other retrieved hardware from the sea off the Sicilian coast. There are **Egyptian and Punic** remains in rooms to either side, and beyond, the larger ivy-clad cloister is devoted to **Roman** sculpture, notably a giant enthroned Zeus on the left. Rooms at the far end contain numerous carved early Greek *stelai* and assorted inscribed tablets (including one from Roman Taormina recording expenses charged by the town's magistrates).

Beyond here, the material is almost entirely **Greek**, beginning with the assembled stone **lion's head water-spouts** from the so-called 'Victory Temple' at Himera (5C BC), the fierce animal faces tempered by braided fur and a grooved tongue which channeled the water, and leading on to the highspot of the museum, the adjacent **Salone di Selinunte**. This gathers together the rich stone carvings (or metopes) from the various temples (known only as Temples A–G) at Selinunte on the south west coast – a vital stop if you intend to visit the site itself (see p.267). Sculpted panels from the friezes which adorned the temples, they're appealing works of art, depicting lively mythological scenes. The earliest and least impressive, single panels from the early 6C BC, sit under the windows on the right and represent the gods of Delphi, the Sphinx, the rape of Europa, and Herakles and the Bull. The reconstructed friezes opposite, from Temples C and (more fragmentary) from F, catch the eye more: vivid works from the 5C BC, like Perseus beheading Medusa with a short sword, his legs in profile but his head and torso facing directly out in archaic style. The most technically advanced tableaux are those in the frieze at the end of the room, from the early 5C BC Temple E, portraying a lithe Hercules fighting an Amazon, the marriage of Zeus and Hera, Actaeon savaged by three ferocious dogs, and Athena and the Titan. There's additional interest in the bronze *kouros* in the middle of the room – a small and strong-featured statue found in a tomb at Selinunte – and in the female heads, three on either side of the door, taken from Temple E.

The remaining rooms on the ground floor deal with funerary art, several 3–2C BC sarcophagi painted with graphic battle-scenes. You have to retrace your steps to the small cloister for the steps up to the **first floor**, which also has plenty to occupy a lengthy dawdle: lead water-pipes with stop-cock retrieved from a site at Términi Imerese (p.84), some 12,000 votive terracotta figures, and a few delicately carved stone heads found at Solunto (p.77). There's more Greek sculpture (including a fragment of the frieze from the

Parthenon) and a reconstructed Roman mosaic pavement as well. But pick of the lot here are two rich bronze sculptures – the naturalistic figure of an alert ram (3C BC) from Siracusa, once one of a pair (the other was destroyed in the 1848 revolution), and a glistening, muscular study of Hercules subduing a stag, found at Pompeii.

Across via Roma: to La Cala

There's an immediate change in style and surroundings once you cross back over via Roma and head towards the water. The area around the docks suffered gravely during the last war, particularly the late-16C church of **Santa Zita**, on quiet via Squarcialupo, which was badly bomb-damaged. It's since been restored, and inside you'll see some flamboyant polychrome marbling and good sculpture by Antonello Gagini. But you'd do better to visit the marvellous oratory behind, the **Oratorio del Rosario di Santa Zita** (ring the bell 11am–noon, or ask in the church in front, San Mamiliano, 8–11am & 4–5.30pm), containing some of the wildest flights of Giacomo Serpotta's rococo imagination – a dazzling confusion of allegorical figures, bare-breasted women, putti galore, scenes from the New Testament, and, at the centre of it all, a rendering of the Battle of Lepanto. Take time to absorb the details of this tumultuous landscape, especially the loving care with which he depicted individual figures – the old men and women, melancholy boys perched on the ledge – and notice Serpotta's symbol on the left wall: the golden snake. Striking wealth indeed when you step outside and consider the area around.

Via Squarcialupo continues down to **piazza XIII Vittime**, where there's a monument commemorating thirteen Palermitans shot by the Bourbons in the 1860 revolt, and some of the city's medieval walls. The whole of the area around is rather forlorn: to the south, the shored-up buildings just back from the water have ground floors given over to car repair workshops, the rooms open to the road and stuffed full of every kind of vehicular wreckage.

The depressed inertia of these streets spreads south to the thumb-shaped inlet of the old city harbour, **La Cala**. Once the main port of Palermo, stretching as far inland as via Roma, the rot set in during the 16C when silting caused the water to recede to its current position. All the heavy work eventually moved north west, to docks off the remodelled post-war streets (site of the Stazione Marittima), and La Cala has been left to the few fishing-boats that still work out of Palermo. It's interesting to stroll around the marine clutter at least once, and there are excellent views over the little harbour to Monte Pellegrino in the distance.

Along Corso Vittorio Emanuele: from Quattro Canti to the water

There's a markedly different character to the quarter south of La Cala, bounded by via Roma and the Corso. Worst hit by the war and allowed to decay since, this area holds some of the poorest streets in the city, within some of the most desolate urban landscapes imaginable. Towards the water along **Corso Vittorio Emanuele**, high narrow streets peel off to the left and right, mostly dark and forbidding. One, via A. Paternostro, cuts away to the right to the 13C church of **San Francesco d'Assisi** (daily 7–11am), whose well-preserved portal, picked out with a zig-zag decoration, is topped by a wonderful rose window – a harmonious design that is, for once, continued inside. All the Baroque trappings have been stripped away to reveal a pleasing stone interior, the later side-chapels showing excellently worked arches – the fourth on the left is one of the earliest Renaissance works on the island, sculpted by Francesco Laurana in 1468. To the side of the church, at via Immacolatella 5, the renowned **Oratorio di San Lorenzo** contains another of Giacomo Serpotta's stuccoed masterpieces, intricately fashioned scenes from the lives of St Lawrence and St Francis. Sadly, it's likely to remain closed for some drastic restoration work in the foreseeable future.

Back on the main road, the Corso runs straight down to the water, with the harbour of La Cala to the left, overlooked by the church of **Santa Maria della Catena**, named after the chain that used to close the harbour in the late 15C. The Corso ends at the Baroque gate, the **Porta Felice**, begun in 1582 as a counter-balance to the Porta Nuova, visible way to the west. Indeed, from here you can judge the extent of the late medieval city, which lay between the two gates. The whole area beyond the Porta Felice was flattened in 1943, and has since been rebuilt as a fairly ugly promenade, the **Foro Italico**, complete with small amusement park, from where you can look back over the harbour to Monte Pellegrino.

Piazza Marina

Double back through the gate and bear left into **piazza Marina**, a large square which skirts around the tropical **Giardino Garibaldi** – another venue for the city's elderly card-players, who gather around green baize tables at lunchtime for a game. Reclaimed from the sea in the 10C, subsequently used for jousting tournaments and executions, and now surrounded by decaying palazzi, every corner of the piazza is worth exploring. The second largest of Palermo's palaces, the **Palazzo Chiaramonte**, flanks the east side of the square: from 1685 to 1782 it was the home of the Inquisition, before becoming the city's law courts – a function it only abandoned in 1972. It's also being restored, and you can't get in, though the more determined can apply for the key at the *Rettorato*, the university administration office in piazza Marina. Otherwise you'll have to be content with peeking through the gates of the delicately arched inner courtyard and admiring the severe facade.

Behind the palace is the derelict shell of the Palazzo Butera, whose 17C facade faces out over the Foro Italico. Via Butera lies behind it (on the right, just before Porta Felice) and at no.1 is the engaging **Museo delle Marionette** (Mon–Sat 10am–1pm & 5–7pm, Sun 10am–1pm; free, ring for entrance), Palermo's definitive collection of puppets, screens and painted scenery. A traditional Sicilian entertainment, puppet theatres have all but died out on the island (though you can still see performances in Palermo, p.66). Based around French and Sicilian history and specifically the exploits of the hero Roland (Orlando), performances nearly always depict dashing knights – Orlando, Rinaldo, and friends – combating Saracen invaders, usually culminating in a great battle. With a commentary often delivered in dialect, you don't follow the lines so much as the short, sharp action – frenetic battle-scenes awash with blood and cries, as Orlando single-handedly slays the enemy and saves the day. It's all great fun, and on Saturdays in summer the museum puts on free shows (the *Spettácolo dei pupi*) at 5pm.

La Kalsa and the Galleria Nazionale

Planned and built by the Saracens, today the quarter of **LA KALSA** (from the Arabic, *khalisa*, meaning 'pure') is old, shattered and – even in daylight – vaguely threatening. Its centre is a huge World War II bombsite, still lived in, but with scarred and gutted buildings on all sides: on maps, it just appears as a blank space. It goes without saying that this is one of Palermo's more notorious areas, young bag-snatchers on speeding Vespas adding to the thrills. Coming here at night would be a big mistake, and although daytime tourists are hardly strangers to the area, given the surrounding attractions, they have been known to be hit by missiles from catapults at dusk.

One reason for braving the district is the **Palazzo Abatellis**, via Alloro 4, a 15C building which still retains elements of its Catalan-Gothic and Renaissance origins, notably in its doorway and courtyard. Revamped since the war, it now houses the **Galleria Nazionale** (Mon–Sat 9am–1.30pm, Sun 9am–12.30pm; L2000), which houses an excellent medieval art collection.

The **ground floor** contains sculpture, beginning with an incredibly intricate door-frame which once adorned a Palermitan mansion, the 12C wooden carving all Arabic, and leading on to the works of 15C sculptor **Francesco Laurana** (room 4): his white marble bust of *Eleonora d'Aragona* is a calm, perfectly studied portrait. Another room is devoted to the work of the Gagini clan, mostly statues of the Madonna, while the only non-sculptural item is a magnificent 15C **fresco**, the *Triumph of Death*, by an unknown (possibly Flemish) painter. It's a chilling study, Death cast as a skeletal archer astride a galloping, spindly horse, trampling bodies slain by his arrows. He rides towards a group of smug and wealthy citizens, apparently unconcerned at his approach; meanwhile, to the left, the sick and the old plead hopelessly for oblivion.

The **first floor**, devoted to painting, is unusually comprehensive, with no shortage of excellent Sicilian art, the earliest (13–14C) displaying marked Byzantine characteristics, including a 14C mosaic of the Madonna and Child, eyes and hands remarkably self-assured. Later 15C paintings and frescoes are all vivid and imaginative in their portrayal of the Coronation of the Virgin, a favourite theme. This floor also contains some notable highlights, not least a collection of works by the 15C Sicilian artist, **Antonello da Messina**: three small, clever portraits of Saints Gregory, Jerome and Augustine (with a rakish red hat), and an indisputably powerful *Annunciation*, a placid depiction of Mary, head and shoulders covered, right hand slightly raised in acknowledgment of the (off-picture) angel Gabriel. There's a second view – looking down – of the *Triumph of Death* and some important Flemish works too, such as an immensely detailed Mabuse tryptych of the Virgin and Child, surrounded by some extraordinarily ugly cherubs.

There's more work by the Gagini family, sculpted fragments and reliefs, in the 15C church of **La Gancia** (Mon–Sat 8–9.15am, Sun 8am–1pm), next door to the gallery. From here, via Alloro runs south west, past a succession of ailing palazzi, before feeding into a confusing jumble of squares, principally piazza Aragona and **piazza Croce dei Vespri** (marked by a cross for the French who died in the 1282 Sicilian Vespers rebellion). In piazza Croce dei Vespri stands the huge entrance to the **Palazzo Valguarnera Ganci**, where Visconti filmed the ballroom scene in *The Leopard*; you may be able to get in by bribing the porter. Close by is piazza della Rivoluzione, from where the 1848 uprising began. From this last piazza, **via Garibaldi** leads south, marking the end of the route that Garibaldi took in May 1860 when he entered the city (he marched north, up Corso dei Mille and into via Garibaldi). Here, at via Garibaldi 23, the immense, battered 15C **Palazzo Aiutamicristo** keeps bits of its original Catalan-Gothic structure, while the little street (via Magione) around the side of the palace leads to the lovely church of **La Magione** (Mon–Sat 7–11am & 4–6pm, Sun 7.30am–12.30pm), approached through a palm-lined drive. Built in 1151, the simple Norman church was subsequently given to the Teutonic knights as their headquarters by Henry VI. Today, it's strikingly sparse, inside and out; the reason becomes clear as you step around the back to look at the finely worked apse. You're standing on the very edge of the worst bits of La Kalsa here, the area (due to its proximity to the port) subjected to saturation bombing during World War II: La Magione, like many of the other historical buildings around, survives only through a combination of luck and piecemeal restoration.

Palermo's best central park, **Villa Giulia**, is just a few minutes' walk away, along via Lincoln: an 18C garden which provides an escape from the traffic. Attractions include planned, aromatic gardens, a kiddies' train, bandstand, deer and ducks, though to the city's shame, there's a lion roaring pitifully from a small concrete cell. There's also a Botanical Garden (Mon–Fri 9am–noon, Sat 9–11am), next door to the park.

Out from the centre

Even if you have no time to see everything in the old centre there are several targets beyond, on the outskirts of the modern city, which warrant investigation. Some, like the **ethnographical museum**, shouldn't be missed on any visit to Palermo; others have a low-key interest for fans of the **Norman** period; while one, the **Cappuccini monastery**, is decidedly ghoulish, for the strong of stomach only.

The Parco della Favorita and Museo Etnográfico Pitrè

To the **north**, around three kilometres from piazza Castelnuovo, lies the city's grandest park, the **Parco della Favorita**: a long, wooded expanse at the foot of Monte Pellegrino, with sports grounds and stadiums at one end and formal gardens laid out a couple of kilometres beyond. The grounds were originally bought by the Bourbon king, Ferdinand, in 1799, during his exile from Naples, and for three years he lived here in the **Palazzina Cinese** (closed to the public), a small Chinese-style pavilion. This is just inside the main entrance, beyond piazza Niscemi, and bus #14 or #15 runs right the way here, from viale della Libertà.

Next door is the third of the city's showpiece museums, the **Museo Etnográfico Pitrè** (daily except Fri 9am–1pm; L1000): *the* exhibition of Sicilian folklore and culture on the island. There's all the work traditionally associated with Sicily, perhaps most spectacularly a wealth of brightly painted carts (*carretti*) and carriages, some several hundred years old. Mostly, they're two-wheeled vehicles, from barrows to horse-drawn wagons, and in the past people's status was judged by the skill and extent of the decorations on their carts. On each, every available inch – sometimes including the spokes and undercarriage – is covered with geometric patterns and historical, chivalrous scenes from the story of the Paladins. There's a reconstructed puppet theatre too (with performances in the summer; ask at the EPT), and dozens of the expressive puppets, scenery backdrops and handbills lining the walls. But also fascinating here is the attention paid to less well-known aspects of Sicilian handicrafts and cultural life: whole rooms are devoted to a series of intricately sculpted and painted terracotta figures; wooden *ex-voto* (votive) tablets depicting the often gruesome death of the dedicatee; and sundry dolls, games, tapestries, tools, bicycles, painted masks – even a great, flowery iron bedstead.

Other remnants of Norman Palermo

The best Norman buildings are, with a couple of exceptions, in and around the old town area of the city. But to be thorough in tracking down the rest of Palermo's Norman relics you'll have to poke around the **southern** and **western** outskirts: built-up areas that were once rolling parkland owned by successive kings. Be warned that most of what survives, however, is for the moment probably either locked or under restoration.

Bus #24 runs west to **La Zisa** (from the Arabic, *el aziz*, 'magnificent'), a huge palace begun by William I in 1160, and later finished by his son William II. Built as a king's retreat, along North African lines, palaces like La Zisa languished in great private estates, stocked with beautiful planned gardens and rare and exotic animals. Apparently, a raid on the palace by disaffected locals in 1161 released some of the wild animals, something that probably came as a bit of a shock to William's neighbours. Today, La Zisa is surrounded by modern apartment blocks and though the exterior is well-preserved, the marvellous Islamic design of the interior is out-of-bounds while long-term restoration work continues. To the south, about a kilometre beyond the Porta Nuova, at Corso Calatafimi 100 (opposite via Quarto dei Mille), **La Cuba** (Wed & Sun 9am–noon) is the remains of a slightly later Norman pavilion that formed part of the same royal park. Today it's irritatingly surrounded by an army barracks, which accounts for the limited opening hours, though in any case the inside has little left of its former elegance. On the outside there's some blind arcading, an Arabic inscription, and the traces of a water-gate, which would have been used when the royal pavilion stood in the middle of an artificial lake. Bus #8/9 or #9 runs past it, and continues up the Corso to **La Cúbula** (on the right, at the end of via Aurelio Zancla, between nos. 443 and 459 on the main road). This domed kiosk, once a summer-house in the extensive grounds of La Zisa, now looks rather uncomfortable in the midst of the modern apartments that dwarf it on all sides.

Bearing in mind the restoration works, you might find more of interest south east of the centre in the well-restored 11C domed church of **San Giovanni dei Lebbrosi** (Mon–Sat 4.30–6.30pm, Sun 8–11.30am), reachable on bus #11, #26 or #31 from the northern end of Corso dei Mille. Just off the Corso, at via Cappello 38, it's one of the oldest Norman churches in Sicily, reputedly founded in 1070 by Roger I. Its name (St John of the Lepers) derives from the building nearby which was once a leprosy hospital. Back down the Corso, the route Garibaldi and his 'Thousand' (hence Corso dei Mille) took into the city in 1860, you reach the stranded **Ponte dell'Ammiraglio**. Built in 1113 by George of Antioch, founder of La Martorana, the slender bridge once straddled the river Oreto, though the water has since been diverted. On the night of the 27 May 1860 it figured as a brief stand of the Bourbon troops as Garibaldi marched into Palermo.

Last Norman attraction is the cemetery-surrounded church of **Santo Spirito** (daily 9am–noon), to the west of San Giovanni – take bus #2, #18 or #42 from Corso Tukory to the Cimitero Sant'Orsola. Founded in 1173, it's been restored to its original, rather severe state. Here, in 1282, began the massacre of the **Sicilian Vespers**, ostensibly sparked off when a French officer insulted a bride on her way to church. The ringing of the vesper (evensong) bell was the signal to drive the French out of Sicily; most were eventually slaughtered by the oppressed islanders.

The Cappuccini monastery

Out of all the attractions on the edge of Palermo, the **Convento dei Cappuccini** (Mon–Sat 9am–noon & 3–5pm; donation expected), is probably the most intriguing, reachable by taking bus #27 (from Corso Vittorio Emanuele) south west to via Pindemonte and walking for a few (signposted) minutes. For several hundred years this monastery retained its own burial ground, placing its dead in catacombs under the church. Later, responding to requests and bequests from rich laymen, many others began to be interred here, right up until 1881. The bodies (some 8000 of them) were preserved by various chemical and drying processes – including dehydration, the use of vinegar and arsenic baths, and treatment with quick lime – and then placed in niches along various corridors, dressed in the suit of clothes that they had previously provided for the purpose. Descending into the catacombs is like having a walk-on part in your own horror film. The rough-cut stone corridors are divided according to sex and status, different caverns reserved for men, women, the clergy, doctors, lawyers and surgeons. Suspended in individual niches and pinned with an identifying tag, the bodies are vile, contorted, grinning figures, some decomposed beyond recognition, others complete with skin, hair and eyes, fixing you with a steely stare. Those that aren't arranged along the walls lie in stacked glass coffins, and, to say the least, it's an unnerving experience to walk among them. Times change, though, as Patrick Brydone noted in his late-18C *A Tour Through Sicily and Malta*:

> *Here the people of Palermo pay daily visits to their deceased friends . . . here they familiarize themselves with their future state, and chuse the company they would wish to keep in the other world. It is a common thing to make choice of their nich, and to try if their body fits it . . . and sometimes, by way of a voluntary penance, they accustom themselves to stand for hours in these niches . . .*

Of all the skeletal bodies, saddest are the many remains of babies and young children, nothing more than spindly puppets. Follow the signs for the sealed-off cave which contains the coffin of two-year-old Rosalia Lombardo, who died in 1920. A new process, a series of injections, preserved her to the extent that she looks like she's asleep – after nearly seventy years. Perhaps fortunately, the doctor who invented the technique died before he could tell anyone how it was done: Rosalia's sister, now an old woman, comes to visit her 'sleeping' sister every year.

Eating

You can **eat** well and cheaply in Palermo, either snacking in bars and at market stalls or sitting down in a score of good-value pizzerias and restaurants throughout the old town. The local speciality is *pasta con sarde*, macaroni with fresh sardines, fennel, raisins and pine kernels.

Breakfast, snacks and markets

Almost any bar or pasticceria is a good bet first thing in the morning, with **breakfast** pastries fresh from the bakeries. But for something more substantial than just *cornetti*, one of the best places to head for is the *Extra Bar*, via Ruggero Séttimo 107, which has masses of cakes and ice-cream and hot food too. The bar inside the *Pizzeria Bellini* (piazza Bellini; see below) starts serving snacks – including pizza slices – early; or try the *Ferrara* (piazza Giulio Césare 6), just to the left of the railway station, and the *Bar Self Service*, Corso Vittorio Emanuele 244, which both offer complete lunches (around L6500–7000) and more substantial fast-food snacks.

For authentic **Sicilian fast-food**, *Antica Focacceria San Francesco*, via A. Paternostro 58 (off Corso Vittorio Emanuele, opposite the church of San Francesco; closed Mon) is an old-time pizzeria (open since 1834) with marble-topped tables and floor, cast-iron surroundings and fresh pizza slices at around L1200 a go. There's a bar, too. Get good **sandwiches**, either toasted or filled rolls, at *Panineria*, via Trabia 47 (off via Maqueda, close to Teatro Mássimo), or *Paninomania*, via Maqueda 162. You're going to want **ice-cream** at some stage and while you can buy it just about anywhere, it's worth tracking down the *Gelateria La Martorana*, Corso Vittorio Emanuele 198.

Some of the best snacks are on sale in Palermo's **markets**, mostly traditional take-away food – chopped boiled octopus, bread rolls filled with sliced fried liver, cooked artichokes, as well as bread, fruit and vegetables. Best is the Vucciria market, off via Roma between Corso Vittorio Emanuele and the San Domenico church, but there's also food on sale in piazza del Cármine (the Ballarò market, p.50) and along via Sant'Agostino (p.53).

Restaurants

Cheapest option for a sit-down meal, the most popular **pizza** restaurants get packed at the weekends, full of young people intent upon a night out rather than just a meal. Easily the best is the *Pizzeria Italia*, via Orologio 54 (off via Maqueda, just before Teatro Mássimo) where large queues develop quickly. There's also the *Trattoria dal Pompiere* at via Bara 107 (the next parallel street north) – same cheap prices, fancier pine tables. More expensive, though still good, and with a full restaurant menu too, is *Peppino* (piazza Castelnuovo 49), run by the same people who own the *Bellini*, in piazza Bellini, a fairly pricey choice just for pizza, but with outdoor tables underneath La Martorana church. *Le Caprice* at via Cavour 42, isn't as swanky as it looks, and, again, has other food besides pizzas.

For full-blown **meals**, the city's best bargain is the *Trattoria-Pizzeria Enzo*, via Maurolico 17/19 (closed Sat, very close to Stazione Centrale), which serves excellent food in hefty portions at daft prices. There are other budget places around the station, too, like the basic but good *Trattoria Trápani* in piazza Giulio Césare; or try the small *Trattoria Azzurra*, via dei Bottai 54 (off Corso Vittorio Emanuele before piazza Marina), which has a long list of cheap pasta dishes and healthy fish meals. You can eat outside a little further on, in piazza Marina itself: avoid the shoddy *La Cambusa* in favour of *Il Cotto e il Crudo* (closed Tues) – on the expensive side but with a good menu. Best of the *al fresco* dining is at the marvellous *Shangai* (not Chinese but Italian, at Vicolo dei Mezzani 34; closed Mon), which has a restaurant terrace with a bird's eye view of the Vucciria market, a great place for lunch – down the steps before San Antonio church, across the square, and the entrance is on the right down a dingy back-street. Other cheap central choices are *Hostaria da Ciccio*, via Firenze 6 (off via Roma at the southern end) and, though rather sad and empty most of the time, *Ca d'Oro*, at Corso Vittorio Emanuele 256–8, where you can eat in splendid isolation overlooking the main road (closed Sun). One **to avoid** is the *Taverna di John*, at via Sperlinga 57 – well-advertised, but its pizzas are dear and there's no local wine, just expensive bottled stuff.

Vegetarians will find *Il Mirto e la Rosa* (closed Sun) at via Príncipe di Granatelli 30 (off Piazza Florio) decent but rather pricey. **Non-Italian food** is all but impossible to find in Palermo: the *Al Duar* (via E. Amari 92; closed Mon) has a *Completo Tunisino* (couscous and the like) for L11,000; and the *Hong Kong* around the corner at via M. Amari 28 serves inauthentic, expensive and ungenerous portions of Cantonese food.

If you have stacks of cash to blow – upwards of L60,000 a head – the *Charleston*, piazza Ungheria 30 (closed Sun), is Palermo's most celebrated **high-class restaurant**, with dreamlike cooking. Between mid-June and late September, the restaurant shifts to the beach at Mondello (see p.69).

Drinking, nightlife and entertainment

After dark and over much of the city, Palermo's frenetic lifestyle stops, pedestrians flit quickly through the shadows, and the main roads are given over to speeding traffic and screaming police sirens. What **bars** there are in the city centre tend to close around 9pm, which suggests you should head out to **Mondello** beach resort – which is where everyone else will be at night during the summer. But in the newer parts of the city, around viale della Libertà, a sort of nightlife continues unabated, with an energetic *passeggiata* and cruising cars blasting away like mobile discotheques. If none of this is your scene, then there is more cultural **entertainment** to be had back in the city centre.

Bars and nightlife

Bars drift in and out of fashion and you'll have to follow the crowds to find the present favourite, but *La Bottiglieria* (closed Sun) has quite a loyal following; it's on the corner of via Daita and via Mazzini, a few minutes' walk up viale della Libertà from piazza Castelnuovo. Apart from wine (cheapest L3000 a bottle), it has good snacks, and gives a chance to watch the smart set at play. Other, more central watering holes include the *Pinguino* (via Ruggero Séttimo 86), which has excellent ice-cream, famous milk-shakes and a range of non-alcoholic cocktails, or *Liberty*, a spaghetteria on via Cerda, off via Maqueda, which serves food and is open until late. Traffic-free via Príncipe di Belmonte has bars and pasticcerias for an outdoor, early evening drink: *Brinkhoff's* is fairly popular, offering crepes and beers and open after midnight. Staggering home, you can get a late drink at a stand-up stall on via Roma: marked *Birra Messina* it's at via Venezia, just before the Teatro Biondo. If you need sobering up, try the sharp, fresh lemon juice, a speciality.

If it's **discos** and **video bars** you're after, there are a couple of establishments along via Generale Arimondi (beyond the Giardino Inglese), or you'll have to venture further out to the new, northern section of the city, where there are several along viale Strasburgo. In summer, though, all this can only be second-best to a **night at Mondello** (see p.69), with buses connecting the city to the beach all night.

Music, theatre, cinema and puppet shows

To check what's on in Palermo, it's always worth looking in *Un Mese a Palermo* and *L'Ora*, see p.41, although live entertainment is hard to come by outside the 'cabaret shows' at the businessmen's clubs. There's no major **rock music** venue and top British and American bands rarely make it further south than Naples, though the *comune* has lately been staging open-air rock events in the summer, usually in the Giardino Inglese and other green spaces – watch out for posters around the city for details. The Politeama Garibaldi theatre, in piazza Ruggero Séttimo, puts on a pretty fair **classical music** programme throughout the year, while there are often free classical and **jazz** events at the Teatro Golden, via Terrasanta 60 (bus #18 from via Roma). See *Listings* below.

Palermo and its surroundings have a stack of other **theatres**, worth checking out if you speak Italian. In particular, the Teatro Tenda Zappalà in Mondello (viale Galatea) features experimental theatre productions throughout the summer. **Cinemas** show the latest films dubbed into Italian, and the main screens are on via Cavour and via E. Amari. There's an *English Film Club*, too, which shows new releases at the *Metropolitan Cinema*, viale Strasburgo 356 (☎091-502.278); L5000 entry, fifty per cent *ISIC* discount.

Best night out, though, and something you should do at least once, is a visit to the **puppet theatre**. There are tourist performances at the Museo Etnográfico Pitrè (p.61) and Museo delle Marionette (p.58), but try to get to one of the surviving back-street puppet theatres for a genuine experience: search out the ones at via Bara all'Olivella 95, close to the archaeological museum; Teatro Carlo Magno, opposite Santa Zita (every evening at 9pm); and vicolo Ragusi 6, off Corso Vittorio Emanuele, close to the cathedral (2–3 weekly at 9pm). Tickets are around L4000–5000 each; check on performances at the theatre or the EPT.

Listings

Airlines *Alitalia* (viale della Libertà 39; ☎091-601.9111); *British Airways* (c/o *Gastaldi*, via E. Albanese 7; ☎091-300.863); *KLM* (via A. Gravina 8; ☎091-331.207); *Pan-Am* (c/o *Fratelli Cosulich*, via M. Stabile 114–118; ☎091-588.297); *SAS* (via Cavour 70; ☎091-581.884); *TWA* (via E. Albanese 7; ☎091-302.881).

Airport bus Fifteen daily departures to Punta Raisi airport from the terminal at via I. Lumia, behind the Politeama theatre. First bus 5.30am, last bus 9.15pm; L3300, 45min journey.

American Express c/o *Giovanni Ruggeri*, via E. Amari 40 (☎091-587.144); Mon–Fri 9am–1pm & 4–7pm, Sat 9am–1pm.

Banks and exchange Banks are open Mon–Fri 8.20am–1.20pm; larger branches also open 2.45–3.45pm. Most will exchange all travellers' cheques. There's an exchange office at Stazione Centrale (daily 8am–1pm & 4–8pm).

Beaches Nearest sandy beach at Mondello (p.69); others further west at Sferracavallo and Isola delle Fémmine (see p.74).

Bookshops Large selection of English books from *Feltrinelli*, via Maqueda 457, opposite Teatro Mássimo (closed Mon morning). Also from *Libreria Flaccovio*, via Ruggero Séttimo 33.

Bus terminals *Ala-Vit*, via Rosario Gregorio 25 (for Caltanissetta); *AST*, piazza Lolli (for Bagheria, Santa Flavia) and piazza Marina (for Balestrate, Corleone, Lercara Friddi, Ragusa, Montelepre, Castelbuono, Cómiso, Módica, Términi Imerese, Partinico); *Autolinee Gallo*, via Rao 17 (for Sciacca); *Autoservizi Salemi*, piazza Marina (for Castelvetrano, Marsala, Mazara del Vallo, Salemi); *Autoservizio Verga*, piazza Marina (for Partinico/

Álcamo/Calatafimi); *Camilleri*, via P. Balsamo 32 (for Agr
Lincoln 42 (for Agrigento); *Prestia & Comandè*, Stazione Cen
and Piana degli Albanesi); *Randazzo*, via P. Balsamo (for Cácca
piazza Marina (for Balestrate, Partinico); *SAIS*, via P. Balsamo 16 (fo
Caltanissetta, Catania, Enna, Piazza Armerina, Gela, Messina, Siracusa,
Cefalù, Gangi, Petralia, Polizzi Generosa, Términi Imerese); *Segesta*, via
Balsamo 26 (for Rome, Trápani, Álcamo, Partinico); *Stassi*, piazza Marina (for
Corleone).

Car problems *ACI*, via delle Alpi 6 (☎091-266.293).

Car rental *Avis* (Punta Raisi airport; ☎091-591.684; and via Príncipe di
Scordia 12–14; ☎091-333.806); *Europcar* (via Cavour 77a; ☎091-321.949); *Hertz*
(via Messina 7; ☎091-331.668); *Holiday Car Rental* (via E. Amari 83–85; ☎091-
325.155); *Interrent* (via Cavour 61; ☎091-328.631); *Maggiore* (Punta Raisi
airport; ☎091-591.688; via Agrigento 27–33; ☎091-297.128); *Sicily By Car* (via
M. Stabile 6a; ☎091-581.045).

Chemist All-night service at via Roma 1, via Roma 207 and via Príncipe di
Belmonte 110. Other chemists operate a rota system, with the address of the
nearest open chemist posted on the door of each shop.

Club Alpino Siciliano via P. Paternostro 43 (☎091-581.323). For hiking
information, maps and details of mountain refuges; and see *Maps* below.

Consulates All the nearest consulates are in Naples or Rome. *UK*, via Crispi
122, Naples (☎081-663.511); *Australia*, via Alessandria 21–25, Rome (☎06-
841.241); *Eire*, via del Pozzetto 108, Rome (☎06-678.2541); *New Zealand*, via
Zara 28, Rome (☎06-851.225).

Emergencies Dial ☎113 (general); ☎112 (police); ☎091-222.966 (road accident); ☎091-587.333 (fire brigade).

Ferry companies *Grandi Traghetti* to Genova and Livorno (via M. Stabile
179; ☎091-587.832); *Siremar* to Ústica (via Francesco Crispi 120; ☎091-
582.403); *Tirrenia* to Naples, Genova and Cágliari (via Roma 385; ☎091-
585.733).

Garages *Aiutami Cristo*, via Garibaldi 41, in La Kalsa; *Di Giandomenico*, via
Oreto 18, behind Stazione Centrale; *Central Garage*, piazza Giulio Césare 43.
Around L4000 a night to leave a car.

Gay info Contact *ARCI Gay* (☎091-324.917/8) at the cultural wing of the
Communist Party's youth section. An information centre and meeting place is
planned at vicolo Istituto Pignatelli 6 (off piazza Don Sturzo, behind the
Politeama theatre), open 5pm–late.

Hospital *Cívico Regionale Generale*, via Carrabia (☎091-592.122). For emergency first aid, call ☎091-321.860.

Jazz For information on jazz happenings contact *Associazione Siciliana per la
Musica Jazz* (also known as *Brass Group*) at via Villa Heloise 21; ☎091-
294.165).

...dries at *Campana*, via Cuba 2 (off Corso ... from piazza della Vittoria); and *Supersecco*, via ...rtà, bus #1, #3, #19 or #25 to viale d'Annunzio).

... Centrale (open daily 24hr; L1000 a day) and ... 7–9.30am, 10am–4.30pm & 5.30–8.30pm; L800 a ...

...or hiking in the Monti Madonie from the *Istituto* ... 16 (☎091-320.346).

News... ... newspapers and magazines from the newsagents at the top of via ... Séttimo, junction with piazza Ruggero Séttimo/piazza Castelnuovo. Local listings in the afternoon daily, *L'Ora*.

Petrol station All-night service at *Mobil*, viale della Regione Siciliana (south west up Corso Vittorio Emanuele/Calatafimi and then turn right).

Police The *Questura* in piazza Vittoria has an *Ufficio dei Stranieri* for specific complaints (☎091-210.111). Tourist police at piazza S. Sepolcro 1 (☎091-616.1361).

Post office Main post office is in the Palazzo delle Poste on via Roma; poste restante at counter 15. Open Mon–Fri 8.10am–7.30pm, Sat 8.10am–1.30pm.

Samaritans Dial ☎091-328.692.

Supermarket *Standa* at via Roma (junction with via Divisi).

Taxis To call a cab, phone *Radiotaxi* ☎091-513.311; otherwise, ranks at piazza Castelnuovo, piazza Giulio Césare, piazza Verdi, piazza dell'Indipendenza.

Telephones Offices at via Lincoln, directly opposite the railway station (*ASST*,open daily; 24hr); piazza Ungheria (*SIP*, daily 8am–9.15pm), off via Ruggero Séttimo; and via Princípe di Belmonte 92 (*SIP*, daily 8am–8pm). Reversed charge calls from the first office only.

Travel agent *CTS*, via Sammartino 79 (☎091-332.209); Mon–Fri 9am–1pm & 4–7.30pm (off via Dante, between piazza Lolli and piazza Castelnuovo). Discounted tickets and *ISIC* cards. *Transalpino* have an office at Stazione Centrale, open Mon–Fri 8.30am–6.30pm, Sat 8.30am–12.30pm.

Women's movement Contact *ARCI Donna* at via Dante 44 (☎091-588.994) or *Unione delle Donne Italiane* (*UDI*) at via Siracusa 16 (☎091-329.604).

AROUND PALERMO

Any respite from Palermo's noise is welcome: take the time to get out of the city at least once. The easiest trips, to **Mondello** and **Monte Pellegrino**, can fill in a few spare hours whenever you like, though Palermitans tend to pack both destinations to the gills on summer Sundays. The other retreat, to the cathedral town of **Monreale**, demands more serious attention: you could see it in an afternoon, but consider a full day (and possibly a night) to get the most out of it and the surrounding valley. Less demanding is a jaunt west to the small family resorts that line the **Golfo di Carini**, a change in pace from the frenetic action at Mondello. Side-trips east, to **Bagheria** and **Solunto**, won't occupy more than half a day out from the city; and you could always see them as a stop on the route out of Palermo, along the Tyrrhenian coast. However, one of the most diverting excursions from Palermo, especially if you're around at Easter, is the trip south to the Albanian settlement of **Piana degli Albanesi**, couched on an upland plain in thoroughly pleasant surroundings.

Bus and train services to all these places are good, and details are given in the text and in *Travel Details*. For a real change of air, though, jump on a ferry or hydrofoil out to the island of **Ústica**, as little as an hour and a quarter from the city. With good, clean swimming and a lazy feel to it, it's the sort of place you may want to hole up for a few days, before returning to the action in Palermo.

Mondello

Regular buses run the eleven kilometres to **MONDELLO**, the best route (#3) passing through ACQUASANTA and then skirting the coast below Monte Pellegrino as far as VALDESI. From here, a marvellous two-kilometre sandy **beach** curves round to the small resort, tucked under the mountain's northern bluff. The beach is the main attraction, though Mondello does have a tiny working harbour, a jetty from which you can try your luck fishing, and the remnants of a medieval tower. Come in the day and you can split your time nicely between the beach and **eating** on the seafront, a major occupation here. There's a line of trattorias – some with outdoor terraces – where the fish is displayed in cases, temptingly fresh. None of them are particularly cheap, but one of the best is *da Totuccio*, via Torre 26, which has a fine *antipasto* table and some unusual shellfish dishes, like *zuppa di vóngole*. If you feel like really splashing out, *Le Terrazze* is the offshore platform in the middle of the bay, to which Palermo's swanky *Charleston* restaurant (see p.64) transfers between mid-June and late September – probably the best dining experience in Sicily. At the other end of the scale, you can grab some excellent **snack food** from the waterfront stalls – *pasta con sarde*, deep-fried vegetables, shrimps and whitebait – putting together a hefty meal for L4000–5000, and then hitting the beach.

Stay late and summer nights at Mondello are fun, the venue for Palermo's *passeggiata*. The bars in the main square are packed, the roads around blocked with cruising cars full of the local youth, and open-air discos add a bit of excitement. In winter it's more laid-back and rarely busy, but the restaurants and snack stalls are still open and it usually stays warm enough to swim until well past the end of the season.

There are several **hotels** in Mondello, but all are impossibly full in summer. If you do fancy staying, ring first: the cheapest is the *Villa Azzurra*, via Stesicoro 14 (☎091-450.362; L33,000), a couple of blocks back from where the bus turns around. To **get to Mondello**, bus #3 skirts Monte Pellegrino to the beach (see above), while #14 or #15 (and, summer only, bus #6) head there through the city's north western suburbs, all caught from via Maqueda or viale della Libertà, a half-hour's ride. If the night-bus fails to materialise, a taxi back to the centre will set you back just under L30,000.

For other beaches within reach of the city, on the Golfo di Carini, see below.

Monte Pellegrino: mountain and sanctuary

North of the city, a clear landmark visible from the port area, is the massive bulk of **Monte Pellegrino**, the mountain which splits Palermo from the bay at Mondello. It was occupied as far back as 7000 BC: Palaeolithic incised drawings were found in the *Grotta d'Addaura* on Pellegrino's northern slopes and there are casts of some of the best in the Museo Archeologico in the city. Today, the mountain is primarily a target for Sunday picnickers, though it also attracts its fair share of pilgrims, coming to visit the shrine of **Santa Rosalia**, the city's patron saint. William II's pious niece, Rosalia, renounced worldly things and fled to the mountain in 1159. Nothing more was heard of her until the mid-17C, when a vision led to the discovery of her bones on Pellegrino. Pronounced sacred relics, the bones were carted around the city in procession in a successful attempt to stay the ravages of a terrible plague, a ceremony which is re-enacted every 15 July – when there's a torchlight procession to the saint's sanctuary – and again on 4 September.

The **ride to the mountain** is extremely impressive (bus #12 from via Filippo Turati, by the Politeama theatre), providing wide views over Palermo and its plain, the winding road climbing through a green belt of trees, cacti and scrub. It's a half-hour journey, and the bus drops you right outside the **Santuario di Santa Rosalia** itself, in a small parking area boxed in by tacky souvenir stands, cafés and vendors flogging every kind of religious kitsch. You enter through a small chapel, built over a deep cave in the hillside where the bones of Rosalia were discovered in 1624. Inside, the water trickling down the walls is supposedly miraculous, channeled by steel plates, while fancy lighting pinpoints a bier containing a reclining golden statue of the saint. Goethe, when he came, thought it 'so natural and pleasing, that one can hardly help expecting to see the saint breathe and move'. Certainly the saint's expression is realistic, though she seems rather smug, too – an effect perhaps induced by the huge pile of bank notes stacked up beside her, offerings from the faithful, who can make the whole thing a bit of a scrum at times. The so-called museum of the saint's life next door is value-for-money, especially when you realise that most of the awful exhibits are for sale.

A small road to the left of the chapel leads to the cliff-top promontory – a half-hour's walk – where a more restrained statue of Santa Rosalia stares over the sprawling city. Another path, leading up from the Santuario to the right, takes you to the top of the mountain, 600m high, and around a forty-minute walk. Elsewhere, all around the trails that cover Monte Pellegrino, whole families are camped out beside their cars, eating lunch from trestle tables and studiously ignoring the 'No Campfire' signs, while the kids make swings out of rope tied between the trees. It's a nice place to spend a day. Heading back, wait until the heat drops and descend by the **Scala Vecchia**, a stepped path which twists from the road by the sanctuary all the way down to Le Falde, near the site of the city's exhibition ground, the *Fiera del Mediterraneo*. On the way, you can make a short diversion to the old *Castello Utveggio* hotel for more marvellous views, and regain the road at the bottom to pick up a bus back to the city centre. Some people *walk up* the same route, a recipe for gut-busting if there ever was one.

Monreale

Beach and mountain are alright for an hour or two out of the city, but the major excursion is to **MONREALE**, a small hill-town eight kilometres south west of Palermo which commands unsurpassed views down the *Conca d'Oro* valley, the capital shimmering in the distant bay. Norman Lewis called the valley ' . . . the greatest and most glorious orchard and market garden in the world', noting that although ' . . . there was nothing of gold about it except the roofs of houses on nearby slopes, it frothed, bubbled and exploded with the voluptuous greenery of millions of trees and plants'. This panorama from the 'Royal Mountain' is alone worth making the trip for, though the real draw is not this, but the mighty Norman cathedral, hidden further in among the houses.

Bus #9 or #8/9 runs frequently from Palermo's piazza dell'Indipendenza (outside the Porta Nuova), the journey through the western suburbs and up the valley taking around twenty minutes. From the bus-stop, trace winding via Roma through the compact town and you'll soon drop down (five minutes' walk) into piazza Vittorio Emanuele, where the **Duomo** (Mon–Sat 8am–12.30pm & 3.30–7pm, Sun 8.30am–12.30pm) flanks one side atop a sea-facing shelf of land. The rather severe, square-towered exterior, though handsome enough, gives no hint of what's inside: the most extraordinary and extensive area of Christian medieval mosaic-work in the world, the apex of Sicilian-Norman art.

The cathedral, and the town that grew up around it in the 12C, both owe their existence to young King William II's rivalry with his powerful Palermitan archbishop, the Englishman, Walter of the Mill. Work had started on Walter's fine cathedral in the centre of the city in 1172. Determined to quickly break the influence of his former teacher, William endowed a new monastery in his royal grounds outside the city in 1174, and its abbey church – this cathedral – was thrown up in a matter of years. Already exempt from taxes and granted other privileges, the church consolidated its position when Monreale was made an archbishopric in 1183, two years before Walter's cathedral was finished. This unseemly haste had two effects. A highly personal project, Monreale's power lasted only as long as William did: though he wanted to create a royal pantheon, he was the last king to be buried there; and later, when Roger II's tomb was removed from the cathedral at Cefalù, it went to Walter's cathedral in Palermo. But the speed with which the Duomo at Monreale was built assisted the splendid uniformity of its most famous relic, its interior art – a galaxy of coloured mosaic pictures bathed in a golden background.

The **mosaics**, almost certainly executed by Greek and Byzantine crafts-men, are a magnificent achievement, completed in perhaps only ten years. Despite the sheer size of the decorated interior (102m by 40m), the gleaming mosaics form a circular and reinforcing picture, from which it's possible to read the Testaments straight from the walls. Once inside, your eyes are drawn immediately over the wooden ceiling to the all-embracing half-figure of Christ in benediction in the **central apse**. It's an awesome and pivotal mosaic, the head and shoulders alone almost 20m high, face full of compassion, curving arms with outstretched hands seemingly encompassing the whole beauty of the church. Underneath sits an enthroned Virgin and Child, attendant angels and, below, the ranks of saints – each subtly coloured and identified by name. Interesting here is the figure of Thomas à Beckett (marked *SCS Thomas Cantb*, between Silvester and Laurence), canonised in 1173 (just before the mosaics were begun), and presumably included as a political show of support by William for the Papacy – an organisation for which Walter of the Mill's lay supporters, the nobility, held no brief. The two **side-apses** are dedicated to Saints Peter (right) and Paul (left), the arches before each apse graphically displaying the martyrdom of each – respec-tively, an inverse crucifixion and a beheading. The **nave mosaics** are no less remarkable, an animated series that starts with the Creation (above the pillars to the right of the altar) and runs around the whole church, while the darker **aisle mosaics** depict the teachings of Jesus. Most scenes are instantly recognisable: Adam and Eve, and Abraham on the point of sacrific-ing his son; positively jaunty Noah's ark scenes showing the ship being built, recalcitrant animals being loaded aboard, Noah's family peering out of the hatches; the Feeding of the Five Thousand; and the Creation itself, a set of glorious, simplistic panels portraying God filling His world with animals, water, light ... and Man.

It's difficult to keep your eyes off the walls but it's worth roaming the whole building. Above the two thrones (royal and episcopal) are more mosaics: William receiving the crown from Christ (less graceful than a similar picture, of Roger, in La Martorana, p.50) and the king offering the cathedral to the Virgin. Both William I and William II are buried here in side chapels, the cathedral's progenitor in the white marble sarcophagus to the right of the apse.

Ask at the desk by the entrance and someone will let you climb up the **tower** (L2000) in the south west corner of the cathedral. It's especially appealing since the steps give access to the roof, for marvellous views of the cloisters (see below), and then continue around the church and upwards, to leave you standing right above the central apse – an unusual and precarious vantage-point. Back inside, tickets for the **treasury** (L2000) are sold from the same desk.

Although all its real artistic attractions are inside, the cathedral's solid exterior merits a closer look too, particularly the enormous triple **apse** – a polychromatic jumble of limestone and lava, supported by slender columns and patterned by a fine series of interlacing arches. You have to circle the cathedral to see this, down a street to the left of the entrance. And it's certainly worth visiting the **cloisters** (Mon–Sat 9am–7pm, Sun 9am–1pm; L2000), part of William's original Benedictine monastery. The formal garden is surrounded by an elegant arcaded quadrangle, 216 twin columns supporting slightly pointed arches – a legacy of the Arab influence in Sicilian art. Look closely at the carved capitals of the 12C columns and you'll see that no two are the same: on one, armed hunters do battle with winged beasts, another has two men lifting high a casket of wine, elsewhere are flowers, birds, snakes and foliage, while around the whole facade of the arches, geometric shapes dip and dance from column to column. A single column in the south west corner even forms a little fountain, in its own quadrangle. Entrance to the cloisters (*Chiostro dei Benedettini*) is from piazza Gugliemo, in the corner by the right-hand tower of the cathedral.

Monreale: other things . . . and some practicalities

After you've seen the cathedral, there's a lot to be said for just strolling the dense latticework of steep streets – especially in the early afternoon when few people are about. At some point, wander into the grounds of the new convent (18C) behind the cloisters for the views from the **belvedere**, straight down the valley. The convent itself now contains the **Istituto Statale d'Arte per il Mosaico** (daily 8.30am–noon) which displays Pietro Novelli's fine 17C painting of St Benedict. Otherwise, while away time in the couple of bars in piazza Vittorio Emanuele, overlooking a fountain and palm trees.

There are two **hotels** in Monreale itself, the expensive *Carrubella Park Hotel*, via Umberto I (☎091-640.2187; L57,000 with bath), and the other, more reasonable, *Il Ragno* (☎091-419.256; L35,000 with bath), out of the centre in località Giacalone. But if you're really set on staying in the area, see SAN MARTINO DELLE SCALE, below, which is a better bet. For **eating**, tourism has shoved the prices up to an alarming degree, though *Trattoria da Peppino* (closed Fri) is better than most, down a side-street off piazzetta Giuseppe Vaglica (follow via Roma from the cathedral) – it does pizzas too, in the evenings. Further up via Roma, in via San Castrense (at no.50), the *Ostaria delle Lumache* (closed Wed) is not bad either, while the *focacceria* next door has light snacks. Information is available from the **EPT** (Mon–Fri 9am–1pm & 4–8pm, Sat 9am–1pm; ☎091-640.2448), in the cathedral square.

Around Monreale: San Martino delle Scale and Báida

Seven kilometres out of Monreale, on the road to San Martino, keep your eyes open for the finely preserved 12C Norman castle on the right, known as the **Castellaccio**, topping a hill above the road. Once a fortified monastery built by William II, 19C neglect made way for the Sicilian Alpine Club who have kitted it out as a mountain refuge, though if there's anyone at home they'll let you in to look around the castle for L500. It's worth the twenty-minute scramble up for the views, which stretch over to the impressive white monastery at nearby **SAN MARTINO DELLE SCALE**. An ancient religious settlement, it's been taken over in recent years as a summer hill resort – holiday homes and Sunday-trippers are much in evidence. But the Benedictine monks are still there, and it's worth visiting their **Abbazia di San Martino** (Mon–Sat 4.30–7pm, Sun 9am–1pm & 5–7pm), supposedly founded by Gregory the Great in the 6C, just to see the grand 18C marble staircase; the rest of interior is rather bland. Ring ahead and San Martino is a pleasant place **to stay**, most economical of the two hotels the *Messina*, at via della Regione 90 (☎091-418.153; L25,000).

During the summer, fairly regular **buses** run between Palermo (from piazza Verdi, by the Teatro Mássimo) and San Martino, through the wooded 'Paradise Valley'. The eastern entrance to the valley is at BOCCADIFALCO, only five kilometres out of the capital; and from here a road leads two kilometres north to **BÁIDA**. A 10C Saracen village (*baidha* is Arabic for 'white'), the convent here was built in the 14C by monks from the Castellaccio, and the church too is interesting, retaining its ochre facade from its 15C construction, together with an earlier apse, and a statue of St John the Baptist, wrought by Antonello Gagini; ask for the custodian at via del Convento 41. Báida is a pretty village, ringed by hills, and again there are direct buses from Palermo; #22 (red) from piazza Verdi, or #23 from piazza dell'Indipendenza.

West: the Golfo di Carini

If you're looking for a **beach** to while away a few hours, then the small succession of holiday resorts along the **Golfo di Carini** is perfectly adequate, and certainly less exhaustingly trendy than Mondello. In fact, given their proximity to the capital, these small fishing ports are surprisingly undeveloped. Better still, they're sheltered by the huge mass of Monte Gallo to the east and protected from the waste ejected into the sea from the city by virtue of their location, tucked safely around the corner of the headland.

The nearest, adjacent towns of **SFERRACAVALLO** and **ISOLA DELLE FÉMMINE** are the best bet, the latter uncomfortably close to a cement factory on one side, though it's quickly forgotten once you're inside the town. The isola in question is a tiny offshore islet. Both places run to **campsites** – the closest official camping spots to the city: the two in Sferracavallo are listed on p.43; those in Isola delle Fémmine are only open in the summer months – *La Scogliera* (☎091-867.7397) and, a kilometre west of town, *La Playa*, which has a sandy beach. Regular local trains stop in Isola delle

Fémmine, while buses #16, #19 (both from Stazione Centrale) and #28 (from the Politeama theatre) come out this way, too.

The train stops at other resorts on or just in from the coast, and there are more summer campsites around, at CAPACI and CINISI. The western promontory, **Punta Raisi** is home to Palermo's airport, said to be controlled by the Mafia, who freight stocks of heroin, processed in factories deep in rural Sicily, out to the States.

The inland town of **CARINI** (buses and trains) has a clutch of 16C churches, and what would be a first-rate visitable **castle**, were it not in a pitiful state of decay, closed and forgotten. The battlemented fortress dates from Norman times and was subsequently held by some of Sicily's leading feudal dynasties: in 1508 a famous murder occurred here, immortalised in an anonymous contemporary poem considered to be the highest example of Sicilian popular versifying, *La Baronessa di Carini*.

Sinners and saints: Montelepre and Partinico

A very minor road climbs eleven kilometres south of Carini to the small town of **MONTELEPRE** (reachable direct from Palermo by bus). There's nothing to bring you to this backwater, except for its associations. To Sicilians, Montelepre is instantly familiar as the birthplace and home of the notorious bandit **Salvatore Giuliano** (1922–1950), who hid out in the hills and caves around here, slipping into town at night to see family and friends. Not only was he hunted by the *Carabinieri*, but platoons of hand-picked soldiers combed the *maquis* for him, and as his ambitions and legend grew, so did his charisma, enhanced by such madcap gestures as writing to President Truman offering the annexation of Sicily to the United States, in a last-ditch attempt to sever the island from the Italian state. As such he was a folk-hero to the Sicilian people, embodying their hopes and frustrations more than any other individual in recent history. He was betrayed and killed, his body found in a courtyard in Castelvetrano, south of here, on 5 July 1950. No one knows exactly what happened or who was responsible for his death, though his cousin and deputy, Gaspare Pisciotta, chose to confess to the crime. Many doubt that he was the one who pulled the trigger, and Pisciotta himself was on the verge of making revelations at his trial that would have implicated high-ranking Italian politicians, when he too was assassinated in his cell at Ucciardone prison. Whatever the truth, there's a pungently Sicilian flavour to the affair, full of betrayal and counter-betrayal, heroes and villains, and Giuliano's legend has since grown to Robin Hood dimensions, nowhere more so than in his 'home' territory around Montelepre. As his biographer Gavin Maxwell was told: 'They should change the name of that village, really – anything else but Montelepre would do. No one can look at it straight or think straight about it now – it just means Giuliano.'

Montelepre is only one of a whole arc of villages to the south west of Palermo where poverty and desperation have long been ingrained. Outlawry is deeply rooted, not just in its romantic guise of banditry, but in the more sinister network of mutual interests and organised criminality that bind politicians and *mafiosi* together. As gripping a story as Giuliano's is that of **Danilo Dolci**, and his campaign for relieving some of the burden weighing down the people of **PARTINICO**. Around ten kilometres south west of Montelepre (and an hour by train from Palermo), this dreary and distressingly poor town is only distinguished for its connections with this social reformer, the 'Sicilian Gandhi', who founded his first self-help and education centre here and campaigned tirelessly to have a dam built locally – something that was resisted at every turn by the Mafia and their political clients who controlled the existing water supplies. For more on Dolci, and on the villages along the Golfo di Castellammare – with which Partinico properly belongs – see p.244.

East: to Bagheria and Solunto

You're likely to see both Bagheria and the ancient ruins at Solunto as easy half-day trips from the capital; regular **buses** (*AST* from piazza Lolli) and frequent local **trains** swing out of Palermo and cut eastwards, across Capo Zafferano, stopping in both towns.

Bagheria

It's **BAGHERIA** that provides the first spark of interest on the run out through Palermo's uninspiring eastern suburbs. Just fourteen kilometres from the city, it quickly established itself as a 17C and 18C summer retreat, the Palermitan nobility sitting out the oppressive heat in a series of Baroque country villas scattered across town. Most are privately owned, however, and you'll need to find someone in the grounds (or ring the bell) to be allowed in. Access to the notorious **Villa Palagonia** is easier: it's on piazza Garibaldi (Mon–Fri 9am–12.30pm & 5pm–1hr before sunset; weekends 11am–12.30pm & 4pm–1hr before sunset; L1000), along the main Corso Umberto, ten minutes' walk from the railway station. Among the travellers who have expressed shock at the eccentric menagerie of grotesque gnomes, giants, gargoyles, and assorted mutants in the villa was Patrick Brydone, the 18C traveller, who wrote:

> . . . *the seeing of them by women with child is said to have been already attended with very unfortunate circumstances; several living monsters have been brought forth in the neighbourhood. The ladies complain that they dare no longer take an airing in the Bagaria; that some hideous form always haunts their imagination for some time after: their husbands too, it is said, are as little satisfied with the great variety of horns.*

Ferdinand, Prince of Palagonia, was responsible for all this, a hunchback who – in league with the architect Tommaso Napoli – took revenge on his wife's lovers by cruelly caricaturing them. The grounds are still amply furnished with the deformed monsters, though only 62 of the original 200 statues remain. Climbing an impressive stairway watched over by a menacing eagle that surmounts the pediment, the palace itself holds the *Salone degli Specchi* – its ceiling covered with mirrors – and some good marbling. However, the chairs with uneven legs and the cushions concealing murderous spikes, which so offended Goethe's sensibilities when he visited in 1787, are sadly no more.

Further up Corso Umberto, the more restrained Villa Trabia and **Villa Valguernara** (also by Napoli) come as something of a relief after this madness, the latter displaying Bagheria's most sumptuous facade, pink and festooned with a royal coat of arms, Attic statues by Marabitti, and views out towards the sea. Villa Valguernara's oval courtyard was one of the settings used in the Taviani brothers' film *Kaos*. Just when you thought you'd left the weirdness behind, **Villa Butera**, at the end of Corso Butera, has within its grounds a building (the *Certosa*) containing a collection of wax figures including (who can say why?) Nelson and the former British Prime Minister, Harold Acton, dressed in Carthusian robes. Legend has it that their creator, Ercole Branciforti, had promised the erection of a Carthusian abbey in return for the granting of a prayer, and took the crafty way out when the prayer was answered.

A little further out from the centre (back to the railway station and over the level-crossing, 300m to the right), the **Villa Cattólica** holds a good gallery of 20C art (Tues–Sat 9am–7pm; L1000) featuring Bagheria's most famous son, Renato Guttuso (1912–1987), whose brilliant use of colour and striking imagery made him one of Italy's most important modern artists for a time.

Solunto

You could well combine a trip to Bagheria with a tour around the Greco-Roman town at **SOLUNTO**, one stop further on the train (the station is called SANTA FLAVIA-SOLUNTO-PORTICELLO). Cross over the tracks and walk down the main road towards the sea; after 300m there's a signposted left-turn, from where it's another twenty minutes' walk up the hillside to the **site** (Tues–Sun 9am–1hr before sunset; L2000), beautifully stranded on top of Monte Catalfano. Ancient Solus, a Phoenician settlement, was founded originally in the 4C BC, though the town was later Hellenised, and finally surrendered to Rome after the First Punic War, changing its name to Solentum. There's a small **museum** at the entrance to the site, worth a quick glance before you ascend the excavated streets, which peep out from under a tangle of thistles, dandelions and other wild flowers. The visible ruins mostly date from the Roman period, notably the impressive remains of wealthy houses which line the hillside. One, with a standing column, was built on two floors, the stairs still visible, and retains a simple mosaic floor. The main street, named via dell'Agora, leads past more houses and shops to the *agora* itself, a piazza with nine recessed rooms at the back, clay-red coloured. Above it, the fragmentary ruins of a theatre and a smaller odeon can be seen, deliberately sited so as to give marvellous views away to the coast. And beyond the *agora* are the remains of a water cistern and storage tanks, necessary as Solentum had no natural springs. It was, and is, a glorious spot, looking out over the coastline: the fishing villages below are split by a small bay, and guarded at one end by the medieval **castello di Sólanto**.

With your own transport you can return to Palermo along the coastal route from Santa Flavia, through **PORTICELLO** village, where there's a summer-only **hotel**, the *Guttilla* (☎091-957.544; L35,000 with bath), above a restaurant which overlooks the beach; ring ahead, as it's popular. Past the stuck-out thumb of Capo Zafferano, it's about another five kilometres to **ASPRA**, from where you can see the whole of the gulf of Palermo ahead of you. If you fancied **staying**, there's a cheap *locanda* here; *Locanda Primavera*, at via Aiello 11 (☎091-878.6328; L14,000). Otherwise, one road runs the couple of kilometres or so south to Bagheria, another west back into the city.

South: Piana degli Albanesi

Half an hour's bus ride south out of the capital takes you to the upland plain where **PIANA DEGLI ALBANESI** sits placidly above a pleasant lake, a million miles from the manic goings-on in Palermo. Founded by 15C Albanians, uprooted from their homes in flight from the Turkish invasions, the 6000 inhabitants here follow the Orthodox rite (though they acknowledge the authority of the Pope), and proudly retain many of their old traditions. It's most spectacular in Piana at Easter, when the small town is full to the brim with people come to admire the handsome costumes, black with gold brocade on Good Friday, brightly coloured on Easter Sunday. If you can't make it then, try to come on Sunday mornings when there are traditional Orthodox services in one of the three churches lining the main street. A couple of kilometres south of the town, the artificial lake lies in a beautiful setting, surrounded by mountains, a good venue for a picnic and a lazy siesta.

If you want a decent walk, you could go on a bit further (four kilometres from Piana, to the right of the lake) to the mountain pass south west of town, **Portella della Ginestra**, scene of one of the most infamous episodes in recent Sicilian history. On 1 May 1947, when the Albanians and villagers from neighbouring San Giuseppe Jato had assembled for their customary May Day celebrations, gunfire erupted from the crags and boulders surrounding the plain, killing eleven and wounding 55, many of them children. This massacre was the work of the bandit Giuliano, whose virulent anti-Communist feelings were exploited by more sinister figures high up in the political and criminal hierarchy: only two weeks previously, the people of Piana degli Albanesi, together with most other Sicilians, had voted for a Popular Front (left-wing) majority in the regional parliament. The cold-blooded kilings erased at one stroke the bandit's carefully nurtured reputation as defender of the poor and friend to the oppressed (see *Historical Framework* and, above, Montelepre).

To get to Piana degli Albanesi, there are several daily **buses** from Palermo, from Stazione Centrale (only two on Sun), and the last one back leaves at 7.45pm (11.45am on Sun). The route takes you through **ALTOFONTE**, once the extreme southerly end of Roger II's royal park and still enjoying a grand view of the *Conca d'Oro* bowl. The **Chiesa Madre** in piazza Umberto gives onto the remains of the cupola-topped royal chapel from this period, though it's been much-changed since then; ask at the sacristy if you want to see it.

Ústica

A volcanic, turtle-shaped island, a lonely sixty kilometres north west of Palermo, **ÚSTICA** is one of the more appealing destinations away from the capital, ideal for putting your feet up for a few days. Colonised originally by the Phoenicians, the island was known to the Greeks as *Osteodes*, or 'ossiary', a reference to the 6000 Carthaginian corpses they found here, abandoned to die on the island after a rebellion. Its present name is derived from the Latin *ustum* – 'burnt' – on account of its blackened, lava-like appearance. Never a particularly attractive place to live, exposed and isolated, Ústica had a rough time throughout the Middle Ages, its sparse population constantly harried by pirates who used the island as a base. In the Bourbon period the island was commandeered as a prison for political enemies, and even as late as the 1890s the few inhabitants were nearly all exiled prisoners: during World War II, Antonio Gramsci, the great theorist of the Italian Communist Party, was interned here.

Today, tourism has rescued the island without altogether spoiling it. Though lacking sandy beaches, its greatest draw is the surrounding limpid waters, ideal for **snorkelling** and skin-diving, which attract an international meeting of scuba enthusiasts every July. Part of the coastline has been designated a 'Natural Marine Reserve', and one of the attractions touted by the locals is 'fish-watching'. On land, Ústica's fertile nine square kilometres are just right for a day's ambling, and it's easy, too, to take a **boat trip** to tour the many grottoes that puncture the rugged coastline. A fishing-boat from the quay will cost about L50,000 for four people; or hire a motor-boat from the *Hotel Stella Marina*, see below – prices are infinitely negotiable. The hotel also rents out **mopeds**, though these are hardly necessary as there's an efficient **minibus** service (L600, pay on board) that plies the island's one circular road every 45 minutes or so. In any case, it doesn't take much more than a couple of hours to walk round the entire island.

Around the island

The first thing you should do on arrival is climb up to the **Castello Saraceno**, right behind the square and beyond the fancy cross at the end of via Calvario. This easy twenty-minute walk leads to an interesting old fort, pitted with numerous cisterns to catch the precious water, and provided with rock-cut steps, which give you a good initial view of the island's layout. From here you can see Ústica's highest point, the **Guardia dei Turchi** (244m), at the summit of a ridge that cuts the island in two, and topped by what looks like a giant golf-ball – in fact a meteorological radar system. You can climb up here from the town in about 45 minutes: up from the square, left at the Municipio, and straight ahead on the cobbled path, cutting off to the right at the end. If you're desperately lazy, you can hire **donkeys** for the same trip at L15,000 each, from Signor Palmisano (☎091-844.9106); ask around the town's bars.

The best **bathing points** are off the rocks on the western shore. Try **Punta Spalmatore**, below the old *torre*, or – below the nearby lighthouse – **Punta Cavazzi**, where there's a *piscina naturale*, a perfect, sheltered pool of sea-water which can get uncomfortably crowded in high season. There's excellent snorkelling at **Punta di Megna**, on the other side of the Marine Reserve, and at the offshore rock of **Scoglio del Médico**, where the clear water's bursting with fish, sponges, weed and coral. Otherwise, choose your own spot. The more cultivated southern coast is best seen by boat as the road runs inland here.

Some practical details

To **get there, ferries** and **hydrofoils** each operate roughly once daily from Palermo (from the Stazione Maríttima), the cheapest passage L10,600 one-way by ferry, hydrofoils twice the price in less than half the time; tickets from *Siremar*, via Francesco Crispi 120. See *Travel Details*.

ÚSTICA TOWN, the island's only port, is where you'll find the cheaper **places to stay**, though be warned that they fill up quickly: most reasonable are the *Locanda Castelli*, at via San Francesco 16 (☎091-844.9007; L15,000), the *Clelia*, via Magazzino 7 (☎091-844.9039; L35,000 with bath), and the *Stella Marina*, via C. Colombo (☎091-844.9014; L37,000). There are plenty of opportunities to **rent rooms**, either through a lettings agency, *Agenzia Osteodes*, piazza Umberto 3 (☎091-844.9210), or direct from the fishermen in the port; just ask around for *cámere*. You can get more information at the **Pro Loco** in the main piazza Vito Longo (daily 9am–1pm, 6–8pm). If you want to visit the **Museo di Archeologia Sottomarina**, also in the main square, contact Padre Carmelo at the church, an acknowledged expert in the field who can give you a guided tour of the exhibits.

festivals

January
6 Orthodox Epiphany procession at PIANA DEGLI ALBANESI; traditional costumes and the distribution of oranges. Similar goings-on at MEZZOJUSO to the south east.

Easter
Holy Week Traditional Orthodox processions and celebrations at PIANA DEGLI ALBANESI, best on Good Friday and Easter Sunday; and also at MEZZOJUSO.

April
23 Costumed processions at PIANA DEGLI ALBANESI to celebrate St George's Day.
Last week Annual World Windsurfing Festival at MONDELLO; races, food, drink and entertainment.

July
11–15 The festival of Santa Rosalia in PALERMO. A procession of the saint's relics, fireworks and general mayhem.

August
21 A colourful horseback parade, *la cunnatta*, at MARINEO, on the Corleone road.

September
4 Pilgrimage to Monte Pellegrino in PALERMO in honour of Santa Rosalia, patron saint of the city.
Last week Annual International Tennis Tournament in PALERMO.

travel details

Trains
From Palermo to Milazzo/Messina (up to 16 daily; 3hr/3½–6hr); Caltanissetta/Enna/Catania (5; 1½hr/2hr/3hr 10min); Agrigento (11; 2½hr); Trápani (10; 2hr); Castelvetrano/Mazara del Vallo/Marsala/Trápani (10; 2hr/2½hr/3hr/4hr); Bagheria/Solunto/Términi Imerese (hourly; 10min/13min/35min); Isola delle Fémmine/Capaci/Carini (hourly; 30min/40min/45min); Naples/Rome (4–8 daily; 10hr/13hr).

Buses
From Palermo to Catania (hourly; 2hr 40min); Messina (1 daily; 4½hr); Trápani (hourly; 1¾hr); Siracusa (4 daily Mon–Sat; 4¾hr); Agrigento (3–4; 2¼hr); Enna (2–4; 1hr 50min); Piazza Armerina/Gela (2; 2¾hr/3hr 40min); Caltanissetta (3–6; 2hr); Noto/Pachino (2 Mon–Sat; 5¾hr/6½hr); Caltagirone (2; 4hr); Bagheria (hourly; 20min); Términi Imerese (5 daily Mon-Sat; 40min); San Martino delle Scale (5 Mon–Sat, 1 Sun; 30min);

Carini (every half-hour; 40min); Piana degli Albanesi (9 daily Mon–Sat; 2 Sun; 30min); Cefalù/Castelbuono (2 Mon–Sat; 1hr/1hr 40min); Nicosia (2–4; 3¼hr); Rome (1; 12¾hr).

Ferries

From Palermo to Ústica (6–7 weekly; 2¾hr); Livorno (3 weekly; 18hr); Genova (4 weekly; 23hr); Naples (1 daily; 11hr); Cágliari (1 weekly; 12½hr).

Hydrofoils

From Palermo to Ústica (1–2 daily; 1¼hr); Naples (3 weekly; 5hr 20min); summer services to Cefalù (3 weekly; 1hr 10min) and the Aeolian Islands (1–2 daily; 3½hr to Lipari).

From Ústica to Naples/Capri (June to Sept 3 weekly; 4hr/5½hr); Favignana/Trápani (June to Sept 3 weekly; 2hr/2½hr).

Planes

From Palermo to Milan (3 daily; 1hr 40min); Rome (8; 1hr 10min); Naples (1; 45min); Genova via Cágliari (1; 2¾hr); Lampedusa (2; 45min); Pantelleria (1; 35min).

CHAPTER TWO

THE TYRRHENIAN COAST AND AEOLIAN ISLANDS

P
ractically the whole of Sicily's northern shore, the **Tyrrhenian coast**, is dedicated to holidaying. At its best it's an eye-catching succession of deserted, rocky coves, sandy strips and citrus groves. But all too often these are eclipsed by a monotonous ensemble of new villas and hotel developments. In summer the beaches can get as congested as the road that runs through the numerous small coastal towns and villages, although out of season there's plenty of room to breathe.

At any time of year, the major distraction is **Cefalù**: a beach resort *par excellence*, whose medieval cathedral contains some of the best mosaic-work you'll find on the island. Cefalù aside, though, the Tyrrhenian coast's attractions are pretty low-key. A good day's wandering can be spent in and around **Términi Imerese**, including a trip out to the hill-top stronghold of **Cáccamo**, which has the biggest and best-preserved of Sicily's Norman castles. And other brief excursions can be made into the **Madonie** and **Nébrodi** mountains – to the hiking and skiing grounds south of Cefalù, or to venerable old inland towns, little-touched by the mayhem on the coast. Everywhere, too, the Tyrrhenian coast is dotted with archaeological remains, the most complete of which is the cliff-top site of **Tyndaris** in the east.

You'll have to brave some pretty ugly industrialisation around the fortified town of **Milazzo** to launch out to the offshore **Aeolian Islands**. Reached by ferry or hydrofoil, this ruggedly diverse chain of seven islands is one of Sicily's real treats: lashed by the sea in winter and often cut off from the mainland by heavy seas, the summer offers hiking and swimming surrounded by some of the most unspoiled of Sicilian landscapes.

THE TYRRHENIAN COAST

The **Tyrrhenian coast** is more accessible than much of the Sicilian seaboard. There's a good **train** service right the way along the coast, making it easy to stop off in any of the seaside resorts that take your fancy. **Cefalù** is an obvious target – though too obvious in summer, when you'll find hotel space difficult to come by. Its fine beach and rocky setting provide the sort of views that attract artists in droves, and it's one of the few package-tour destinations from Britain. Still, it's worth battling with the crowds to spend at least a day there. And you could always base yourself instead at the decent, smaller resorts to the east, like **Sant'Agata di Militello** and **Capo d'Orlando**, also served by train.

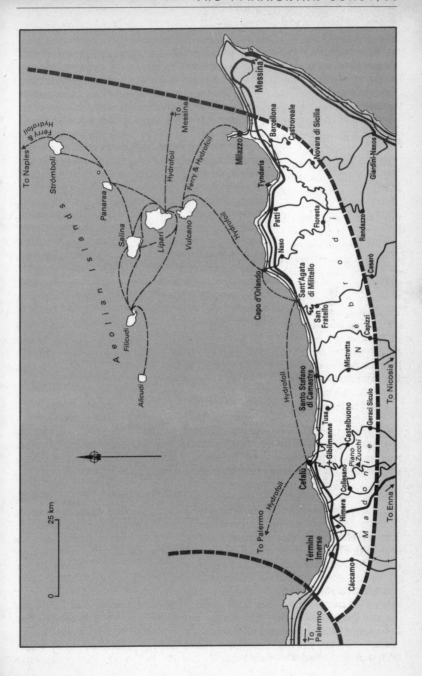

Head **inland** from the coast, into the Madonie and Nébrodi mountains, and you soon leave the crowds behind. There are some good hikes to be done in the hills between **Castelbuono** and **Piano Battáglia**, while further east you can break your off-coast excursions at atmospheric hill towns, especially **Mistretta**, **San Fratello** and **Castroreale**. You can get to most of these places by **bus** from various points on the coast, though a car is useful for continuing on into Sicily's interior.

Train is much the best way to see the coast. **Driving** can be slow, especially where there's still no autostrada – specifically the seventy kilometres between Cefalù and Sant'Agata, which the traffic files through at a snail's pace along the twisting SS113: no fun at night. Where the A20 autostrada does exist, it's a toll road. If you fancy a more leisurely mode of travel, *SNAV* operate a useful (though limited) **hydrofoil** service in summer, from Palermo to the Aeolian Islands, taking in Cefalù, Capo d'Orlando and Sant'Agata di Militello; see *Travel Details* for full schedules.

Términi Imerese, Cáccamo and ancient Himera

First stop out of Palermo is TÉRMINI IMERESE, though if you're driving, keep an eye open for the **Chiesazza**, the ruin of a Norman church built by Robert Guiscard in 1077 and once annexed to a Basilian monastery. As you pass by, it appears stranded by the side of the motorway (on the left, after the exit for ALTAVILLA MILICIA) – much the best vantage-point from which to view it. Don't bother pausing to take a closer look.

Términi Imerese

Fifteen kilometres further on, **TÉRMINI IMERESE** has the magnificent backdrop of Monte Calógero rearing behind, and a seafront marred by some of the only industry you'll see this side of Milazzo. Términi was originally settled by Greeks from Zancle (Messina) in the 7C BC, and subsequently grew in importance as it absorbed the influx of survivors from the destroyed city of Himera, thirteen kilometres to the east (see p.87). Later, as Therma Himeraia, it flourished under the spa-loving Romans, and today the town is still famous for its waters, reputed to be good for arthritis and pasta-making. The main reason to come here, though, is for the excursions you can make from Términi: easy bus rides to Cáccamo, in the hills south of town, and to the site of ancient Himera, to the east.

Términi: the upper town

The town splits into two parts, upper and lower, the **upper town**, Términi's centre, linked to its lower part by long, gracefully-stepped lanes, and dignified by a spacious piazza, where the **Duomo** is the most prominent building. The facade of this 17C creation is embellished by four statues (a century older) and a fragment of Roman cornice below the bell-tower; inside, there's a

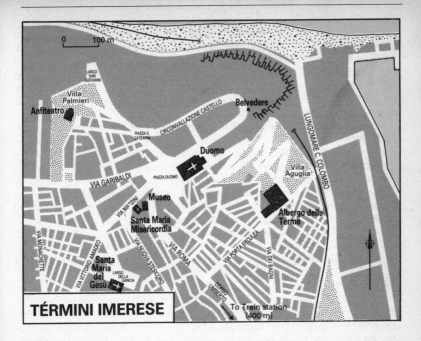

painted 15C crucifix and some 18C sculptures by Marabitti, notably his *Madonna del Ponte* in the chapel on the left of the choir. Walk on, past the duomo, to the palm-fringed **belvedere** to take in the excellent panorama over the lower town, port and sea, mercifully unobscured by the industrial tangle below. Back across the piazza, the small 15C church of **Santa Caterina d'Alessandria** has an old pointed arched doorway surmounted by a crude relief: the church is generally locked, but if you're lucky you'll get to see some frescoes of the saint's life inside, with captions in the local dialect. Just a few steps around the corner from here, the **Villa Palmieri** has some Roman remains scattered among its lush vegetation, including the remnants of the **Anfiteatro Romano**, parts of which also stretch out along the other side of the road near the Porta Palermo, the former entrance to the city.

Before you leave the upper town, it's worth strolling down via Museo Cívico, over from the cathedral. On the right, the **Museo Cívico** itself (Tues–Sun 9am–2pm; L2000) has mainly archaeological material (including finds from Himera) and a small gallery of paintings. Although there's not much else to detain you, the steep, cracked streets below the duomo are pleasant to explore; and you could also track down a couple of noteworthy paintings tucked inside two of Términi's other churches. **Santa Maria della Misericordia**, just past the museum, will probably be locked but contains the town's only important artistic treasure, a 15C tryptych of the *Madonna with Child and Saints*. Further on down, in largo della Gancia, **Santa Maria di Gesù** has a fine Renaissance wooden panel hidden behind its altar, from around 1400, showing St George slaying the dragon.

The lower town: all the practicalities

Términi's **lower town** has less of interest: shaded and cool, its narrow streets play host to a congested mass of traffic, people and grocery stores. Still, it's here that you'll **arrive**, and where you'll find all the town's hotels and restaurants.

The **railway station** is off our map, south east of the town centre: turn right outside, walk past piazza Crispi and down Corso Umberto e Margherita to reach via Roma, the stepped street which climbs to the upper town. Local and long distance **buses** arrive and depart from immediately outside the station. If you're going to see Cáccamo or Himera (or both), you'll probably need to **stay the night**, and there are a couple of cheap options over the road from the station, best of which is the *Locanda Roma*, vicolo di Stefano 12 (☎091-814.1566; L14,000); otherwise, try the basic (though dearer) *Locanda Elena*, via Aurora 12 (☎091-811.523; L20,000), further to the right. The nearest **campsites** are at BUONFORNELLO, around fifteen kilometres east of town: take a bus from outside the railway station for either *Torre Battilamano* (☎091-940.044) or *Villagio Himera* (☎091-940.240), the latter of which has cabins available for rent; both open all year.

Eating places are bunched around the massive *Albergo delle Terme*, near the port – a modern hotel covering the point where Términi's thermal waters issue forth at a constant 42°C. Opposite, the *Tris* trattoria (closed Sat) is the best value in town, while nearby (further up via Porta Erculea and on the left) *La Petite Marseilles* serves shellfish under the stars and within sight of the sea. In the network of alleys winding off piazza Bagni (where via Porta Erculea meets via dei Bagni) there are more decent places; try *Da Giovanni*, in via delle Verdure (closed Sat).

Cáccamo

Buses from Términi's railway station run regularly to **CÁCCAMO**, ten kilometres south, amid green hills and the first of many inland towns hereabouts worth going out of your way for. Its remarkable **castello** is the main draw, and is the first thing you see as you approach – a chalk-white array of towers and battlements dominating the town and commanding the heights above the deep San Leonardo river valley. Built in the 12C, but much modified since and today under scaffolding, the 130-roomed castle nonetheless presents an imposing front. If the gate isn't open, ring at Corso Umberto 6 (the door nearest the war memorial opposite the main entrance), from which Signor La Rosa will emerge to guide you up inside the walls, through three gateways to the main keep. One of the oldest sections contains the *Sala della Congiura*, the chamber where the barons' plot against William I ('the Bad') was hatched in 1160. Entrance to the castle is free, but a tip is appreciated, as you'll be reminded by the hand-written signs liberally scattered along the route.

When you've had your fill of the castle, take time to stroll around the jumble of houses and squares that make up the town. It's little more than an overgrown village, disturbed only by the weight of traffic along the one main street, and at some stage you'll fetch up at the secluded piazza del Duomo behind the castle crag. Here sits an enclave of faded buildings, presided over by Cáccamo's **Chiesa Madre**, dating in part from 1090, though rebuilt in the 15C, and now heavily Baroque in character. The reliefs around the sacristy door are attributed to Francesco Laurana, the Renaissance sculptor who has left his mark all over the region, particularly in Palermo. The best decoration, though, is over the main portal – a 17C tablet depicting St George and the Dragon.

If you're heading **for Palermo**, there's a handy 2pm bus to the capital from Cáccamo; otherwise the last bus back to Términi leaves at 5.10pm.

Ancient Himera

The site of Greek **Himera** is a short bus-ride from Términi Imerese – if you're driving take the Buonfornello exit from the autostrada. It was the first Greek settlement on Sicily's northern coast, founded in 648 BC as an advance post against the Carthaginians, who controlled the west of the island. The town inevitably became a flashpoint, and in 480 BC the Carthaginian leader Hamilcar landed a huge force on the coast nearby, with the intention of taking Himera and very probably the rest of Sicily at the same time. But, pitted against the combined armies of Akragas (Agrigento), Gela and Syracuse, the invading force was demolished and Hamilcar himself perished – either assassinated by Greek spies before the battle, or killed when he threw himself onto the pyre afterwards, depending on whose version you read. The outcome of the battle marked a significant upheaval of the classical world – and, in the case of Sicily, a new balance of power, with the Greeks in the ascendant. But their glory was short-lived: in 409 BC Hamilcar's nephew, Hannibal, wreaked his revenge and razed the city to the ground, the surviving citizens fleeing west to what is now Términi Imerese.

All that's left of the important Chalcidinian settlement that once stood here is one ruined monument: a massive **temple** erected to commemorate the defeat of the Carthaginians. It's ordinary enough, a conventional Doric construction, with six columns at the front and back, and fourteen at the sides. Interestingly, though, the two stair-wells on either side of the entrance to the *cella*, or sanctuary, suggest the involvement of craftsmen from Akragas in its construction. Despite the paucity of the actual remains, the solitary ruin does have a powerful appeal. It's said to stand on the very site of the 480 BC battle and after the victory some of the rich Carthaginian spoils were pinned up inside.

The acropolis lay to the south of the temple, inland, and though excavations have uncovered a necropolis and some smaller temples, much work remains to be done at the site. You can see some of the items dug up from the area in the newly built **antiquarium** (daily 9am–2pm; free) above the site, including some of the striking lion's head water-spouts that drained the temple's roof. There are more of these in the archaeological museums in Términi and, better presented, Palermo.

Hiking and skiing in the Monti Madonie

By car, Buonfornello is also the autostrada exit you need to take for an excursion into the **Monti Madonie**: keep on the coast road and head south at CAMPOFELICE DI ROCCELLA. By **bus** (from Palermo or Términi) you can get as far as COLLESANO, beyond which you have to hitch or walk the fifteen kilometres south to **Piano Zucchi**, first of the upland plains hereabouts that supports a winter sports industry. The *palermitani* come here in winter to ski on the surrounding slopes. In summer, it's just as attractive to come for the pleasant hiking, and if you want more than a few hours in the hills, you can **stay** at the *Rifugio Orestano* (☎0921-62159; L18,000 per person full board at L43,000); though ring first to check for vacancies.

Ten kilometres further on, **Piano Battáglia** is the best base for visiting the highest of Sicily's peaks after Mount Etna, and the only other resort (apart from Etna) equipped for winter sports. It's a very un-Sicilian-looking place, with Swiss-type chalets and even Alpine churches, the area equally popular for summer picnics and for winter skiing. As well as **hikes** to the two highest peaks, Pizzo Antenna Grande (1977m) and Pizzo Carbonara (1979m) – see below – there's a good choice of less ambitious walks along the region's numerous paths, and one to CASTELBUONO (see p.93). If you want to stay at Piano Battáglia, there's a handful of **hostels** around, best of which is the *Rifugio Marini* (☎0921-49.994; L10,000 per person), right in the centre of the plain. It offers full board at L31,000 per person – worth taking as there's nowhere else in the area to eat, and no shops – and also hires out **skiing equipment**. Otherwise, in the summer there are plenty of **freelance camping** possibilities in these hills.

From Piano Battáglia you can continue south along good minor roads to POLIZZI GENEROSA (p.212) or PETRALIA SOTTANA (p.212), though without a car you'll have to walk – sixteen kilometres and twenty-five kilometres respectively. Or you can head back down towards the coast, by-passing Collesano and following the minor road due north for CEFALÙ – close on a fifty-kilometre hike.

The hike to Pizzo Carbonara from Piano Battáglia (2hr)

From *Rifugio Marini*, cross the plain to come out onto the road; turn right and immediately left, winding uphill to reach a small footpath ascending steeply along the main valley. Continue for an hour and round the spur, turning into the river valley. The level path enters a small wood; on leaving this you'll see a zigzag path rising on the opposite bank. Continue along this for twenty minutes and you'll find yourself looking down on Piano Zucchi; otherwise, leave the path and cut up the head of the valley to reach the open uplands, dotted with deep depressions and beechwoods. Continue in the same direction until wooden crosses mark the rounded summit of **Pizzo Carbonara** – head for it by any convenient route. On a very clear day you can see Etna's peak from here.

Cefalù

Despite the recent attentions of *Club Med* and a barrage of modern building outside town, **CEFALÙ** remains a fairly small-scale fishing port, partly by virtue of its geographical position – tucked onto every available inch of a shelf of land underneath a fearsome crag, the *Rocca*. Roger II founded a mighty cathedral here in 1131 and, as befitting one of the most influential early European rulers, his church dominates the skyline, the great twin towers of the facade rearing up above the flat roofs of the medieval quarter, the whole structure framed by the looming cliff. Naturally, it's the major attraction in town, but most visitors are also tempted by Cefalù's fine curving sands – the main reason why the holiday companies have moved in in such great numbers in recent years. Still, it's nothing like as developed as Sicily's other package resort, Taormina: the crowds are manageable, even in summer, and outside July and August you could do worse than make Cefalù your base for a few days, especially if you're attracted by the hiking possibilities in the hills to the south.

The town

It's worth making a bee-line for the **Duomo** (daily 9am–noon & 3.30–7pm; free) first thing in the morning if you want to avoid the tour-coach hordes. Apocryphally, it was built in gratitude by Roger who found refuge at Cefalù's safe beach in a violent storm, though it's more likely that the cathedral owed its foundation to his power struggle with Pope Innocent II. Shortly after his coronation, Roger had allied instead with Anacletus, the anti-pope, whose support of Roger enhanced the new king's prestige. Roger's cathedral benefited from Anacletus' readily-granted exemptions and privileges, its conception at once rich and showy, something that's obvious 850 years later. Quite apart from the massive, fortress-like exterior, inside, covering the apse and presbytery, are the earliest and best-preserved of all the Sicilian church mosaics, dating from 1148.

Unfortunately, the full power of the interior remains muted while the cathedral undergoes long-term restoration (a thorough 'de-Baroquing'), and you can't for the moment approach the mosaics as was intended, down the length of the impressively columned nave (which is completely boarded off). Only the choir and apses are currently visible, accessible through a courtyard to the right of the facade. The **mosaics** follow a familiar pattern: Christ Pantocrator, right hand outstretched in benediction, open Bible in the left, dominates the central apse; underneath is the Madonna flanked by archangels, then the Apostles. Though nowhere near as extensive as at Monreale (p.71), these mosaics are equally affecting and, most interestingly, display a quite different artistic tradition. Forty years older than those in William's cathedral, they are thoroughly Byzantine in concept: Christ's face is elongated, the powerful eyes set close together, the outstretched hand flexed and calming; the archangels have their heads tilted towards the Madonna. When you've seen the pictures here, and noted the two marble thrones on either side of the choir, head back outside and through a little gate for an exterior view of the triple apse – hemmed in by the soaring cliff.

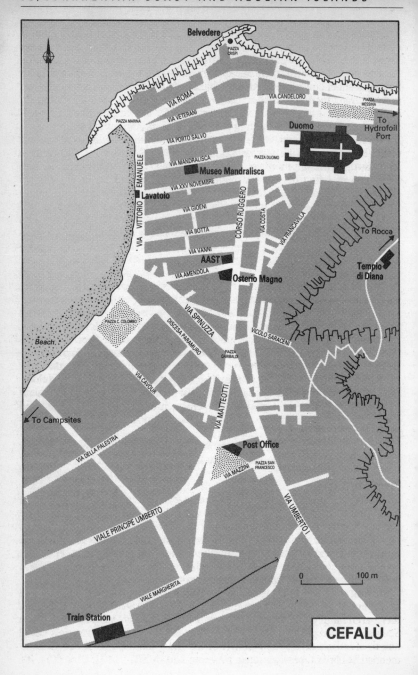

CEFALÙ

Cefalù's ageing, tangibly Arabic, central tangle of streets provides an immediate incentive for some strolling around town. Piazza Duomo itself is always lively, especially in the early evening. Just around the corner, at via Mandralisca 13, the **Museo Mandralisca** (daily 9am–12.30pm & 3.30–6pm; L1500) houses a small collection of quality objects, its two great works the wry and powerful *Portrait of an Unknown Man*, by the 15C Sicilian master Antonello da Messina, and a quirky Greek *krater* (4C BC) showing a robed tuna-fish salesman, knife in hand, disputing the price of his fish with the buyer.

From the museum, walk down towards the water and the little harbour off piazza Marina; when it's quieter, say at lunchtime, this part of Cefalù repays long dawdles through its alleys – rows of washing stretched between houses, fishermen mending nets in the high vaulted boathouses along via Vittorio Emanuele. Back past piazza Marina and off via Roma, a **belvedere** gives onto the old Greek walls of Cefalù, mostly covered and incorporated into a 16C bastion; the other way, down via Vittorio Emanuele, is a relic of the Saracen occupation – the **lavatoio**, a rather smelly bath-house at the bottom of a curving staircase. Frankly, though, these sights are no more than excuses to poke around this atmospheric area, each of the parallel streets off narrow Corso Ruggero lined with attractive buildings in various stages of well-tended decay. One of the most impressive is the **Osterio Magno**, on the corner of via Amendola and the Corso, the surviving portion of a medieval palace.

Meanwhile, the long sandy **beach** beyond the harbour beckons – one of Sicily's best and offering marvellous views over the red roofs of the town. A much more energetic pastime would be to climb **the mountain**, the *Rocca*, following the steps at the side of the *Banco di Sicilia* in piazza Garibaldi. A steep twenty-minute clamber takes you to the so-called **Tempio di Diana**, a megalithic structure adapted in the 5C BC by the addition of classical doorways, their lintels still in place. Keep to the left of the temple and a path continues upwards, right around the crag, through pinewoods and wild fennel. Further on, it dips in and out of a surviving stretch of medieval walls to the sketchy fortifications at the very top, which look down to the coasts on either side of the headland. You can then cut down to the temple and rejoin the path back into town, the whole walk taking about an hour.

Practical details

The **railway station** is south of the town centre, ten minutes' walk from the main Corso Ruggero; all local **buses** leave from the square outside the station. The three-times-weekly summer **hydrofoil** service (from Palermo or Lípari/Vulcano in the Aeolians) docks in the little port to the east of town, a twenty-minute walk away around the headland. The **AAST** (Mon–Fri 8am–2pm & 4.30–7.30pm, Sat 8am–2pm; ☎0921-21.050) is at Corso Ruggero 77 and doles out free maps and accommodation lists.

Staying over can prove expensive in summer (if you can find space in any of the hotels), though it's easy and pleasant outside peak season. Officially, there aren't any private rooms for rent in town, though ask at *Maria Testa Souvenirs* in piazza Duomo – you may strike lucky. Elsewhere, there's a real dearth of budget accommodation, the only thing that fits the bill the recommended *Locanda Cangelosi*, at via Umberto I 26 (☎0921-21.591; L16,000) – it's just off piazza Garibaldi and only has five rooms, so get there early. Otherwise, try *La Giara*, via Veterani 40 (☎0921-21.562; L38,000); the *Pensione Santa Dominga* (☎0921-22.124; L27,000), next to the more expensive hotel of the same name on via Gibilmanna (the extension of via Umberto I); or the *Terminus*, via Gramsci 2 (☎0921-21.034; L36,000), just to the left of the railway station. Note that in high season, July and August, these prices can rocket. You may be better off **camping** – the nearest sites are three kilometres out of town, beyond the beach, just off the SS113 (and behind the *Club Med* complex): *Camping Costa Ponente* (☎0921-20.085), with a swimming pool, and *San Filippo* (☎0921-20.184), open all year, are right next to each other.

There are dozens of **places to eat** scattered around town, though most are overpriced and mundane. One that isn't is the *Arkade Grill*, via Vanni 9 (off Corso Ruggero), which has a small Tunisian menu as well as cheapish pasta and good local wine. **Vegetarians** could do worse than to sample the massive self-service *antipasto al buffet* in the restaurants along the lungomare. You get a plateful for around L5000 at either *Da Nino*, the best, or *Da Saro al Gabbiano*, and both places serve pizzas in the evening as well.

Into the hills: Gibilmanna, Castelbuono and some hiking details

There are some good half-day excursions to be made into the green **Monti Madonie**, south of Cefalù, and for once the public transport services make them easily accessible. Closest, just fourteen kilometres from town (buses from Cefalù's piazza Garibaldi), is the **Santuario di Gibilmanna**, in a spot made sacred by the Arabs who recorded miraculous deeds by the Madonna on the hillside. The sanctuary is the goal of pilgrimages which culminate on September 8 each year, though there are usually people around throughout the summer, picnicking amid the cypress trees if not praying. Avoid the beginning of September and it can be a nice alternative to staying in Cefalù: there's one **hotel**, the *Bel Soggiorno* (☎0921-21.836; L26,000).

Another good road (and regular bus) climbs further into the mountains, running up the green valley and dipping over the first range of hills, to **CASTELBUONO**, a forty-minute ride. It's a comely town, spread across the lower reaches of the surrounding mountains, and sheltering behind the squat 13C keep of its **castello**: inside, there's a small stuccoed chapel, the work of Giacomo Serpotta, and a museum. The steep, crooked streets of Castelbuono – dotted with elaborate fountains and shady piazzas – encourage a stroll, and there are some fine churches, too, like the 17C Matrice Nuova, sitting at the back of its pretty little palm-planted square.

There's good **hiking** country beyond Castelbuono: if you want to base yourself here, stay at the *Ariston*, via Vittimaro 20 (☎0921-71.321; L25,000), right in town. To stretch your legs, head up the road towards GERACI SICULO and half an hour's walk gives you splendid views back over the town and castle. There's a superb hike from Castelbuono to Piano Battáglia (see below), or you could keep on the road as far as **GERACI SÍCULO** itself, 25km from Castelbuono, sitting under the brow of its hill and marked by a ruined 11C castle. Buses come this way, too, from Cefalù twice a day, passing through Castelbuono, and you can complete the trans-mountain route by staying on until GANGI, another 25km (see p.212).

On foot from Castelbuono to Piano Battáglia

To manage this hike easily in a day, you'll have to base yourself at the snug *Club Alpino Siciliano* **refuge**, the *Francesco Crispi* (☎0921-72.279; L12,000 per person, L30,000 per person full board), two hours' strenuous walk above Castelbuono, in the Milocca forest; follow the steep winding road out of town for half an hour beyond the posh *Hotel Milocca*.

From the refuge, keep on the jeep path, leaving the woodlands after half an hour to reach Piano Sempria, where there's another refuge on the right (though it's usually closed). Carry on to a small plain surrounded by four minor peaks, with crosses on each of the summits. There's a wire fence on the left, which you should climb over, and then continue over stony ground in the same direction for fifteen minutes until the large rounded peaks appear: one kilometre ahead (due west) is Pizzo della Principessa (1977m), topped with an antenna; further away to the left (south west) is conical Monte Ferro. Take the wooded Zotofonda valley between these two and you'll reach Piano Battáglia (p.88) in around three hours.

If you're intent upon other serious walks in the hills around here, get details of the local refuges from the AAST in Cefalù before you go; there's no shortage of places to pitch a tent. For the hike described above, it's a good idea to have a contoured **map**, available from the *Istituto Geográfico*, via Siracusa 16, Palermo (L3000); photocopies from the *Ufficio Técnico* in Castelbuono's town hall.

East to Capo d'Orlando . . . and more inland routes

The best stretches of the Tyrrhenian coast all lie **east of Cefalù**: clean sand and stony beaches, backed for the most part by extensive groves of orange and lemon trees. The train stops at several small, attractive seaside resorts – **Castel di Tusa**, **Sant'Agata** and **Capo d'Orlando** – where there's often cheap accommodation. There are buses south, too, into the hills, the **Monti Nébrodi**, from various points on the coast: short runs worth making if only for a breath of fresh air away from the popular beaches.

Castel di Tusa, Santo Stéfano and Mistretta

Some 25km east of Cefalù, the village of **CASTEL DI TUSA** has the remnants of a defensive castle, some good rocky beaches, and a couple of places to stay; something you might want to do as the resort is smaller and quieter than most along this stretch. There's a **hotel**, the *Al Kawarib*, close to the sea on via C. Battisti (☎0921-34.295; L34,000), and there's a **campsite** (*Lo*

Scoglio, open May to Sept; ☎0921-34.345). Three kilometres up the road (there's no bus), on the way to the inland parent village of TUSA, are the sparse ruins of **Halaesa** (daily 9am–1hr before sunset; free), a 5C BC Sikel settlement that enjoyed some success under Rome until despoiled by the *praetor* Verres. You can just about make out the chequered layout of the streets, remains of the *agora*, and – at the highest point – foundations of two 3C BC temples, with lofty views down over the Tusa valley.

More frequent trains stop at **SANTO STÉFANO DI CAMASTRA**, a coastal resort famed locally for its colourful ceramic-work – as you can't fail to realise as soon as you get anywhere near the town. Santo Stéfano is awash with gift shops, plates, jugs and decorative pottery piled high along the sides of the roads; you can pick up some good articles – though haggle hard for the best bargains. It's not the prettiest of the resorts on this coast, but Santo Stéfano does have a cheap **place to stay** if you're stuck for the night – the *U Cucinu* (☎0921-31.106; L14,000) – and the usual selection of fish-restaurants and pizzerias, catering for the Italian tourists who stay here.

Just to the west of Santo Stéfano, a high viaduct flies off sixteen kilometres inland to the first and biggest of the **Nébrodi** hill-villages, **MISTRETTA** – reached by bus from Santo Stéfano. This has a handsome old centre of 18C and 19C buildings unspoiled by modern construction, a 17C cathedral that has the hoary look of a medieval monument and a population largely composed of brown-suited pensioners milling around outside their veterans' associations. It's also one of the few opportunites you'll get to stay overnight in the Nébrodi hills, an alternative in high season to taking your chances down on the noisy coast – sleep at the *Sicilia*, via Libertà N. 128 (☎0921-814.63; L25,000).

The road from here rolls on over the range to NICOSIA, 28km south (see p.210), reachable by a regular daily bus which afterwards doubles back into the mountains to the small village of CAPIZZI, isolated amid vernal woods and meadows.

Sant'Agata and San Fratello

Back on the coast, **SANT'AGATA DI MILITELLO** is one of the livelier Tyrrhenian resorts, busy and noisy in summer with the mainly Italian tourists it attracts. Its wide landscaped promenade supports a little fun-fair, there's a very long pebbled beach, and the remains of a dumpy castle have been turned into a pizzeria. The small fishing fleet working off these shores means you get excellent fish in the local restaurants, and if you want to stay, there's the *Locanda Miramare* (☎0941-701.773; L16,000), next to the railway station – though this is, admittedly, fairly grotty.

One bus a day from Sant'Agata slinks south over the mountains to CESARÒ (see p.211), the first part of the meandering route taking in **SAN FRATELLO**, just fifteen kilometres from the coast. This large village was once populated by a Lombard colony, introduced to Sicily by Roger II's queen, Adelaide di Monferrato, and still retains Gallic-Italian traces in the local dialect. Best time to come here is on the Thursday and Friday of Holy Week, before Easter, for the *Festa dei Giudei*, or 'Feast of the Jews' – a unique *Carnevale*-type celebration in the post-Lent period, when the rest of the Catholic Church is in mourning. Actually, it appears to be the opposite of a Christian festival, with the locals adorning themselves in red devil's costumes, masked and hooded, complete with black tongues and horses' tails (a reminder of their traditional trade of horse-raising), all to the cacophonic accompaniment of trumpets, bells and drums. Needless to say, the ecclesiastical authorities take a dim view of these proceedings, but have been unable to stop them, making do with having the Easter Sunday church congregations in suitably contrite and sober mood.

If you're not around for the festival, make for the Norman **chiesa di Santi Alfio, Filadelfio e Cirino**, isolated on top of a hill at the entrance to the village (follow the rough track from the cemetery): a good place for a picnic. The church is dedicated to three brothers horribly martyred by the Romans: the first had his tongue torn out, the second was burned alive, and the third hurled into a pot of boiling tar.

San Marco d'Alunzio to Capo d'Orlando

Seeing any more of the coast between Sant'Agata and CAPO D'ORLANDO, or the hills beyond, isn't really on without your own transport. Buses are too few and far between to be much good for day-trips, although regular buses do leave Sant'Agata for **SAN MARCO D'ALUNZIO**, five kilometres away just inland: an impressively sited village. Called Aluntium by the Romans, San Marco had already been established in Greek times, and its principal point of interest, the **Tempio di Ércole** recalls that era, an evocative shell that was converted into a church by Robert Guiscard. It has since been deconsecrated, though something of its sacred aura remains thanks to its imposing position high above the coast. Later religious monuments, particularly the church of **Sant'Agostino**, with an interesting Renaissance sarcophagus and a *Madonna* attributed to Antonello Gagini, make San Marco somewhere you could easily spend a couple of hours roaming around; there are also the fragmentary remains of a **castle** where members of the Hauteville family (Sicily's Norman rulers) once resided.

A short drive along the coastal road brings you to the turn-off for **FRAZZANÒ**, fourteen kilometres up in the mountains, beyond which lies the Basilian church and monastery of **San Filippo di Fragalà**, a fortress-like structure built by Count Roger in the 11C. With high walls enclosing a courtyard, this is sadly abandoned and falling apart, but you can tiptoe over the crumbling floors and peer into the narrow cells, examine the faded Byzantine frescoes on the walls of the church, and enjoy the views from the ramparts. If there's no one around to let you in, try around the back for an open door.

Occupying a headland which was the site of an historic defeat for the Aragonese king, Frederick II, at the hands of a group of rebellious barons in 1299, **CAPO D'ORLANDO** is a busy town surrounded by good rocky and sandy **beaches**, especially on its eastern side (around the SAN GREGORIO area). It's the last major resort on this stretch of coast and if you're sufficiently charmed by the beaches you might well want **to stay**: the *Piave*, via Piave 125 (☎0941-901.562; L30,000 with bath), is the most reasonable of the town's several hotels, and frequent buses run to a well-equipped **campsite** four kilometres to the west, the *Santarosa* (☎0941-901.524; June to Sept). For

information, ask at the kiosk on the seafront (open in the summer only) or the Pro Loco in via Vittorio Veneto.

Inland from here, the oddly named town of **NASO** ('nose') sits at the end of a twelve-kilometre bus-ride, where you can see (just before entering the town, up a steep lane on the left) the partly ruined **convento dei Minori Osservanti** – 15C, with an interesting tomb of the same period decorated with allegories of the six virtues. The road continues up, another 33km, to **FLORESTA**, lying on a grassy plain and, at 1275m, Sicily's highest village, then down to RANDAZZO (p.162) and the foothills of Mount Etna.

Roman remains at Patti, Tíndari and San Biagio

East of the cape, the coast is more built-up, the unremarkable towns merging into one long conurbation. **PATTI**, however, thirty kilometres on, possesses an important relic in the shape of a 4C AD **Roman villa** – east of the town, close to the railway station and under a motorway viaduct. The extensive site (daily 9am–1hr before sunset; free) contains a few mosaics and the remains of a bath-house. At the top of the town, Patti's **Cattedrale** has a powerful *Madonna* by Antonello de Saliba, and, in the right transept, the tomb of Adelasia, much-loved first wife of Roger I, with the date of her death inscribed at the bottom, 1118.

The villa is the first of a series of Roman remains in the area, and from Patti's main square you can catch a bus (around three daily) to the most complete of the classical ruins, at **TÍNDARI**, eleven kilometres to the east.* Originally founded in 396 BC, **Tyndaris**, as it was known, was one of the last Greek settlements in Sicily, built and fortified by settlers from ancient Syracuse as a defence against Carthaginian attacks along this coast. Almost impregnable on its commanding height, the town prospered even under Rome, when it was given special privileges in return for its loyalty.

As the bus climbs the hill to the site, though, you could be forgiven for thinking you'd come to the wrong place, since the first thing you see, glistening from its cliff-top position, is the **Santuario di Tíndari**, a lavishly kitsch temple erected in the 1960s to house the much-revered *Madonna Nera*, or Black Madonna. A plaque underneath this Byzantine icon boasts *Nigra sum, sed hermosa* ('I am black, but beautiful'): reference to the esteem in which she has been held for a thousand years, since the icon miraculously appeared from the east, subsequently performing a series of miracles, such as producing a soft mattress in the nick of time to save a child who was hurtling to the rocks below. There's always a commotion here, with thousands of pious pilgrims thronging daily to the sanctuary to pay their respects, and especially around the Black Madonna's feast-day on 8 September.

* There are direct buses, too, from Messina to Tíndari, an hour and a half's trip: Monday to Saturday, two daily.

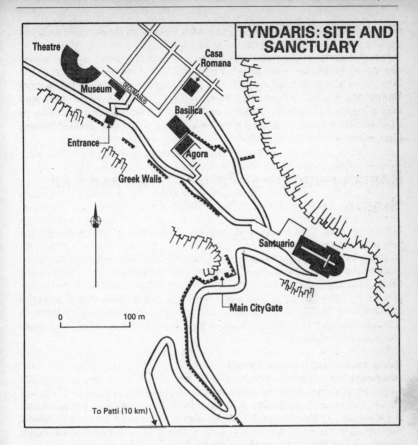

TYNDARIS: SITE AND SANCTUARY

Theatre

Casa Romana

Museum

DECUMANUS

Basilica

Entrance

Agora

Greek Walls

Santuario

0   100 m

Main City Gate

To Patti (10 km)

  The **archaeological site of Tyndaris** (daily 9am–1hr before sunset; free)
lies at the end of a path which starts in front of the sanctuary. Most of the visible remains are Roman, including some houses and shops along the main
street, the *decumanus* – one of them (probably a *caldarium*, or bath-house)
with traces of plumbing still surviving – and an impressive **basilica** at the
eastern end. Strictly an entrance to the *agora* lying beyond (in the area now
covered by tourist shops), this building was subjected to restoration in the
Fifties which provoked much ire on account of the modern materials used.
But it still retains a certain grandeur, undiminished by the cement, and you
can clearly make out the manner of its construction, bridging Greek and
Roman building techniques and designed in such a way that the central
gallery could be shut off at either end and used for public meetings, with the
market traffic diverted along the side-passages. Some of the sculpture which
was found in the niches here is now in the archaeological museum in
Palermo.

The *decumanus* has streets running off it, and at the bottom of one is the **Casa Romana**, a Roman house in good condition with mosaic floors. At the other end of the main street, the **teatro**, cut into the hill, boasts a superb prospect over the sea, with views as far as the distant Milazzo promontory. A part of the scene-structure remains from the original 3C BC Greek edifice, but most of the rest is Roman, dating from the Imperial Age when the theatre was converted for use as a gladiatorial arena. Later, the theatre was partly dismantled to furnish stone for the **city walls** that once surrounded the settlement, of which a good portion remains. You'll have seen some of them on the road up, including the ancient city's **main gate**, built on the same 'pincer' design as the one at the Euryalus castle outside Siracusa.

The **museum** on the site (daily 9am–2pm; free) contains some of the best finds from the excavations, including a massive stone head of Augustus. There's also a reconstruction of the theatre's scene-building, and some 18C watercolours showing how the basilica looked before its overhaul. Ask here for information on the **classical dramas** staged in the theatre during the summer months.

If you're especially interested, and have your own transport, another short drive away along on the coastal road east of Tíndari are the more modest Roman remains at **SAN BIAGIO**, right on the SS113. The recent excavation of a 1C AD **Roman villa** here (daily 9am–1hr before sunset; free) revealed interesting evidence on the construction of baths, but above all it's the vivid mosaics that make this worth stopping for – and one in particular, depicting a fishing scene at sea.

Seeing the sites: practical details

There are two railway stations within reach of the main sites: PATTI-SAN PIERO PATTI station is the stop for Patti; for Tyndaris you can either take a bus from Patti station direct to the site or stay on the train for a few more kilometres to OLIVERI-TÍNDARI, from where it's about a three-kilometre (uphill) walk. Without a car it's easy to get stranded; if you do, there are a couple of **campsites** and some (expensive) **hotels** near Patti railway station, and one very cheap place to stay in Oliveri – *La Corda* on via Spiaggia Mare (☎0941-33.140; L12,000).

Away from the coast: to Castroreale

From San Biagio, two choice inland routes branch off into the **Monti Nébrodi**, the first of which, the SS185, is the only road in the province connecting the Tyrrhenian and Ionian coasts, leading to GIARDINI-NAXOS (p.139). This is one of the finest routes on the island, climbing gently into the hills through some handsome countryside to **NOVARA DI SICILIA**. You could make a convenient lunch-break at this small town, in the *Pineta* **trattoria** (just off the main square, largo Bertolami), which serves cheap and abundant portions. The dense woods above, with expansive views over the sea, are a favourite spot for the locals, who come out here on a Sunday, armed to the teeth with picnic hampers and portable stoves, though there are enough shady nooks and glades to find your own space. The road climbs to 1270m before descending, in sight of Etna's dramatic slopes, to FRANCAVILLA and CASTIGLIONE (see p.141).

Back on the coast, you can make a detour at the uninteresting BARCELLONA to the Peloritan hill-town of **CASTROREALE**,* eight kilometres to the south. Favoured by Frederick II of Aragon, who came here for the hunting, the town enjoys magnificent views over the hills and out to sea. At its highest point is a tower, the one remaining fragment of Frederick II's fort, built in 1324 and subsequently ruined by earthquakes. The tower, just off the end of the main Corso Umberto I, now houses an *IYHF* **youth hostel** (☎090-905.247; open all year); you can enter to climb up to the top even if you're not staying.

The rest of Castroreale is creakingly medieval, and half the fun is just strolling along the quiet, sloping streets, and dropping in at the couple of basic bars for a drink. If it's at all possible, aim to spend the night in town, either at the hostel or, rather better, down at the **Collegio dei Redentori**, an old and depopulated Redemptionist monastery, now used as a seminary and conference centre – excellent value at L8000 per person; another L4000 gets you a good meal cooked by the sole remaining monk, eaten in hall with him and the abbot. It's located on a bend of the road as you enter the village (below the cross on the right).

Milazzo

If it wasn't for the industry besieging **MILAZZO** – first major town on this coast after Términi – it wouldn't be a bad-looking place. Most people, though, are put off by the unsightly oil refinery that produces a constant yellow smog overhead, and only stop long enough to get out again, taking the first ferry or hydrofoil to the Aeolian Islands (see below). But Italian tourists know Milazzo well, and regularly crowd the beaches and campsites strung along the thin finger of land behind the town.

The town

If you're in a hurry, Milazzo's easy enough to handle. You could be on an outward-bound ferry or hydrofoil within thirty minutes of arriving: **buses** stop right on the quayside, while the **railway station** is a few hundred metres further down, set back from the water. **Sailings** to the Aeolians operate daily, and are frequent enough to make it unnecessary to book, although bear in mind that there is a reduced service between September and June – see below for more information and *Travel Details* for frequencies.

---

* To get to Castroreale, get off at Barcellona railway station and make for the bus station – straight down the road ahead, turn left at the second set of traffic lights, and keep straight on for 200m. If you don't want to wait for the bus (the last one leaves at 6.15pm), it shouldn't be difficult to hitch out of Barcellona (keep going straight out of the railway station to get out of town), or even walk, by following the Longano river valley upwards for about three hours – the steep bit's at the end.

With an hour to spare before or after your Aeolian trip, you might choose at least to visit the rambling old castle that caps Milazzo's acropolis. Historically, the site's strategic importance made it one of the most fought-over towns in all Sicily. The Greeks arrived in 716 BC, after which the town was contested by successive armies, from the Carthaginians to the Aragonese. It even became a base for the British during the Napoleonic Wars, while fifty years later Garibaldi won a victory here that set the seal on his conquest of Sicily. Via San Francesco climbs up from the northern end of the port, into the heart of the old town, surrounded by massive walls. To appreciate the citadel's size, carry on walking round to the north side, where the formidable defences erected by the Spanish still stand almost in their entirety. The **castello** itself (guided tours hourly: Oct to end Feb 9am–noon & 2.30–3.30pm, March to end May 9am–noon & 3–5pm, June to end Sept 10am–noon & 3–7pm; free) is steeped in military history: built by Frederick II in the 13C on the site of the Greek acropolis and on top of Arab foundations, it was enlarged by Charles V, and restored by the Spanish in the 17C. Inside the castle walls you'll see the **Vecchio Duomo** – presently closed for restoration – a central Norman keep, the old *Sala del Parlamento* and the remains of the Palazzo dei Giurati, later converted into a prison. A museum is to be installed within these crumbling walls, but until then it's enough to admire the sheer views down to the sea from the ramparts.

Milazzo has a couple of other churches worth looking at. Directly opposite the castle's entrance, the Dominican **chiesa del Rosario**, together with its convent was formerly a seat of the Inquisition, while below, in the new town, the silver-domed **Duomo Nuovo** has some excellent Renaissance paintings in the apse: four panels of the Saints Peter, Paul, Rocco and Thomas Aquinas; between the last of these, an *Adoration of the Child* by Antonello de Saliba; and an *Annunciation* by Andrea Giuffrè above that.

Practical details

Milazzo's **Pro Loco** is at piazza Duilio 14 (Mon–Sat 8.30am–12.30pm, 4–8pm; Sun 9am–noon); you can also telephone from there, if you need to book a hotel in the Aeolians. The **shipping agencies** are all down by the harbour, including the two major ones – *Siremar* for ferries and hydrofoils, *SNAV* for hydrofoils only; you can also buy hydrofoil tickets at the quayside kiosk before boarding. If you want to leave a car in Milazzo, there's a convenient choice of **garages**, though all are on the expensive side: prices vary according to length of stay – expect to pay L6–12,000 a day. All are dependable, but try the *Garage Sicilia* on via Siro Brigiani for good rates.

If you need to **stay** in Milazzo, and you really could spend time in worse places, the *Cosenz* (☎090-928.2996; L30,000) in the street of the same name is reliable; nearer to the port, the *Capital*, via G. Rizzo 23 (☎090-928.3289; L35,000) is another choice. Otherwise you could move further along the thin promontory, where three or four well-equipped **campsites** are grouped around the headland of **Capo Milazzo**, six kilometres out of town. Cheapest is the *Agriturist* (☎090-928.2838), a twenty-minute bus ride, though only open June to September. There are plenty of good **beaches** all around here, but the sandiest is close to the centre of town, on Milazzo's western, less developed side (at the end of via Colombo).

THE AEOLIAN ISLANDS

The **Aeolian Islands**, or Isole Eolie, are a mysterious apparition when glimpsed from Sicily's northern coast – sometimes it's clear enough to pick out the individual white houses on their rocky shores, at other times they're murky, misty and only half-visible. D.H. Lawrence, on his way to Palermo by train in bad weather, thought they resembled ' . . . heaps of shadow deposited like rubbish heaps in the universal greyness'. The sleepy calm that seems to envelop this archipelago masks a more dramatic existence: two of the islands are still volcanically active, and all are buffeted alternately by ferocious storms in winter and waves of tourists in summer. But their unique charm has survived more or less intact, fuelled by the myths associated with their elemental and unpredictable power. Volcanoes have always been identified with the mouths of hell, and it was here that the smith Vulcan had his workshop: Zeus's son (known to the Greeks as Hephaestos), Vulcan was the god of fire and metal-working, and one of the islands is called after him. Another takes its name from Liparus, whose daughter Ciane married Aeolus, ruler of the winds and master of navigation; Aeolus in turn lending his name to the whole archipelago. The winds were kept in one of the Aeolians' many caves, and Odysseus was presented with a bag of them on his travels, which blew his ship straight back to port when opened by his curious crew.

The more verifiable **history** of the islands is equally eventful. The first settlers exploited the volcanic resources of the islands, above all the abundance of obsidian, a hard glass-like stone that can be worked to produce a fine cutting-edge and was traded far and wide, accruing enormous wealth to the archipelago. The islands were drawn more closely into the Greek ambit by the arrival in about 580 BC of refugees from the wars between Segesta and Selinus (Selinunte). Welcomed by the inhabitants, these errant Greeks organised themselves into two groups: those who cultivated the land and settled the smaller islands, and those who defended their settlements from Etruscan pirates, in turn preying on other shipping. The land was held in common, and the loot divided. This system was so successful that their contributions to the sanctuary at Delphi rivalled even those of great Syracuse.

The islands subsequently changed hands several times before being abandoned to the frequent attacks of wide-ranging North African pirates, culminating in the terrible slaughter that took place in 1544 at the hands of Khair ed-Din, or Barbarossa, who consigned to slavery all the survivors of the massacre – a figure estimated to have been as high as 10,000. Italian unification saw the islands used as a prison for political exiles, a role that continued right up to World War II, with the Fascists exiling their political opponents to Lípari. The last political detainee to be held here was, ironically, Mussolini's own daughter, Edda Ciano, in 1946.

Emigration, especially to Australia, had reduced the Aeolian population to a mere handful of families by the late 1950s, when the arrival of the first hydrofoil signalled salvation by a nascent tourist industry. Agriculture has largely been abandoned, and the economic revival today is based purely on tourism (though Lípari's pumice industry has recently expanded), with hotels sprouting on previously barren ground, and running water and electricity installed almost everywhere. During the summer months at least, you'll not be alone here, especially on the central islands of **Vulcano**, **Lípari** and **Salina**. All are pretty well known to an increasing throng of devotees, and prices are verging on the exclusive side: food is expensive, a glass of water (like food, imported) can set you back L1000, and you'll pay over the odds for **accommodation** – if you can find it. When it's scarce, in high season (Easter and July/August), you'd be wise to phone in advance. Outside of these times, you can usually find bags of space; **renting rooms** can turn out to be an economical option, there's a fine **youth hostel** on Lípari, and **campsites** on Vulcano, Lípari and Salina – but camping rough is illegal.

At the right time of year, there's a lot to be said for spending some time on the Aeolian Islands: each has a distinct identity, they're easy to explore using the frequent ferry and hydrofoil traffic plying between them, and all are embraced by beautiful clean sea, of a limpid quality you won't find anywhere else along the coast of Sicily. Sandy **beaches** are sparse, and the ones there are are ash-black, but if you can get access to a boat, you'll find no shortage of secluded coves, and snorkelling opportunities are plenteous everywhere. For something completely different, a trip up to **Strómboli**'s seething crater is an unforgettable experience, while a sojourn on one of the minor isles of **Filicudi** and **Alicudi** will give you a taste of what it what was like twenty – or a hundred – years ago: unsophisticated, rough and beautiful.

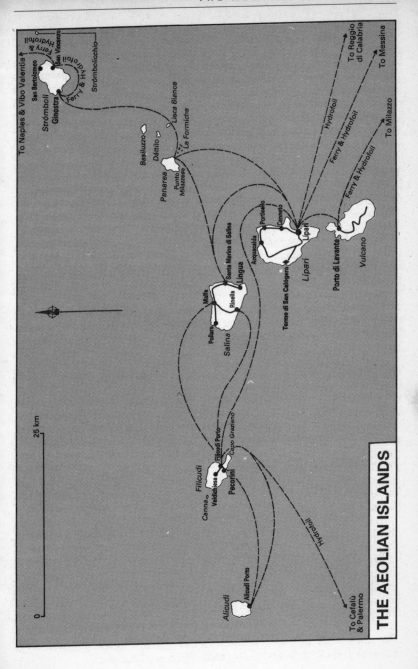

THE AEOLIAN ISLANDS

Getting there ... and getting around

You can **get to the Aeolian Islands** from numerous points along the Italian or Sicilian coasts. There's a fairly regular **hydrofoil** service in summer from Palermo and Cefalù (see *Travel Details*, p.81 and p.117); a twice-daily summer service from Capo d'Orlando (p.95); a daily service from Messina (p.120) and Réggio di Calabria; and **ferries and hydrofoils** leave several times weekly from Naples and Vibo Valentia, on the Calabrian coast (see the box below for all connections from outside Sicily). But access is easiest **from Milazzo** (p.99), with year-round ferries and hydrofoils connecting the port with all the islands several times a day (less frequently in winter). Ferries and hydrofoils from Milazzo call first at Vulcano, followed by the main island, Lípari, which is connected by ferry and hydrofoil to all the other islands; from Naples or Vibo Valentia, Strómboli is the first port of call, while from Palermo, some routes take in Filicudi and Alicudi first.

Whichever way you come, you'll find it useful to get hold of **timetables** at the tourist offices in Milazzo or Messina: *SNAV* and *Siremar* are the main operators, the first just for hydrofoils (*aliscafi*), the second for hydrofoils and ferries. Ferries (*traghetti*) take about twice as long, but are half the price and more enjoyable. In winter especially, the hydrofoils are more prone to cancellation due to bad weather, particularly services to the more distant islands. From Milazzo, ferry **tickets** cost L5,600 one-way to Lípari, L11,800 on the hydrofoil, returns exactly double; one-way tickets to the islands beyond Lípari cost L3–10,000 more (by ferry) and L5–20,000 more (by hydrofoil). Note that Lípari is the hub of the Aeolians' ferry and hydrofoil system: you may need to return to Lípari to catch onwards services to one of the other islands.

Once you're there, **getting around** is usually no problem, with most of the islands small enough to be easily negotiable on foot, and Lípari and Salina equipped with good public-transport links. These two islands are the only ones where you might consider taking a car, but it's expensive and somewhat unnecessary (there are garages to store your car in Milazzo); a bicycle would be more apt, and you can **rent bicycles, mopeds and scooters** at L10–35,000 a day – see the text for details.

Connections to the Aeolian Islands from mainland Italy

SNAV hydrofoils from Réggio di Calabria (approx 2hr 20min): June to Sept 4 daily, Oct to May Mon–Sat daily at 1.35pm.

SNAV hydrofoils from Vibo Valentia (approx 1hr 30min): mid-July to mid-Sept Tues–Sat daily at 8.40am.

SNAV hydrofoils from Naples (approx 5hr): June to Aug daily at 3.15pm, Sept daily at 2.45pm.

Siremar ferries from Naples (approx 8hr): Oct to March Wed & Sat at 7am, beginning to mid-June & mid- to end Sept Tues, Thurs & Sat at 7am, mid-June to mid-Sept Tues, Thurs & Sat at 7am, Mon & Fri at 7.30am.

For all connections to the Aeolians from within Sicily, see Travel Details, chapters 1, 2 and 3.

Lípari

LÍPARI is the busiest, the most popular and the most diverse island in the archipelago. Arriving by sea at its main town – also called Lípari – gives a pleasant foretaste of what is to come: a thriving little port, dominated by an impressive castle on an acropolis which effectively divides the town into two. The road which circles the island from here takes in several much smaller villages, some good beaches, and excellent views out to its neighbouring islands, which are all within easy reach.

Historically, it has always been Lípari that has guided the development of the Aeolians. After obsidian had been superseded by metals, the island's prosperity in classical times was based on its sulphur baths and thermal waters, which still today attract many of the island's visitors. Its alum too was much prized, found more abundantly here than anywhere else in Italy. Today, with a population of over 10,000, its economy is bolstered by an expanding pumice industry in the north of the island, though the main money-spinner is inevitably the island's natural beauty, which brings in tourists by the boat-load.

Arriving and getting around the island

Hydrofoils dock at the Marina Corta while **ferries** steam straight past the fort to dock at the Marina Lunga, a deep-water harbour, beyond which a long beach curves away to the north. If you're only staying long enough to transfer from hydrofoil to ferry, the most direct way is up the main Corso Vittorio Emanuele and across to the other main street of via Garibaldi, or vice-versa. If you have time, drop in on the **AAST** (Mon–Sat 8am–2pm, 4.30–7.30pm; ☎090-981.1410) at Corso Vittorio Emanuele 253 (though soon to be transferred across the road), which will provide you with a useful hotel list, good for all the Aeolian Islands, and will also phone ahead to check on accommodation vacancies. To get a decent map of the islands you'll have to buy one on the Corso – a bit steep at L5000, but full of information.

Lípari's **buses** all leave from a stop by the Marina Lunga, and there are at least nine daily (three on Sunday) to every village on the island; full timetables are printed by the stop, and see *Travel Details*. This is also the site of the island's only **petrol stations**, and the couple of **scooter and bike hire** shops are fifty metres further up on via Marina Lunga – expect to pay up to L35,000 a day for a Vespa, excluding petrol; you'll have to leave your passport as security.

The town

Lípari's sights are concentrated in its citadel, or **upper town**, protected by the sturdy walls of the **castello**. Most of what remains of this formidable structure is 16C Spanish, though it incorporates fragments of earlier medieval and even Greek buildings. Until the 18C, this was the site of Lípari town, and still contains the **Duomo**, along with the dilapidated ruins of several churches, giving the place a forgotten, spectral air. The most impressive approach to the

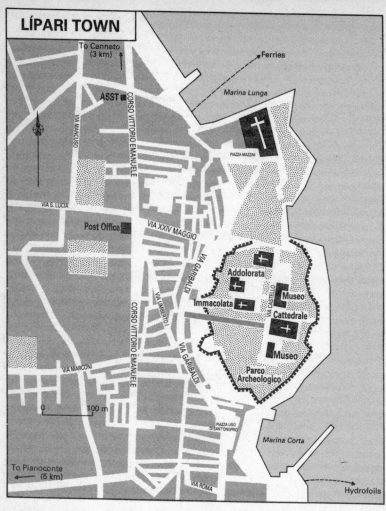

LÍPARI TOWN

To Canneto
(3 km)

Ferries

Marina Lunga

ASST

CORSO VITTORIO EMANUELE

VIA MANCUSO

PIAZZA MAZZINI

VIA S. LUCIA

Post Office

VIA XXIV MAGGIO

VIA GARIBALDI

Addolorata

Museo

VIA CASTELLO

Immacolata

Cattedrale

VIA UMBERTO I

CORSO VITTORIO EMANUELE

VIA GARIBALDI

Museo

VIA MARCONI

Parco
Archeologico

0   100 m

PIAZZA UGO
DI SANT'ONOFRIO

To Pianoconte
(5 km)

Marina Corta

VIA ROMA

Hydrofoils

upper town is from via Garibaldi, from which long steps cut right through the thick walls, bringing you up to the duomo itself: all about lie scattered the **excavations** of superimposed layers of occupation, from the Neolithic to the Roman age, a continuous record covering almost 2000 years. It's a unique sequence, providing archaeologists with heaps of finds that have enabled them to date other Mediterranean cultures. But you won't make much sense out of the wide trench exposing these fragments of Bronze Age and Iron Age huts without going into the superb **Museo Eoliano** (Mon–Sat 9am–2pm, Sun 9am–1pm; free), housed in buildings scattered around the cathedral; one of Europe's most important prehistoric and classical collections.

On the right of the cathedral, the 17C bishop's palace contains the **first part** of the museum, its displays laid out chronologically from the earliest examples of Aeolian pottery to later vivid figurative work, like the lid of a *bothros*, or sacred repository of votive articles, embellished by a reclining lion, from the mid-6C BC. The **second section** of the museum, on the left side of the duomo, holds principally classical and Hellenic material, some imaginatively set in reconstructions of the sites where they were found. The last rooms hold the most splendid items: shelves of decorated vases – some from Paestum showing a variety of satyrs, gods, queens, clowns and courtiers, from the first half of the 4C BC. One room has a good collection of small terracottas grouped in theatrical scenes, and the oldest and most complete range of Greek theatrical masks in existence. Look out, too, for the series of etchings on the way out, by the English sea-captain, W. H. Smyth, showing views of the Aeolians and other Sicilian scenes in 1823. The **other sections** of the museum across the road are dedicated to the rest of the islands, and include some lovely vases from Salina, finds from sites on Panarea and Filicudi, and a wealth of vulcanological material. At the end of the road, the **Parco Archeologico** (Mon–Sat 9am–1pm & 4–6pm) has some Greek and Roman tombs, and a modern Greek-style theatre where concerts and plays are performed between July and September. There's a nice look-out over rooftops and the Marina Corta from here.

There's nothing else specific to see in Lípari town, though you can spend time mooching around the small, packed streets, a lively array of chic boutiques interspersed with fishing-tackle shops. The best place to while away an afternoon is at the **Marina Corta**, where the constant coming and going of hydrofoils, taxis, bikes and people can be safely observed from the cool haven of parasol-covered bars. Other bars deeper in the town's warren of streets have live music until late at night in the summer.

Sleeping, eating and practical details

There's more choice of **accommodation** in Lípari than any of the other islands, though you can still find yourself stuck for a room in high season, especially in the cheaper range. If you've equipped yourself with an accommodation list, don't hesitate to wave it in front of hotelkeepers' faces if they try to overcharge, although sometimes they'll simply oblige you to take breakfast and add another L5000 to your bill.

Of the cheaper hotels, there's the *Locanda Salina*, via Garibaldi 12 (☎090-981.2332; L25,000), and the *Europeo*, Corso Vittorio Emanuele 98 (☎090-981.1589; L35,000), both on a main drag, and often full. A better possibility is the quiet and well-kept *Neri* at via Guglielmo Marconi 43 (☎090-981.1413; L36,000), down an alley off the Corso (after no.85). Another good option is to **rent a room**, from around L30,000 for a double in winter (up to twice this in summer). You may be asked to spend a minimum of two nights (or a week in summer), but it can still work out cheaper than a hotel, given that you'll nearly always get something with a shower and a kitchen – a distinct advantage given the price of restaurant food here. Look for notices in shop windows, or ask around in the harbour bars; the *Residence Fiorentino*, via Giuseppe Franza 9 (☎090-981.2136), is a good, friendly, family-run place.

Lípari's **youth hostel** (☎090-981.1540; March to Oct) is marvellously situated in the castle: good value and great views, though again busy in July and August; out of season, they're unlikely to hassle you about being a member. If you're **camping**, the island's only site is at CANNETO, three kilometres north of town (see below).

The town's numerous **restaurants and pizzerias** – many of them open-air – come in varying degrees of expensiveness, though some have (often poor) tourist menus at around L15,000. Even the cheaper places have exorbitant twenty per cent service charges that'll boost your bill. If you're looking for a decent pizza, though, *Il Corsaro*, on via Marina Lunga, isn't at all bad; or there's a bakery next to the *Standa*, on the Corso – both places you should definitely visit if you're self-catering. You'll see the locals eating at the exclusive *Filippino*, in piazza Municipio in the upper town, or the more modest *La Nassa* on via Giuseppe Franza (open May to Oct only).

You can **telephone** from the shop opposite the *Esso* station in via Marina Lunga, or, when it's closed, in via Maurolico (open till 9pm, noon on Sun). The **post office** is in Corso Vittorio Emanuele, where there are also several **banks**.

Around the island

Buses leave Lípari town approximately every hour for the **rest of the island**, no part of which is more than half an hour's ride away. If you're not weighed down you could easily walk the short distance north to the nearest village, **CANNETO**, in about an hour – much less if you choose to go through the tunnel, though this is a bit hair-raising on foot. A long pebbled beach fronts the village itself, though most opt for the expansive sandy **beach** lying at the end of a path just to the north of here, the island's finest. It retains its name, *Spiaggia Bianca*, though its whiteness is rapidly becoming a distant memory as the pumice dust which covered it gets washed away by the winter storms; nevertheless it's worth making a day's expedition for, and is a good reason to stay in Canneto itself. **Camping** rough is feasible if you're discreet, though you might prefer the facilities available at the *Baia Unci* campsite (☎090-981.1909; April to Sept), which you'll have passed on the way into the village. And Canneto has several reasonable *pensioni*, best of which is the *Giallorosso* (☎090-981.1358; L30,000), overlooking the sea and right above the village's best **trattoria**.

Stay on the road and it's only another three or four kilometres to the great pumice works of La Cava at **CAMPOBIANCO**. More uses for this volcanic debris are being found all the time, and it's presently used in such diverse products as toothpaste, light bulbs, construction materials, jeans (for bleaching), and most recently, fertiliser. Years of accumulation of pumice sediment on the seabed below have turned the water a piercing aquamarine colour – very enticing, and instantly accessible by sliding the thirty metres or so down the brilliant white mountains of dust formed by the quarrying. This is nothing new to the islanders and other *conoscenti*, who've been doing it for years;

indeed the pumice-chute was used for one of the closing scenes in the Taviani brothers' epic film *Kaos*.

Above Campobianco, a path leads up the slopes of **Monte Pilato**, thrown up in the eruption from which all the pumice originally came. The last explosion occurred in around 700 AD, leading to the virtual abandonment of Lípari town and creating the obsidian flows of *Rocche Rosse* and *Forgia Vecchia*, both of which can be climbed. Although overgrown with vegetation, you can still make out the outline of the crater at the top, and you may come across the blue-black veins of obsidian. Despite its quite different appearance, it's almost identical in composition to pumice, and it's the presence of obsidian on Lípari that makes the island's beaches sparkle.

Below Campobianco, a road drops to the stony **beach at PORTICELLO** – more good swimming – and then curls round to face Salina on Lípari's northern shore. From here the road descends a couple of kilometres to **ACQUACALDA**, a one-street village with two or three basic, homely trattorias and, unexpectedly, **rooms** to rent – contact Mondello Carmelo in via Rocche (☎090-982.1003).

Following the coast west from Lípari town, you can walk to the vantage-point for one of the Aeolian Islands' most stunning vistas. Climbing the three kilometres through lush and fertile country, you'll know you're at **QUATTROCCHI** when Vulcano and the spikey *Faraglioni* rocks, which puncture the sea between the two islands, sweep into view to the south. The curious name of this spot ('Four Eyes') is said to derive from the fact that newly-wedded couples traditionally come here to be photographed, so gracing every shot of this memorable place with two pairs of eyes.

Keep on the road to **PIANOCONTE**, a fragmented village which has a couple of popular restaurants: they're at their best in the evening when they serve pizzas too. Just before the village, a side-road slinks off down to the old Roman thermal baths at **SAN CALOGERO**. It's a particularly nice route to follow on foot, across a valley and skirting some impressive cliffs, the baths right at the end of the road. Lengthy excavations here have unearthed a great deal of archaeological material, particularly from the Mycenean age (15C BC), and even if the spa-hotel is still closed you should be able to take a look around the site, and walk down the path to the sea below.

Vulcano

Only a few minutes south of Lípari by ferry or hydrofoil, separated by the kilometre-wide channel *Bocche di Vulcano*, is the island of **VULCANO**. Closest of the Aeolians to the Sicilian mainland, it's the first port of call for services from Milazzo, and you don't have to disembark to experience the sulphurous, rotten-egg smell that sometimes hits you before you've even reached the small port – disconcerting if you're not expecting it. The island's **Gran Cratere** hangs menacingly over its inhabited northern tip, its plume of vapour a constant reminder of its silent power, though this very old volcano is in the last, smoking phase of its life, and unlikely to spring anything more harmful than the nasty smell.

That said, the volcano was threatening enough to dissuade anyone from living here before the 18C, since when there have been some hasty evacuations. In the last century a Scot called Stevenson bought the island to exploit the sulphur and alum reserves, but all his work was engulfed by the next major eruption. Although the volcano's last gasp of activity occurred between 1886 and 1890, its presence permeates the island, giving Vulcano a more primeval flavour than any of the other Aeolians. Everything here is an assault on the senses, the outlandish saffron of the earth searing the eyes, as violent as the intense reds and orange of the iron and aluminium sulphates that leak out of the ground in the summer, to be washed away with the first autumn rains.

However, none of the jet-setting Italians who come to bronze themselves on Vulcano's superb beaches are discouraged, and numerous villas and some sprawling luxury hotels make this the most exclusive of the Aeolian islands. Don't let this put you off: if you can't find a place to stay here, or can't afford the prices, Vulcano still offers a good day out, with some of Sicily's stranger volcanic enticements and the best **beach** in the entire archipelago, fifteen minutes' walk across the narrow neck of land separating **PORTO DI LEVANTE** (where the ferries dock) and **PORTO DI PONENTE**. Here, a perfect arc of fine black sand lines a bay looking onto the towering pillars of rock that rise out of the channel between Vulcano and Lípari – the setting for some unforgettable sunsets.

On the way to the beach you'll pass Vulcano's famed **fanghi**, or mud baths: more exactly one pool, containing a thick yellow soup of sulphurous mud, in which people come to wallow, caking every inch of their bodies with the stuff. This surreal performance is all part of a long tradition – specifically for skin and arthritic complaints – though the degree of radioactivity here makes it inadvisable to immerse yourself for any length of time, and unsuitable for young children or pregnant women. Avoid contact with the eyes (it stings like hell) and take off any silver or leather jewellery, which will be ruined forever, even just by coming into contact with the sand hereabouts. When you've had enough of the mud, hobble over to rinse yourself off in the nearby sea where the water itself is hot, and you need to take care in order not to get scalded.

If you're spending time on Vulcano, there are a couple of brief **hikes** worth doing: one to the **Gran Cratere**, an hour's walk up, where you can observe the acrid volcanic emissions at close quarters and enjoy some lofty views from the 400m peak; the other to **Vulcanello**, the volcanic pimple just to the north of the port, thrown up out of the sea in a famous eruption in 183 BC, and joined to the main island by another flurry of activity a few centuries later. The birth of Vulcanello excited enthusiasm in the high society of the time: it was witnessed by some of the greatest luminaries of the 2C BC, and described by Pliny, Livy and Strabo. The **Valle dei Mostri** here – literally the 'Valley of the Monsters' – is an area of lavic rock formations, blackened and sculpted by the elements.

From Porto di Levante, Vulcano's only road runs eight kilometres south, past **Monte Saraceno** (481m, with views as far as Alicudi and the Sicilian coast), to the extensive **Piano**, the only plain of any size in the Aeolian

Islands. A straggling path leads from here to the hamlet of **GELSO**, stranded on Vulcano's south coast. Gelso is Italian for 'mulberry' and they're cultivated here, along with capers. As the hamlet is virtually cut off from the rest of the island, most of its provisions have to be transported here by sea.

Some practicalities

There are cheapish **rooms** to let at Porto di Levante, though most are only available in the summer months. Best choice is the amenable *Casa Sipione* (☎090-985.2034; L35,000 with bath), at the end of a path beside the church; otherwise try *Casa Fioritan* on via Levante (☎090-985.2006; L35,000). On the Porto Ponente side, there's *Orsa Maggiore* (☎090-985.2018; L40,000 with bath). In all cases, ring first, and expect prices to shoot through the roof in summer. The **campsite** (*Sicilia*; ☎090-985.2164; June to Sept), is close to the port. More information can be had at the **AAST** (June to Sept Mon–Sat 8am–2pm; ☎090-985.2028) at Porto di Levante, opposite the *Siremar* ticket agency. The cost of **food** on Vulcano is exorbitant, but if you must eat here, the *Gabbiano Bianco* on the main road is one of the cheapest options.

Salina

SALINA's ancient name, *Didyme*, or 'twin', refers to the two volcanic cones that give the island its distinctive shape. Both volcanoes are long extinct, but their past eruptions, combined with plenty of water – unique in the Aeolians – have endowed Salina with the most fertile soil of all the islands, vigorously cultivated to produce excellent capers and delicious *malvasia* wine.

You'll **arrive** either at the main port, **SANTA MARINA DI SALINA**, or RINELLA, a little fishing village on the south coast (see below). A bus service connects them, taking in the island's other villages as well. Santa Marina is the better place to stay, with some nice seafront bars and a choice of **accommodation**: the *Punta Barone* (☎090-984.3172; L30,000) is right by the sea, but you're likelier to find room at *Mamma Santina*, via Sanità 26 (☎090-984.3054; L25,000), further from the front and signposted off the main street – clean and friendly, the view from its wide terrace compensates for its distance from the port. Or you can **rent a room** from Giovanna Iacono on via Francesco Crispi (☎090-984.3096; L26,000).

From Santa Marina you can do a wonderful seven or eight kilometre **walk** through the centre of the island, to below the peak of **Monte Fossa delle Felci**, the archipelago's highest at 962m. In the central plain of **Valdichiesa**, the path trails off south at the sanctuary of **Madonna del Terzito** – highly wooded, cultivated, and with fine views over the sea – taking in the nondescript village of LENI and finishing at **RINELLA**. There's little to keep you here but the island's one **campsite** (*Tre Pini*; ☎090-984.2155; June to Sept).

Alternatively, you could head two or three kilometres down the road from Santa Marina to **LINGUA**, a tiny cluster of hotels and trattorias facing the shore of Lípari. A good choice here for **accommodation** is *'A Canna* (☎090-984.3161; L25,000), though out of season you'll be able to take your pick from a number of options. At the end of the road is the salt-lagoon from which

Salina takes its name, and there's a narrow **beach**; you'll find others along the road, though this isn't the best island for expanses of sand.

Back the other way, following the road north and then west from Santa Marina, **MALFA** has a good beach below it, stony but picturesquely backed by ruined fishermen's houses. This is the island's biggest town, steeply sloping towards a tiny mole at the bottom and equipped with a couple of decent trattorias and one **place to stay**, the *Villa Orchidea* in via Roma (☎090-984.4079; L25,000). The only other village on the island is **POLLARA**, a few kilometres further west, raised on a cliff above the sea and occupying a crescent-shaped crater from which Salina's last eruption took place, 13,000 years ago.

You can **rent bicycles** (L10,000 a day), **mopeds** (L18,000) and **Vespas** (L20,000) from a shop just outside Santa Marina (two minutes' walk from the port), on the road to Lingua, useful for exploring the island though some of the roads make cycling a bit of an effort. Look out on your wanderings for the exotic violet-flowered **capers**, and the abundant **vines** that carry the **malvasia** grape. You'll come across these two traditional Aeolian specialities on every island, but, while caper production is still flourishing, *malvasia* wine has fallen victim to the general depletion of agriculture, and most of what you drink will have been imported from Sicily. Only in Salina can you still taste the authentic sulphurous taste of this sweet and strong honey-coloured wine. If you want to buy a bottle, expect to pay around L15,000.

Panarea

PANAREA, to the east, is the smallest island of the Aeolian archipelago, at just 3km by 1½km, and the prettiest, surrounded by clusters of outlying islets that provide some of the best swimming hereabouts. Inhabited since Neolithic times, Panarea also holds one of the region's most important archaeological sites, easily accessible on the dramatic Punta Milazzese.

No cars can squeeze onto the island's narrow lanes to disturb the tranquillity, though heavily loaded three-wheelers are common. To really enjoy Panarea you need a boat, which will enable you to explore the uninhabited western side and connect you with the rocks and islets offshore. You should be able to hire one at the jetty – not too expensive if you share it with others; very roughly, expect to pay around L15,000 per person. Panarea's downside is that its cosy intimacy has made it into something of a ghetto for the idle rich, putting it almost on a par with Vulcano on the exclusivity scale. Nevertheless, you can find cheap accommodation here, and it's worth a couple of lazy days sampling the island's pleasures, even if you have to bring your own sandwiches.

You'll find many of the cheaper **hotels** around the jetty area of **SAN PIETRO**, biggest of the island's three settlements. Try the *Locanda Stella Maris* (☎090-983.163; L17,000) or the *Locanda Rodà* (☎090-983.006; L20,000). It's also always worth asking around for **rented rooms**, but bear in mind that the supply of accommodation in Panarea in July and August does not meet the demand. Though illegal, you could get away with **camping** on the island's one sandy **beach** if you're desperate, half an hour's walk south of San Pietro. You'll find a number of adequate and rather expensive **trattorias** along this path, one directly above the beach, rather rough-and-ready but nicely situated overlooking the bay. This would be a useful place to ask about **rooms**, too.

High above the beach, on the other side, is the headland of **Punta Milazzese**, where a Bronze Age village of 23 huts was discovered in 1948. This beautiful site overlooking two rocky inlets is thought to have been inhabited since the 14C BC and pottery found here (displayed in Lípari's museum) shows a distinct Minoan influence – fascinating evidence of an historical link between the Aeolians and Crete that goes some way to corroborating the legends of contacts between the two in ancient times.

North of San Pietro, you'll pass evidence of volcanic activity in the gushing hot springs and steaming gas emissions (*fumarole*) all the way to CALCARA where the road ends.

But above all, be sure to make a trip out to Panarea's own archipelago, the largest islet of which is **Basiluzzo**, formerly inhabited but now only used for caper cultivation. Next down in size, and nearest to Panarea, **Dáttilo** points a jagged finger skyward, and has a minuscule beach; or there's better swimming at **Lisca Bianca**, where the tranquil water is sheltered by **Bottaro** opposite. Nearby **Lisca Nera** and **Le Formiche** ('the ants') are mere wrinkles on the sea surface, though a constant hazard to shipping.

Strómboli

The most spectacular of all the Aeolians, **STRÓMBOLI** is little more than a volcano thrust out of the sea. This most active outlet of the volcanic belt throws up showers of sparks and flaring rock at regular intervals of about twenty minutes, though only visible at night – occasionally from as far away as the Calabrian coast. It was Strómboli's crater from which Professor Lindenbrook and his colleagues emerged in Jules Verne's *Journey to the Centre of the Earth*.

Undaunted, people have always lived under the skirts of this volcano, and the communities of **Ginostra** and the straggling parishes of SAN VINCENZO, SAN BARTOLO and PISCITÀ – often grouped together as **Strómboli town** – exist in a charmed world, their white terraced houses adorned with bougainvillea and wisteria, remote from the fury of the craters above. Plumbing is at best rudimentary, especially in Ginostra, on the far side of the island, which is dependent on wells for its water supply, and the majority of houses have no electricity at all. But despite this Strómboli, too, has become something of a chic resort, with a couple of first-class hotels and some swish open-air discos.

Strómboli town ... and boat trips around the island

Most people choose **STRÓMBOLI TOWN** as a base, better equipped with beaches, and with a wider choice of accommodation and restaurants. Two roads lead off from the port area, one along the seafront, the other ascending to the main street, where you'll find most of the bars, shops and cheaper **hotels**. The first one you see along here, the *Pensione Roma*, is not a bad option, with doubles at L35,000 and distant views of the sea; alternatively, ask at *La Nassa* discotheque (down one of the alleys leading to the sea) for one of their good clean rooms – though slightly more expensive. Or you can go further along the main street to *Villa Petrusa* (☎090-986.045; L25,000), beyond the church in the square – the nearest this string of houses gets to a centre. Further along this meandering main road, you come to the parish of **SAN BARTOLO** and, just beyond **PISCITÀ**, the island's best ashy **beach**. If you want to **eat** moderately cheaply, the *Villa Petrusa* does an adequate dinner for about L15,000 a head.

Strómboli town also offers the best chance of arranging a **boat tour** of the island. According to season and numbers, it'll cost around L15,000 a person, and is worth it for the sea-views of the volcano, including the dizzy *Sciara del Fuoco* (see below), and an excursion to Strómboli's basalt offspring, **Strombolicchio**, a couple of kilometres out. You can climb the two hundred or so steps leading up this colossal battlemented rock to the lighthouse on its top, a lonely vantage-point.

The volcano

Piscità is a starting-point for the **ascent of the volcano**. Guides for this are available – ask at your hotel or telephone ☎090-986.093/080/175 for the official *Club Alpino Italiano* guides – though there's no reason why you shouldn't do it alone: it's not dangerous and it's easy enough to find your way. In hot weather you'll appreciate the value of setting out in the early morning or evening, though to see the full display, take a sweater (it gets cold and windy up there), sleeping bag and torch, and bed down in one of the lava shelters. It'll take between 2½ to 3½ hours to reach the summit, but make sure you arrive in daylight: the last bit's the trickiest. Otherwise, just follow the markers, and don't drink your water too soon – you'll need it. On the way you'll pass the frighteningly sheer volcanic trail that channels all the lava outflows, known as the **Sciara del Fuoco**, plunging directly into the sea. At the top, the fiery explosions can vary in intensity, but it's always a fairly impressive performance, the noise alone something like an express train thundering directly below you. Ignore the warning signs at your peril.

Ginostra

For the descent, you might choose to come down on the other side, to **GINOSTRA**. The path, skirting a desolate lunar landscape of tormented rocks and fine black dust, is steeper and more tiring than that to Strómboli town, and less well-marked – keep your eyes open for the red dots at all times – though it's quite a bit shorter (about two hours). Once there, you could kick around this peaceful hamlet, eat at one of the trattorias, and either take one of the Strómboli-town-bound hydrofoils or the rough path leading along the seashore. If you decide to stay here, the *Petrusa* (☎090-981.2305; L17,000) has large rooms with their own terraces and wells; otherwise, there's always the possibility of finding **rooms** to let.

Filicudi and Alicudi

Out on a limb, the two wildest of the Aeolian Islands, **Filicudi** and **Alicudi**, have most to offer those looking for a quiet time. Supporting tiny populations who make ends meet by fishing and little else, they are extremely remote and have very basic facilities: fine places to come to unwind, though neither has very good bathing unless you can get hold of a boat. Between June and September there are daily hydrofoil connections between the islands and Lípari, yet it's surprising how few people bother to make the trip. Even out of season, when services are reduced – and if the weather turns, you're in danger of being stuck on them for days – the islands are seductive, with a slow rhythm and a refreshing absence of other tourists.

Filicudi

FILICUDI, the bigger of the two islands, is the closest to the main pack, an hour by hydrofoil from Lípari, its small harbour dominated on one side by a hotel complex that's closed for eight months of the year. If you're looking for **accommodation**, you couldn't do better than *La Canna* (☎090-984.4187; L25,000), in the *Rocche Ciauli* district of the island, best approached by climbing the steep path to the left of the hotel at the port: clean rooms opening on to a spacious terrace with a magnificent view down to the bay below. You can eat well and cheaply here too, better than at the two or three trattorias down by the portside. If you're heavily loaded, walk or hitch along the road instead, a hairpinned kilometre from the beach.

The road forks at *Rocche Ciauli*: either up to the dispersed central village of **VALDICHIESA**, its houses mostly derelict; or switching down to the other coast where the village of **PECORINI** straggles down to the sea. Beyond Pecorini, you can continue on round the island, and scale the 774m **Fossa dei Felci**. Filicudi's mountain slopes are all painstakingly lined with stone terracing, a monument to former agricultural activity, but now serving only to reduce soil erosion.

Much nearer the port, an easy ten-minute climb from the stony beach (turn right at the rock), is the archaeological site at **Capo Graziano**, where the remains of a dozen or so oval huts mark the spot which gave its name to the local Bronze Age culture that immediately preceded Panarea's Punta Milazzese, 18–13C BC. You can visit this small site (discovered in 1952) at any time – a calm but unspectacular spot from which the finds are on show at the museum in Lípari.

You could see a lot more of Filicudi by hiring a boat, giving you the chance to explore the island's uninhabited northern and western coasts. **Punto Perciato**, to the west, has a fine natural arch, and nearby you can visit the **Grotta del Bue Marino**, the 'Seal Grotto', a wide rocky cavity 37m long by 30m wide, its walls of reddish lava barely visible in the pitch black of the interior. A little further out to sea, the perpendicular **Canna** is a startling sight, a rugged and solitary obelisk 71m tall, the most impressive of all the *faraglioni* of the Aeolian Islands.

Alicudi

The precipitous shores of **ALICUDI** are also pierced by numerous caves, and nosing around these is just about the only entertainment this isolated island (the furthest from Lípari) can provide. The island forms a perfect cone, though Alicudi's ancient name *Ericusa* was the word for the heather that still stains its slopes purple in spring. Its rocky isolation has in the past been exploited by the Italian goverment, using the island as a prison for convicted *mafiosi*, but now it's virtually abandoned by all but a few farmers and fishermen, giving the place a relaxed pace: nothing happens on Alicudi, but that, presumably, is its virtue.

From the only village on the island, **ALICUDI PORTO**, a path leads north to the ruins of a castle, nearing the 675m summit of the mountain, **Filo dell'Arpa**. There's one **hotel**: the *Ericusa* (☎090-981.2370; L32,000), though fishermen are usually willing to put you up in a private room if you ask around. You can **eat** at the *Ericusa* too.

festivals

Easter
Holy Week On the Thursday and Friday, bizarre happenings at SAN FRATELLO, the *Festa dei Giudei*, with processions and devil's costumes.

June
Start of the theatrical performances and concerts at the castle in MILAZZO; they run through until August.

August
2nd Sunday A medieval procession, *La Castellana*, in CÁCCAMO, composed of five hundred characters representing all the notables in the town's history from the 11C to the 19C.
24 Procession of San Bartolomeo's statue and relics in LÍPARI town on the Aeolians. Celebrations, too, on ALICUDI.

September
8 Informal pilgrimage to the sanctuary of the Black Madonna at TYNDARIS. Pilgrimage, too, at GIBILMANNA, south of Cefalù.

October
Horse fair in SAN FRATELLO.

travel details

Trains
From Términi Imerese to Cefalù/Santo Stéfano/Sant'Agata (hourly; 30min/1hr/1½hr); Palermo (half-hourly; 30min).
From Sant'Agata to Capo d'Orlando/Patti/Oliveri-Tíndari/Barcellona/Milazzo (14 daily; 15min/30 min/45min–1hr/1hr–1hr 40min/2hr); Milazzo (6; 1hr).
From Milazzo to Palermo (half-hourly; 2½–3hr); Messina (hourly; 45min).

Buses
From Términi Imerese to Cáccamo (Mon–Sat 10 daily, Sun 1; 30min); Buonfornello (several daily; 20min); Cefalù (Mon–Sat 1; 30min);

Palermo (Mon–Sat 5; 40min); Castelbuono (Mon–Sat 2; 1hr 40min).
From Cáccamo to Términi Imerese (Mon–Sat 8 daily, Sun 1; 30min); Palermo (2; 1hr).
From Cefalù to Gibilmanna (1–3 daily; 30min); Castelbuono (3–6; 40min); Geraci/Gangi (2; 1hr 25min/2hr); Petralia (1; 2hr); Términi Imerese (1; 30min); Palermo (2; 1hr).
From Castelbuono to Geraci/Gangi (1–2 daily; 1hr 20min); Isnello/Collesano/Campofelice/Términi Imerese/Palermo (Mon–Sat 1; 30min/55 min/1¼hr/1hr 40 min/2¼hr).
From Santo Stéfano to Mistretta (3–6 daily; 40min); Nicosia (Mon–Sat 1, change at Mistretta; 2hr 50min).

From Sant'Agata to San Fratello/Cesarò (1 daily; 20min/1½hr).

From Patti to Tíndari (3 daily; 20min).

From Barcellona to Castroreale (7 daily; 30min, less frequent on Sun).

From Milazzo to Messina (hourly; 40min).

From Lípari town to Canneto (Mon–Sat 9 daily, Sun 3; 10min); Acquacalda (Mon–Sat 7, Sun 2; 30min); Quattrocchi/Pianoconte/Quattropani (Mon–Sat 8, Sun 2; 15min/20min/30min).

Ferries

From Milazzo (June to Sept) to Vulcano/Lípari/Salina/Panarea/Strómboli/Naples (5 weekly; 16½hr); Vulcano/Lípari (2 daily; 1½hr/2¼hr); Salina (2; 3½hr); Filicudi/Alicudi (4 weekly, 4½hr/6hr).

From Milazzo (Oct to May) to Vulcano/Lípari/Salina/Panarea/Strómboli/Naples (2 weekly; 20hr); Vulcano/Lípari (1 daily; 1½hr/2¼hr); Salina (2; 3½hr); Filicudi/Alicudi (2 weekly, 4½hr/6hr).

From Lípari (June to Sept) to Milazzo (4 daily; 2hr); Vulcano (4; 30min); Salina/Panarea/Strómboli/Naples (5 weekly; 14hr); Salina (1–2 daily; 50min); Filicudi/Alicudi (5 weekly; 2hr 25min/3hr 45min).

From Lípari (Oct to May) to Milazzo (1–2 daily; 2hr); Vulcano (3; 30min); Salina/Panarea/Strómboli/Naples (2 weekly; 14hr 15min); Salina (1–2 daily; 1hr); Filicudi/Alicudi (4 weekly, 2hr 25min/3hr 45min).

Hydrofoils

From Cefalù (mid-June to end Sept) to Palermo (3 weekly; 1hr 10min); Vulcano/Lípari (3 weekly; 1hr 50min/2hr 10min).

From Capo d'Orlando (mid-June to end Sept) to Sant'Agata/Vulcano/Lípari/Panarea/Strómboli (2 daily; 15min/1hr 20min/1hr 35min/2hr 5min/2hr 35min).

From Milazzo (June to Sept) to Vulcano/Lípari (half-hourly; 40min/55min); Salina (8 daily; 1hr 25min); Panarea/Strómboli (6; 2½/3hr); Filicudi/Alicudi (1; 2hr/2½hr); Naples (1; 4–6hr).

From Milazzo (Oct to May) to Vulcano/Lípari (6 daily; 40min/55min); Salina (4; 1hr 20min); Panarea/Strómboli (6 weekly, 2½/3hr); Filicudi/Alicudi (1 weekly, 2hr/2½hr).

From Lípari (June to Sept) to Palermo (2 daily; 3½hr); Cefalù (3 weekly; 2hr 10min); Capo d'Orlando/Sant'Agata (3 daily; 1hr/1½hr); Milazzo (half-hourly; 55min); Messina/Réggio di Calabria (4 daily; 1hr 30min/2hr); Vibo Valentia (Wed–Sun 1 daily, 3hr); Naples (1 daily, 5½hr); Vulcano (every 45min; 10min); Salina (12 daily; 15min); Panarea/Strómboli (10; 30min/1hr); Filicudi/Alicudi (4; 1hr/1½hr).

From Lípari (Oct to May) to Messina/Réggio di Calabria (2 daily; 1hr 30min/2hr); Milazzo/Vulcano (7; 1hr/10min); Salina (4; 20min); Panarea/Strómboli (4 weekly; 30min/1hr); Filicudi/Alicudi (3 weekly; 1hr/1½hr).

CHAPTER THREE

THE NORTHERN IONIAN COAST

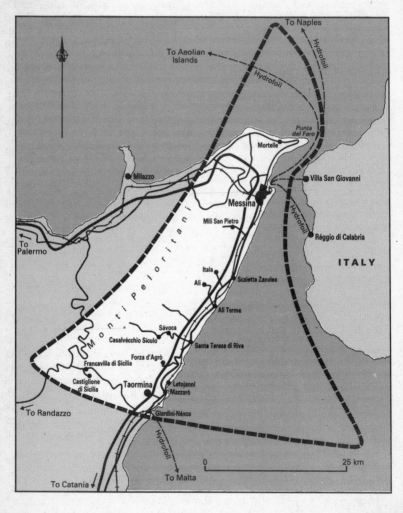

Hemmed in by the mountains, Sicily's **northern Ionian coast** is the island's most visually exotic strip, crammed with some of the most brilliant displays of colourful vegetation you'll see anywhere on this flower-filled island. Perhaps not surprisingly, it's crowded by an almost unbroken ribbon of development, and is one of Sicily's most popular resort areas, with both Italian and foreign tourists lured by the stunning views down to a turquoise sea.

Just across the busy Straits from mainland Italy, **Messina** is for many the first taste of Sicily, and your initial impulse may be to move on quickly. Apart from its own meagre merits, however, there are some enticing spots within easy reach of here, to the mountains behind, or around the cape to the beaches on the Tyrrhenian side. Otherwise, keep on south, where you'll find some unspoilt **hill-villages** amid the woods and craggy uplands of the Monti Peloritani. These seem as secure today from the tourist hordes as they were in the past from piratical raids, two or three of the villages enlivened by impressive Norman churches built by Count Roger in the 11C to consolidate his grip on the island. Further down, the only road penetrating any distance inland takes in the **Alcántara valley** and its spectacular gorge, before heading up to the gnarled old town of **Castiglione di Sicilia**.

There are sandy **beaches** – and resorts – aplenty all the way down the coast, and you'd do well to avoid the area in July and August if you want a bit of elbow room. Even outside these months there's a fairly high level of saturation-tourism in the area's most illustrious resort, **Taormina**. Undeniably pretty, it was a simple hill-village as little as fifty years ago, set apart from others in the Peloritani range only by virtue of its fine ancient theatre. Now it's a high-profile, high-class tourist centre, packed in summer but still retaining enough small-town charm to merit at least a day-trip.

Messina and around

MESSINA may well be your first sight of Sicily, and from the ferry it's a fine one, stretching out along the seaboard, north of the distinctive hooked harbour from which the city took its Greek name – *Zancle*, or 'sickle'. The natural beauty of its location, looking out over the Straits to the forested hills of Calabria, is Messina's best point and the city itself presents a duller view from close-quarters: a bland sequence of characterless new buildings lining long, traffic-choked streets that are used as a racetrack by drivers who can claim to be the most reckless in Sicily. But the city's unedifying appearance is not entirely its own fault: the congestion is largely the result of the surrounding mountains that squeeze the traffic along the one or two roads which link the elongated centre with the northern suburbs; and Messina's modern aspect is more a tribute to its powers of survival – in the face of a record of devastation that's high even for this disaster-prone island.

The greatest damage has been caused by the unstable geological belt on which Messina stands, responsible for a series of catastrophic **earthquakes**. The most notable of these occurred in 1783 and – still within living memory of some *messinesi* – 1908, when the shore sank by half a metre overnight, and

84,000 people lost their lives. The few surviving buildings, along with everything that had been painstakingly reconstructed in the wake of the earthquake, were once more destroyed when Allied bombardments gave Messina the dubious distinction of being the most intensely bombed Italian city during World War II.

Today the remodelled wide streets and low, reinforced buildings guard against future disasters of a natural kind, but make for a pretty uninspiring spectacle. The few monuments that remain, chiefly, the **Duomo** and the nearby **Chiesa Annunziata dei Catalani**, though worth investigating, won't take up more than a morning's worth of ambling: but take more time to see the treasure trove of art contained in the **Museo Regionale**, one of Sicily's best collections and making up for what the rest of Messina lacks. Otherwise the city's pleasures are to be found in kicking around its portside promenade and absorbing the endlessly changing views across the Straits. If you're here in summer, you'll see the passage of the tall-masted *felucche*, or **swordfish boats**, patrolling the narrow channel, attracted to these rich waters from miles up and down the Italian coasts. You can enjoy their catch the same day in a good choice of restaurants either in town, or a little way north, at **Ganzirri**, where the lakeside fish restaurants provide welcome relief from Messina's motor madness. Beyond, and around the corner of **Punto del Faro**, at **Mortelle**, where the city's main lidos are, you can swim by day and play till late in the good bars and pizzerias.

Arrival, information and getting around

Trains from the mainland are carried across the Straits on *FS* **ferries**, and it takes a good hour for them to reassemble at Messina's **Stazione Maríttima** (see *Getting There*). If you're changing trains or stopping at Messina, you might as well disembark and walk the hundred metres on to the main **Stazione Centrale**, at piazza della Repubblica, also where most of the **local and long distance-buses** arrive and depart. (Although **buses to Milazzo for the Aeolian Islands** leave from the nearby *Giuntabus* office, via Terranova 8, at the junction with viale San Martino.)

Drivers and pedestrians using *FS* ferries also disembark at the Stazione Maríttima, while those on the private *Caronte* **ferries** pull in further up, on via della Libertà , ten minutes' walk from the centre. This is marginally more convenient for the slip-road to the Palermo (A20) and Catania (A18) **autostradas**: drivers arriving off the *FS* ferries should head up viale San Martino (well signposted). **Hydrofoils** (from the Aeolian Islands or Réggio di Calabria) dock at the terminal in the port area.

Messina's **EPT** (Mon–Sat 9am–1pm; ☎090-777.0731) is outside the railway station on the right, useful for a map and hotel lists. Many of Messina's hotels are scattered around this area (see below), and it's a short walk to piazza Cairoli and the broad viale San Martino, the shopping centre of town, where you'll find the best of Messina's restaurants.

Most of the **city buses** leave from piazza della Repubblica: take #8, #27 or #28 for the museum, #8 or #28 for Ganzirri, #28 for Mortelle (other bus routes are specified in the text); hourly **night buses** take over after 11.30pm. Tickets cost L600 apiece, available from most *tabacchi*. Messina is also an

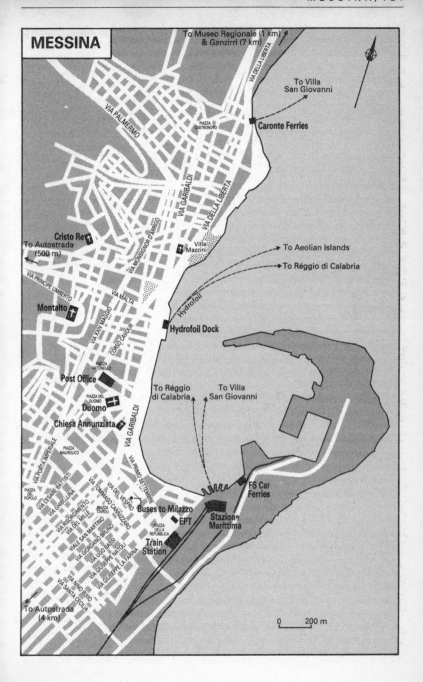

MESSINA

To Museo Regionale (1 km)
& Ganzirri (7 km)

VIA DELLA LIBERTA

To Villa
San Giovanni

Caronte Ferries

VIA PALMERMO

PIAZZA
CASTRONOVO

VIA GARIBALDI

VIA DELLA LIBERTA

VIA MONSIGNOR D'ARRIGO

Cristo Re
To Autostrada
(500 m)

Villa
Mazzini

To Aeolian Islands

To Réggio di Calabria

VIA PRINCIPE UMBERTO

VIA MALTA

Hydrofoil

Montalto

VIA XXIV MAGGIO

CORSO CAVOUR

Hydrofoil Dock

PIAZZA
ANTONELLO

Post Office

PIAZZA DEL
DUOMO

Duomo

VIA GARIBALDI

Chiesa Annunziata

To Réggio
di Calabria

To Villa
San Giovanni

PIAZZA
MAUROLICO

VIA PORTA IMPERIALE

VIA PRIMO SETTEMBRE

PIAZZA
DEL
POPOLO

VIA CESARE BATTISTI

VIA GHIBELLINA

VIA TOMMASO CANNIZZARO

VIA DEL VESPRO

PIAZZA
CAIROLI

FS Car
Ferries

Buses to Milazzo

EPT

VIA RISORGIMENTO

VIA DEL MILLE

VIA SAN MARTINO

VIA GIORDANO BRUNO

VIA UGO BASSI

VIA GIUSEPPE NATOLI

VIA GIUSEPPE LA FARINA

Stazione
Marittima

PIAZZA
DELLA
REPUBBLICA

Train
Station

VIA NINO BIXIO

VIA SANTA CECILIA

To Autostrada
(4 km)

0   200 m

easy city to negotiate **on foot**: you could walk to the museum, for example, in about 45 minutes from the station.

Finding a place to stay

Of Messina's cheaper **hotels**, the nearest to the station are on via N. Scotto, an alley to the left of piazza della Repubblica: try the *Mirage* at no.1 (☎090-293.8344; L30,000) or the *Touring*, no.17 (☎090-293.8851; L30,000), both rather shabby affairs, but adequate. You can do far better by walking into the centre of town, and trying the *Roma*, right on piazza del Duomo at no.3 (☎090-775.566; L15,000), though you might want to phone ahead as it fills quickly. Otherwise, go up a grade to the *Monza*, viale San Martino 63 (☎090-773.755; L40,000).

There's an unofficial (non-*IYHF*) **youth hostel** some 25km down the coast at ALÌ (see p.128), and the only **campsite** you'll find in the Messina area, *Il Peloritano* (☎090-844.057; May to Oct), is situated inconveniently far out beyond Punto del Faro on the northern coast (bus #28 to RODIA, from the railway station). Otherwise to camp you'll have to go as far west as Milazzo, or south to SANT'ALÉSSIO, both about forty minutes away (see *Travel Details* for bus schedules).

The city

Messina's most important monument, the **Duomo**, is symbolic of the city's phoenix-like ability to recreate itself from the ashes of its last disaster. Standing defiantly at the bottom of its spacious piazza, it's the reconstruction of a 12C cathedral erected by Roger II, one of a series of great Norman churches that included the sumptuous cathedrals of Palermo and Cefalù. Formerly, the building dominated medieval Messina, and was the venue for Archbishop Palmer's marriage of Richard the Lionheart's sister Joan to the Norman-Sicilian, William II. But, devastated by the 1908 earthquake, it was rebuilt in the years following World War I, only to fall victim to a fire-bomb in 1943 that reduced it once more to rubble. What you see today is mostly a faithful copy, which took years to complete, with few elements remaining of the original fabric.

The Romanesque facade is its best aspect, its lower part mostly authentic and dominated by a richly decorated late-Gothic **central portal**, extravagantly pointed, with good detail, and flanked by two smaller contemporary doors. Inside, almost everything is a re-creation, from the marble floor to the painted wooden ceiling. The **mosaic-work** in the three grand apses holds most interest, though it pales into insignificance beside the island's other examples of the genre, and only the mosaic on the left – of the Virgin Mary with Santa Lucia – is original. All the same, try to find someone to switch on the lights, as the works then take on a majesty that's entirely lost in the gloom which normally shrouds the cathedral's interior. There's little else here that pre-dates the 20C, apart from some salvaged tombs, handsomest of which is that of Archbishop de Tabiatis from 1333, on the right of the altar and heavily graffitied.

Back in the piazza, the detached **campanile** claims some attention, particularly when the hours strike – best of all at noon, when you get the full mechanical performance. The bell-tower, like the cathedral, is something of a fake, looking much older than its 55 years, though it can safely claim to be the largest astronomical clock in the world. On the side facing the cathedral two dials show the phases of the planets and the seasons; above them a globe shows the phases of the moon; while facing the piazza, the elaborate panoply of moving gilt figures, activated on the hour, half-hour and quarter-hour, range from representations of the days of the week and the four ages of man to Dina and Clarenza, the two women who saved the city from a night-attack by the Angevins during the Wars of the Vespers. There's a lion, too – Messina's ancient emblem – that unleashes a mighty roar over the city at midday, quite alarming if you're not expecting it.

In front of the cathedral and its bell-tower, spare a glance for the **Fontana di Orione**, a fountain daintily carved in the mid-16C by Montorsoli, a Florentine pupil of Michelangelo. It depicts Orion, the city's mythical founder, surmounting a collection of cherubs, nymphs, and giants, and surrounded by four figures (representing the rivers Nile, Ebro, Camero and Tiber) reclining along the balustrade.

Just back from the duomo, the truncated section of the 12C **Chiesa Annunziata dei Catalani** squats below pavement level, Messina's only surviving example of Arabo-Norman church-building. The blind arcading around the apses and the Byzantine-style cupola are the perfect antidote to the ugly cement facade surrounding its three portals, and the interior is suitably simple, with the transept and apse true to their original construction. In front, a martial statue by the sculptor Andrea Calamecca (Calamech) stands half-hidden under the trees, showing a proud Don Giovanni of Austria, victor of the Battle of Lepanto. (The victorious Christian fleet sailed from Messina in 1535.)

From here, it's a short stroll to the **harbourside**, with its combination of constant activity and compelling vistas over the Straits. It's Sicily's deepest natural harbour and a port of call for freighters and cruisers of all descriptions, as well as for frequent NATO warships. But the greatest traffic consists of ferries, endlessly plying back and forth, which – until the much-talked-about bridge across the Straits comes into being – are Sicily's chief link with the mainland.

The rest of Messina's unremittingly modern centre won't take up much of your time, though the area around **piazza Cairoli** is the place for shopping and bustling evening promenades. You'll feel less cramped, however, when you head out north, past older fishermen's houses backing onto short sandy strips, to the city's marvellous **Museo Regionale** at via della Libertà 465 (Mon–Sat 9am–1.30pm, Tues, Thurs, Sat also 4–7pm, Sun 9am–1pm; L2000; buses #8, #27 or #28 from the railway station or anywhere along via Garibaldi or Corso Cavour). This thoughtfully laid-out museum is a repository for some of Messina's greatest works of art, many of them carefully rescued from earthquake rubble, and includes what is perhaps Sicily's finest collection of 15–17C art.

It's the earlier rather than the later material that claims your attention, basically the items in the first few rooms. The collection starts with some lovely Byzantine work, larded with a good helping of Gothic, well-evident in a 14C tryptych of the *Madonna with Child between Saints Agatha and Bartholomew*, and a remarkably modern-looking wooden crucifix from the 15C, with a sinuous, tragic Christ. It's **room 4** that you'll want to spend most time in, with marvellous exhibits of 15C art, notably an ethereal statue of the *Madonna and Child*, attributed to Francesco Laurana, and the museum's most famous exhibit, the *Saint Gregory* polyptych, by Sicily's greatest native artist, **Antonello da Messina** – a masterful synthesis of Flemish and Italian Renaissance styles that's a good example of the various influences that reached the port of Messina in the 15C (for more on Antonello, see Palermo p.59 and Cefalù p.91). The statue of *Scilla*, the classical Scylla who terrorised sailors from the Calabrian coast (as described in Homer's Odyssey), is on display in **room 6**; it's an alarming spectacle, with contorted face and eyes awash with expression. Sculpted by Montorsoli in 1557, it was once adjoined to an imperious figure of Neptune in the act of calming the seas, a copy of which stands on the seafront just up from the hydrofoil terminal. Of the museum's remaining works, the most noteworthy are a couple of large shadowy canvases by **Caravaggio** in the suitably darkened **room 10**, commissioned by the city in 1604, the best of which is the atmospheric *Raising of Lazarus*.

Eating, nightlife ... and ferragosto

Messina has a good choice of **restaurants**, either cheap and fast – as befitting a port and transit-point – or offering a more relaxed ambience. If you're here in summer, you should splash out a bit and sample the swordfish, freshly caught and a local speciality; May and June are the best months for this, before the water gets too warm.

If you're at the station and waiting for a train, or just hungry after arriving, the *Trattoria Firenze* has good-value meals, always open and conveniently situated in via del Vespro, just across piazza della Repubblica. Behind piazza Cairoli at via Ugo Bassi 157, *Pippo Núnnari* (closed Mon) has a well-deserved reputation for providing the best stand-up meals in Messina; try their *arancini*, with butter and cheese or meat fillings. On the other side of the square, at via dei Mille 88, the *Pizzeria del Capitano* (also closed Mon) has the best pizzas in town, with fast service, and low prices. Further up viale San Martino, there's a bunch of more serious eating-places on or around via Santa Cecilia. Try *Number One* at via Risorgimento 192 (closed Wed) – and see the old photos of what Messina used to look like before the earthquake – or *Lo Squalo*, a trattoria on the corner of via Ghibellina and via Nino Bixio (closed Sun). At the end of the street, *La Capanna* (closed Tues), on via Césare Battisti, is a focus for students from the nearby university residence block and generally quite convivial, with a range of snacks. Further up and behind via Battisti (around piazza del Pópolo) are two or three fairly rough trattorias with rock-bottom prices.

Messina by night can be extremely beautiful, especially from the high **via Panoramica** – from which, with the city at your feet, there's a long, sparkling view across to mainland Italy. From the centre, the closest section of this route is the viale Príncipe Umberto stretch, where there are bars and pizzerias around two floodlit sanctuaries (Cristo Re and Montalto) and plenty of scope for some pleasant evening strolling. In summer, **free classical concerts** are often held up here behind the Cristo Re, while back down in the centre, the Villa Mazzini shows **free films** – usually starting at 8.30pm – though it tends to get crowded. Watch out for posters giving details of all of these, or ask at the EPT. (There are more free films at Mortelle, half an hour away, and a better selection of fish restaurants around the lake at Ganzirri, twenty minutes up the road – for both of which see below).

If you're in Messina in mid-summer, you might catch the festivals around the feast of the Assumption, or **ferragosto**. Although all the villages on both sides of the Straits hold festivals around this time, with some pretty spectacular fireworks lighting up the sky on any one night, Messina's festivities are grander, beginning around 12 August, when two plaster giants (*giganti*) are wheeled around town, and finally stationed near the port opposite the Municipio. These are said to be Messina's two founders, *Mata* and *Grifone*, one a white female, the other a burly Moor, both mounted on huge steeds. On *ferragosto* itself, August 15, another towering carriage, the *Vara*, is hauled through the city centre: an elaborate column supporting dozens of papiermaché *putti* and angels, culminating in the figure of Christ stretching out his right arm to launch Mary on her way to heaven. This unwieldy construction is towed on long ropes, pulled by hundreds of penitents – semi-naked if they're men, all in white if they're women – and cheered on by thousands of people along the way. The whole thing is a sweaty and frenetic performance, finishing up at piazza del Duomo, where flowers are thrown out to the crowds, many of whom risk being crushed in the mad scramble to gather these luck-bearing charms. Late at night, one of Sicily's best **firework displays** is held on the seafront near via della Libertà .

Listings

Airlines *Alitalia* c/o *A. Meo & Figli*, via del Vespro 52–4 (☎090-719.192).

Airport Nearest at Réggio di Calabria (internal services only).

Ambulance ☎090-293.1840.

Bus companies *AST* via Natoli 20 (for Forza d'Agrò, Itala, Ali Terme and Patti); *Giuntabus*, via Terranova 8 (for Milazzo); *Meo M.*, viale San Martino 20 (for Tíndari); *SAIS*, piazza della Republicca (for Palermo, the coast south to Taormina and Catania).

Car problems *ACI*, via L. Manara 23 (☎090-293.3031).

Car rentals *Avis*, via Vittorio Emanuele 35 (☎090-58.404); *Hertz*, via Vittorio Emanuele 113 (☎090-363.740); *Maggiore*, via T. Canizzaro 46 (☎090-775.476); *Sicilcar*, via Cavalieri della Stella (☎090-46.942).

Chemist All-night service in via Palermo.

Ferry tickets All tickets across the Staits are on sale at kiosks at the respective terminals; for Malta (leaving from Réggio di Calabria), buy tickets from *Tirrenia Navigazione* (via Garibaldi 146; ☎090-43.095).

Hospital *Ospedale R. Margherita*, viale della Libertà (☎090-363.615).

Police *Carabinieri* at via Monsignor d'Arrigo (☎112); road accidents ☎090-771.000; anything else at the *Questura*, via Plácida 2 (☎090-43.101/42.510)

Post office Main office at piazza Antonello (behind the Municipio).

Taxi Ranks at piazza Cairoli (☎090-293.4880); Corso Garibaldi (☎090-46.880).

Telephones Offices at the railway station (open daily until 9.45pm) or via Natoli 57 (open daily until 8pm).

Ticket agency Travel and theatre, including Taormina's Greek theatre, at *Lisciotto Viaggi* at piazza Cairoli 221 (☎090-719.001)

Around Messina

There are several mountain or coastal destinations not more than half an hour away from the centre of Messina by bus or car, all well worth a visit to get the most out of the city. If you're driving, you might wish to follow the high-level via Panoramica north rather than the congested coastal road, though this is the route the buses take (#8 or #28), passing areas that must have once justified their idyllic names of PARADISO, CONTEMPLAZIONE and PACE. The buses make a stop in **GANZIRRI,** which in summer especially becomes the hub of milling crowds, hanging around the excellent bars and attending the nightly **Italian pop concerts** held throughout August.

There used to be mussel-farming on Ganzirri's lake, though nowadays the water has grown decidedly murky. But you can still eat plenty of fresh shell-fish, swordfish or whatever else has been hauled in that day by the many boats operating around here. Most of the **trattorias** are squeezed into the wedge of land between lake and sea, and you can eat outside at nearly all of them, with lakeside views: try the *Trattoria alla Marinara* (closed Mon), or, around the corner, the *Trattoria del Mare* (closed Wed), both relatively cheap. Further up, the *Anfora Blu* is a good pizzeria with a garden and a choice of views – lake or sea. Keep going along this road (keeping right, towards FARO) and you'll find the cosy little *Trattoria Minico* (closed Tues): good food though not particularly cheap prices.

Here, **Punto del Faro** is the very tip of Sicily, the nearest point to Italy where the lighthouse (the *faro*) is dwarfed by the towering pylon supporting the massive cables that tether the island to the mainland. Here, too, was where the legendary **Charybdis** once posed a threat to sailors – along with Scylla on the opposite shore – still remembered in the locality's name of CARIDDI.

A couple of kilometres further up the road, **MORTELLE** is the focus in summer for Messina's bronzed youth, who throng the lidos and **beaches** and fill the air with the drone of a thousand motorbikes. Apart from some sleek bars and pizzerias, there is the *Arena Green Sky* (opposite the *Due Palme* pizzeria), which shows **open-air films**, with free performances nightly at 8.30pm, and late performances at 10.30pm of more contemporary films that you have to pay for. Westwards from Mortelle is a succession of sandy beaches and beach-towns, best of which is **ACQUALADRONE** (bus #28 from Messina's railway station).

Inland from Messina, the ridge-top of the **Monti Peloritani** offers the best vantage-point of the Tyrrhenian and Ionian coasts, and also has some good walking in the woods. To reach the ridge, take the old Palermo road from via Garibaldi in the city (bus #29). On the way, you can make a stop at the old monastery of Santa Maria della Valle, better known as **La Badiazza**. Secluded in a deep gully, this old Benedictine monastery lies at the end of a twenty-minute walk along a dirt road leading off to the right just before via Palermo passes under the autostrada. The monastery dates from the 12C, but was reconstructed after a fire in the 14C and later abandoned. Today, recently restored, it has recovered its formidable fortress-like appearance, and looks quite capable of withstanding a corsair raid.

You can wander through the pinewoods around here, but they are thicker further up the SS113 (via Palermo); from there you can take a left turn at the crossroads at **Colle San Rizzo** (where the bus stops), then it's another ten kilometres south to reach the **Monte Antennamare** sanctuary, a shabby building in a sublime spot (1124m high). Back at Colle San Rizzo, you could make a round-trip of it by descending north to CASTANEA, another wooded area favoured by hunters, and down to the Tyrrhenian coast at SPARTA, on the Messina road.

The coastal route to Taormina . . . and into the hills

There's no shortage of beaches on the coastal strip **south of Messina** if you delve in between the closely packed houses that line this stretch. They're nothing special near the city, but once beyond the suburbs there's a few low-key seaside resorts that would do for an hour or two if you were desperate for a swim. Along the coast, it's best to take the **train** that traces the shoreline pretty much all the way: on a clear day there are hearty views across to Calabria, while the ragged cliffs on the other side are covered with acres of prickly pears. The slower buses, on the other hand, stick to the back-streets of the successive towns and villages – a largely unedifying ride and excruciatingly slow. This is also true for **drivers**, though the toll motorway (the A18) is a fast alternative, plunging through some fairly dramatic scenery as it cruises above the sea. You don't have to stick with the coast all the way, though: there are some short trips to be made **into the hills** on the way. There are good **bus services** from some of the coastal resorts for these, and there should be no difficulty in hitching, or even walking, if you've the time.

Mili San Pietro to Ali Terme

Messina's ungraceful suburbs extend almost as far as the motorway turn-off at TREMESTIERI. Shortly beyond, a minor road leads off inland from MILI MARINA to **MILI SAN PIETRO** (bus #9 from Messina's railway station), a nondescript little place two kilometres up the road. As the village swings into view, the grey cupolas of the monastery-church of **Santa Maria** are just visible below the road on the right. The Basilian monastery of which this was a part was founded by Count Roger in 1082, but is now abandoned – irreverently occupied by assorted farmyard animals and permeated by their pungent rural smells. The church survives just – its exterior displaying some nice interlaced blind arcading on one wall, and a semicircular apse. But the inside is derelict and not particularly interesting, although it's said to contain the burial place of Roger I's son, Jordan; ask at the church in the centre of the village for the key.

Seven or eight kilometres further down the coast, **SCALETTA ZANCLEA** is a popular resort with an impressive 11C **castle** at its highest point, containing some heraldic knick-knacks. The key is kept at the *comune*. The next village down, ITALA MARINA, has an inland parent, **ITALA**, two and a half kilometres up the road from the coast, just beyond which – over the bridge on the road to CROCE – is the church of **San Pietro e Paolo**. Built by Roger in 1093 in thanksgiving for a victory over the Arabs, this has features in common with Santa Maria in Mili San Pietro, and provided the model for the church near Casalvécchio Sículo built eighty years later (see below). But this domed, red-brick construction has been restored and is still in use, indeed the best time to see it is before the 11am service on Sunday morning – otherwise contact the priest at no.26 on Itala's main street for the key.

If you're stuck for **somewhere to stay** along this stretch, **ALI TERME** – a village known since antiquity for its sulphur baths – has a couple of cheap hotels, the *Terme Granata Cassibile* (☎0942-715.029; L20,000) and *Terme Marino Giuseppe* (☎090-715.031; L20,000). There's also a **youth hostel** at ALÌ, rather remote at the end of a twisty six-kilometre road which climbs high above the Ionian coast – frequent *AST* buses from Messina, last one at 8pm. The rudimentary hostel is in a converted church in piazza Spirito Santo, up one of the alleys behind the rough marbled Chiesa Madre; it has beds for L6000.

Santa Teresa di Riva and Sávoca

Ten kilometres south of Ali Terme, **SANTA TERESA DI RIVA** is the first recognisable resort on this stretch, with an oversized beach and a few trattorias. Though the town itself is nothing to shout about, it's a useful jumping-off point for the foothills of the **Monti Peloritani: buses** leave from here for SÁVOCA and CASALVÉCCHIO SÍCULO; ask the driver of the Messina-Catania bus to put you off on the seafront (the lungomare Santa Teresa), and Sávoca is signposted to the left, the bus-stop for the village one block back from the sea on the corner of a crossroads.

It's a winding four-kilometre run up to **SÁVOCA**, a peaceful village, evocatively sited: houses and three churches perch on the cliffsides in clumps, a tattered castle (originally Saracen) topping the pile. Two pincer-like streets, via San Michele and via Chiesa Madre, reach around to their respective churches, the grandest the square-towered 13C **Chiesa Madre**. Sitting on a tiny ridge between two opposing hills, it's a fine vantage-point, looking down the valley to the sea and across the surrounding hills. Spare a glance, too, at the house next door, lovingly restored and displaying a 15C stone-arched double window. It's one of many in the village that have had a facelift as outsiders move in to snap up run-down cottages as second homes. These days, Sávoca is within the Taormina commuter-belt and most of the people who live here work elsewhere, something that's to its advantage: during the day the streets and hillside alleys are refreshingly empty – the medieval atmosphere still intact.

Signs in the village point you to the **Cappuccini monastery**, whose catacombs (*catacombe*: Oct to March Tues–Sun 9am–noon & 3–5pm, April to Sept daily 9am–1pm & 4–7pm; free) contain a selection of gruesome mummified bodies. These are the remains of local lawyers, doctors and the clergy: two to three hundred years old, they stand in niches dressed in their 18C finery, the skulls of less-complete colleagues lining the walls above. Ask the custodian and you'll probably be shown the church treasury as well, which has a small collection of liturgical books and 17C and 18C bibles (it's appreciated if you leave a small donation on the way out). More off-beat delight is at hand in the village's *Bar Vitelli*. An appealing 18C wood-panelled, stone-flagged building, it (and the village) was used as the scene of Michael Corleone's wedding feast in Coppola's film of *The Godfather*. There's a still of Marlon Brando inside, tables on the terrace outside.

Sávoca has a popular **trattoria**, *La Pineta*, but nowhere to stay – a shame really, but you could easily see the village (and the rest of the route, described below) on a day-trip from Taormina or Messina, provided you time the buses right.

Casalvécchio Sículo . . . and a walk back to the coast

The only road beyond Sávoca (and the same bus from Santa Teresa) careers another two kilometres along the ridge to **CASALVÉCCHIO SÍCULO**, which if anything has even better valley-views from its terraces. There's not much to detain you here, except the quiet village atmosphere, but walk through Casalvécchio and, after about five hundred metres, a rough road drops away to the left (signposted), snaking down into a lush, citrus-planted valley. It's about a twenty-minute hike to the Norman monastery of **Santi Pietro e Paulo**, gloriously sited on a high bank above the river. Built in the 12C, its battlemented facade and double domes are visible from a distance through the lemon groves, and the church betrays a strong Arabic influence, particularly in the polychromatic patterns of the exterior. If it's locked, there should be someone around in one of the adjacent buildings with a key.

Either head back up to the main road and wait for the return bus to pass, or continue downhill for a longer **walk**, beyond the monastery to the river Agro. It's about another hour's tramp, alongside the wide (and mostly dry) riverbed to RINA, back towards the sea. The main (SS114) coastal road is signposted from Rina and in another twenty minutes, through a small tunnel, you're back in Santa Teresa, on the Messina-Catania bus route.

Sant'Aléssio and Forza d'Agrò

The only other worthy diversion into the hills is just a few kilometres south, where the turn-off at **Capo Sant'Aléssio** gives the first views of TAORMINA. The cliffs here support a sturdy castle and though you can climb up to it, you can't get in – it's been for sale for years. Four kilometres inland of here, atop a corkscrew road, is **FORZA D'AGRÒ** (reached, by *AST* bus from Messina and Taormina) – like so many Sicilian villages, a breezy place defiantly crumbling all around its mostly elderly inhabitants, and with little left of the Norman **castello** which crowns it. It's a memorable clamber up to the top: the streets become ever more perilous, the stone cottages increasingly neglected and held together by rotting spars of wood. One push, it seems, would bring the whole lot down. The lower parts of the village are better maintained, but not much – hi-fi and clothes shops tucked into tiny cottage interiors, and a couple of churches locked and decrepit.

Still, it's close enough to Taormina to attract the tour-coaches, which deposit their passengers in the village square, where there's a couple of bars to help idle the time away. There's even **somewhere to stay** if you are so inclined, the *Souvenir* (☎0942-751.114; L27,000, L35,000 with bath) on via Belvedere – not at all bad value.

Otherwise, if you're energetic enough, make the descent back down to the main coastal road and Capo Sant'Aléssio, where you can pick up the Messina-Catania bus. Or, one kilometre north of the cape, there's a railway station at **SANT'ALÉSSIO SÍCULO** village, a small resort with a wide beach and a few cheap accommodation possibilities. There's a **campsite** close to Sant'Aléssio, too, the *Forza d'Agrò Mare* (☎0942-36.418; open June to Sept), at Località Buzzurratti.

Taormina and around

TAORMINA, high on Monte Tauro and dominating two grand, sweeping bays below, is Sicily's best-known resort, the whole town devoted to – and dependent on – the top-notch international tourism which flaunts through its streets from April to October. You'd be wrong, though, to avoid Taormina because of this: it's certainly expensive to stay here, but the veneer of exclusivity is only skin-deep, and at heart the small town still can't seem to believe its good luck. Certainly there's enough left of its hill-village charm to make it a worthy stop, especially if you hole-up at one of the cheaper nearby beach-resorts. And although Taormina itself has no beach, the outstanding remains of the classical theatre and the sheer beauty of the town's site amply compensate. Among many passing travellers arrested by Taormina, Goethe and D.H. Lawrence are the two big names touted by the tourist office; Lawrence was so enthusiastic about Taormina's prospect and climate that he lived here (1920–1923), in a villa at the top of the valley-cleft behind the theatre.

Despite the intrusion of contemporary tourists, Taormina retains much of its late-medieval character. The one main traffic-free street is an unbroken line of 15–19C palazzi and intimate piazzas; its churches are unobtrusive and attractive; and there's an agreeably crumbly castle and rows of flower-filled balconies. The downside is that between June and August it can get supremely crowded: the narrow alleys are filled shoulder-to-shoulder with tourists, while the beaches below town simply seethe. April, May or September are better, but to avoid the crowds completely come between October and March, when it's usually still warm enough to swim, and the spring brings with it flamboyant displays of all kinds of flowering plants.

You can always escape the throngs in the surrounding hills, too: there are several good walks to be done, including a trip up to the neighbouring village of **Castelmola** and the mountain behind it. Most people, though, are content to see and be seen on the excellent **beaches** which punctuate the coastline below Taormina. Easiest to reach, on foot or by cable-car, are the small, stony stretches around **Mazzarò**, though for decent expanses of sand you'll have to travel further – to **Giardini-Naxos**, around a fifteen-minute bus-ride away. You'll not avoid the crowds in either of these places, nor in the small resorts further north and south along the coast, but Giardini-Naxos might be a more realistic base for your beach-going: cheaper and less pretentious than Taormina in every way.

Taormina: arrival and information

Trains pull up at Taormina-Giardini station (where there's a left-luggage office) on the water's edge, way below town. It's a very steep thirty-minute walk from here up to Taormina: turn right out of the station and, after 300m, left through a gap in the buildings, signposted *Centro*. Much better (certainly if you have luggage) is to arrive by bus – from Messina or Catania – or take one of the fairly frequent local buses up the hill, roughly every forty-five minutes from outside the railway station. Taormina's **bus terminal**, where they all stop, is on via Luigi Pirandello. Alternatively, a **taxi** ride from the railway station to the town costs around L10,000. Arrivals from Malta on the summer **catamaran** service dock in Giardini-Naxos (see p.139), from where you take the local bus up to Taormina.

The main street, **Corso Umberto I**, runs right through town, from Porta Messina to Porta Catania at the other end. The useful English-speaking **AAST** is in the Palazzo Corvaja, off piazza Vittorio Emanuele (Mon–Fri 8am–2pm & 2.30–7.30pm, Sat 8am–noon; ☎0942-23.243). Pick up a free map, accommodation listings and bus timetables, and programmes for summer events in the theatre. In summer, the **EPT** also has an office, at Corso Umberto I 144 (Mon–Fri 9am–1pm & 5–8pm, Sat 9am–1pm; ☎0942-237.51).

Finding a place to stay

Finding a **bed** between June and September is a time-consuming business without a reservation. Only a handful will be both available and affordable, so start looking early. Late arrivals can usually persuade the AAST to ring round for available rooms, though this way you don't get to see them first.

Good possibilities are along **via Bagnoli Croce**, alongside the public gardens: cheap rooms at no.66 (L12,000 each) – very small but with incredible views from the roof-terrace, and one room has a small kitchen; the *Villa Pompeii* at no.88 (☎0942-23.812; L20,000); and the *Il Leone* at 124–126, above the pizzeria (L22,000). A big step-up in price gets you a room at the pleasant *Pensione Elios* at no. 98 (☎0942-23.431; L49,000 with bath).

Other budget options are *Villa Liliana*, via Dietro Cappuccini 4 (☎0942-24.373; L22,000), close to the AAST; the *Columbia*, via Iallia Bassia 11 (☎0942-23.423; L23,000); the handy but overpriced *Casa Ingegnere* (☎0942-25.480; L30,000), next to the Teatro Romano; and, with excellent views, the *Pensione Svizzera* at via Pirandello 26 (☎0942-23.790; L37,000 with bath), just up from

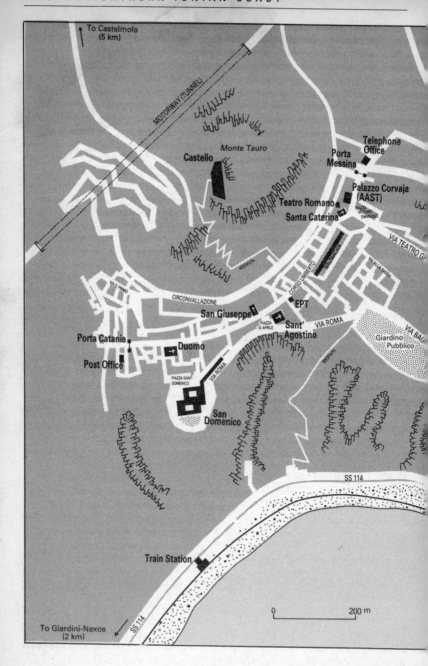

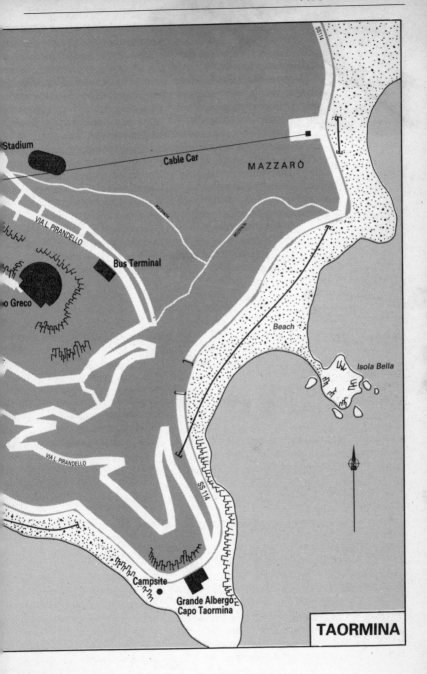

TAORMINA

the bus terminal. If you want to stay on, or just off, the main **Corso** try the recommended *Palazzo Vecchio*, Salita Ciampoli 9 (☎0942-23.033; L34,000 with bath); the *Friuli*, Corso Umberto 19 (☎0942-25.313; L27,000); the *Trinacria*, Corso Umberto 99 (☎0942-23.723; L36,000 with bath); or the *Cuscona*, Corso Umberto 238 (☎0942-23.270; L29,000).

We've given the official **high-season** prices but it's worth bearing in mind that in the frantic summer months, everywhere – these places included – can more or less charge what they like: it's a good idea to take the first reasonable place you're offered and check the rest later. It can also be worth enquiring at the AAST about **furnished apartments**, rented out by the month only in summer but for negotiable periods in winter. There are dozens all over town, all with bathroom and kitchen facilities, and off-season prices start at around L100,000 a week – though in summer you're talking about at least L1 million a month. There are some nice, reasonable apartments for rent on Salita dei Gracchi, off the main Corso by piazza IX Aprile; information from the AAST.

If everywhere is full, or you prefer to be nearer the beach, you'll have to try GIARDINI-NAXOS (also a good place to eat), MAZZARÒ (p.138) or **camp**. The campsite, *San Leo* (☎0942-24.658), is open all year, on the cape below town (next to the *Grande Albergo Capo Taormina*): take any bus running between Taormina and the railway station. There are two other sites nearby, too, at LETOJANNI (see p.138).

The town

Don't come all the way up to Taormina if all you really want to do is to hit the beaches (see p.138–40). They're a bus or cable-car ride from town and if you're just passing through, it's much easier to get to them from the coastal road: walk or take a bus from Taormina-Giardini railway station.

As for Taormina itself, whenever you come you shouldn't miss the **Teatro Greco** (daily 9am–1hr before sunset; L2000), signposted from just about everywhere, at the end of via Teatro Greco. Vincent Cronin (in *The Golden Honeycomb*) thought the theatre was ' . . . deluged to distraction with multiple beauty . . . sited by connoisseurs', and certainly it's a considered choice, the theatre carved out of the hillside and giving a complete panorama of southern Calabria, the Sicilian coastline and snow-capped Etna – a glorious natural backdrop for the audience.

Despite its name, the existing remains are almost entirely Roman. Founded by Greeks in the 3C BC, it was rebuilt at the end of the 1C AD, a period when Taormina enjoyed great prosperity under Imperial Roman rule, and the reconstruction completely changed the theatre's character. The arched apertures, niches and columns of the impressive Roman scene-building, for example, must have obscured the views of Etna, which presumably were a major reason for the theatre's original siting. Likewise, Imperial Roman drama was strictly gladiatorial, so the stage and lower seats were cut back to provide more room and a deep trench was dug in the *orchestra* to accommodate the animals and fighters. Still, it all adds to the interest, and you'll want to scramble up and down the seats of the *cavea*, as well as poke around the high vaulted rooms on either side of the scene-building – all of which is best done in the early morning or near closing-time if you want to avoid the high season crowds. You can't fault the acoustics either, and in summer (July and August) the theatre hosts an international film festival and various concerts and plays – tickets and information from the AAST. A **museum**, close to the entrance, with relics of Roman Taormina, is currently being restored, possibly open some time in 1989.

There's little else that's vital in town and, really, Taormina's attractions are all to do with strolling along the flower-decked streets and stepped alleys, and window-shopping in the converted ground floors of Corso Umberto's 15C palazzi. If you want more direction to your wanderings, a few other vestiges of Roman and medieval Taormina warrant a look. A much smaller brick-built *Odeion*, known as the **Teatro Romano** (originally used for musical recitations), is half-buried under the adjacent church of **Santa Caterina**, next to the AAST: peer down at it through the railings from outside and then enter the church to take a closer look at bits of the theatre exposed in the floor of the nave. Opposite is the fine 14C **Palazzo Corvaja**, decorated with inlaid black and white lava and encompassing an attractive courtyard staircase. You can usually get into the main hall, where the Sicilian 'parliament' met in 1410 to choose a successor to the Aragonese line, and there are concerts and exhibitions held inside throughout the year. Further up the Corso, off a side-street to the left (via Naumachia), is the long niched wall of a Roman **water cistern** – the sunken garden here occupied by a restaurant and barber's shop.

Centre of town is **piazza IX Aprile**, with its restored 12C **Torre dell'Orologio**, a clock-tower you can walk right through. The views here, from a terrace overlooking Etna and the bay, are splendid, though don't sit down at the inviting outdoor cafés unless you have a substantial bankroll. Both churches in the square, low-key and unassuming, indicate how small-scale Taormina was until fairly recently. Squat 15C Sant'Agostino is now a library, while **San Giuseppe** tops the steps at the back of the piazza – its 17C facade curiously decorated with plaques depicting skull-and-crossbones.

Through the clock-tower is the oldest part of Taormina, and the narrow Corso is awash with stately palazzi, now neatly displaying shoes, clothes and local lace in their lower windows. The battlemented **Duomo**, originally built in the 13C, though restored since, isn't of vast interest, typically subdued in design – and fronted by a pretty 17C fountain. Steps to the right lead to a patchy, enclosed Roman mosaic, badly faded, just above piazza del Duomo. Head the other way, behind the square and cathedral, and a street drops down to the impressive **convento di San Domenico**, now a luxury hotel and containing a contemporary cloister (which you can't get into) and a restored church-hall adjoining it (which hosts the odd concert). Though you'd never know to look at it, the convent was badly bombed during World War II, when it was commandeered as the headquarters of Field-Marshal Kesselring.

That's it as far as the Corso and the surrounding alleys are concerned. A left turn out of one of the old town gates, Porta Messina, leads in a few minutes (down via Cappuccini and via Fontana Vecchia) to the villa in which **D.H. Lawrence** lived for three years in the 1920s – the *Fontana Vecchia*, now a private house, marked by two cypress trees. Otherwise, if you haven't yet had your fill of views, there are endless places in town where you can revel in them. Easiest target is the **Giardino Pubblico** (open dawn to dusk) on via Bagnoli Croce. Or with more time to spare, it's worth hiking up to the tumbledown medieval **castello** above Taormina, where the panoramas take in the town and theatre as well as the coastline. There's a very steep path which leads up from the Circonvallazione, past the cliff-top cross of Madonna della Rocca, the climb taking around half an hour.

Eating, drinking and nightlife

Eating in Taormina can be very expensive. Several places offer a limited-choice *pranzo turístico*, usually around L15,000 a head, but it rarely includes a drink. At the budget end of the scale, there are a couple of unspectacular pizzerias outside Porta Messina, while the only vaguely cheap restaurant (L12–15,000 each including wine) is the basic but good *Trattoria da Nino*, via Pirandello 37. *Il Baccanale* in piazzetta Filea (end of via Bagnoli Croce) has slightly higher prices but you get to sit outside. If money is no object, there are lots of places where you can get a great meal – good fish especially – though watch out for the steep service charges. Favourites are the *Gámbero Rosso*, via Naumachia 11, with outdoor tables and some unusual pasta dishes, and the wonderfully chic *Vicolo Stretto* at vicolo Stretto 6, up the slimmest of alleys off the Corso by piazza IX Aprile. If you're really loaded (or maybe just for afternoon tea) brave the forbiddingly posh entrance to the *Granduca*, Corso Umberto 170, a restored 15C palazzo whose dining-room looks out over the bay below town.

Otherwise, there's a daily indoor **market** (mornings only, not Sun) off via Dietro Cappuccini, a *Standa* **supermarket** outside the Porta Catania (and to the right) and – over the road from the supermarket – a take-away spit-roast chicken place. Best **bars** for a quick drink, or a coffee and a pastry, are either the one immediately above the supermarket; a larger affair with outdoor tables opposite the post office (closest to the Porta Catania); or *Tony's*, down the Corso and just past the duomo.

Taormina's **nightlife** might seem dauntingly exclusive at times, but it isn't really: just dauntingly dear and in fact rather tame. Be prepared to pay heavily for drinks in the few discos and video-bars – all of which are as good, or bad, as each other. It's probably nicest to sit and **drink** in one of the pavement cafés, the best and most popular in piazza IX Aprile and piazza Vittorio Emanuele/largo Santa Caterina. Again, though, they're not cheap and budget-conscious travellers could simply join Taormina's swanky *passeggiata*, or take a bus down to Giardini-Naxos for an evening waterfront stroll – by no means the worst way to spend an evening.

Listings

Banks and exchange At the *Banco di Sicilia*, Corso Umberto 91; open Mon–Fri 8.30am–1.30pm & 3–4pm. Also, an exchange office at Corso Umberto 145 (July to Sept Mon–Sat 9am–1pm & 4.30–8.30pm, Sun 9am–1pm; rest of the year Mon–Sat 9am–12.30pm & 4–7.30pm; closed Thurs all year).

Chemist There's an English-speaking chemist on the corner of piazza IX Aprile (no.1).

First Aid Call ☎0942-23.149.

Petrol stations Several on via Luigi Pirandello.

Police *Carabinieri* at piazza Badia 4 (☎0942-23.105).

Post office Just outside the Porta Catania.

Scooters Available to rent from *California*, via Bagnoli Croce 86, or from the gift shop behind the AAST, overlooking the Teatro Romano. Around L25,000 a day plus petrol.

Taxis Ranks in piazza San Pancrazio and piazza Vittorio Emanuele; around L10,000 to the railway station.

Telephone calls Make them from inside the *Avis* rent-a-car office (Mon–Sat 8.30am–12.30pm & 4.30–7.30pm, Sun 9am–12.30pm), via San Pancrazio 6, outside the Porta Messina on the left.

Around Taormina: inland, and the coastal towns and beaches

For a good day out from Taormina, away from the crowded streets, it's an idea to head **inland**, up into the hills surrounding the nearby village of **Castelmola**. Less energetically, the **coastline** below Taormina, north and south, is appealing – a mixture of grottoes, rocky coves and good sand beaches – although too much of it is either sectioned-off as private lidos (which you have to pay to use; around L5000 a day), or simply gets very packed in summer. Little communities – not quite villages – have developed around the bay to the north, while to the south **Giardini-Naxos** is very much a separate town, with its own holiday trade and nightlife. Indeed, rooms are plentiful, and you might well want to stay in one of the numerous *pensioni* right on the beach, rather than up in Taormina.

Inland: Castelmola and Monte Vénere

After taking in Taormina's castle, you could always just continue to follow the road (or the marked path) further up to **CASTELMOLA**, five kilometres above and seemingly sprouting out of the severe crag beneath it. It's around an hour's climb on foot to the village (though there are buses too, from Taormina); its role these days seems to be as a drinks-stop for view-seeking mobile tourists. It's a tiny place, just one cobbled road, some lean-to houses and the remnants of a long-demolished castle. But it makes a handsome stop and there's a fine bar in the lilliputian piazza. Even some places to eat, too, and two cheapish **hotels** if you fancied spending the night up here; either the *Panorama di Sicilia*, via de Gasperi 44 (☎0942-28.027; L35,000 with bath), or the *Villa Sonia*, via Porta Mola 9 (☎0942-28.082; L28,000).

Another couple of hours' walk beyond are the heights of **Monte Vénere** (885m) – take the path behind Castelmola's cemetery – where usually the only other people around are the shepherds. **Returning to Taormina**, through Castelmola, you can vary your route back. At the crossroads just out of Castelmola, a road leads off around Monte Tauro and across the other side of the valley: keep bearing right and you'll eventually end up on via Fontana Vecchia, which finishes up in town – around a two-hour stroll. Less of a hike is the path (signposted 'Taormina') which leads steeply down behind the castle, passing D.H. Lawrence's house away up on the left and entering town on via Cappuccini.

North: Mazzarò, Spisone and Letojanni

The closest beaches to town are the extremely popular pebbled coves at **MAZZARÒ**, easily reached by a **cable-car** (*funivia*) service – L1000 each way, every fifteen minutes from via Pirandello in Taormina. There's also a steep **path** which starts just below the cable-car station. Whichever way you arrive, the water here is remarkably clear and you can hire pedal-boats to explore the local grottoes. Of the two beaches, the southernmost is usually the most packed, fronting its much-photographed islet, the **Isola Bella**; while the little bay to the north (*Spiaggia Mazzarò*) is emptier and shelters a very reasonable restaurant, the *Trattoria Il Barcaiolo*, whose terrace looks out over beached fishing-boats. If you're still searching for a bed, there are a dozen small **hotels** here, too, ranged along the main road and above the beaches, though get the AAST to ring for you first from Taormina: cheapest are *La Conchiglia* in piazzale Funivia (☎0942-24.739; L28,000), near the cable-car station, and *Villa Moschella*, via Nazionale 240 (☎0942-23.328; L32,000). If you've got wheels, you may want to come down to Mazzarò in the evening and **eat**: the main road above the Isola Bella has a couple of restaurants with terraces and outdoor tables, while back along the road (south, towards Capo Taormina) is one of Sicily's few Chinese restaurants – the *Drago d'Oro*, via Nazionale 114: not cheap but worth the money for a change.

The beach-bars and restaurants at **SPISONE**, north again, are also accessible by path from Taormina, this time from below the cemetery in town (off via Guardiola Vecchia). It's around half an hour's walk, though there are also buses which make the trip from Taormina's bus terminal, passing Isola Bella and Mazzarò on the way.

From Spisone, the coast opens out and the beaches get wider. **LETOJANNI**, five kilometres from Taormina, is a little resort in its own right, with some rather more ordinary bars and shops, and a few fishing-boats on a sandy beach. In summer it's as busy as anywhere else on this stretch, but it wouldn't be a bad place to **stay** out of season: there are several cheapish *pensioni* in the village – try along via L. Rizzo – and two nearby **campsites**: *Paradise International* (☎0942-36.306), open March to October, and *Euro Camping Marmaruca* (☎0942-36.676), open all year.

Along the seafront, one of Letojanni's *pensioni* – *Da Peppe* (☎0942-36.159; L32,000) – also has a good **restaurant** over on the beach, where Peppe himself presides over the kitchen from behind a bushy beard: it's a great place to eat fish, well worth the steepish prices. Regular buses head back to Taormina, passing Spisone and the Isola Bella, and trains link the village with Taormina-Giardini station.

South: Giardini-Naxos and Recanati

Roomier and better for swimming are the sands south of Taormina, principally at **GIARDINI-NAXOS**. The wide, curving bay – easily seen from Taormina's terraces – was the launching-point of Garibaldi's 1860 attack on the Bourbon troops in Calabria and, equally significantly, the site of the first Greek colony in Sicily. An attractive and obvious stop for ships sailing between Greece and southern Italy, there was a settlement here by 734 BC, named *Naxos* after the Greek island from which the colonists came, though it was never very important. The **excavations** (daily 9am–1hr before sunset; free) are very low-key – a long stretch of ancient, lava-built city wall, two covered kilns and a sketchy temple – but it's a pleasant walk there through the lemon groves: take the bus from Taormina to Naxos/Recanati and follow the signs (*Scavi*). Right on the cape, Capo Schisò, in between two restaurants, is an inconspicuous **museo archeologico** (Mon–Sat 9am–2pm, Sun 9am–1pm; free), which houses some of the finds.

Giardini itself, the sprawling town backing the beach, is an excellent alternative to Taormina as a source of accommodation and food. Prices tend to be a good bit cheaper and in high season, if you've arrived by train, it's probably worth trying here first; again, though, starting early in the day is a good idea. Recommended **places to stay** are the endearingly antiquated *Moderno* (L20,000), opposite the station, and, left out of the station and just before the railway bridge, the *Locanda Roma*, via Roma 21 (☎0942-52.137; L17,000). But there are loads of other possibilities, from *pensioni* to swanky hotels, and if our choices are full, or don't appeal, just take a walk along the seafront and see which of the others have room, as well as looking out for *cámere* signs above the trattorias. Another option if you intend to stay in the area for some time is to take a **furnished apartment**. Like Taormina, they're cheaper in winter and rented by the month only in summer, but the prices here are a good bit more realistic: ask in *Immobiliare Naxos* (☎0942-51.184), via Vittorio Emanuele 58; they speak English. For other information, there's an **AAST** on the seafront, via Tysandros 76 (Mon–Sat 9am–1pm & 4–7pm; ☎0942-51.010).

If you're on any kind of budget, you're better off **eating** in Giardini too, as the pizzerias and restaurants are consistently better value than in Taormina. Best and cheapest is the friendly ristorante-pizzeria attached to the *Lido Europa* (opposite the Chiesa Immacolata, via Tysandros), and there are fine pizzas, a big *antipasto* table and fresh pasta at *Fratelli Marano*, via Naxos 181. Other good choices are the *Arcobaleno*, via Naxos 169; *Taverna Naxos*, via Tysandros 108, which has a very cheap *menu turístico*; *Da Angelina*, via Schisò (next to the museum) with outdoor tables overlooking the bay; and the *Calypso*, via IV Novembre 267, opposite the petrol station. Of the **bars**, try the ice-cream and *granite* at the *Bar Europa* on via Naxos.

Buses run half-hourly to Giardini from Taormina, the last one at 9.30pm. Last one back to Taormina is at 9pm, from the stop outside the *Lido Europa* on the seafront.

Around the cape, the next bay south is largely taken up by the holiday village of **RECANATI**. This is the end of the line for buses from Taormina and, though the beach here is fairly long, it's not at all an attractive target.

Almost without exception, every building is either a package-tour hotel or a block of holiday apartments, and it's a long walk to Giardini for a decent bar or restaurant.

The Alcántara valley

Buses from Taormina-Giardini railway station (and twice daily from Taormina itself) motor a few kilometres south and then turn inland to coast through the pretty **Alcántara valley**. It's an hour's ride all told, east into the green hills beyond Taormina, and the bus stops at several small towns, many crowned with ruined medieval castles. The first places you reach, **TRAPPITELLO** and **GAGGI**, are new and uninviting dormitory suburbs for Taormina and Giardini. But if you're mobile (the last bus back to Taormina is at 5pm), Trappitello at least has the attraction of perhaps Sicily's best rural **restaurant**, inside the *Azienda Sant'Antonio* farm, just outside town and above the road to Gaggi (on the right). All the food and wine is reared, grown and made on-site: there's usually ravioli stuffed with wild boar and celery, and if you stick to the grand self-service *antipasti* and the fresh pasta rather than the roast meats, it works out fairly reasonably. There's a supermarket here, too, if you want to take back some home-made cheese and wine.

The Gole di Alcántara

On the other side of Gaggi, the valley is immediately more attractive, the road snaking into the hills, and the railway line carried over a viaduct which crosses the Alcántara river (the name, Alcántara, is a corruption of the Arabic word for bridge). For the most part it's fertile, green countryside, gentle hills supporting a profusion of citrus groves, olive trees and wild flowers, while the road runs over and alongside the river past isolated farms.

Twenty minutes beyond Gaggi, get the bus driver to let you off at the **Gole di Alcántara**, a vast geological cleft in the hillside. The deep, grey-green gorge, with a silent frog-filled river at the bottom, invites a splash around, and there's a bar and restaurant above if you want them. There are steps down from the main road (beyond the official entrance) or a lift (L1500 return) on the site, which also rents out thigh-length wellies (L3000) for some serious gorge-wading. This is enormous fun, though without the wellies (or at least some strong, gripped plastic shoes) it would be very difficult to get beyond the first swirling, rocky pool. Once inside, it can get very hairy indeed, with freezing waterfalls and soaring stone walls providing the obstacles, and it takes about an hour to clamber as far up the gorge as you can get.

Francavilla and Castiglione

You could walk from the gorge, or pick up the next bus on to **FRANCAVILLA DI SICILIA**, four kilometres away, alongside the river and overlooked by the few surviving walls of its hillside castle. There's a path up to the ruins, and although much of the town is newly built there's a fair amount of interest in the couple of old central streets, and in walking up to the convent which peers over town and river. You might want **to stay** in

Francavilla, both for the scenery and the fact that it has the area's only hotels: the *Centrale* (☎0942-981.052; L22,000) on the main road through town, and the *d'Orange Alcantara* (☎0942-981.374; L37,000) on the way in from the Gole di Alcántara, the latter used in the summer by package-tourists holidaying around Taormina.

There's a **railway station** in Francavilla, for local trains back to Taormina or west to RANDAZZO (see p.162), while the bus keeps on to **CASTIGLIONE DI SICILIA**, five kilometres above. This is an old and decrepit mountain settlement, the numerous church spires and the solid, rock-built castle an inviting target as the bus inches up the switchback road. It's easy to spend a couple of hours just wandering the quiet streets, which meander up as far as a small piazza at the top of town containing a bar and a barber with a sign in English offering 'fashion' haircuts. The town was a formidable medieval stronghold as the doughty castle remains attest.

If you're heading back to Taormina, you can either hang around for the return bus to Giardini (it leaves from outside the bar at via Regina Margherita 174, back down the hill from the piazza), or – better – walk down the hill to Francavilla, an easy hike, and pick up a bus or train from there. (Castiglione's railway station, incidentally, is miles away, impractical for visiting the town.) The walk takes around an hour, and at the bottom of the crag, on the way into Francavilla, you cross a sturdy medieval bridge. Just beyond here, at the back of the factory at the side of the road, is the sad ruin of a **Byzantine church**, one of several in the area left to rot.

Beyond the Alcántara valley: some day-trips

There are a handful of **round-trip** alternatives from Taormina if you want to make a day of it. Infrequent buses from Castiglione head to CATANIA (p.143), or two a day go on to Randazzo to the west, from where it's an hour by local train back to Taormina-Giardini. With your own wheels (or on foot), it's around nine kilometres through Castiglione to LINGUAGLOSSA (p.163), where you can pick up the round-Etna railway – a journey described in the next chapter. One last possibility for those with their own transport is to return to Francavilla, from where the SS185 climbs up into the Monti Peloritani, and to NOVARA DI SICILIA, and then down to the Tyrrhenian coast. Both town and route are covered on p.98.

festivals

January
1–6 Christmas and New Year celebrations in TAORMINA. Puppet shows, folk-singing and concerts, ending on Twelfth Night.

February/March
Carnevale Carnival celebrations in TAORMINA and GIARDINI-NAXOS: processional floats, fireworks and music for three days.

May
Last week Puppet shows, a parade of painted carts and folk-singing in TAORMINA's most traditional festival.

July
21–30 International Film Festival in TAORMINA, with screenings in the Greek theatre.

31 onwards Dance, drama and music; all performances held in the Greek theatre in TAORMINA; runs until September.

August
12–14 Procession of the *Giganti* in MESSINA (p.125).

15 *Ferragosto* procession and fireworks in MESSINA (p.125).

December
20 onwards Christmas celebrations in TAORMINA. Puppet shows, folk-singing and concerts.

travel details

Trains

From Messina to Taormina/Catania (approx every 40min; 1hr/1½hr); Milazzo/Cefalù/Palermo (up to 16 daily; 40min/2¾hr/3½–6hr); Naples (13; 6½hr); Rome (7; 9hr); Milan (5; 14hr).
From Taormina to Messina (approx half-hourly; 1hr); Catania/Siracusa (13 daily; 45min/2¼hr); Francavilla di Sicilia (3–6; 25min); Randazzo (3–5; 1hr).

Buses

From Messina to Scaletta/Ali Terme/Santa Teresa di Riva/Sant'Aléssio/Letojanni/Taormina (Mon–Sat half-hourly, Sun 6 daily; 25min/35min/55min/1hr 5min/1hr 15min/1½hr); Itala (Mon–Sat 16; 35min); Forza d'Agrò (Mon–Sat 1; 1½hr); Taormina/Catania (Mon–Sat 11, Sun 5; 1½hr/3hr); Giardini-Naxos/Randazzo (Mon–Sat 4; 55min/2¼hr); Catania by autostrada (Mon–Sat hourly, Sun 9; 1hr 35min); Catania airport (2 daily; 1hr 50min); Milazzo (9 daily by autostrada, Mon–Sat 11 by local road; 30min–1hr); Tíndari (Mon–Sat 2; 1½hr); Patti (Mon–Sat 5; 1hr 10min); Palermo (1; 4½hr); Rome (1; 9½hr).
From Taormina to Giardini-Naxos/Recanati (roughly half-hourly in summer, less in winter and Sun; 15min/25min); Isola Bella/Mazzarò/Spisone/Letojanni (roughly half-hourly in summer, less in winter and Sun; 10min/12min/15min/25min); Trappitello (3–5 daily; 20min); Gole di Alcántara/Francavilla/Castiglione (Mon–Sat 2 daily; 40min/55min/1hr 10min); Forza d'Agrò (2–3; 30min); Castelmola (5–6; 20min).
From Taormina-Giardini (railway station) to Gole di Alcántara (Mon–Sat 9 daily; 25min); Francavilla/Castiglione (Mon–Sat 6; 40min/55min); Randazzo/Bronte/Cesarò (Mon–Sat 3; 1hr 20min/1hr 40min/2hr 20min).
From Santa Teresa di Riva to Sávoca/Casalvécchio Sículo (Mon–Sat 5 daily, 3 Sun; 20min/30min).

Ferries

From Messina to Villa San Giovanni (*FS* every 45min, *Caronte* every 20min, less at night; 35min); Réggio di Calabria (*FS* 10 daily; 50min).

Hydrofoils

From Messina to Réggio di Calabria (Mon–Fri every 40min, Sat hourly; 15min); Vulcano/Lípari (4 daily in summer, 2 in winter; 1¾–3hr); Naples (1 daily in summer; 6hr).
From Giardini-Naxos catamaran service to Malta (June to Sept 2 daily Mon and Sun; 2¾hr).

CHAPTER FOUR

CATANIA, ETNA AND AROUND

Bang in the middle of the Ionian coast, **Catania** is Sicily's second largest city, and a point of arrival for most of the island's foreign visitors, who land at the airport just outside. But unlike other stops on the mostly pretty, indented shoreline, Catania is by no means a prime tourist destination: there's heavy industry here, a large port and some depressing suburbs, glimpsed as you edge in on the train. That said, it's a lively city with a uniformly grand architecture bestowed upon it after the late 17C earthquake which wrecked the whole region. Making full use of the local building-material (lava), the 18C architect Giovanni Vaccarini gave the city a lofty, noble air; and today, despite the neglect of many of the churches and the disintegrating, grey mansions, there's still much of interest. Delving about throws up lava-encrusted Roman relics, surviving alongside some of the finest Baroque work on the island. The university, the first in Sicily, adds a youthful feel to the streets, and there's some good, cheap accommodation and restaurants.

Excursions from the city take in the villages around the town of **Acireale**, small-scale resorts with good swimming from the rocks and fresh fish in the trattorias. A longer trip, still using Catania as a base, is the run to **Lentini** and its ancient Greek ruins. But the most rewarding expedition is to drive or take a bus a few kilometres north to **Mount Etna**, Europe's highest volcano. Still active, its massive presence dominates the whole of this part of the coast – the towns and villages around, like Catania, built from the lava it periodically ejects. A road and a small single-track railway, the **Circumetnea**, circumnavigate the lower slopes, passing through a series of hardy towns, like **Randazzo**, almost foolishly sited in the shadow of the volcano and surrounded by swirls of black volcanic rock. Reaching the top, or at least the lower craters below the summit, is possible too, either on foot or by mountain-bus – heady experiences both.

CATANIA AND THE COAST

First impressions don't do much at all for **Catania** – on an initial encounter possibly the island's gloomiest spot. Built from black-grey volcanic stone, the central streets can feel suffocating, dark with the shadows of grimy, tall Baroque churches and palazzi. The influence of Etna is pervasive, in the buildings, in the brooding vistas you get of the mountain at the end of Catania's streets – even the city's main thoroughfare is named after the volcano.

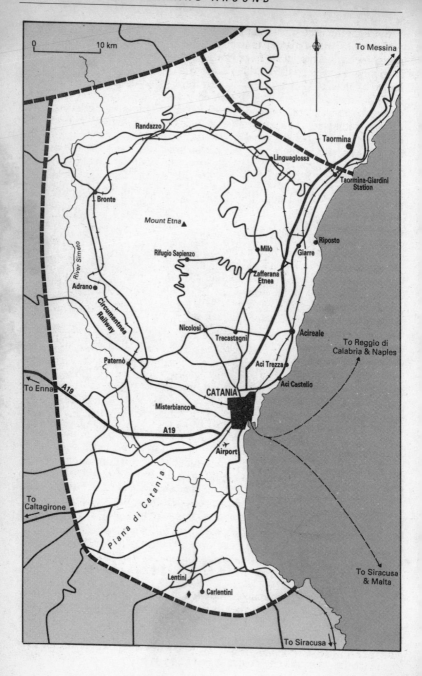

0   10 km

To Messina

Randazzo

Taormina

Linguaglossa

Taormina-Giardini
Station

Bronte

Mount Etna ▲

Rifugio Sapienzo

Milò

Riposto

Giarre

Zafferana
Etnea

River Simeto

Adrano

Circumetnea
Railway

Nicolosi

Trecastagni

Acireale

To Reggio di
Calabria & Naples

Paternò

Aci Trezza

Aci Castello

To Enna   A19

CATANIA

Misterbianco

A19

Airport

To Caltagirone

Piana di Catania

To Siracusa
& Malta

Lentini

Carlentini

To Siracusa

But fight the urge to cut and run: Catania is one of the most intriguing of Sicily's cities, with a **history** to match. Some of the island's first **Greek colonists**, probably Chalcidians from Naxos, settled the site as early as 729 BC, becoming so influential that their laws were eventually adopted by all the Ionian colonies of Magna Graecia. Later, the city was one of the first to fall to the **Romans**, under whom it prospered greatly, and, unusually for Sicily, Catania's surviving ancient relics are all Roman. In the early Christian period Catania witnessed the martyrdom of **Agatha**, who, having rejected the improper advances of the *praetor*, Quintianus, was put to death in 252. She was later canonised (becoming the patron saint of Catania) and it was her miraculous intervention that reputedly saved the city from complete volcanic destruction in the 17C. Even with the the saint's protection, Catania has had its fair share of disasters: Etna erupted in 1669, engulfing the city in lava, and the **earthquake** of 1693 devastated the whole of south eastern Sicily.

Given these repeated catastrophes, the **modern city** is overshadowed in terms of historical monuments by Palermo. Still, there are some remarkable Baroque churches – dating from the 18C rebuilding of the city – and the stumpy remnants of its medieval castle. It's also the only large urban centre outside the capital, though unlike Palermo, Catania is first and foremost a business-like, commercial city, with the island's busiest market and some of Sicily's best food. And, while drivers usually choose to see the volcano from the prettier towns and villages hereabouts, if you're travelling by public transport you'll have to leave for Etna from Catania itself.

Catania is a major transport terminus, not only for buses and trains south to Siracusa, but also for travel west, including services to Enna, Agrigento and Palermo. Before moving on, it's worth taking day-trips out to the nearby towns and villages: there's a diverting **coastal route north**, through small bathing resorts, to Baroque **Acireale**; while **south** of Catania you can make a quick escape to the good beaches fronting the gulf, behind which lies the flat and mostly uninhabited **Piana di Catania**, the fertile plain that traditionally fed the city. At the plain's southern extremity sits **Lentini**, on the site of one of the earliest Greek colonies to be founded in Sicily.

Arrival and orientation

The **airport**, *Fontanarossa*, is five kilometres south of the city, and is the entry-point of most charter flights to Sicily. If you're not on a package and don't have a coach to meet you, bus #24 leaves from right outside, running to the central piazza del Duomo; a taxi from the rank outside the airport will cost around L25,000 for the same journey. **Ferries** from Naples, Réggio di Calabria and Malta (and hydrofoils from Malta) dock on the Molo Vecchio, just off via Dusmet, from where it's a short walk to piazza del Duomo. (See *Listings* for ferry company details.)

All mainline **trains** use Stazione Centrale in piazza Giovanni XXIII, north east of the centre. If you're changing on to the narrow-gauge Etna train (see below, p.160), the **Stazione Circumetnea** is on Corso delle Province (ticket office at no.13), just off Corso Italia, fifteen minutes' walk up via della Libertà from piazza Giovanni XXIII. **Regional buses** to/from Acireale, Nicolosi, Etna (Rifugio Sapienza), Zafferana Etnea and Lentini all stop on the other side of piazza Giovanni XXIII; buses to/from Piazza Armerina stop on via Luigi Sturzo, just to the left of the square; all other regional and **island-wide buses** stop in piazza Bellini, a few minutes' walk from piazza del Duomo. See *Listings* and *Travel Details* for further bus information.

As far as **orientation** goes, you'll need little more than our map and your own two feet to get around the city. Most of the sights are confined within a small area, the centre of which is piazza del Duomo – just a twenty-minute walk from the railway station. From here, via Etnea steams off north, lined with the city's most fashionable shops and cafés; fish market and port lie behind to the south; the best of the Baroque quarter to the west.

Information and getting around

For information, there's an **EPT** office (June to Sept daily 7am–9.30pm, rest of the year Mon–Fri 9am–1pm & 4–7pm; ☎095-531.625) inside the railway station: very helpful, with accommodation listings, free maps and English-speaking staff. The main office (Mon–Fri 9am–noon & 4–7pm, Sat 9am–noon; ☎095-312.124), on the other hand, is harder to find – it's signposted off via Etnea, down via Pacini, at largo Paisello 5, in an unmarked office block. There's also an **information office** at the airport (Mon–Fri 9am–noon & 1–8pm; ☎095-341.900), again with free maps and accommodation lists.

You'll rarely need to use the **city buses** in Catania itself, though they'll save you a walk into the centre from the station – and you'll have to jump on one to get to the airport and the campsites. There are **stops** immediately outside the railway station: #27, #29, #33, #36, #39 and #42 run into the centre, along via VI Aprile and via Vittorio Emanuele to piazza del Duomo; #24 goes to the airport. Other central pick-up points are piazza del Duomo and piazza Stesicoro (where you can catch most of the buses already listed); and behind the Porta Uzeda (below piazza del Duomo), where there's a stop for bus #24 (airport) and #27 and #D (campsites). **Tickets** are valid for one journey (L700), two hours (L900) or nine hours (L1200), available from *tabacchi* or the booth by the terminus outside the railway station.

Finding a place to stay

Catania has plenty of cheap hotel **accommodation**, making it a good base for seeing the area. Most of the the places listed below (in alphabetical order) are fine, if sometimes a bit basic, and out of season you may even be able to negotiate prices lower than these. If you're reading this before you arrive in Catania, bear in mind that you could cut costs further by writing ahead to book space in the city's student hostel during summer – see *Basics* for more details. You should know, too, that parts of Catania have a reputation for violence (see below) and where we don't consider the hotels or the area to be particularly safe for single women, we've said so. In summer it's wise to ring ahead, especially for the recommended hotels.

Hotels

Pensione Centrale, via Pacini 17 (☎095-310.983; L20,000). Nice rooms, close to the Carlo Alberto market – but the back-street location doesn't make this the best choice for single women.

Pensione Duomo, via Garibaldi 9 (☎095-340.195; L22,000). Handy for the central sights, average rooms.

Centrale Europa, via Vittorio Emanuele 167 (☎095-340.271; L25,000). Like the *Savona* (see below) over the road, a safe choice for women.

Corona, via Crociferi 81 (☎095-327.708; L15,000): inside the courtyard and it's the door on the right. Good location and a popular place which fills quickly in summer, *but* the proprietor is a racist and if you're black this *pensione* will probably be 'full'.

Pensione Gresi, via Pacini 28 (☎095-322.709; L22,000 includes shower). One of the best, clean and friendly, close to the Villa Bellini.

Holland International, via Vittorio Emanuele 8 (☎095-532.779; L27,000 with shower); at the eastern end. Cheapish double rooms above the courtyard of a nice palazzo, on the way into town from the railway station.

Moderno, via Alessi 9 (☎095-326.250; L50,000 with bath), between piazza Università and via Crociferi. Nice, well-kept rooms in a good central location.

Roma, via della Libertà 63 (☎095-316.167; L35,000 with bath). Modern, well-appointed rooms, close to the railway station.

Rubens, via Etnea 196 (☎095-317.073; L22,000). Best budget choice if you want to stay on the the main via Etnea, though always busy.

Sangiorgi, via A. di Sangiuliano 237 (☎095-320.641; L24,000). Fairly seedy around here at night, though the hotel is fine.

Savona, via Vittorio Emanuele 210 (☎095-326.982; L25,000). Well-placed, close to piazza del Duomo on a main road, and OK for single women.

Camping

Campsites are all a bus-ride out of the city: it's worth getting one of the longer-validity tickets if you want to come straight back after pitching your tent. Bus #27 from the railway station or Porta Uzeda, and #D (summer only) from via Etnea/Porta Uzeda head to the long beach south of Catania where there are three big campsites, all with cabins available, along viale Kennedy. Of these, *Villagio Souvenir* (☎095-345.440; June to Sept), at no. 71, is the cheapest. The others are *Villagio Turístico Internazionale* (☎095-340.880; open all year), at no. 47; and the *Europeo* (☎095-591.026; June to Sept), no. 91.

Smaller-scale is *Camping Jonio* (☎095-491.139; open all year), to the north of the city, at OGNINA (see p.156): you'll need to take two buses, the #43 from the railway station to piazza Europa and the #34 from there; the campsite is at via Villini a Mare 2.

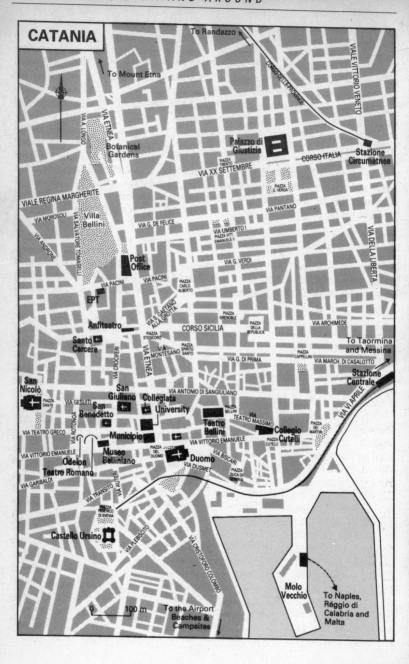

The city

You could see the whole of central **CATANIA** in a busy day's strolling, certainly while long-term restoration projects keep the best of the churches and monasteries and the only major museum in the city closed to the public. But the city really deserves more time if you can spare it: in any case, the opening times of what is accessible are usually restricted, and there's vigorous street activity in the swarming markets or along the main via Etnea well worth staying to enjoy. Something to be aware of as you potter around the crumbling back-streets of the Baroque town is the high incidence of **petty crime**. Catania has a well-deserved reputation for thievery and, while the main streets are safe enough, don't flash money and cameras around too obviously in the more run-down areas or the markets, and avoid badly-lit roads at night. (See our accommodation listings for safe places to stay.)

Around piazza del Duomo

Catania's main square, **piazza del Duomo**, at the the bottom of via Etnea, is a handy orientation point: from here, most things of interest are only a few minutes' walk away. It's also one of Sicily's most engaging piazzas, rebuilt completely in the first half of the 18C by the Palermitan, Giovanni Battista Vaccarini, who was made Catania's municipal architect in 1730. He surrounded the square with elegant buildings, like the **Municipio** on the northern side, finished in 1741, providing some relief from the grandeur by adding the central **elephant fountain**: an 18C lava elephant supporting an Egyptian obelisk on its back. This has become the city's symbol, and features an inscription, *Agatina Msshepl* – apparently an acronym for 'The mind of Saint Agatha is sane and spontaneous, honouring God and liberating the city.'

Cross over to the piazza's eastern flank for Vaccarini's grandest project, the **Duomo** (closed noon–5pm). Originally founded by Count Roger in the 11C, only the marvellous medieval apses, beautifully crafted from volcanic rock, survived the 1693 earthquake. They are viewable through the gate at via Vittorio Emanuele 159. Vaccarini's heavy Baroque touch is readily apparent from the imposing facade, on which he tagged granite columns filched from Catania's Roman amphitheatre. The interior is no less grand, adorned by a rich series of **chapels**: the *Cappella di Sant'Agata* (to whom the cathedral is dedicated) is to the right of the choir, and houses the relics paraded through the city on the saint's festival days; next to it, entered through a fine 16C doorway, is the *Cappella della Madonna*, with a Roman sarcophagus which holds the ashes of the Aragonese kings – Frederick II, Louis and Frederick III. It's worth looking in the sacristy too, for a fresco depicting the disastrous 1669 eruption of Mount Etna, completed only eight years after the event, while a wander through the rest of the church reveals the uncovered medieval foundations and ancient columns. The tomb of the composer Bellini, a native of the city, is set in the floor before the second column on the right as you enter, inscribed with a phrase from his opera, *La Sonnambula*.

Via Vittorio Emanuele II cuts across the piazza, its eastern arm running towards the sea. Opposite the cathedral, the church of **Sant'Agata** (usually locked) is another of Vaccarini's creations, though this time the rococo interior dates from after his death. More interesting, slightly further on, is the little **piazza Plácido**, with an 18C church of the same name and a house, at via Vittorio Emanuele 140, that was the home of early 19C Catanese erotic poet Domenico Tempio. The blackened doorway is decorated with some fairly raunchy figures of men and women playing with themselves. Further east, past the **Collegio Cutelli**, distinguished by Vaccarini's round courtyard, via Vittorio Emanuele ends in piazza dei Mártiri – marked by a statue of Saint Agatha atop a Roman column, looking over the harbour.

Back in piazza del Duomo, head for Catania's noisome open-air **market**, at its best early in the day, either by walking down through the towering late 17C Porta Uzeda and bearing right, or by crossing the piazza and nipping down the steps behind a marble fountain. This takes you right into the action – usually over by the early afternoon but until then almost frightening in its intensity. A medieval warren of narrow streets spreads around the fish market (the *Pescheria*), slabs and buckets full of twitching fish, eels and shellfish, some of which – mussels and sea-urchins – you might be offered, cut open, to try. There are endless lanes full of vegetable and fruit stalls, too, as well as bloody butcher's tables and one or two excellent lunchtime trattorias (see p.153).

The roads wind from here through a dilapidated neighbourhood to an open space (piazza Federico di Svevia) punctured by the **Castello Ursino**, once the proud fortress of Frederick II. Originally, the castle stood on a rocky cliff, over the beach, but following the 1669 eruption, which reclaimed this entire area from the sea, all that remains is the blackened keep – desperately neglected and surrounded by a shallow moat filled with all kinds of dumped junk. The Museo Cívico is housed inside but it's being rearranged and no one expects it, or the castle, to be open for years. Houses heareabouts are in a fairly ruinous state, too, and you might as well head back towards the centre (following via Auteri). It's easy to miss **piazza Mazzini**, straddling via Garibaldi, a dingy arcaded square that must have been much prettier once, constructed from 32 columns which originally formed part of a Roman basilica.

Via Crocíferi: Baroque churches, Bellini and Roman remains

Just north of piazza Mazzini is perhaps the most interesting section of the city – a tangle of churches, narrow 18C streets and archaeological remains which begins as you cross over via Garibaldi and walk up to via Vittorio Emanuele II. Everything close by is big and Baroque, and even the narrow **via Crocíferi** – which strikes north from the main road under an imposing arch – is lined with some arresting religious and secular buildings, little changed since the 18C. Amble up the street and you can peer in the courtyards of the palazzi (one with a plantation of banana trees) and poke around the churches

– best of which is **San Giuliano**, about halfway up on the right, which has a facade by Vaccarini and an echoing elliptical interior.

Back at the bottom of the narrow street, opposite San Francesco church, the house where the composer Vincenzo Bellini was born in 1801 is now open as the **Museo Belliniano** (Mon–Fri 8.30am–1.30pm, Sun 8.30am–12.30pm; free), an agreeable little collection of photographs, original scores and other memorabilia. Bellini composed his first work at six, and was only 34 when he died in Paris; his body was transported back to Sicily to be buried. He notches up several tributes around the city, including a piazza, Catania's main theatre and park, and the ultimate accolade, *spaghetti Norma*. Cooked with tomato and aubergine sauce, and named after one of Bellini's operas, it's a Catanian speciality.

Step west, along via Vittorio Emanuele to the **Teatro Romano** (daily except Mon 9am–1hr before sunset; free), at no.266, a surprisingly large chunk of Roman hardware to have survived the city's 18C refit. Built of lava in the 2C AD, on the site of an earlier Greek theatre (it may be marked *Teatro Greco* on some maps), much of the seating and the underground passage-ways are preserved, though all the marble which originally covered it has disappeared; adjacent, there's a smaller **Odeon**, originally used for music and recitations. If the gate is locked you can get a view of it by walking around the block and doubling back on the higher via Teatro Greco.

The other way down via Teatro Greco, west, leads to **piazza Dante**, a pretty crescent of houses, some of whose ground floors contain little work-shops – cabinet-makers, metal workers – open to the pavement. Opposite is the unfinished facade of **San Nicolò**, its grim 18C exterior studded by six enormous, lopped columns. The biggest church in Sicily (105m long), it's currently being restored but there's usually someone around in the early morning to show you the stark interior: undecorated save for the sculpted choir stalls and a meridian line drawn across the floor of the transept, embel-lished with zodiacal signs. The custodian will probably show you the sacristy, too, but it's doubtful whether you'll be able to climb up to the dome – a shame, as it used to provide one of the best views over the city. The church is part of the adjoining Benedictine **convent**, also under restoration and with equally impressive dimensions – it's the second-largest convent in Europe after Mafra in Portugal. Officially, you can't get in, but there's a gate to the left of the church, through which are the remains of some **Roman walls** and, behind, the massive conventual buildings: from here, you can at least see part of the Baroque exterior, rich in sculpted ornamentation. If you can persuade a workman to open the gate into the convent itself, there are two lovely court-yards beyond, the first containing an overgrown cloistered garden.

Along via Etnea

Most of the other city sights are ranged around the long and busy **via Etnea**, which runs north from piazza del Duomo and out of the city. Following its full length would eventually lead you right to the foothills of Mount Etna – and from the street's northern end there are much-trumpeted views of the peak in the distance. Mostly, you'll be concerned with the southern stretch of via

Etnea, the liveliest section lying between piazza del Duomo and the Villa Bellini (see below): an out-and-out shopping street, recently pedestrianised and none the worse for it, good for browsing and a coffee at one of the popular brightly polished bars.

Nearly all the notable buildings and churches are on the **west side** of via Etnea. Past the Municipio, the first square off the street (piazza dell'Università) holds the main building of the **University**, founded by the Aragonese kings in the 15C. The earthquake postponed its completion until the 1750s, Vaccarini – again – responsible for the attractive courtyard. Further on, **piazza Stesicoro** marks the modern centre of Catania, an enormous square split into two by via Etnea, and a useful point to pick up buses. The western side is almost entirely occupied by the sunken, black remains of Catania's **Anfiteatro Romano** (railed off but visible), dating back to the 2C or 3C AD. Built from lava blocks, the amphitheatre could hold around 16,000 spectators – quite a formidable size – and from the church steps above the square you can see the seating quite clearly, supported by long vaults. Although much is still concealed under the surrounding buildings, it's the grandest of Catania's Roman remains. More modest is the little 12C church of **Santo Cárcere** (Mon–Fri 8–11am & 4–7pm, weekends 8am–noon), above its own square nearby (reached from via Cappuccini). With strong defensive walls, it was built on the site of the prison where Saint Agatha was confined before her martyrdom at the hands of the Romans, and a custodian will let you in to the 3C crypt – now bright and cosy with electric candles and velvet chairs. More sinister is the chapel's medieval stone doorway, topped by evil, grinning, sculpted heads and ape-like creatures.

Back on via Etnea it's not far to the **Villa Bellini**, just beyond the post office: a large, ornamentally laid-out public garden which provides a welcome touch of greenery, and even the occasional concert in the summer. There's more seclusion, too, in the **Orto Botánico** (Mon–Sat 9am–1pm), a botanical garden at the northern end of the park, across piazza Roma.

There's precious little on the **east side** of via Etnea worth the legwork. Mostly modern, the gridded shopping streets march off towards the sea and the only time you're likely to be around here is having arrived on the Circumetnea train, which deposits you right in the middle of Corso delle Province, in the north of the city. Further south, the area around **piazza Carlo Alberto** is worth exploring, a long rectangular square which hosts the *Fera o Luni* market (daily except Sun), replete with fruit and vegetables, household gear and clothes. This is a good area to eat, particularly at lunchtime, though – the market aside – there's little else of interest in the streets around. Once beyond via Antonio di Sangiuliano, you're back in the old-town area of Catania, and the only real draw here is **piazza Bellini**, a strange conglomerate of buildings from some diverse architectural periods. A wide flight of steps leads up to a crumbling church, there's a Fascist-built office block and – overshadowing the lot – the bulky **Teatro Bellini**. Finished in 1890, its elaborate facade leans over the square and during the opera and concert season (winter and spring) you can usually take a quick look inside before the performances begin; programme details from the box office inside.

Eating, drinking, nightlife and culture

You'll rarely do better for **eating** than in Catania: fresh fish is a speciality, and there are some good restaurants about, from budget places in the markets to expense-account jobs in the modern city. The presence of students means that the **bars** and **nightlife** are fairly lively too, while Catania hosts one of Sicily's best religious **festivals** every February.

Food: markets, snacks and meals

Catania's two main **markets** are detailed in the text, great places to wander and munch from a variety of fresh fruit stalls, stand-up cafés and snack bars. Outside these areas, and at other times, there's an abundance of places to get **breakfast** and other **snacks**, best and most central of which is the *Centrale*, via Etnea 123, a busy tavola calda with a full range of snacks. The *Fast Food* is a bar-pizzeria-birreria at via Antonio di Sangiuliano 283 (corner of via Etnea), which sells pizza slices to take away and has seating inside. Around San Martino's day (November 11), the Catanese make *crispelle* – fritters of flour, water, yeast, and ricotta or anchovies: a good place to sample some is *Friggitoria Stella*, via Monsignor Ventimiglia 66. More snacks, pastries and ice-cream from *Savia*, Catania's finest, and *Spinella*, its next-door rival, at via Etnea 302, opposite the main entrance to the Villa Bellini. Of the **bars**, handiest is the *Bar Università* in piazza dell'Università (no.21), which sells good milkshakes and fresh-fruit drinks; and the kiosks along via Umberto I, offering a thirst-quenching Catanian speciality: mineral water with or without salted, crushed lemon (*selz con/senza limone e sale*). There's **late-night** eating, at the *Rosticceria Pistorio*, viale M. Rapisardi 237, a continuation of viale Regina Margherita, west of the Villa Bellini; bus #21 from piazza Stesicoro.

For **full meals**, consistently best value are the trattorias in the markets. Try the friendly *Trattoria Trípoli*, via Pardo 30 (lunchtime only and closed Tues), down in the fish market near piazza del Duomo, off via Garibaldi: it's one of two opposite each other, this one without a menu in the window and run by a woman who dishes-up complete meals, including wine, for under L15,000 a head. The other market, the *Fera o Luni* in and around piazza Carlo Alberto, offers several more good choices: best is the *Ristorante Rápido*, via Corridoni 17, off via Pacini, usually with fresh tuna and a bargain L8000 *pranzo completo*. There's also a ristorante-pizzeria at the via Pacini end of the street which offers a good, cheap daily menu; and a new **Chinese** restaurant opposite, *La Grande Muraglia*, via Pacini 83.

Other central inexpensive options include *La Pigna Verde*, via Carcaci 15, off via Etnea; the quiet *Trattoria Calabrese*, on via Penninello, down the steps at the end of via Crocíferi, with a tourist menu for L14,000; and *Da Aldo* (closed Mon), piazza G. Sciuti, first-left off via Pacini coming from the Carlo Alberto market – a popular place at lunchtime for quick grills. One place that certainly isn't cheap, but is renowned as Catania's **best**, is *La Siciliana*, way up in the north of the city at viale Marco Polo 52a (closed Sun evening and Mon), and serving marvellous pasta dishes – a full meal costs around L50,000 a head; bus #22 north, up via Etnea from piazza Stesicoro. Back in the centre,

La Zagara, via L. Capuana 32 (east of piazza Vittorio Emanuele, off via M. Ventimiglia) is a decent **macrobiotic** restaurant.

Nightlife and culture . . . and the Festa di Sant'Agata

To check out all the options, a free weekly arts and entertainment guide, *Fine Extra*, is available from *Nievski's* bar (see below) – in Italian, but comprehensive and comprehensible. For more general info about what's on where, get a copy of Catania's daily newspaper, *La Sicilia*, which has city entertainment listings, available from kiosks all over the centre.

At night, serious **drinking** goes on in *La Cantinaccia*, a birreria-ristorante on the corner of piazza Europa and via Messina. *Nievski's*, on via Alessi (off via Crocíferi), intriguingly describes itself as a 'pub alternativo'. For more of the same, *The Other Place Pub* is at via E. Reina 18 (just off piazza Università; closed Mon); and *Engisa*, piazza Michelangelo, decked out in art nouveau style, is out in the modern city, bus #35 from Corso Sicilia.

As far as cultural entertainment goes, there are occasional open-air **concerts** – jazz and classical – held in the summer in the Villa Bellini; and the Catania **jazz festival** runs from November to April, with gigs in the Teatro Metropolitan, via S. Euplio (parallel to via Etnea, next to the Villa Bellini) and Teatro Nuovo, via Re Martino (bus #23 from piazza Stesicoro). The *Cine-Club Ariston*, via Balduino holds foreign **film seasons** (in the original language) from November to May; bus #22 from piazza Stesicoro to via Giuffrida. Of the city's **theatres**, the Teatro Mássimo Bellini (p.152) is the most famous: the opera season starts in December and runs through until May; musical recitals are held before that, roughly October to December. You'll have to go elsewhere to see plays: either to the Teatro Stábile, via Rasa 3 (off viale Mario Rapisardi; bus #21 from piazza Stesicoro) or, for more alternative productions, to Teatro Musco, via Umberto 312 and Teatro Nuovo (see above) – though all performances are in Italian. You might be able to make more of a **puppet-show** performance, but this involves leaving Catania and heading out to ACIREALE (see below), an easy evening excursion.

One of Sicily's best **festivals**, the *Festa di Sant'Agata*, takes place in Catania between February 3 and 5. A golden statue of the saint is dragged through the streets, there are fireworks in piazza del Duomo, special stalls in via Etnea selling festival nougat and sweets, and the highlight of the event is the procession of the *Cannaroli* – long candles, up to six metres high, carried for hours at a time by groups representing the different trades. A prize is given to the group which holds out the longest.

Listings

Airlines *Air France* (Corso Mártiri della Libertà 188; ☎095-532.210); *Alitalia* (Corso Sicilia 111; ☎095-252.333); *Air Malta* (via M. Ventimiglia 117; ☎095-317.674); *British Airways* (Corso Mártiri della Libertà 38; ☎095-313.755); *Lufthansa* (Corso Italia 72; ☎095-533.138); *Pan Am* (via M. Ventimiglia 117; ☎095-325.183); *TWA* (Corso Mártiri della Libertà 38; ☎095-321.119).

Airport Buses Buy tickets for bus #24 into the centre from the airport *tabacchi*; note that buses from Catania to Agrigento and Enna make a stop at the airport. Direct services, too, from the airport to Messina and Milazzo (for the Aeolian Islands); see *Travel Details*.

American Express Cash cheques and collect mail at *La Duca & C.*, via Etnea 63; Mon–Fri 9.30am–1pm & 4.30–8pm, Sat 9am–12.30pm.

Bus terminals *AST* has two terminals: outside the railway station for services to Acireale, Etna (Rifugio Sapienza) and the locality; piazza Bellini for Caltagirone, Módica, Siracusa. Other operators are *Etna Trasporti*, via Luigi Sturzo 236 (to Gela, Licata, Piazza Armerina, Ragusa); *Fratelli Scionti*, via Terranova, off piazza Mártiri (to Augusta); *SAIS*, piazza Bellini (to Messina/Taormina, Enna, Agrigento, Caltanissetta, Palermo, Nicosia, Siracusa, Noto, Pachino).

Car hire *Hertz* (☎095-341.595) and *Holiday Car Rental* (☎095-346.769) at the airport; *Avis*, via San Giuseppe La Rena 87 (☎095-347.116); *InterRent*, via Firenze 104 (☎095-444.063); *Maggiore*, piazza G. Verga (☎095-310.002).

Chemists Night chemists at via Etnea 274 (☎095-317.053), via Vittorio Emanuele II 54 (☎095-531.400) and Corso Italia 105 (☎095-383.536).

Club Alpino Italiano At via Vecchia Ognina 169 (off viale della Libertà): for climbing advice, information and maps of Mount Etna.

Emergencies Call ☎095-375.050 for an ambulance.

Etna Organised day-trips to the volcano from *CIT*, via A. di Sangiuliano 208, Catania (☎095-317.393).

Exchange There's an exchange office, *Agenzia Cambio*, at via S. Maria del Rosario 2, off piazza dell'Università (Mon–Fri 8.30am–1pm & 3.30–7.30pm, Sat 8.30am–1pm).

Ferry tickets *Tirrenia Società Navigazione* (piazza Grenoble 26, ☎095-316.394) for services to Réggio di Calabria, Naples, Siracusa and Malta. Note also there's a new summer catamaran service to Malta: ask in any travel agent, and see *Travel Details*.

Hospital Casualty at the following hospitals: *Ospedale Generale Garibaldi*, piazza S. Maria di Gesù (☎095-322.344); *Santa Marta*, via Clementi 36, (☎095-310.433); *S. Tomaselli*, via Passo Gravina 185, (☎095-330.333).

Left luggage At the railway station, open 24hr, L1000 per day.

Post Office and Poste Restante at via Etnea 215, close to the Villa Bellini; Mon–Sat 8am–8pm.

Swimming pool *Piscina Comunale* at viale Kennedy (near the campsites; bus #27 or #D).

Taxis Ranks at the railway station, piazza Duomo and piazza Stesicoro; to call a cab, ring ☎095-330.966.

Telephones *SIP* at via S. Euplio 118 (daily 8am–10pm). Telephone offices also at the airport daily (8am–8pm) and (24hr) at via A. Longo 54 (next to the botanical gardens).

Travel agents *Elisea* travel agency, Corso Italia 31; *CTS*, via Balduino 38 (Mon/Wed/Fri 9.30am–1pm & 5–7pm, Tues & Thurs 9.30am–1pm). Both deal in *BIJ* tickets and cheap flights, etc.

North of the city: the coastal route

Although all the good sand beaches are to the south of Catania, it's the coast **north of the city** that's the most popular holiday area. The lava streams from Etna have reached the sea many times over the centuries, turning the coastline into an attractive mix of contorted black rocks and sheer coves, excellent for swimming. Consequently, what was once a series of small fishing villages, stretching from **Ognina** as far as **Acireale**, is now a fair-sized strip of hotels, lidos and restaurants, idle in the winter but swarming in summer with trippers from the city. It's an appealing coastline, easily reached by *AST* bus from outside the railway station, and while some of the villages – like **Aci Castello** – are really only worth a visit when the summer is well under way, Baroque Acireale warrants a day trip from Catania at any time.

It's an area that has taken well to imaginative interpretation. The 19C Sicilian novelist, Giovanni Verga, set his masterpiece *I Malavoglia* in and around the village of Aci Trezza; and some of the better-known of the Homeric myths have been ascribed to this locality. The prefix 'Aci', given to a number of settlements here, derives from the local river Aci, said to have appeared following the death of the herdsman Acis at the hands of the giant, one-eyed Polyphemus.

Ognina, Aci Castello and Aci Trezza

Bus #34 from Catania's piazza del Duomo runs right the way to **OGNINA**, a small suburb on the northern outskirts of Catania. Built on lava cliffs formed in the 15C, it's an easy break from the city: there are a few restaurants here, overlooking the little harbour, as well as a campsite.

To go any further north you'll need to change onto one of the frequent *AST* buses, which run up the coast to Acireale, stopping first in **ACI CASTELLO**, nine kilometres from the city. Here, as the name suggests, there's a **castle** (Tues–Sun 9am–1pm & 3–5pm, summer 5–7.30pm; free), a lofty 13C building that rises above the sea in splinters from a volcanic rock crag. It was the base of the rebel Roger di Lauria in 1297 and is remarkably well-preserved, despite many volcanic explosions and the destruction wrought by Frederick II of Aragon, who took the castle from Roger by erecting a wooden siege-engine adjacent. In town, there are a couple of small trattorias, handy for lunch, while the ragged coastline to the north is popular for sunbathing and swimming: in summer, a wooden boardwalk is built over the lava rocks here and you pay a small fee to use the changing-rooms and showers.

Aci Castello marks the beginning of the so-called *Riviera dei Ciclopi*, named after the jagged points of the **Scogli dei Cicopli** which rise from the sea just beyond the town. Homer wrote that the blinded Polyphemus slung these rocks, broken from Etna, at Ulysses as he and his men escaped from the Cyclops in their ships. The three main sharp-edged islets present an odd sight (the largest sticking some 60m into the sky) and it's a good half-day's diversion to get off the bus at Aci Castello, and walk the couple of kilometres north along the rough coast to **ACI TREZZA**. Here, right opposite the rocks, on the lungomare, is a fine **restaurant**, *I Faraglioni* – in a posh four-star hotel, but with great views and food. If you want to stay in the area, there's a **campsite** at Aci Trezza; *Camping Galatea* (☎095-631.026; June to Sept), right on the coast, at via Livorno 148.

Acireale

ACIREALE, sixteen kilometres from Catania, is marvellously sited, high above the rocky shore and the surrounding lemon groves, something best appreciated from the public gardens at the northern end of town: from here you can look right back along the *Riviera dei Ciclopi*. Known since Roman times as a spa centre, Acireale's sulphur baths (*Terme di Santa Vénera*) are still in use, though visitors these days are more likely to be attracted by the town's striking examples of Sicilian Baroque in the crowded central streets. This, the fourth successive town on the site, was rebuilt directly over the old lava streams after the 1693 earthquake. As in Catania, the result is a planned town-centre which relies on a few grand buildings, a handsome square and some long thoroughfares for its effect.

All the finest buildings are right in the centre, on and around piazza del Duomo. The restored **Duomo**, with its extravagant tiled spires, still retains a good Baroque portal; it's the bigger of two churches in the open square. Over the way, facing the piazza from via Romeo, is the long **Municipio**; a little further down, in piazza Vigo, the church of **San Sebastiano** sports an elaborate balustraded facade, decked-out with a barrage of statues; and straight up from piazza del Duomo is the grand **Palazzo Musmeci**, in piazza San Domenico. It won't take long to whip around this compact enclave of decorative Baroque work and once you've done that, there's little else to detain you in town though you might derive some small interest from the art and historical collections in the **Pinacoteca Zelantea** (Mon–Fri 10am–1pm & 3–6pm, Sat 10am–1pm; free), just off piazza San Domenico.

A visit to Acireale really pays dividends if you come at *Carnevale* (see p.26), when it hosts one of Sicily's best **festivals**, flower-decked floats and fancy-dress parades clogging the streets for five noisy days. There's more traditional entertainment, too, in Acireale's surviving **puppet theatre**: currently, there are performances during August and September, every Tuesday at 9pm, at *Opera dei Pupi*, via Alessi 7; check with the AAST (see below).

Some practicalities

You can get to Acireale by **train**, though the railway station is well to the south of town, near the sulphur baths, and it's a long walk into the centre along Corso Vittorio Emanuele. It's better to arrive by **bus**, either locally from Catania or stopping off on the *SAIS* Catania-Messina route: local buses stop along the main Corso Umberto, or at the ranks outside the public garden, at the end of the Corso; the Messina buses pass piazza del Duomo. If you need information, the **AAST** is at Corso Umberto 177 (Mon–Fri 9am–1pm & 4–7pm; ☎095-604.521). With Catania so close, you shouldn't need to **stay** in Acireale, though if you're stuck the *Pattis*, via Libertà 9 (☎095-605.181; L28,000), is the cheapest option – on the way into town from the railway station. Around festival time, everywhere in town will be full.

There's hardly anywhere decent to get a meal in Acireale. Best bet – and something that's worth doing anyway if you've got time to kill – is to stroll the couple of kilometres downhill to the tiny hamlet of **SANTA MARIA LA SCALA**, where there's a harbour full of painted fishing-boats, a tiny church and three or four **trattorias** overlooking the small bay. It's about half an hour's walk, down via Romeo (to the side of the Municipio), across the main road and then down the path to the water. You might fancy the **campsite** nearby, too; *Camping La Timpa* (☎095-894.420; open all year), via Floristella 25, next to the sea.

South: across the Piana di Catania

There's a real paucity of places to stop south of the city, certainly compared to the good day-trips to be made to the north. Partly, this is down to geographical factors, much of the land a vast, largely uninhabited plain, the **Piana di Catania**. Known to the Greeks as the Laestrygonian Fields after the cannibal Laestrygones who was reputed to live there, it's a fertile region, rich agricultural land full of citrus trees and other crops. You'll head across here on the way to Siracusa, or taking the motorway to Enna, and it's a pretty enough ride through the windmill-dotted flat fields, but the only features of interest lie on the very fringes of the plain. Closest to Catania are the good sand **beaches** which line the wide Golfo di Catania, reached by taking buses #24, #27 or #D from the city; there are also three big campsites here which front the sea, see p.147.

Lentini

LENTINI, half an hour or so out from Catania, has a long pedigree that puts it among the earliest of the Greek settlements in Sicily, and the first of all the inland colonies. Established in 729 BC as a daughter-city of Naxos, Lentini (Leontinoi) flourished as a commercial centre for two hundred years, before falling foul of Hippocrates of Gela. Later, the city was absorbed by Syracuse, sharing its disasters but never its prosperity. It was Leontinoi's struggle to assert its independence, by allying itself with Athens, that provided the pretext for the great Athenian expedition against Syracuse in 415 BC. Another attempt – this time an alliance with the Carthaginians during the Second Punic War – resulted in the Romans beheading 2000 of its citizens, a measure that horrified the whole island, as no doubt it was intended to do. By the time Cicero got round to describing the city, Lentini was 'wretched and empty', though it continued as a small-scale agricultural centre for some time, until the great earthquake of 1693 completely demolished it.

Some of the ancient city survives today as an extensive archaeological site, a couple of kilometres out of the modern town, and Lentini itself has a good collection of finds in the town's **Museo Archeologico** (Mon–Sat 9am–2pm; Sun 9am–1pm; free), which should be visited first in order to make any sense of the site. It's in piazza del Liceo, close to the central piazza del Duomo, and includes artefacts from all stages of Lentini's long history, though some of the best have been appropriated by the museums at Catania and Siracusa. All the same, you'll see plenty of examples of the local pottery, a graphic reconstruction of the ancient city's south gate, and plans of the site itself.

The **Zona Archeologica** (daily 8am–1hr before sunset; free) is a twenty-minute walk north, between the modern town and nearby CARLENTINI, on the Catania-Lentini bus route. Or take buses #1 or #2 from Lentini's railway station, and get off at piazza San Francesco on the outskirts of Carlentini. The site is five minutes' signposted walk away, spread over the two hills of San Mauro and Metapíccola. The first of these is the more interesting, holding the ancient town's acropolis and substantial remains of a vast necropolis nearby, from which most of the museum's contents come. You'll see the pincer-style **south gate** immediately, part of a well-conserved system of fortifications that surrounded the ancient town. After about 600 BC, Leontinoi expanded over the opposite hill of Metapíccola, though the remains here are very scanty: the foundations of a Greek temple, and some scattered huts belonging to an earlier native village, mentioned by Thucydides. Together, the hills make a good couple of hours' rambling.

Back in modern Lentini there's not much else that might induce you to prolong your visit, though if you need a **place to stay**, the *Carmes* hotel, via Vittorio Emanuele III 10 (☎095-901.902; L26,000), isn't a bad deal, near piazza del Duomo. Lentini has two good **ristorante-pizzerias**: the *America*, piazza delle Resistenze 27, and the *Ben Kenia*, on via Gela; low-price set menus at both. **Arriving by bus**, you'll be deposited near the cathedral, from where it's an easy walk to the museum. **Train arrivals** would do well to take a city bus to the centre of town (#3 or #4); if you want to do the twenty-minute walk, go left out of the station and up the long main road (via Riccardo Valentini), turning right at the end into via Vittorio Emanuele, and left at the *IP* service station for the museum.

MOUNT ETNA

Mount Etna is one of the world's largest volcanoes, and dominates much of Sicily's eastern landscape, its smoking summit a familiar feature when travelling in this area. The main crater is still dangerously active: as late as 1985, an eruption destroyed local roads and threatened the mountain refuge that is the main base for trippers up to the top. Earlier eruptions, stretching right back into antiquity, have done far worse – devastating Catania, repeatedly ripping up the cultivated fields and farms, with the lava flows even reaching the sea on several occasions. Yet the volcano remains a remarkable draw for travellers, and really demands that you set aside at least a day to see it.

If you're pushed for time you'll have to make do with the glimpsed views of its peak and hinterland from the **Circumetnea railway**, a circular route from Catania to Riposto which provides one of Sicily's most fascinating rides. It passes through some intriguing settlements: medieval **Randazzo** is the only place you might want to stop over, but there's interest in the towns of **Paternò** and **Adrano**, both with fine castles, while **Linguaglossa** is the base for Etna's ski resorts. If you're driving, you can follow exactly the same route as the railway, around the volcano, a minor but perfectly adequate road sticking close to the line.

There are interesting villages, too, on the **south eastern** side of Etna, worth stopping in for their proximity to the lower craters: **Nicolosi** is an important ski-centre and within walking distance of craters blown open in the 17C. But skirting the foothills of the volcano can only be second-best to **the ascent** to the top, a trip worth every effort to make. Although you're not allowed to reach the main crater itself, getting to the ones just below is possible and not at all dangerous.

The Circumetnea railway: Catania to Riposto

The **Circumetnea railway** (*Ferrovia Circumetnea*) is a private line, 114km long, which runs around the base of the volcano through fertile vegetation – citrus plantations, vines and nut trees – and past (often through) the strewn lava of recent eruptions. It's a marvellous ride, across Etna's foothills with endless views of the peak, starting in Catania and circling Etna as far as Riposto on the Ionian coast. There's only thirty kilometres between the two places if you go on the direct coastal route, which means that you can circumnavigate the volcano and get back to Catania on the same day: if you make the entire trip, to Riposto, allow around five hours, plus another half an hour back to Catania. *InterRail* passes are not valid on the railway, and tickets for the whole route (though not including the coastal trip back to Catania) cost L4,600 one-way, L8,600 return: buy them on the train, or visit the Circumetnea office in Catania, at Corso delle Province 13 (see *Travel Details* for schedules). Incidentally, the office is also the place to find out about a couple of related **side-trips** from Catania, organised by *Ferrovia Circumetnea*: there's a daily 9am bus (July to Sept) which heads to the hill resort and ski-base of Piano Provenzana, with a wine-tasting on the way, and costs L14,000 return (back in Catania around 9pm); while every Sunday in winter (Jan to April), skiers can take a bus (7am, return 4.30pm) to the same place, for L7,000 return. Piano Provenzana is covered on p.165.

Something to note is that **accommodation** in the towns around Etna is scarce, so if you're going to stop over anywhere, plan – and ring – ahead; see the text for details of hotels.

Catania to Bronte

The first part of the route runs out through Catania's grim suburbs, **MISTERBIANCO** the first stop. Soon, though, the first of the citrus- and olive-groves are visible and, by the time you reach **PATERNÒ**, you're well within sight of Etna's southern slopes. A lively town in the valley of the river Simeto, Paternò clusters around its main street, via Vittorio Emanuele, its railway station at one end, a medieval **castello** at the other. Founded by Count

Roger in 1073, this is largely 13C (though much restored) and it's worth going into for the view from the terrace at the top – the reason the Germans used it as an observation post during World War II. They proved hard to dislodge and 4000 people died here during the subsequent aerial bombardment. There's one **hotel** in Paternò, the *Sicilia*, via Vittorio Emanuele 391 (☎095-841.700l; L40,000 with bath), though it's rather grumpily run and usually full.

Ten kilometres further on, **BIANCAVILLA** was founded by Albanian refugees in 1480. The area around is devoted to growing oranges, and small sideroads from here run up through the orchards and on to the higher, south western slopes of Etna – a nice little diversion if you're coming this way by car. **ADRANO**, close by, is one of the more interesting stops hereabouts, built over the site of ancient Adranon, a town founded by Dionysius the Elder – parts of the Greek lava-built **walls** are still visible in town, though they're barely distinguishable from later fortifications. Much more impressive is the **castello**, another of Count Roger's creations and, like Paternò, squat, solid and battlemented. Inside there's a small **museum** (Tues–Sat 8.30am–1pm, Sun 9am–noon) with finds from local sites, including early Bronze Age pottery. Take a look, too, in the **Chiesa Madre**, next to the castle, which has some good artwork inside, though the outside is disfigured by an unfinished modern campanile. The old centre of Adrano provides a fairly pleasant wander, with its spacious gardens and faded churches; for **lunch**, try *La Posata* trattoria, in piazza Mercato, near the Giardino della Vittoria.

If you're travelling under your own steam, there are a couple of possible side-trips from Adrano. Around eight kilometres west, near CÁRCACI, the **Ponte dei Saraceni** is a 14C bridge which arches over the river Simeto (at the end of the first road on the right after Cárcaci; keep to the right). And south west of town, on the SS575 (before it meets the SS121 to Catania), is **Eurelios**, a massive solar-energy centre at the foot of a volcanic plateau on the same river. It's the biggest in Europe, completed in 1982, and there are **free guided tours** if you arrive between 9am and 1pm, or 2pm and 6pm, Tuesday to Sunday.

Between Adrano and Bronte are some of the best views of Etna, as the railway line and road climb ever closer to the lava flows that have marked the landscape further north. **BRONTE** lies about halfway along the Circumetnea route, its rather shabby, amorphous aspect belying its noble past. Founded by Charles V in 1535, many echoes of its original layout survive, particularly in the town's numerous battlemented and pointed campanili which top its ageing churches. The town gave its name to the dukedom bestowed upon Nelson, the English admiral, in 1799, and his ducal seat (the Castello Maniace, see below) is a few kilometres north of town. Otherwise, Bronte's sole claim to fame these days is as the centre of Italy's pistachio-nut production, the plantations around town accounting for 85 per cent of the country's output. It's also a handy jumping-off point for an extended trip into the interior of Sicily, buses heading to CESARÒ, from where a fine route cuts west into the Nébrodi hills – covered in chapter 6.

Back on the Circumetnea, beyond Bronte the pistachios give way to walnuts and chestnuts, and the train passes the huge lava flow of 1823 which came close to destroying the town. A little further on, **MALETTO** is the highest point on the Circumetnea line. From here, a very minor road leads west – or there are regular **buses** from Bronte – to the **Castello Maniace** (Tues–Sat 10am–12.30pm & 4–7.30pm, Sun 10am–1pm), founded as a convent in 1174 on the site of a victory over the Arabs by George Maniakes, when he was attempting to regain the island for Byzantium. The 1693 earthquake destroyed much of the building, but the estate was given to Lord Nelson as part of his dukedom, granted by King Ferdinand in gratitude for British help in repressing the Neapolitan revolution of 1799, which had forced the Bourbon court to flee to Palermo. Nelson never got round to visiting his Sicilian estate and his family cut their last links with the property in 1978 – it's now owned by the *comune*. Maniakes' walled castle and the fallen lava-built church are both undergoing long-term restoration, but you can gain entry to the well-tended garden, English in style but for the presence of palm trees.

Randazzo

Closest town to the volcano's summit as the crow flies, **RANDAZZO** is easily the most interesting stop on the route. The dark medieval town is built entirely of lava and despite being dangerously near Etna, it has never been engulfed – though an eruption in 1981 came perilously close; the lava flow is easily visible just outside town. Randazzo was also one of the main forward positions of the German forces during their defence of Sicily in 1943 and everything in town was bombed to bits. But the churches and buildings from the wealthy 13–16C period have been meticulously restored, and there's great interest in its dingy authentic streets.

In medieval times three churches took it in turns to act as cathedral, a sop to the three parishes in town whose inhabitants were of Greek, Latin and Lombard origin and had little in common. The largest, **Santa Maria**, in the main Corso Umberto, is the modern-day holder of the title, a severe Catalan-Gothic structure incorporating chunks of volcanic rock. Better is the church of **San Martino**, further up the road on the northern edge of town, which features a 14C campanile, cracked and moss-ridden. Across the square, the blackened tower which forms part of the old city walls is all that survives of Randazzo's castle. From the 15C until about fifteen years ago, it did duty as a prison, though it's soon to open as the town's museum.

Randazzo practicalities

Arriving in Randazzo on the Circumetnea line, walk straight down the road in front of you to reach the central piazza Loreto; the medieval town is down via Umberto and away to the left. The **bus station** is a couple of blocks back from piazza Loreto, towards the Circumetnea station (down via Vittorio Véneto). There's a regular *FS* **railway station** too, from which you can catch frequent trains to the coast, at Taormina-Giardini, an hour away. It's another block over from the bus station.

If you wanted to break the journey around Etna, Randazzo is the best place to get **lunch**: *La Veneziana*, in via del Santuario, behind the *Scrivano* hotel (see below) isn't particularly cheap but has excellent food. (Incidentally, avoid the well-signposted *La Trottola*, which is dire and pricey.) Randazzo has a lively *passeggiata* up and down Corso Umberto, a street with some nice, old-fashioned bars (like the *Arturo*). However, the only **accommodation** is uninspiring: the tatty *Motel Scrivano* (☎095-921.126; L32,000) behind the *Agip* petrol station on via Regina Margherita, off piazza Loreto.

East to Riposto

The lava flows around Randazzo are quite clearly defined, and from the train you'll see great rivers of volcanic rubble cluttering the slopes. Occasionally, all that survives of a former orchard or vineyard is the wall, visible through the wreckage. Naturally, the views of Etna are magnificent this close to the summit – just fifteen kilometres away. Road and rail stick close together around the northernmost stretch of the route, passing the station at CASTIGLIONE DI SICILIA (a good five kilometres from the town, see p.141) and, shortly after, running into **LINGUAGLOSSA**. It's the main tourist centre on Etna's northern slopes, but for all that a quiet town during the summer, with locals' bars lining the cobbled streets, and extensive pine forests out of the centre, good for a ramble. It's a different story in winter when Linguaglossa becomes a busy **ski centre**, although all the equipment, ski-schools and ski-lifts are out of town, fifteen kilometres further up the mountain, at Piano Provenzana (see p.165); information from the helpful Linguaglossa **Pro Loco**, in piazza Annunziata (daily 9.30am–12.30pm & 4.30–7.30pm). If you're going to **stay** in town in summer, there should be no problem finding space; try the *Hotel Centrale* (☎095-643.548; L20,000) in piazza Municipio, just down from the Pro Loco. And there's even a campsite, though again it's out of town, ten kilometres up the road to Piano Provenzana.

Back on the train, after a fairly uneventful forty-minute ride – all the best views of Etna have been and gone – the Circumetnea route ends on the coast at the twin-town of GIARRE-RIPOSTO. There's no reason to linger here longer than the time it takes to change stations for your onward transport: it's a sprawling, largely modern town, split between gridded **GIARRE** (which has its own *FS* railway station as well as a Circumetnea stop) and, down the long, main Corso Italia, the shabby port area of **RIPOSTO**. To switch onto the main *FS* line (for **trains** to Taormina or Catania) walk the short distance from Riposto's Circumetnea station to Corso Italia and bear left up the hill into Giarre – the mainline station is signposted up on the right after about ten minutes. For **buses** to Taormina, Messina and Catania, keep going straight uphill to the piazza in front of Giarre's grand Duomo. It would be hard luck indeed to get stuck here for the night; if you do, head for the cheap *Sicilia* (☎095-931.868; L26,000 with bath), via Gallipoli 444, near the mainline station. At the bottom of Corso Italia, around piazza San Pietro, there are a few bars, a couple of trattorias and views over the working boatyard. Much more attractive, if you're mobile, is to head up the coast, three kilometres north, to FONDACHELLO, where there are two seaside **campsites**; *La Zagara*, via Spiaggia 127 (☎095-966.979; June to Oct), and *Mokambo*, via Spiaggia 131 (☎095-938.731; April to Sept), signposted from just about everywhere on this stretch of coast. Both also have cabins available for rent.

The volcano: its foothills . . . and an ascent

Although the Circumetnea route takes in some fairly adventurous scenery, you get little impression of Etna as an active volcano except for the odd lava flow. This can only really be gleaned by making the effort to roam around the **northern and south eastern foothills**, much closer to the summit than the towns on the Circumetnea route – though without your own transport the effort can be considerable. Still, it's not impossible to get around the foothills and craters by public transport, and there are buses from Catania that link some of the villages, notably **Zafferana Etnea** and **Nicolosi**.

The major attraction, though, is a trip to the **summit** of what, at 3323m high, is a fairly substantial mountain – the fact that it's also an active volcano only adds to its fascination. Etna was just one of the places that the Greeks thought to be the forge of Vulcan, a fitting description of the blustering and sparking from the main crater. The philosopher Empedocles studied the volcano closely, living in an observatory near the summit. This presumably terrifying existence was dramatised by Matthew Arnold in his *Empedocles on Etna*:

> *Alone! –*
> *On this charr'd, blacken'd melancholy waste,*
> *Crown'd by the awful peak, Etna's great mouth.*

Certainly, it all proved too much for Empedocles, who in 433 BC jumped into the main crater in an attempt to prove that the gases emitted would support his body weight.

Of the scores of recorded **eruptions** since that of 475 BC (described by Pindar), some have been disastrously spectacular: in 1169, 1329 and 1381 the lava reached the sea, while in 1669, the worst year, Catania was wrecked and its castle surrounded by molten rock. In this century, the Circumetnea railway line has been repeatedly ruptured by lava flows, the towns of the foothills threatened and roads and farms destroyed, and in 1979, nine tourists were killed by an explosion on the edge of the main crater.

This unpredictability means that it's no longer possible to get close to the main crater. An eruption in 1971 destroyed the observatory supposed to give warning of such an event; another in 1983 brought down the cable-car which provided access – not the first time this had happened. There are plans to re-open the cable-car, but at present access is by ten kilometres of rough track. All this is not to say you'll be in any danger, provided you heed the warnings as you get closer to the top.

Approaches: around the northern and south eastern foothills

If you're short on time and not mobile, the easiest way to see the volcano and climb its slopes is by **organised tour** from either Catania or Taormina. These are usually full-day tours, including transport there and back, an accompanied trip up to the craters, and protective clothes and boots – around L50,000 per person, plus another L15,000 for lunch if you want it. Of the

agents, try *CIT*, via A. di Sangiuliano 208, Catania (☎095-317.393), at Catania airport; and Corso Umberto 101, Taormina (☎0942-23.301); and see Piano Provenzana, below.

Otherwise, with your **own transport**, there are several **approaches** to the craters. Some of the best scenery is on the **north side** (signposted *Etna Nord*), from the road that leads up from Linguaglossa (see p.163). A tortuous fifteen-kilometre road corkscrews up past the skiing pistes of **Piano Provenzana**; the settlement of Mareneve beyond doesn't exist anymore, despite still being marked on most maps. In the summer (July to Sept), a daily bus from Catania unloads its passengers at Piano Provenzana, giving them plenty of time for lunch and the opportunity to reach some of the craters higher up by jeep – a trip that will take around three hours and cost another L20,000. If you're around anyway, you should be able to find space on the jeep; otherwise the walking around here is especially good, and you'll have no trouble staying at the *Clan dei Ragazzi* (☎095-643.611; June to Sept) **campsite**: it's in the pinewoods, five kilometres below Piano Provenzana. If you're coming to ski, book accommodation in Linguaglossa well in advance.

A lower, more direct road leads south from Linguaglossa past various old lava flows – of 1852, 1950 and, near FORNAZZO, of 1979 – to **MILÒ**, fifteen kilometres away. Here, there are impressive views of the Valle del Bove above – see p.167 for more views of this, from the top. Maps show a road from Milò which climbs north west, up the volcano to the *Rifugio Citelli* and back towards Linguaglossa, but it's currently blocked by a landslide. You should be able to get some of the way up, though, for more striking views of the summit and the coastline below.

By **public transport**, the only practicable routes into the foothills are on the **south side** of Etna (signposted *Etna Sud*), frequent buses running out of Catania to the nearby villages. Most pleasant of these is **ZAFFERANA ETNEA**, an hour from Catania and surrounded by vineyards and citrus groves. It's a bracing place, with an 18C air to its central buildings and churches, and it makes for a leisurely stop: drinking coffee in the bar on the corner of the elegant central piazza. Zafferana is acquiring a reputation as a low-key hill resort: certainly, there's some good walking to be done in the green hills behind the village, a couple of **hotels**, and a **campsite**, the *Mareneve* (☎095-951.396; open all year), two or three kilometres out of town on the road to Milò. One bus daily (9.20am, not Sun) leaves Zafferana for Rifugio Sapienza (see below), running along a fine road which cuts due west, twisting further up towards the main craters on Etna.

The other easily reached village from Catania is **TRECASTAGNI**, whose main church, the **Chiesa Madre**, is a fine Renaissance building, probably designed by Antonello Gagini and affording marvellous views over the coast from its elevated position. Frankly, though, you're hardly likely to come here for just these; better, if you're mobile, to see Trecastagni as a coffee-stop.

NICOLOSI, a tidy little town just to the west of Trecastagni, is rapidly being developed as a winter ski resort, and is a far more attractive target, with several hotels and some good places to eat. At around 700m, it's pretty brisk in Nicolosi even in summer, and the area around boasts some good walking possibilities. Best of these, certainly if you're going no further, is the hike up to the **Monti Rossi** craters, around an hour each way. Formed in the eruption of 1669, they're the most important of the secondary craters which litter the slopes of the volcano.

Nicolosi is the last main stop before the steeper slopes begin – a good place to pick up information. There's a small **information office** at via Etnea 65 (daily 8.30am–1pm, summer also 4–7.30pm; ☎095-914.206), the main road that runs through town. The **hotels** in Nicolosi are a fairly expensive bunch, though there are some exceptions: try the *Monti Rossi*, via Etnea 179 (☎095-911.000; L22,000), or the *Belvedere*, via Etnea 110 (☎095-911.406; L15,000). The *Monti Rossi* is some way out of town, but it has a traditional wood-fired **pizza** oven which warms the place up in the evenings. If you're **camping**, *Camping Etna* (☎095-914.309; May to Sept) is on via Goethe, signposted from town.

The ascent

Although there are frequent *AST* buses to Nicolosi from Catania, only one (8.05am, from outside Catania railway station) continues to the mountain refuge/hotel which marks the end of the negotiable road up the south side of Etna. It's a bizarre ride. Beyond Nicolosi, the green foothills give way to wooded slopes, then to bare, black and grey seas of volcanic debris, spotted with hardy, endemic plants, the yellow-green *Spino Santo* and Etna violets – the only things to grow on the heights of the volcano. Everywhere, the slopes are dotted with earlier, spent craters, grass-covered on the lower reaches, no more than black pimples further up.

At **RIFUGIO SAPIENZA**, 1400m below the summit, the road ends in a car park, below which are several small, extinct volcanoes and craters which you are free to wander around and into. Further up there's a row of souvenir shops, flogging ashtrays made of lava and the like, a couple of over-priced restaurants and the *Rifugio Sapienza* itself (☎095-911.062l; L35,000). In 1983 and 1985, small-scale eruptions led to the evacuation of guests from the refuge: good photographs inside show it surrounded by the lava streams, the sky glowing red. If you've arrived with your own transport and it's late, this is the best place to **spend the night**, though it's wise to ring ahead and book. Otherwise, arriving on the early morning bus, you'll have enough time to reach the top and get back for the return bus to Catania – it leaves around 4pm from the refuge. Failing that, it's not impossible to cadge a lift down with someone.

Until the cable-car re-opens, there are **two ways up** from the refuge. You can either take one of the tough-looking *SITAS* **minibuses** from outside the old cable-car station (tickets inside, L28,500 each; April to Oct/Nov only), a two-hour return-trip which gives you half an hour clambering around just below the main crater. Or you can **walk**, following the rough minibus track. Really it all depends on finances and time: walking up will take between three to four hours, the return obviously a little less. However you go, take warm clothes, good shoes or boots and – especially if you wear contact lenses – glasses to keep the flying grit out of your eyes.

The volcano is a lunar landscape, the ground under your feet alternately black, grey or red depending on the age of the lava. The more recent stuff lies in great folds, earlier minor craters signposted as you climb; below, the red roofs and green fields of the lower hills stretch away to the sea. Even in winter, the snow on the southern side tends to lie only in patches, partly melted by the heat of the rocks. *

On the way up, the minibus makes a short stop at the **Valle del Bove**, an enormous chasm almost twenty kilometres in circumference, its lava walls 900m high. A massive rent in the side of the volcano, its sunken flank comprises a sixth of the entire surface area of Etna – only one of many mind-boggling photo-opportunities on this trip.

The highest you're allowed to get (on foot or in the bus) is 2900m, from where you can visit the so-called **Torre del Filósofo**, a tower said to have been the home of Empedocles, but more likely a memorial built by the Romans to celebrate the Emperor Hadrian's climb to the summit. From the turn-around point for the minibus you look up to the summit, smoke puffing from the **south east crater** immediately above. Though there's only a rope across the ground to prevent you from climbing further, it would be foolish to presume that nothing serious would happen to you if you did – gaseous explosions and molten rock are common this far up. Higher still is the **main crater**: depending on the weather conditions you'll see smoke from here too, and, if you're lucky, spitting explosions. If you've walked, you'll be glad of the **bar** set up in a wooden hut at the minibus stop, one of the more peculiar places in the world to get a cappuccino.

---

* Over on the northern side, where hollows in the ground are filled year-round with snow, the ice used to be cut, covered with ash and then transported to the rest of the island, the mainland, and even Malta, for refrigeration purposes – a peculiar export which constituted the main source of revenue for the Bishop of Catania, who owned the land until comparatively recently.

festivals

January
15 Festival of San Mauro in ACI CASTELLO.
17 Festival of Sant'Antonio in NICOLOSI.

February
3–5 *Festa di Sant'Agata* in CATANIA: boisterous street events, fireworks and food stalls, and the procession of the saint's relics; see p.154.

February/March
Carnevale Five days of processional floats, flowers and traditional music in ACIREALE – one of Sicily's best annual events. Smaller-scale affair at PATERNÒ.

March/April
Easter Good Friday procession in ACIREALE in traditional costume. Easter Sunday ceremony in ADRANO, the *Diavolata* – a symbolic display showing the Archangel Michael defeating the Devil.

May
9–10 Traditional hi-jinks at TRECASTAGNI: a pilgrimage by athletic souls who, barefoot and shirtless, run the main road linking Catania to the sanctuary at Trecastagni; as well as costumes, painted carts etc.

July
19–26 Festival commemorating Santa Vénera in ACIREALE.
24 *Pesce a Mare* festival at ACI TREZZA: if the EPT is to be believed, 'a fisherman pretends to be a fish and excitedly the local fishermen catch him.' Unmissable.

August
15 Procession of the *vara* in RANDAZZO: an 18m-high column with decorative figures representing the Assumption.

November
11 San Martino's Day celebrations in CATANIA.

December
Christmas week Display of 18C cribs in ACIREALE.

travel details

Trains
From Catania to Lentini/Siracusa (hourly; 30min/1½hr); Acireale/Giarre-Riposto/Taormina/Messina (every 40min; 15 min/30min/1hr/1½hr); Enna/Caltanissetta (9 daily; 1½hr/2½hr); Palermo (4; 3¼hr); Caltagirone/Gela (9; 2hr/2hr 40min).
From Randazzo to Taormina (3–5 daily; 1hr).

Circumetnea trains
From Catania to Paternò, Adrano, Bronte, Maletto, Randazzo (11 daily; 2hr 10min).
From Randazzo to Linguaglossa, Giarre, Riposto (8 daily; 1¼hr).

Buses
From Catania to Acireale/Giardini-Naxos/Taormina (6–14 daily; 40min/1hr 25min/1hr 40min); Acireale (half-hourly; 30min); Rifugio Sapienza (1 daily at 8.05am; 2hr); Nicolosi (hourly; 40min); Trecastagni (6–10 daily; 40min); Fornazzo (for Milò, 6 Mon–Sat, 2 Sun; 1¼hr); Zafferana Etnea (hourly, 5 Sun; 1hr); Messina (6–12 daily; 3hr 10min; and hourly, Sun two-hourly by A18 autostrada; 1hr 35min); Palermo (hourly; 2hr 40min); Enna (4–7 daily; 1hr 20min); Agrigento (2–4; 2hr 50min); Lentini (hourly, Sun 6; 30min); Augusta (Mon–Sat 11, Sun 3; 50min); Siracusa (Mon–Sat 7, Sun 1; 1¼hr); Noto/Pachino (Mon–Sat 5, Sun 1; 2¼hr/3hr); Caltagirone (Mon–Sat 7; 1½hr); Piazza Armerina (Mon–Sat 5, Sun 2; 2hr); Gela (Mon–Sat 7, Sun 2; 2hr); Ragusa (4–8; 3hr).
From Catania airport to Milazzo (June to Sept, not Sun, 1 daily at 3.30pm; 2hr); Enna (2–5 daily; 1hr 10min); Agrigento (2–3; 2½hr); Messina by autostrada (1–2 at 9.30am and 7pm; 2hr).
From Randazzo to Maletto/Bronte/Cesarò (Mon–Sat 3 daily; 20min/30min/1hr); Giardini-Naxos/Messina (Mon–Sat 4; 1hr 20min/2¼hr).
From Bronte to Castello Maniace (Mon–Sat 5 daily; 20min).
From Lentini to Siracusa (Mon–Sat 9 daily, Sun 1; 40min).

Ferries
From Catania to Siracusa/Malta (3 weekly; 2¼hr/8½hr); Réggio di Calabria (3 weekly; 3¼hr); Naples (1 weekly; 15hr).

Hydrofoil
From Catania to Malta (June to Sept 2 daily; 2hr 25min).

CHAPTER FIVE

SIRACUSA AND THE SOUTH EAST

S icily's **south east** corner is dense with interest, an area whose historic towns and vigorous scenery merit as much time as you can give it. This has always been one of the island's wealthiest enclaves, reflected in the opulence of its building styles, and especially in **Siracusa** (Syracuse), whose long and glorious history outshines all other Sicilian cities. With its streets displaying examples of the architecture of almost every age, Siracusa has managed to survive the earthquakes that have repeatedly afflicted the area, none so destructive as that of 1693, which affected the whole of the region as far north as Catania. This upheaval did, however, produce one positive and lasting effect: where there were ruins, a confident new generation of architects raised planned towns, displaying a

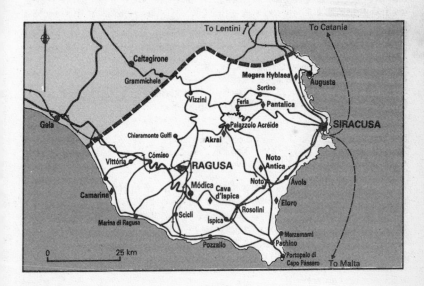

noble but vivacious **Baroque style** – of which **Noto**, **Ragusa** and **Módica** are the most outstanding examples.

In contrast to the refinement of its cities, much of the south eastern landscape is rough and wild, cut through by the **Monti Iblei** and riven by unexpected and often spectacular ravines, or *cave*. Wedged in one of these, **Pantálica**, west of Siracusa, is Sicily's greatest necropolis. Nearby **Palazzolo Acréide** has the best of the classical digs outside Siracusa, while there are several other sites along the coast, often beside uncrowded expanses of sand.

SIRACUSA AND AROUND

Once **Siracusa** was the most important city in the western world. Now, with most of Sicily's business activity located elsewhere and all political power centred on Palermo, the port's only status is that of a mere provincial capital. Yet although Siracusa retains the intimacy of a small town at its heart, it's charged with historical resonance. There's no shortage of things to see, and it's a useful base for visiting any of the other places mentioned below, all on bus routes and few more than 45 minutes from the city.

Like Siracusa, **Augusta**, to the north, is a port centred on an offshore islet, but the similarity ends there. The coast between the two, the **Golfo di Augusta**, has Sicily's greatest concentration of industry, a petrochemical nightmare of immense proportions, almost overwhelming what's left of the old Greek city of **Megara Hyblaea**. Inland, the high mountainous area around **Pantálica**, occupied since the 13C BC, has preserved this ancient necropolis from 20C intrusions, while the nearby town of **Palazzolo Acréide** shelters the site of Greek **Akrai**. You have to head south, though, for the biggest draw in Siracusa's hinterland: the town of **Noto**, whose charms vie with those of the provincial capital, but are dedicated to the perfection of just one artistic style, the Baroque.

The coast around here has plenty of good **beaches**, trailing off into a humdrum series of small resorts dotting Sicily's southern cape, **Capo Pássero**.

Siracusa

More than any other Sicilian city, **SIRACUSA** (ancient Syracuse) has a past that is central not just to the island's history, but to that of the entire Mediterranean region. Its greatest splendour belongs to antiquity: Syracuse established its ascendancy over other Sicilian cities for more than five hundred years and at its height was the supreme power in Europe, with at least three times its present population. Its central position on the major trade routes ensured that even after its heyday the port continued to wield influence and preserve its prestige.

All this is reflected in a staggering diversity of monuments, spanning the Hellenic, early Christian, Medieval, Renaissance and Baroque eras – the styles often shoulder-to-shoulder, sometimes in the same building. Combined with its inspired location, this distracting medley makes Siracusa one of the most enjoyable towns in Sicily to spend time in.

Some history

The **ancient city** grew around Ortygia, an easily defensible offshore island with two natural harbours on either side, fresh springs, and access to extensive fertile plains over on the mainland, from which important trade routes weaved inland. These natural advantages couldn't help but attract settlers, and around 733 BC Corinthian colonists arrived here, apparently at the behest of the Delphic oracle. But it wasn't until the beginning of the 5C BC that the city's political position was boosted by an alliance with Greeks at Akragas (Agrigento) and Gela. With the crushing victory of their combined forces over the Carthaginians at Himera in 480 BC (p.87), and the transfer of Gela's tyrant, **Gelon**, to Syracuse, the stage was set for a century of expansion, and the beginning of the city's long supremacy in the island. The grandest monuments you'll see here are from this period, and more often than not were built by slaves provided from the many victories won by Syracuse's bellicose dictators.

Inevitably, the city's ambitions provoked the intervention of Athens, who dispatched against her one of the greatest fleets ever seen in the ancient world. This **Great Expedition** was scuppered in 413 BC by a mixture of poor leadership and astute defence: 'to the victors the most brilliant of successes, to the vanquished the most calamitous of defeats' commented the historian Thucydides. But Syracuse earned the condemnation of the Hellenic world for its seven-year incarceration of the vanquished Athenians in appalling conditions in the city's notorious quarries, some still visitable today.

Throughout this period Syracuse was in a state of constant tension between a few overweening but extremely capable rulers, and sporadic convulsions of democracy. Occasionally the tyrants displayed a yearning for cultural respectability that sat uncomfortably beside their un-sentimental power-seeking. **Hieron I** (478–466 BC), for instance, described by the historian Diodorus as 'an utter stranger to sincerity and nobility of character', invited many of the luminaries of the age to his court, including **Pindar** and **Aeschylus**, who possibly witnessed the production of his last plays – *Prometheus Bound* and *Prometheus Released* – in the city's theatre. **Dionysius the Elder** (405–367 BC) – 'cruel, vindictive and a profane plunderer of temples' and responsible for the first of the **Euryalus** forts – comically harboured literary ambitions to the extent of regularly entering his poems in the annual Olympic Games. His works were consistently rejected, until the Athenians judged it politic to give him the prize, whereupon his delirious celebrations were enough to provoke the seizure which killed him. His son **Dionysius II** (367–343 BC) dallied with his tutor **Plato**'s 'philosopher-king' theories until megalomania turned his head and Plato fled in dismay. Dionysius himself, recorded Plutarch, spent the end of his life in exile, 'loitering about the fish-market, or sitting in a perfumer's shop drinking the diluted wine of the taverns, or squabbling in the streets with common women'.

Very rarely, the rulers themselves initiated democratic reforms – men such as **Timoleon** (343–337 BC), who arrived from Corinth to inject new life into all the Sicilian cities, and **Hieron II**, who preserved Syracuse's independence from the assertions of Rome by a novel policy of conciliation, abandoning expansion in favour of preserving the status quo. His long reign (265–215 BC) saw the construction of such monuments as the **Ara di Ierone II**, and the enlargement of the **Teatro Greco** to more or less its existing proportions.

With the death of Hieron, Syracuse, along with practically every other Sicilian city, sided with Carthage against Rome in the Second Punic War. For two years the city was besieged by the Romans, who had to contend with all the ingenious contrivances devised for its defence by **Archimedes**, though Syracuse eventually fell in 211 BC, an event which sent shock waves rippling around the classical world. Syracuse was ransacked, and Archimedes himself – the last of the great Hellenic thinkers – was hacked to death, despite the injunctions of the Roman general Marcellus.

Syracuse languished under Roman rule, and shared in the general despoliation of Sicily carried out by the governor Verres. But its trading role still made it the most prominent Sicilian city, and it became a notable centre of early Christianity, as attested by its extensive **catacombs**. Syracuse briefly became the capital of the Byzantine empire when Constans moved his court here in 663 AD, but otherwise the city was eclipsed by events outside its control, and played no active part in all the successive waves of Arab, Norman and other medieval conquerors. The **Castello Maniace** survives from this period, erected by Frederick II, along with some other important vestiges of 14C and 15C building that help to give Ortygia its lavish appearance today. The 1693 earthquake laid low much of the city, but provided the impetus for some of its Baroque masterpieces, notably the creations of the great Siculo-Spanish architect Giovanni Verméxio, who contributed an imposing facade to the **Duomo** – a building which encapsulates the polyglot appearance of modern Siracusa.

Modern Siracusa: orientation

Siracusa today has kept the same general arrangement as it had two and a half millenia ago, with the city divided between its ancient hub, the island of Ortygia, and the four mainland quarters of Achradina, Tyche, Neapolis and – further west – Epipolae. You'll spend much of your time on **Ortygia**, still the heart and soul of Siracusa, and predominantly medieval and Baroque in appearance. The modern city is centred on mainland **Achradina**, now, as in Greek times, the busy commercial centre, traversed by the main street of **Corso Gelone**. North of Achradina, the old residential quarter of **Tyche** holds Siracusa's **catacombs** and its celebrated **archaeological museum**, while **Neapolis** is the site of an **archaeological park**, containing remains of the Greek city's theatres and some extensive quarries. Spread over the ridge to the west of town, **Epipolae** holds the old defensive walls and the solid remnants of the **Euryalus fort.***

---

* Visitors to Siracusa should bear in mind that many of the city's older remains are prone to temporary closure from one year to the next whilst they are renovated. Currently this applies to all the catacombs except those under San Giovanni church, some of the ancient city's quarries, and some sections of the archaeological park.

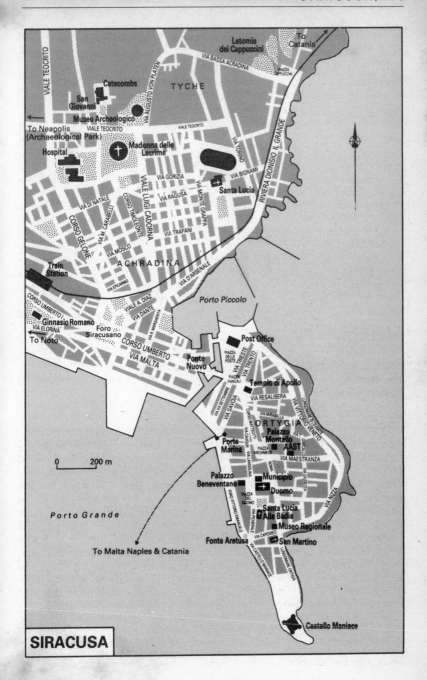

SIRACUSA

Arriving and getting around

Arriving by bus, you'll be deposited in piazza delle Poste on Ortygia, from where it's a five-minute walk either to the island's central square, **piazza Archimede**, or to the broad **Foro Vittorio Emanuele**, where the **ferries** from Naples, Catania and Malta dock. Across the **Ponte Nuovo**, the main bridge linking the island to the mainland, a twenty-minute walk up **Corso Umberto I** will bring you to the **railway station**, where there's a **left-luggage office** (24hr; L1000 a day) if you need to dump your bags. Most of the city's cheaper hotels are around here (see below).

Although much of Siracusa is easy enough to see on foot, you can always avail yourself of the **city buses** when the sightseeing begins to take its toll: the main stops are in piazza Archimede or piazza Pancali/largo XXV Luglio on Ortygia, and along Corso Umberto. One ride costs L600, and relevant routes are specified in the text.

For free maps, accommodation listings and other information, you'll find an **AAST** booth inside the railway station (Mon–Sat 9am–1pm and 3–7pm), but the main office is on Ortygia, at via Maestranza 33 (Tues–Sun 9am–2pm; ☎0931-66.932). The main **EPT** office is at via San Sebastiano 43–45 (Mon–Sat 8.30am–6pm; ☎0931-67.607), and there's also a second office (Mon–Sat 8am–6pm; ☎0931-60.510) housed in a church by the entrance to the archaeological park.

Finding a place to stay

Siracusa's **accommodation** choices aren't spectacular, and in high season you should check-in early, or else make an advance reservation. Also in summer, be prepared to pay another L5000 for obligatory breakfast tacked on to the official prices.

Best-placed is the *Gran Bretagna*, via Savoia 21 (☎0931-68.765; L33,000) – the only hotel in this price-range on Ortygia and often full. Nearest to Ortygia, on the mainland, is the *Hotel Milano*, Corso Umberto 10 (☎0931-66.981; L35,000 with bath). Otherwise, there are several choices close to the railway station: of the row strung along via Francesco Crispi, try the *Aretusa* at no. 75 (☎0931-24.211; L35,000); the *Hotel Centrale*, Corso Umberto 141 (☎0931-60.528; L25,000); or – though rather dingy – the *Pensione Gelone*, via Epicarmo 36 (☎0931-60.004; L25,000), and the *Pantheon*, at via Foro Siracusano 22 (☎0931-60.254; L23,000), the street which tops the Foro Siracusano (signposted from the level crossing).

A much better plan is to head out of town, to the private **youth hostel**, viale Epipoli 45 (☎0931-711.118; L10,000 per person), out at BELVEDERE on the Epipolae ridge, just beyond Euryalus castle. Open all year, it's a clean and relaxed place, with a maximum of four beds per room, serving breakfast and sometimes other meals. Buses #9, #10, and #11 run up here in around twenty minutes from piazza Pancali, the last one leaving at 10pm.

The nearest **campsite** to Siracusa, *Agriturist* (☎0931-721.224; open all year) is five kilometres away, just off the Noto road, turning right after the junction for ARENELLA. It has a few cabins available for rent. If you bus it (#34 or #35 from Corso Umberto) you'll have to walk the last kilometre to the site. There's a second site, posher and near an excellent beach, but it's much further south – twenty kilometres from Siracusa, at FONTANE BIANCHE (see p.184).

Ortygia

The ancient nucleus of Siracusa, **ORTYGIA** best conserves the city's essential spirit. Here are concentrated the artistic vestiges of over 2500 years of history, in a space barely five hundred metres across and a kilometre in length and all within the ambit of an easy stroll through quiet streets and alleys. Although parts of Ortygia have been badly neglected in the past, a recent cleaning-up operation has rescued many of the island's monuments from irreversible damage, helping to restore the old town's lustre.

Across the narrow ribbon of water severing the island from the mainland, the **Tempio di Apollo** is a case in point. This dignified old ruin is thought to have been the first of the great Doric tembles built in Sicily, though not much survives of its 7C or early 6C BC fabric apart from a couple of columns, fragments of others, and part of the south wall of its *cella*. The high arched window in this wall dates from a Norman church that incorporated part of the temple into its structure, and you can make out a dedicatory inscription to Apollo on the reconstituted stereobate. But to get a complete picture of the original temple, you'll have to see the scale-model in Siracusa's museum.

Corso Matteotti leads up from here to Ortygia's central **piazza Archimede**: its centrepiece a 20C fountain depicting the nymph Arethusa (the symbol of Ortygia) at the moment of her transformation into a spring. The square has a couple of Catalan-Gothic palazzi round its sides, a common architectural style in Ortygia; more interesting, however, is to take a look around the corner from piazza Archimede, down the claustrophobic via Montalto, where the **Palazzo Montalto** is sadly shored up and undergoing some radical restoration. You can still admire its facade, graced by immaculate double- and triple-arched windows, and with an inscription dating the building's construction to 1397. This is one of the few surviving examples of the style favoured by the powerful Chiaramonte dynasty, more of which can be seen from the derelict courtyard at the back, where a loggia still stands.

Piazza del Duomo

Ortygia's most impressive architecture, though, belongs to its Baroque period, and nowhere does this reach such heights as in the city's loveliest square, the elongated **piazza del Duomo** – a traffic-free space surrounded by a range of 17–18C buildings, best of all the **Duomo** itself. To get an idea of the great age of this cathedral, walk round to the side on via Minerva to see not just the battlemented west wall added by the Normans, but also the stout Doric columns that form the skeleton of the structure, part of an earlier Greek temple. Although these bones were fleshed-out by later builders, they still provide the church's main proportions, and set a tone of dark antiquity.

The site was already a sacred one when the Greeks started work on an Ionic temple to Athena here in about 530 BC, though this was abandoned when a new temple was begun in thanksgiving for the victory over the

Carthaginians at Himera. The extravagant decoration that adorned this building spread its fame throughout the ancient world, and tantalising details of it have come down to us through Cicero, who visited Syracuse in the 1C BC and listed the temple's former contents as part of his prosecution of the Roman *praetor* and villain Verres, who appeared to have walked off with a good part of them – part of the booty he plundered from many Sicilian temples. The doors were of ivory and gold, and its walls painted with military scenes and portraits of various of Syracuse's tyrants – claimed to be the earliest examples of portraiture in European art. On the temple's roof stood a tall statue of the warrior-goddess Athena, carrying a golden shield which, catching the sun's rays, served as a beacon for sailors out at sea.

Although all this rich decoration has vanished, the main body of the temple was saved further despoliation thanks to its conversion into a Christian church, which was elevated to cathedral-status in 640 AD. A more drastic overhaul was carried out after the 1693 earthquake, when the Norman facade collapsed and was replaced by the present formidable Baroque front. This is in sharp contrast to the more muted **interior** (generally closed noon–4pm), in which it is still the frame of the ancient temple that is prevalent. The aisles are formed by the massive Doric columns, while the *cella* walls were hacked through to make the present arched nave. There's also evidence of the temple in the apse at the end of the north aisle, where you can make out the columned end of the *cella* wall. This apse is actually the one Byzantine element in the building, and stylistic boundaries are further fudged by the presence here of a good statue by the Renaissance artist Antonello Gagini, *Madonna of the Snow*. Other statues by the Gagini clan line the north aisle, where the distorted pillars give some inkling of how close the entire structure came to toppling when the 17C earthquake hit Siracusa. The duomo's south aisle shows more characteristic Baroque effusion in the series of richly ornate chapels, though the first one – actually the baptistery – is from an earlier age. Enlivened by some 12C arabesque mosaics, it contains a Norman font that was cut from a block still marked with a Greek inscription, and is supported by seven bronze lions.

Across from the duomo, on the corner of via Minerva, the **Municipio** displays the foundations of the first Ionic temple that occupied this site in its basement, and there are more fragments from it in two ground floor rooms (ask at the gate). Further down the piazza, the **Galleria Numismática** (Mon–Sat 9am–1pm; L2000) is an important coin collection, tracing ancient Syracuse's rise to wealth and empire, and including commemorative issues following the victories at Himera and Cumae.

Palazzo Bellomo, the Arethusa fountain and medieval Ortygia

Siracusa's tradition of architectural hybridism is again apparent in the **Palazzo Bellomo**, via Capodieci 14, an interesting mixture of 13C and 15C features, with a courtyard that has some 13C arcading and a Spanish-style stairway leading up to the loggia. This and the next-door Palazzo Parisio are the ideal surroundings for the superlative **Museo Regionale d'Arte Medioevale e Moderna** (Tues–Sat 9am–2pm, Sun 9am–1pm; L2000), a small but select display, with mainly sculpture on the ground floor – including some medieval and Renaissance tombs, and the inevitable examples of Gagini expertise – and some exceptional paintings on the first floor. Most famous of these is the *Annunciation* by Antonello da Messina, rescued from a state of advanced decay in a church at Palazzolo Acréide (see p.189), and subjected to some pretty rigorous and controversial restoration. The debate arose over the decision to transfer the painting from wood to canvas, and the whole story of how this was done is meticulously illustrated and explained here, a useful appendage (if you read Italian), though your attention will be principally taken up by the painting itself, still an absorbing image despite the considerable damage.

In nearby via San Martino, the **chiesa di San Martino** is one of Siracusa's oldest churches. Originally a 6C basilica, it was rebuilt in the 14C and smartened up with a good-looking rose window and Gothic doorway. Its dusky interior (open after 5pm) is a treat – plain stone columns leading to a tiny mosaicked half-apse with a 15C tryptych to the right of the choir.

Carry on down via Capodieci to the seafront, where the **Fonte Aretusa** spreads serenely below a small piazza. Mentioned in the original Delphic directions that brought the first Greek settlers here, the number of myths associated with this freshwater spring underlines the strong sentimental links that continued to bind the colonists to their motherland. This was where the nymph Arethusa rose after swimming across from the Peloponnese, having been metamorphosed into a spring by the goddess Artemis to escape the attentions of the predatory river god Alpheus. All in vain, though, for the determined Alpheus pursued her here to mingle with her in a watery form. Other legends declared that the spring's water would stain red at the time of the annual sacrifices at the sanctuary of Olympia, and that a cup thrown into the river there would rise here in Ortygia. More recently, and less apochryphally, Admiral Nelson took on board water supplies from here on his way to the Battle of the Nile. Now that the spot has been planted with papyrus, and filled with bream below the water and ducks above, it's a compulsory stop on the evening *passeggiata*, and the piazza's furnished with a nice selection of (expensive) cafés.

At the end of the dangling limb of land south of here sits the stout **Castello Maniace**, a defensive bulwark erected around 1239 by Frederick II, but named after the Byzantine admiral who briefly reconquered Syracuse from the Arabs in 1038. Unfortunately the solid square keep still retains its military function as a barracks, and access isn't allowed for the moment. Below the Fonte Aretusa is a small garden containing the city's **Acquario Tropicale** (Sat–Thurs, 9am–1pm; L2000), with 33 tanks of tropical fish. The main procession of promenaders takes off from here, extending all the way along the tree-lined **Foro Vittorio Emanuele II**, with rows of bars on one side, and the odd millionaire's yacht on the other. The vast, still pool of the **Porto Grande** spreads out beyond, dotted with fishing-boats, liners and tankers winking under the starlight. At the end of the avenue, to the right, the **Porta Marina** is a remnant of the city's medieval walls, a 15C gateway surmounted by a curlicued Spanish heraldic device.

If you've walked around the sights in a fairly disciplined order, it's well worth taking a couple of hours to do some aimless wandering around the less immediately obvious parts of Ortygia: typically, you'll run across a clutch of good-looking palazzi from different epochs, spread all over the island. The best of these are from the spate of building that took place under the aegis of the Aragonese, such as the **Palazzo Gargallo** (in via Gargallo, off via Maestranza), with a Catalan outer stair, and the **Palazzo Migliaccio** in via Picherale (off piazza del Duomo), its white marble terrace adorned with black lava chevrons. But look out too for the later Baroque constructions, notably in **via Maestranza** itself and **via Vittorio Véneto**, on the eastern side of the island. Connecting this last street with largo XXV Luglio, **via Resalibera** is also worth a stroll, squeezing the occasional church between its tangled rows of houses, or a solitary bar – usually just a room, full of wine barrels and old men, both half-full of the stuff.

Achradina

Modern development in the central mainland quarter of **ACHRADINA** makes it difficult to picture the ancient city that Plutarch wept over when he heard of its fall to the Romans. Much of the new building dates from World War II, when Siracusa was bombed twice over – once by the Allies, then, after its capture, by the Luftwaffe in 1943. But you're likely to be staying in one of the hotels scattered around this part of town, or will pass through on the way to the archaeological museum and park, so you could well drop in on some of these lesser sites *en route*.

You'll certainly become familiar with the rather shabby park-area known as the **Foro Siracusano**. Site of the old town's *agora*, it holds a few paltry columns in a landscaped garden, and is not improved by the grotesque war memorial towering above, a Fascist monument from 1936. On nearby via Elorina, there's a much more interesting relic, the little-visited **Ginnasio Romano** (daily 8am–6pm; free). This was never actually a gymnasium, but a small Roman theatre, probably built in the 1C AD when the ancient city's much grander Greek theatre was requisitioned for blood sports. Make a brief circuit of the well-tended lawn that surrounds the rectangular *cavea*, with the remains of a portico behind it. This once enclosed a small shrine, part of which is still visible. These days the theatre's *orchestra* is flooded from an underground cistern, hindering further excavation, though if anything enhancing the appeal of this forgotten mossy site.

Over on the eastern edge of Achradina, close by the crowded huddle of boats in the **Porto Píccolo**, you'll find a less recognisable ruin, the **Arsenale**, by the railway line. As its name suggests, it was a provisions centre, where ships were refurbished, hoisted up from the port by devices that clamped into the ground – and the slots that engaged them are about the only thing to look at here. A little further up is another low-key sight, the **Edificio Termale**, a Byzantine bath-house claimed to be the very same one in which, in 668 AD, the Emperor Constans was assassinated, knocked on the head by a servant wielding a soap-dish.

From here, via Fuggetta leads up to the modern city's pleasantest square, which takes its name from the **chiesa di Santa Lucia** (daily 9am–noon) lying at its northern end. Built in 1629, the church marks the spot where

Santa Lucia, Siracusa's patron saint, was martyred in 304 AD. Today the church has been methodically stripped of all the treasures that once made it an essential item on tourist itineraries, though you can still visit Giovanni Verméxio's octagonal **cappella di San Sepolcro** outside in the piazza – ask inside the church. The mortal remains of the saint were originally preserved below this chapel, before being carried off to Constantinople by the Byzantine admiral Maniakes in 1038, and later shipped to Venice as part of the spoils plundered by the Venetian 'crusaders' in 1204.

The real disappointment, though, is the lack of access to the extensive network of **catacombs** lying beneath this site, closed to the public until they can be made safe. After the ones in Rome, these constitute the largest system of subterranean tombs in Italy, and are the oldest in Sicily.

Tyche

The entire district of **TYCHE**, which stretches north from Santa Lucia, is riddled with more of these catacombs, on account of the Roman prohibition of Christian burial within the city limits (Syracuse having by then shrunk back to its original core of Ortygia). The warrens were hewn out of the rock, and often followed the course of underground aqueducts, disused since Greek times. All are now inaccessible, apart from those below the basilica of **San Giovanni** (daily 9am–1pm & 2–7pm; free), which lies opposite the EPT at via San Sebastiano, and has been in ruins since 1693. Fronted by a triple arch, the nave is now open to the sky and the interior overgrown, but you can still admire the 7C apse and a medieval rose window. Once the city's cathedral, it was built over the **crypt** of Saint Marcian, first bishop of Siracusa. Steps lead down to the pillar where he was flogged to death in 254; his tomb is here too, along with a modern altar marking the spot where Saint Paul is supposed to have preached, stopping in the city as a prisoner on his way to Rome. **Guided tours** (L2000) of the **catacombs** under the basilica take place on the hour, between 10am and noon, and 4pm and 6pm: these are in Italian but you'll have to go on one to see anything. Numerous side-passages lead off from the main gallery (*decumanus maximus*), often culminating in *rotonde*, or round caverns used for prayer. Entire families were interred in niches hollowed out of these walls and floors, anxious for burial close to the tomb of Saint Marcian. Most of the treasures buried with the bodies have been pillaged, though the robbers overlooked one – an ornate sarcophagus unearthed from just below the floor in 1872, and now on show in Siracusa's archaeological museum.

It's this museum, the **Museo Archeologico** (Tues–Sun 9am–2pm, last entry 1pm; L2000), that forms Tyche's main attraction, just round the corner on viale Teócrito (opposite the monolithic Santuario delle Lacrime recently erected to house a statue of the Madonna which allegedly wept for five days in 1953). From Ortygia, buses #4, #5, #12 (not Sun) and #15 for the museum leave from largo XXV Luglio and run up Corso Gelone and along viale Teócrito. Purpose-built in the grounds of the Villa Landolina, the museum is Sicily's newest and most wide-ranging collection of antiquities, worth a prolonged browse to view the almost indescribable wealth disgorged from archaeological sites throughout the province and beyond. Near the entrance, an explanatory diagram colour-codes the three main sections into which the exhibits are arranged: prehistoric (section A), items from Syracuse, Megara Hyblaea and the Chalcidinian colonies (B), and finds from Gela, Agrigento, Syracuse's sub-colonies and the indigenous Sikel centres, including copious material from the sites of Pantálica and Castelluccio (C).

The museum's most celebrated exhibit is the **Venus Anadiomene**, also known as *Landolina*, after the archaeologist who discovered her in 1804. *Anadiomene* means 'rising from the sea', which describes her coy pose: with her left hand she holds a robe, while studs show where her broken-off right arm came across to hide her breasts. Probably Roman-made in the 1C AD, from a Greek model, the headless statue has always evoked extreme responses, alternately exalting the delicacy and naturalism of the carving, and condemning her 'immodest modesty', her knowing sensual attitude that symbolised the decline of the vigorous classical age and the birth of a new decadence. By the statue's feet, the dolphin, Aphrodite's emblem, is the only sign that this was a goddess.

Among the earlier Hellenic pieces, the museum also has some excellent *kouroi* – toned, muscular youths, one of which (in section B), from Lentini, is one of the most outstanding fragments still extant from the Archaic age of Greek art – around 500 BC. Of the same period, from the colony of Megara Hyblaea, there is a striking image of a mother/goddess in the act of suckling twins, its absorbed roundness expressing a tender harmony as close to earth and fertility rites as the *Venus Landolina* is to the cult of sensuality. Also in this section, look out for some gruesome theatrical masks, while from Siracusa's Christian period there's the finely worked 4C marble sarcophagus from the catacombs below San Giovanni. It held a Roman official and his wife, both prominently depicted and surrounded by reliefs of scenes from the Old and New Testaments.

Neapolis: the archaeological park

NEAPOLIS was the district containing most of the ancient city's social and religious amenities – theatres, altars and sanctuaries – and was thus never inhabited. Today it's encompassed by Siracusa's large **Parco Archeologico** (Tues–Sun 9am–2hr before sunset; L2000), reachable on foot or on buses #4, #5, #6, #8, #11, #12 and #15 from largo XXV Luglio to Corso Gelone/viale Teócrito. The entrance is hidden behind a tawdry circus of souvenir stalls and ice-cream stands, catering for the bus-loads of tourists which arrive every few minutes in the summer.

On your way to the ticket booth you'll pass the ruined base of the **Ara di Ierone II**, a 200m-long altar erected by Hieron II in the second half of the 3C BC, in honour of Zeus Eleftherios, 'the giver of freedom'. Now railed-off to the public, it was the biggest construction of its kind in all Magna Graecia: Diodorus records that 450 bulls were led up the ramps at either end of the altar to be slaughtered. Above plinth-level, little is left standing, though the sheer dimensions of the structure still retain their impact.

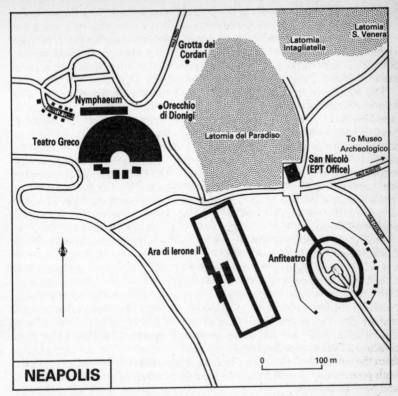

At the end of the lane, the **Teatro Greco** is Siracusa's most spectacular monument. One of the biggest and best-preserved of Greek auditoriums, there's been a theatre on this site since at least the 5C BC, though it was frequently modified and added to at different periods. Most of what you see today is owed to Hieron II, who expanded it to accommodate 15,000 people, in nine sections of 59 rows (of which 42 remain). The inscriptions around the top of the middle gangway – faint but still visible – date from the 3C BC, giving the names of the ruler and his family, with Zeus Olympios in the middle.

Most of the alterations carried out by the Romans were made to adapt the arena for gladiatorial combat, and included extending the *orchestra* by cutting back the first rows of seats. They also installed some marble-faced seats for privileged spectators, and the seventeenth row was removed, possibly to segregate the classes. Nowadays the theatre is used for a milder form of entertainment: concerts and Greek dramas, the latter performed, as in antiquity, in May and June on alternate (even-numbered) years – though not staged early in the morning, as were the original performances; ask at the on-site EPT for details.

Below the Greek theatre sits a smaller structure, known as the **Teatro Lineare** due to its simple, straight design. Nearby are the scant remains of one of the site's most venerated spots, the **Santuario di Apollo**, which once contained a huge bronze statue of the god before this was carried off to Rome by the Emperor Tiberius. Walk back up through the theatre and the high terrace above contains a large artificial grotto, the **Nymphaeum**, fed by water from an ancient aqueduct, where a number of statues were found, now in the museum. To the left of here, the **via dei Sepolcri**, or 'Street of the Tombs', is deeply rutted by the carts that plied to and fro, and is flanked by more votive niches.

Back at the entrance to the theatre, another path descends to the largest of Siracusa's huge pits, or *latomie*, from which the rock for the city's multifarious monuments was excavated. These wide, vertically walled **quarries** also provided a harsh but effective prison for the 7000 Athenian prisoners-of-war, following the fiasco of the Great Expedition. Most were probably kept in the lusciously overgrown Latomia dei Cappuccini, across on Siracusa's eastern seafront in Tyche – now a garden for the Capuchin monks, and closed until the collapsing walls can be bolstered. But this one, here in Neapolis, the **Latomia del Paradiso**, is well worth a look in its own right, mainly for the remarkable cavern known as the **Orecchio di Dionisio**. It owes its name ('Ear of Dionysius') to the painter Caravaggio, who noted its resemblance to a human ear, while the association with Dionysius derives from a story that the tyrant used the cavern's acoustic qualities to overhear the conversations of suspected conspirators. In fact, Dionysius probably had far more efficient means of extracting information, though the sound-enhancing effect is still there, and can be tested by anyone.

A second cave, the geometrically shaped **Grotta dei Cordari**, was used as a work-space by the ancient city's ropemakers, who found that the damp air down here prevented the rope-strands from breaking under stress: you can still see the grooves worn into rock by the twined rope. There are two other quarries in this area, the **Latomia Intagliatella**, with a tall rocky pillar in the centre, and the niched **Latomia di Santa Vénera**, from where a precipitous passage leads off to the **Necrópoli Grotticelle**. This Greco-Roman burial ground includes one grave with a Doric pediment, dubiously imagined to be the tomb of Archimedes.

Keep hold of your ticket for the **Anfiteatro Romano**, through a gate on the right as you leave the park: a large elliptical arena built in the 3C AD to satisfy the growing lust for circus games. One hundred and forty metres long – one of the largest of its kind anywhere – it's encircled by a parapet inscribed with the names of some of the leading citizens of the time, though you're unlikely to get near enough to see this as the interior is out of bounds. The rectangular tank in the centre of the arena is too small to have been used for aquatic displays, and is more likely to have been for draining the blood and gore spilled in the course of the combats. But not before the spectators had had their fill: at the end of the contests the infirm, ill and disabled would apparently attempt to suck warm blood from the bodies and take the livers from the animals, in the belief that this would speed their recovery.

Out from the city: Epipolae, the Ciane river, and Siracusa's beaches

If you're beginning to wilt under the combined onslaught of heat and crowds, Siracusa offers some good possibilities for **half-day trips** out of the centre. Each is a city bus ride away, or, in the case of the Rive Ciane, a boat-ride – though this last would also make a decent walk, once you get off the main road.

Epipolae and the Castello Eurialo

The outlying area of **EPIPOLAE**, seven kilometres west of the city, holds ancient Syracuse's inland military and defensive works. To get here from the centre, take buses #9, #10 and #11 from Ortygia or from Corso Gelone outside the archaeological park, to the village of **BELVEDERE**, a twenty-minute ride.

These heights were first fortified by Dionysius the Elder in about 400 BC, after the Athenians had come so close to taking the city by occupying them a few years previously. Constantly modified and extended over a couple of centuries, what remains today consists of a great wall which marked the city's western limit, and the **Castello Eurialo** (Mon–Sat 9am–6pm, Sun 9am–1pm; free), just before the village on the right. The Euryalus castle is the major Greek fortification in the Mediteranean which is still standing, most of it dating from Hieron II's time, when **Archimedes**, as his General of Ordnance, must have been actively involved in its renovation. Despite the effort and ingenuity that went into making this site impregnable, the castle has no very glorious history: ignored altogether by the attacking Carthaginians, it surrendered without a fight to the Roman forces of Marcellus in 212 BC.

Assailants had to cope with three defensive trenches, designed to keep at bay the new artillery of the time – siege engines and battering rams. The first of the trenches (approached from the west, where you come in) was just within range of catapults mounted on the five towers of the castle's most impressive remain, the **keep**; while in the trench below the keep, you can see the high piers supporting the draw-bridge that once crossed it. All around here, long galleries burrow beneath the walls into the keep, serving as supply- and escape-routes, and also enabling the defenders to clear out by night the material thrown in by attackers during the day. Chambers were also dug out of the rock for use as store-rooms and stables.

Behind the keep is a long, wedge-shaped fortification, to the north of which is the main gateway to the western quarter of the city. This, the **Epipolae gate**, was built indented from the walls, allowing the defenders to shower attackers with missiles, and is reminiscent of the main gate at Tyndaris (p.97), a city that shared the same architects. The longest of the underground passages surfaces here, stretching 180m from the defensive trenches. From the gate, you can stroll along Dionysius' extensive walls, looking down over the oil refineries and tankers off the coast north of the city, and back over Siracusa itself, Ortygia clearly visible, pointing out into the sea.

If you like the look of Epipolae and Belvedere village, don't forget that there's a **youth hostel** here, and a decent **pizzeria** (see p.174 and 185 respectively).

Ciane and the Olympieion

Just south of the city, the **Ciane river** offers a good rustic excursion. The river's source is only ten kilometres inland, forming a pool said to have been created by the tears of the nymph Cyane when her mistress Persephone was abducted into the underworld by Hades. The pool and the riverbanks are overgrown by thickets of papyrus, apparently the gift of Ptolemy Philadelphus of Egypt to Hieron II, making this the only place outside North Africa where the plant grows wild.

You can get to the pool from Siracusa **by car**, taking the road for CANICATTINI BAGNI at the end of viale Paolo Orsi, and following the signs for about five kilometres. But if you want to make the trip **on foot**, following up the lush riverbanks along a good path, take any of the #34 or #35 buses from piazza delle Poste, getting off where the SS115 crosses the Ciane river (immediately after the Anapo river, which runs parallel). This route allows you to drop in on the scant but evocative remains of the **Olympieion**, or Tempio di Giove Olimpico, a Doric temple built in the first half of the 6C BC, of which only two columns and the stylobate remain. The hillock the ruin stands on was a vital strategic point in classical times, and was often occupied by Syracuse's enemies when the city was under attack. The pestilential air of the Lysimelia marshes below saved the day on more than one occasion, infecting the hostile armies with malaria.

In summer, a **boat service** operates off the Porto Grande's *Molo Zanagora*, the most laid-back way to see both temple and pool; it costs around L40,000 to hire the boat, or – if there's a large group of you – L4000 per person. The whole trip takes around two hours (ask for Signor Vella).

The beaches

Since the coast north of Siracusa has become an evil depository for noxious chemicals, the city's main **beaches** all lie to the south. **Buses** (#35 from piazza delle Poste) go direct to **ARENELLA**, the first of the beach resorts and the only sandy stretch in the area, though most of it consists of private lidos (L3000 a day), and all can get horribly crowded. You might prefer the less populous stretches of rock further south, where the inlets create clear pools that are good for snorkelling. You can walk to these easily enough from Arenella, or else drive down the coast (or take bus #34 from piazza delle Poste in Siracusa) to **OGNINA**, and walk back a little way.

If you want to be sure of beautiful surroundings, though, it would be worth heading down a bit further south, to **FONTANE BIANCHE**, whose wide arc of sand provides some of the best swimming on this part of the coast. Bus #34 does the journey here from Siracusa in about half an hour, as do *AST* buses leaving every forty minutes from piazza delle Poste (last one at 8.15pm). Along with a number of bars and trattorias, this popular resort has a good **campsite**, *Fontane Bianche* (☎0931-790.356; April to Oct), but don't expect a lot of action here outside the period from June to September.

Siracusa: all the consuming details

Eating and drinking

There's no shortage of opportunities to spend money in Siracusa, either in the many sit-down bars, or at a choice of trattorias and restaurants. Two of the best **bars** are the outdoor *Porta Marina*, next to the Porta Marina on the Foro Vittorio Emanuele, and the *Bar Del Ponte*, right at the end of the Ponte Nuovo on Ortygia, a good breakfast-stop. Ortygia also has the best **eating-places**: take advantage of the tourist menus available in many of them, around L15,000 excluding drinks. Try the trattoria adjoining the *Gran Bretagna* hotel in via Savoia; in the same street there are a couple of basic **pizzerias** on either side of the road − one of them, *Pizzeria Savoia* (closed Mon) at no. 17, cheap and good, with some raw local wine. For fast service and a rowdy atmosphere, try the *Spaghetteria* in via Scina, an alley between piazza Archimede and Porta Marina, with a huge selection of pasta at L4000 a plate. Otherwise, there's a whole host of pricier joints dotted around Ortygia's streets, like the *Trattoria Campisi*, via del Consiglio 10 (north of the Duomo, down via Landolina and right) for *al fresco* eating. There's a new **vegetarian** restaurant too: *La Foglia* (closed Sun night), in via Capodieci, with some interesting soups and salads; while for **fish** you can't do better than *Pescomare*, just off piazza del Duomo in via Landolina, where you can eat succulent giant clams in an atmospheric plant-filled old courtyard.

Another good place to eat outside in the summer is on the breezy higher ground at **Belvedere**, where the good food and reasonable prices at the *Castello Eurialo* ristorante-pizzeria attract crowds of *siracusani* every night. It's by the entrance to the castle, two minutes' walk from the youth hostel.

Entertainment: puppet shows and concerts

If you're looking for other evening diversions in Siracusa, you might drop by the **puppet theatre** at via Nizza 14, where you can follow the swashbuckling adventures of Orlando and his pals three times a week − a bit touristy but good for a laugh. The performances generally take place in summer only, Tuesday, Thursday and Saturday at 9.30pm (L2000), but contact the AAST/EPT for details. They'll also fill you in on the possibility of seeing **Greek plays** at the Teatro Greco (May to June, on alternate, even-numbered years) in the archaeological park, one of Sicily's finest venues; tickets start at L15,000 on weekdays, L20,000 weekends, though look out for special reductions (down to around L10,000) on specified days. If you miss these, there are **other performances** every year throughout July and August too: jazz, opera, and ballet, attracting some big names, with seats at around L15,000.

Listings

Boat trips Daily in summer around the city's harbours: L4000 a ticket, departures from Molo Zanagora, Foro Vittorio Emanuele.

Buses Main companies are *AST* at piazza delle Poste (for Lentini, Catania, Cómiso, Íspica, Módica, Noto, Pachino, Palazzolo Acréide, Ragusa and Vittória); and *SAIS*, around the corner at via Trieste 28 (for Agrigento, Catania, Messina, Noto, Pachino, Palermo and Taormina).

Car problems *ACI*, Foro Siracusano 27 (☎0931-66.656).

Emergency First Aid Call ☎0931-68.555.

Ferry Services on the Naples/Réggio di Calabria/Catania/Malta route call at Siracusa three times a week; tickets from *Tirrenia Navigazione* at viale Mazzini 4–7, ☎0931-66.956).

Hospital At via Testaferrata (☎0931-724.111).

Police The *Questura* is in via San Sebastiano (☎0931-21.122).

Post office The main post office is in piazza delle Poste, open Mon–Fri 8am–8pm, Sat 8am–2pm.

Taxis Ranks in piazza Pancali (☎0931-60.980), Corso Gelone (☎0931-69.302) and at the railway station (☎0931-69.722).

Telephones The main *SIP* office is at via Brenta 35, close to the railway station (8am–8pm). At night (8pm–8am), use the phones at the *Bar Trápani*, piazza Marconi 19.

North: the coast to Augusta

The coast **north of Siracusa**, the Golfo di Augusta, has been defaced by some of the ugliest industry you'll see in Sicily, filling the air with acrid fumes and the sea with chemicals. These mammoth plants employ one tenth of Siracusa's population, but the scale of this industrial zone – the largest concentration of chemical plants in Europe – has effectively obliterated the coast from any other point of view. Oil tankers hover offshore, while people living in some of the coastal villages have been evacuated and their houses destroyed, their places taken by a mesh of pipes and containers that will seem all too close if you're travelling this route by train. It casts a foul shadow over the area's ancient sites: the Bronze Age tombs of Thapsos on the besieged peninsula of Magnisi are closed off now, and the extensive remains of **Megara Hyblaea** are hidden behind a barrage of alien development, though you can still fight your way through to visit them. Beyond, **Augusta** thrives as an industrial port, but preserves a fine Baroque centre, with beaches to the north out of reach (just) of the emissions.

Megara Hyblaea

You'll have to see the site of **Megara Hyblaea** with your own car, unless you want to walk from MEGARA GIANNALENA station, 25 minutes out of Siracusa. It's a fair hike, though if you're very careful you could reduce it to a kilometre by walking along the rails, and climbing up at the road bridge.

Although the earliest settlers here were Neolithic, it was as a Greek colony that the town prospered, after the Sikel king of Hybla had granted Greeks from Megara (near Athens) this tract of land alongside his own. By the mid-7C BC, the population had done so well out of trade and their high-quality pottery, that they were able to found some minor colonies of their own, including Selinus (see p.267), though their city was eventually submerged by Syracusan ambitions and destroyed by Gelon in 482 BC. In the middle of the

4C BC, the site was resettled and the town flourished again, until it was finally levelled by the Romans in the same avenging campaign that ended Syracuse's independence in 214 BC.

Most of the ruins you'll see at the **site** (always open) belong to the 4C revival, but the fortifications were erected a century later, interrupted by the Romans' arrival. Various buildings – temples, baths, the market place – lie confusingly scattered over a wide area, though this is considered to be the most complete model of an Archaic city still surviving. Your best bet to make head or tail of it is to spend some time in the excellent **Antiquario** (Mon–Sat 9am–2pm, Sun 9am–1pm; free), where illustrations and diagrams put it all into context. However, the best finds, including a statue of a goddess suckling twins and a *kouros*, are in Siracusa's archaeological museum (see above).

Augusta and its beaches

Despite **AUGUSTA's** superficial resemblance to Siracusa – its old centre detached from the mainland on its own islet, surrounded by two harbours – the port has never attained the same importance, and didn't even exist until 1232. Frederick II, who founded the town, characteristically stamped his own personality on it in the form of a castle, though everything else of the medieval town was entirely destroyed by the 1693 earthquake. What's left is a handsome Baroque centre with lots of restaurants and a good hotel – a relief after the rampant industrialisation all around.

You can't miss the **castello** that dominates the causeway leading onto the island, though you're unlikely to get inside: used for years as a prison, it's now awaiting conversion into a war museum. The **Villa Comunale** below is a shady public garden through which all traffic is channeled, including the promenaders who overflow into here from the long and narrow main street, via Príncipe Umberto. Along here is a piazza holding the 18C Duomo, and a solemn **Palazzo Comunale**, its facade crowned by Frederick II's imperial eagle.

Augusta's best **hotel** is right on the square, the *Centrale*, via Príncipe Umberto 126 (☎0931-974.034; L25,000); get a room overlooking the piazza if you can. You won't have any trouble finding a **place to eat**: the Villa Comunale and the main street are bristling with trattorias, but if you want to eat outside you should try *Da Sabina* (closed Tues) on via Xifonia, on the eastern seafront.

If you've got time to explore the **coast to the north**, you'll come across resorts with more good eating possibilities, some decent swimming and a couple of **campsites**. The nearest of these is *A' Massaria* (☎0931-983.078; June to Sept), in **MONTE TAURO**, reachable by hourly bus (#2D) from Augusta's Villa Comunale. Much nicer, though, is the *Baia del Silenzio* (☎0931-981.211; June to Sept), a little further on and overlooking a pretty bay: take the BRÚCOLI bus (also from the Villa Comunale), get off at the signpost before the town and walk the two kilometres to the site. **BRÚCOLI** itself is a small resort with a restored 15C castle, and ominous 'Bathing prohibited' signs that are studiously ignored by locals and tourists alike. You too might chance a swim here: it's far enough round the point to be safe from the Gulf's contaminated waters.

Inland: Pantálica and Palazzolo Acréide

These are two separate day-trips you can make **inland from Siracusa**, both to destinations lying in the folds of the **Monti Iblei**. It's a dramatic landscape, crossed by dry-stone walls and dotted with small villages springing the odd surprise – a crumbly church or an inviting trattoria. Whatever time you spend at the necropolis of **Pantálica** will be mainly taken up by wandering the deep gorge through which the Ánapo river runs. Its refreshing walks are enough to attract weekend picnickers from all over the region – with several thousand tombs hollowed out of the valley-sides providing the occasional diversion. **Palazzolo Acréide** is a mainly Baroque town with a compact Greek and Roman site lying just outside, one of the most interesting of the province's classical sites.

Pantálica

Pantálica is Sicily's greatest necropolis, first used between the 13C and 10C BC by Sikel refugees from the coast. After the 8C BC, this plateau is thought to have been the site of Hybla, whose king invited Megarian Greeks to colonise first Thapsos and then Megara Hyblaea; there are visible remains from this era, but the fascination of the place derives from the five thousand or so tombs hewn out of the gorge below.

The plateau rises between the river Ánapo and its northern tributary, the Cava Grande, and can be approached on foot from either end of the gorge. From Siracusa, buses run to **SORTINO** (every two hours, not Sun) to the north, and **FERLA** (three daily), to the west. Though further from the site, it's Ferla that's the prettiest base, with a good **trattoria** (closed Sun) in its piazza San Sebastiano.

Access to the necropolis is best from below Ferla village: if you're on the bus from Siracusa, ask to be let off at the site's entrance at the bottom of the hill, immediately after crossing the river and before reaching Ferla. The gorge is closed to all private traffic but there's a **free minibus service** that does the whole route in about an hour. It leaves the entrance every 1½ hours on weekdays, every 45 minutes at weekends, making stops along the way. There's no reason why you shouldn't do it on foot though – at least some of the way. You'll soon see the tombs, first just dotting the walls of the valley in clusters, and finally puncturing the whole cliff-face. On the plateau above are the foundations of a building from ancient Hybla: the **Anaktoron**, or prince's palace, with a few stretches of walling nearby. The **tombs** themselves were dug out of the vertical cliff-walls, and the sheer number of them creates an eerie impression. In some were found the traces of several separate skeletons, probably of the same family, and others show evidence of habitation, though much later, when the Syracusans themselves were forced to flee inland from barbarian incursions. The atmosphere is primeval and almost sinister – for Vincent Cronin, even something terrifying: 'Here is Sicily of the stone age, intent on nothing higher than the taking of food and the burial of its dead'. The free play of nature in this ravine embodied for Cronin Sicily's own particular contribution to the man-made wonders bestowed later by the island's conquerors, and as such – symbolised by a honeycomb he came across in one of the caves – the object of the quest described in his book, *The Golden Honeycomb*.

Palazzolo Acréide

Lying on a hill some eighteen kilometres south of Ferla, **PALAZZOLO ACRÉIDE** is the modern successor of the Greek colony of Akrai, founded in the middle of the 7C BC by Syracuse in its first drive inland. The remains of the ancient town lie just outside the modern settlement, an easy walk. Both occupy the higher slopes of a promontory once strategically commanding routes inland, now somewhat stranded from the main road- and rail-links crossing the province. It's a good excursion, though, enabling you to wander the town's knot of small Baroque streets before visiting the site.

Buses from Siracusa pull up in Palazzolo's main square, piazza del Pópolo, and you can take any of the roads leading down from here to reach the heart of the Baroque town. There's not a lot to see here but it's a nice place to wander through, noting the town's opulent Barqoue facades and gargoyled balconies. Palazzolo has a museum worth tracking down too, the **Casa-Museo di Antonino Uccello** (Tues–Sun 9am–2pm; free), tucked away at via Machiavelli 19 (off via Carlo Alberto). The fruit of one man's thirty-year obsession to root out and preserve the culture of rural Sicily, this varied collection of 5000 objects constitutes eastern Sicily's most important documentation of folk art, showing trousseaus, olive-presses, puppets, reconstruc-

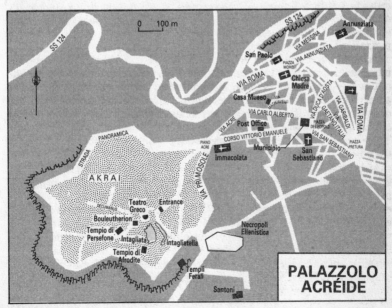

tions of houses and stables, and anything else judged by Uccello to be in danger of extinction.

If you want a quiet alternative to staying in Siracusa, Palazzolo has a cheap **hotel**, the *Ánapo*, Corso Vittorio Emanuele 7 (☎0931-871.093; L23,000), and there's a good **trattoria**, *Da Alfredo* (closed Wed), at via Duca d'Aosta 27.

Akrai: the ancient city

Syracuse chose the site of **Akrai**, its first inland colony, well; it dominated the trade routes into the interior, particularly the *via Selinuntina* to Akragas. The city thrived during the peace and security that characterised Hieron II's reign in the 3C BC, though it declined under the Romans, later re-emerging as an important early Christian centre, as shown by the number of rock-cut tombs in the area – only to be eventually destroyed by the Arabs.

Of the ancient city's visible remains at the **Zona Archeologica** (Tues–Sun 9am–1hr before sunset; free), most complete is the small **Teatro Greco**, built towards the end of Hieron's reign and modified by the Romans. A perfect semi-circle, the theatre held 600, and retains traces of its scene-building. Behind the theatre to the right is a small **senate-house**, or *bouleuterion*, a rectangular construction that was originally covered. Beyond is a 200m-stretch of *decumanus* that once connected the two gates of the city (Porta Siracusana and Porta Selinuntina). Crossed at regular intervals by junctions, and paved in lavic rock, it's in better condition than many of the more recent roads in the area.

The rest of the site isn't as clearly defined and other remains give little impression of their former grandeur. You'll have a job identifying a recently excavated Roman **Tempio di Persefone**, above the theatre, an unusually round chamber, formerly covered by a cupola. Equally fragmentary is the much older **Tempio di Afrodite**, 6C or 5C BC, lying at the head of what was the *agora*. From here you can look straight down into one of the two quarries from which the stone to build the city was taken. Later they were converted into Christian burial chambers, and in the first of them, the **Intagliata**, you can plainly see the recesses in the walls: some of them catacombs, others areas of worship, the rest simply rude dwellings cut in the Byzantine era. The narrower, deeper quarry below it, the **Intagliatella**, has more votive niches, and a relief cut from the rock-face, over two metres long, that combines a typically Greek scene – heroes banqueting – and a Roman one of heroes offering sacrifice. It's thought to have been carved in the 1C BC.

There are more niches and chambers in a lower quarry, the **Templi Ferali**, though you'll have to ask the custodian to let you see this, along with the much more interesting **Santoni** further down (ten minutes' walk from the site). These are twelve rock-cut sculptures of a fertility goddess Cybele, a predominantly eastern deity whose origins are steeped in mystery. Certainly there's no other example of so rich a complex relating to her worship, and the local name tagged to these sculptures – *santoni*, or 'great saints' – suggests that the awe attached to them survived until relatively recently. Carved no later than the 3C BC, these rough, weathered images are protected in individual locked shelters; they represent the *Magna Mater* seated, attended by priests, lions, and other deities.

South to Noto

Fifteen kilometres down the SS115 from Siracusa, the nondescript town of **CASSÍBILE** is known to Italians as the place where, in an olive yard on 3 September 1943, Generals Bedell-Smith and Castellano signed the armistice which took Italy out of the Axis alliance in World War II. A side-road branches off from here for the beach resort of Fontane Bianche (see p.184), while the main road continues on another ten kilometres to **ÁVOLA**. This agricultural town has an old Baroque centre, partly reconstructed on a hexagonal design after earthquake damage. The small **Museo Cívico** at piazza Umberto 17, containing finds from Thapsos, Pantálica and the pre-earthquake town, is closed at the time of writing.

Noto

Six kilometres beyond, **NOTO** represents the apogee of the wholesale renovation that took place following the cataclysm of 1693, a monument to the achievement of a few architects and planners, whose vision coincided with the golden age of Baroque architecture. Although there existed a town called Noto, or *Netum*, in this area for centuries, what you see today is in effect a 'New Town', conceived as a triumphant symbol of renewal.

Noto was flattened on 11 January 1693, and a week later its **rebuilding** was entrusted to a Sicilian-Spanish aristocrat, Giuseppe Lanza, Duke of Camastra, on the strength of his work at the town of Santo Stéfano di Camastra, on the Tyrrhenian coast. Lanza visited the ruins, saw nothing but 'un montón de piedras abandonadas', and quickly decided to start afresh, on a new site sixteen kilometres to the south. In fact, the ruins weren't abandoned, the city's battered population was already improvising a shanty town, and even held a referendum when Lanza's intentions became known, rejecting the call to relocate their city. But partly motivated by the prestige of the undertaking, partly by the need to refurbish the area's defences, Lanza ignored the local feeling, even pulling down their new constructions and the old town's remaining church. With the help of the Flemish military engineer Carlos de Grunemburg, Lanza devised a revolutionary new plan, based on two quarters – one for the political and religious establishment, the other for the people – which were to be almost completely separated from each other. The best architects were to be used: Vincenzo Sinatra, Paolo Labisi and the master craftsman Rosario Gagliardi – not innovators, but men whose enthusiasm and experience enabled them to concoct a celebration of the latest architectural skills and forms. Their collaboration was so complete that it's still difficult today to ascribe some buildings to any one person. Within an astonishingly short time the work was completed, a new city, planned with the accent on symmetry and visual harmony, from its simple street plan to the gracious curves of its buildings. It's easily the most harmonious post-earthquake creation, and for a time, in the mid-19C, the new Noto replaced Siracusa as the region's provincial capital.

This century has seen a deterioration of the town, mainly due to the traffic that thunders through. The local Iblean stone, so workable and suitable for

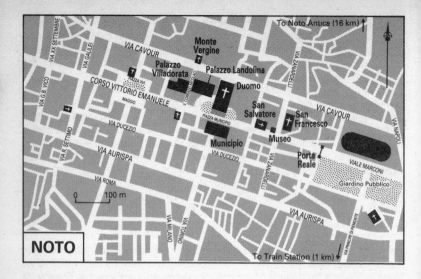

delicate carving, is also highly fragile; but it was not until 1987 that belated restoration work was begun. Heavy traffic was diverted round the outskirts of town, and corroded ornamentation subjected to a thorough cleaning. Some buildings may still be under scaffolding – a pity in a city where the visual aspect is so important – but you shouldn't miss visiting Noto under any circumstances. From Siracusa, it's around half an hour's journey by hourly buses or frequent trains. The **bus** will drop you at the Giardino Pubblico at the eastern end of town; the **railway station** is ten minutes' walk away down via Príncipe di Piemonte.

The centre is best approached through the monumental **Porta Reale**, topped by the three symbols of the town's allegiance to the Bourbon monarchy: a dog, a tower and a swan (respectively, loyalty, strength and affection). The **Corso Vittorio Emanuele** that leads off from here runs through the heart of the lower, patricians' quarter, and is lined with some of Sicily's most captivating buildings. All are a rich honey colour – starting with the formal-looking church of **San Francesco**, to the right, its facade rather dulled by the more flamboyant **Convento del Santíssimo Salvatore** next door. Part of this convent houses the **Museo Cívico**, on the corner, containing finds from Greek coastal sites and material from Noto Antica, but it's currently closed.

A little way up is what is arguably Sicily's finest piazza. Perfectly proportioned, the tree-planted **piazza del Municipio** is the elegant heart of the town, and contains its noblest buildings. Most imposing is the twin-towered **Duomo**, whose splendid facade is raised on a broad, stepped plinth, and whose tone varies from clear white in the morning to a yellowish glow at sunset. Completed in 1776, it's said to have been inspired by models of Borromini's churches in Rome. Opposite, the **Municipio** (or Palazzo Ducezio) is the work of Vincenzo Sinatra, flanked by its own green spaces, the arcaded building presenting a lovely, convex front of columns and long stone balconies. On the far side of the Duomo, the **Palazzo Villadorata** is an eccentric piece of work. Onto a strictly classical front, six extravagant balconies were grafted, supported by the last word in sculpted buttresses – a panoply of griffins, galloping horses and bald and bearded figures with fat-cheeked cherubs at their bellies.

There's a lot more pleasure to be had out of Noto by straying off into the side streets on either side of Corso Vittorio Emanuele, or down the Corso to piazza XVI Maggio and Noto's **market**. Don't leave without visiting the upper part of town, filled with massive monastic houses and the dwellings of Noto's poorer 18C citizens. They had their own church, Gagliardi's **Santíssimo Crocifisso**, in piazza Mazzini. Never completed, the church preserves some treasures from the old town, including a magnificent pair of Romanesque lions, and the only statue in Sicily actually signed by the master-sculptor Francesco Laurana, *Madonna of the Snow*, carved in 1471 (behind the altar on the right).

Noto practicalities
Sleeping possibilites in Noto are limited, with one hotel that's often full, the *Albergo Stella*, via F. Maiore 44 (☎0931-835.695; L32,000), on the corner of via Napoli. If you want a **meal**, the small *Trattoria del Carmine*, via Ducezio 9, does *cucina casalinga*. Get free maps and information from the **EPT** in piazza XVI Maggio, behind the Hercules fountain (April to Oct daily 9am–8pm, rest of the year 8am–2pm & 4–6pm; ☎0931-836.744). Also in the piazza is the **bus stop** for Siracusa and Ragusa; the *FS* bus for PACHINO (see below) leaves from outside Noto's railway station.

Noto Antica
If you've got a car, you could venture out to see the sparse remains of **NOTO ANTICA**, sixteen kilometres north west of town, up the SS287. After passing the convent of Santa Maria delle Scale, turn left, and pass through the gate of a castle. The visible remnants of the old town are confined to bits of wall, and the bric-a-brac held in a makeshift museum at the **Éremo della Madonna della Providenza**. There should be someone around to let you in: it's free, but not very exciting.

The coastal route to Sicily's southern cape

Trains no longer run south from Noto, and if you're travelling **down the coast** you'll have to take the bus to Pachino, either the *FS* service from Noto railway station (twice daily, 2.53pm and 6.16pm; Sun 2.53pm only), or the more regular *SAIS* bus from Siracusa/Noto. If you have a car, though, you'll be able to stop off at some of the remoter beaches along the way.

First stop out of Noto, eight or nine kilometres to the south west, are the ruins of Helorus, or **Eloro**, by the sea – buses for here leave Noto three times daily. This Syracusan colony, founded in the 7C BC at the mouth of the Tellaro river, is still being excavated, but the small site can be seen at any time. It has some city walls, a small theatre, and a sanctuary dedicated to

Demeter and Kore, with the remains of a *stoa*, or portico. It's all very ramshackle, but made all the more attractive by its position bang on the rocky shore. The broad expanse of sand alongside also offers **good swimming**.

If you're driving, there's another secluded **beach** five or six kilometres further south, at the **Torre Vendícari**, an abandoned tower overlooking a crescent of sand that's hidden behind some disused salt pans. It's a bit difficult to find: turn left over a narrow railway bridge, and look out for an old tower.

Pachino and the cape

The lowlands south of here are best reached from the area's main town, **PACHINO**. It's a pleasant enough place, with an outsized central piazza that's lined with bars, and there are regular local buses from here to various coastal resorts. One, **MARZAMEMI** (four kilometres north east), is a resort-cum-fishing port with an old Arab feel to it and a couple of **hotels**: the *Celeste*, via del Porto 7 (☎0931-841.244; L34,000); and *La Conchiglietta*, via Regina Elena 46 (☎0931-841.191; L32,000). The bay here is littered with the submerged hulks of Greek, Roman and Byzantine ships, which foundered on their way round the cape.

Seven kilometres south of Pachino is the larger town of **PORTOPALO DI CAPO PÁSSERO**. In summer it's a fairly lively place, with several bars and discos along the main street and one cheapish **hotel** – *El Condor*, via Vittorio Emanuele 38 (☎0931-842.016; L25,000). You might be able to persuade someone to row you over to the little islet lying just offshore, complete with 17C castle. Otherwise, there's a pleasant day's moseying around to be done in the area: the flat land here is market-garden country, the fields and greenhouses sheltering tomatoes, strawberries and artichokes; the coast – when you can get to it along dusty, unmade tracks – rough and seaweed-scattered. Along the road that leads to the cape, there are two **campsites** (both with cabins and adjacent beaches), within walking distance of Portopalo. The first of these is only a kilometre away, the *Capo Pássero*, (☎0931-842.333; open all year), though you'd do better to go a bit further, to the south eastern point of **Isola delle Correnti**, where the clean and well-equipped *Captain* campsite (☎0931-842.595; June to Sept) sits in happy isolation behind its own unspoiled sandy bay. You're on the southernmost tip of Sicily here, with nothing between you and Africa.

RAGUSA AND THE BAROQUE SOUTH EAST

Aside from the much-vaunted Noto, the best of the Baroque in Sicily's south east is in the **province of Ragusa** – less visited, but providing surprising pockets of grandeur amid the bare hills and deep valleys of the region. The most congenial base for any exploration of the area is **Ragusa**, a busy provincial capital not especially interesting in itself but with two or three hotels and an encouraging, friendly atmosphere. From here, it's easy to reach the other

Baroque towns by train or bus: **Módica** to the south, **Cómiso** and **Vittória** to the west, with smaller examples closer to the coast – like **Scicli** or **Íspica**. This last town is at the end of one of the best **walks** in the region, through the **Cava d'Íspica**, a gorge lined with rock-cut tombs. The **coast** south of Ragusa has a string of small-scale holiday towns, and a couple of ancient sites, interspersed with good **beaches**.

Ragusa

The 1693 earthquake destroyed many towns and cities that were then rebuilt in a different form, but the unique effect on **RAGUSA** was to split the city in two. The old town of Ragusa Ibla, on a jut of land above its valley, was comprehensively flattened, and within a few years a new town emerged, on the higher ridge just to the west. Unlike Noto Antica, Ibla was stubbornly rebuilt, though retaining its medieval appearance; while its new neighbour, known simply as Ragusa, developed along planned, grand lines. Rivalry between the two was commonplace, until 1926 when both towns were nominally reunited, a move which proved to be the kiss of death for Ragusa Ibla. Rapidly depopulated, all the business and industry was relocated to the prosperous upper town, where oil is the latest venture – derricks scattered around modern Ragusa's higher reaches. Ibla meanwhile still survives, a short walk out of the modern centre, an anachronistic appendage to its younger relative.

Ragusa: the upper town

It's in the **upper town** that you'll arrive, buses and trains dropping you a five-minute walk from the exposed **Ponte Nuovo**. The bridge spans a huge cleft in the ridge, and what there is of interest lies across the far side of this. Via Roma runs right into the heart of modern Ragusa, the gridded town slipping off to right and left on either side of the steeply sloping Corso Italia. Just around the corner, above piazza San Giovanni, stands the **Duomo**, conceived on an imposing, symmetrical scale. Finished in 1774, its tapered columns and fine doorways are a fairly sombre background to the vigorous small-town atmosphere around.

Back towards the railway station, underneath the *Standa* supermarket at the Ponte Nuovo, there's an important **Museo Archeologico** (Mon–Sat 9am–2pm, Sun 9am–1pm; free), worth an hour or so of your time. Aside from the usual exhibits – prehistoric flints to late Roman mosaics – the museum deals mainly with finds from the Greek site of Camarina (6C BC), on the coast to the south west (p.201). Especially interesting are the necropolis reconstructions, amplified by photos, and a restored potter's kiln (from a site at Scornavacche), the neat little terracotta figures found around it displayed in separate cases.

As far as Ragusa goes, though, that's about it. Although the new Baroque town received its share of good-looking buildings (like the few grand palazzi down Corso Italia), most of the architects' efforts seem to have gone into keeping the streets as straight as possible and there's little that's all that striking. Ragusa is predominantly a working, commercial town, with an

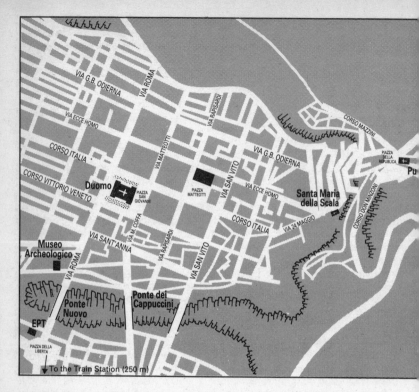

atmosphere to match and perhaps the best of all the diversions are the unusually lively scenes around piazza San Giovanni and the main streets at *passeggiata* time. By 6pm via Roma is packed shoulder-to-shoulder with milling people, the cars forced off the roads for an hour or two while everyone hits the bars and cake shops.

Ragusa Ibla

It's in **RAGUSA IBLA**, the original, lower town that you'll probably while away much of the day. The locked and shuttered buildings of its stepped streets give the impression of a ghost town, and it's much the most interesting part of Ragusa despite the evident abandonment. Head down Corso Italia and the narrow via XXIV Maggio, and from the terrace, by the restored 15C church of **Santa Maria della Scala** (which features the remains of an unusual exterior pulpit), Ragusa Ibla lies beyond and below. It's a mighty view, the weather-beaten roofs straddling the outcrop of rock, rising to the prominent church dome of San Giorgio, which fronts the town like the prow of a ship.

Walking, it'll take about another twenty minutes to descend to Ragusa Ibla itself, following the steps from Santa Maria down beneath the winding road,

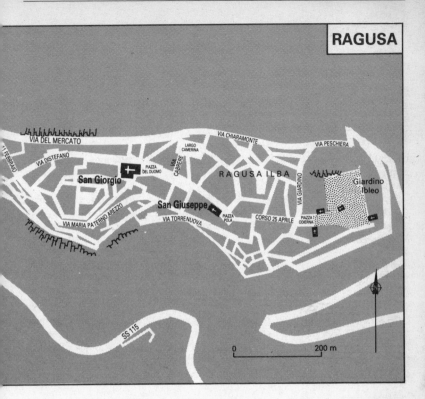

to the chiesa del Purgatorio. Although there are quicker routes into the centre, it's an idea to follow via del Mercato, which hugs the edge of the spur on which the town rests, so that you can look out over the grey valley before cutting back through largo Camerina. This is the best approach for entering piazza del Duomo, for the first excellent views of **San Giorgio**, stridently placed at the top of the square. One of the masterpieces of Sicilian Baroque, the church was designed by Rosario Gagliardi and took nearly forty years to complete. The sloping piazza, split by six palms, ends in broad steps which lead to the church set slightly at an angle. Its three-tiered facade, sets of triple columns climbing up the wedding-cake exterior to a balconied belfry, is an imaginative work, though typically not matched inside. As with Gagliardi's other projects, all the beauty is in the immediacy of the powerful exterior.

The whole town – deathly quiet at lunchtime – is ripe for aimless wandering. Gagliardi gets another credit for the elegant rounded facade and bulging balconies of **San Giuseppe** in piazza Pola, a few steps below San Giorgio, while Corso XXV Aprile continues down past abandoned palazzi to the **Giardino Ibleo** (daily 8am–8pm). The violet-strewn flower beds here set off the remains of three small churches, abandoned in the grounds; and to the right of the garden's entrance there's the surviving Gothic portal of the shattered old church of San Giorgio, the badly worn stone centrepiece depicting a skeletal St George killing the dragon.

If you can't face the walk back to the upper town, bus #1 or #3 makes the trip hourly from piazza Pola.

Ragusa practicalities

All **buses** stop outside the **railway station** in the upper town: bus departure schedules are posted on the wall by the bus park and in the bar over the road (at via Dante 94). A short walk to the left from the station, along the main road, leads to piazza della Libertà, just across which (first left) is the **EPT**, via Natalelli 131 (Mon–Sat 8.30am–2pm; ☎0932-21.421); no one here speaks English, but you should at least be able to grab a free listings booklet which contains a map.

Accommodation is limited to a few hotels in the upper town. The cheapest, *San Giovanni*, via Traspontino 3 (☎0932-21.013; L30,000), is at the railway station end of the Ponte dei Cappuccini; the other good-value choice, the *Mediterraneo* (☎0932-21.944; L42,000 with bath), is just over the Ponte Nuovo on the way into town from the station. The nearest **campsites** are on the coast at MARINA DI RAGUSA (see below), 24km south: *Baia del Sole* (☎0932-39.844/46.495; open all year); and *Villa Nifosì* (☎0932-39.118/51.168; April to Oct) – buses every hour (Mon–Sat) from Ragusa.

As far as **eating** goes, there's a really good, basic trattoria, the *Trattoria Ragusana*, in via San Sebastiano (take via Mariannina Coffa from the south eastern corner of piazza San Giovanni), which has set meals, including wine, for around L12,000. There are a couple of trattorias, too, in Ragusa Ibla, best the *U Saracinu* at via del Convento 9, very close to the church of San Giorgio (April to Sept only, closed Wed).

South: Módica and around

The wild countryside continues to impress as you head beyond Ragusa. The route to **Módica**, half an hour's drive to the south, is a case in point. As the bus swirls down past Ragusa Ibla and climbs through some rugged hills, all the vegetation seems to have been pulled into the valleys below, the tiered slopes bare and rocky – the effect only spoiled by the siting of an asphalt works right on the top, disfiguring the stark hills. Beyond Módica, the train ambles south towards the coast, passing other small Baroque towns like **Scicli**, before reaching **Íspica**, base for an exploration of its gorge.

Módica

MÓDICA is an enjoyable place to spend half a day. A powerful medieval base of the Chiaramonte family, the **upper town** (Módica Alta) is watched over by the magnificent 18C facade of **San Giorgio**, a worthy rival to the church of the same name in Ragusa Ibla. It's thought that Gagliardi was responsible for this too: the elliptical facade is topped by his trademark, a belfry, while the approach is characteristically daring – twin flights of stairs zig-zag up across the upper roads of the town ending in a terrace before the church. From here, or better still from the tight streets above San Giorgio, you can look back over the grey-tiled roofs and balconies of the town, built up two sides of a narrow valley. The **lower town** (Módica Bassa) lies in the valley cleft, traced by the main Corso Umberto I and home to palazzi whose balconies are buttressed by gargoyles, twisted heads and beasts – and to a crop of battered churches.

It's worth making the journey from Ragusa to Módica by **bus** if you can – the train route isn't half as spectacular. Buses pull up on Corso Umberto I, and just down the street, on the left, a side-street flanking San Pietro church leads up to the steps which rise to San Giorgio. To get into the town centre from the **railway station**, walk to the right and, at the ornamental fountain, bear left for the Corso.

Given the price of accommodation in Ragusa, you might well want to stay overnight in Módica instead. There's a very pleasant little **hotel**, the *Albergo Minerva* (☎0932-94.129; L21,000 with shower), tucked up via San Domenico – down the Corso from the bus-stop, left at the first main junction, then via San Domenico is just over the road (via Marchesa Tedeschi), next to the church.

If you're looking for **lunch**, *La Contea*, via Iachinoto 43 (over from the hotel, off the other side of via Marchesa Tedeschi), is a moderately priced restaurant with (unusually inland) fish on the menu. Or there's a good, basic trattoria, *Trattoria Ringo*, at the bottom of town, beyond the fountain, next to the *Esso* petrol station on via Corrado Rizzone. One **bar** worth a look is *Rick's Bar*, entered through the cracked portal of an old palazzo on the main Corso (no. 133) – a trendy cellar drinking-spot.

Scicli, Pozzallo and Íspica

SCICLI, just ten kilometres south (buses and trains from Ragusa and Módica), is dramatically pitched against the bottom of a knobbly bluff, its air of faded grandeur reinforced by the almost exclusively geriatric population. Perhaps because it's off the tourist track, Scicli's profusion of pale yellow 18C churches, balconied palazzi and spacious, empty squares, is being allowed to slip into terminal neglect, though it still retains the graceful line and colour shared by all the region's post-quake towns.

Just off the main piazza, the crumbling **Palazzo Beneventano** features some spectacularly ugly 18C exterior decoration: manic grinning faces with lolling tongues and bald heads tucked under the balconies and clinging to the walls. From the palazzo, via Matrice and via San Matteo lead uphill past the abandoned shell of a chapel to the empty church of **San Matteo**, currently being beautifully restored. Its terrace enjoys grand views over Scicli below, the track then continuing upwards, behind the church, to the remains of a lookout tower. Walk a little way beyond here, to the top of the ridge, and you're standing right above a series of abandoned **cave-dwellings** that litter the hills around, used from Neolithic times until fairly recently: from the vantage-point you can make out bricked-up entrances, caves and doorways, in the tree-dotted cliffs below.

From Scicli the train forges a devious route south, to the coast at **POZZALLO**, a small port with a nice beach and a tangled industrial complex close by. British troops, led by Montgomery, landed here in 1943, joining with the Americans, who had landed further west, to take Gela – the first European ground to be recaptured by the Allies in World War II.

Another ten minutes on, **ÍSPICA** lies at the head of a wide gorge riddled with more Neolithic tombs and cave-dwellings, later used by Sikels, Greeks and early Christians to bury their dead. The gorge, the **Cava d'Íspica**, stretches for twelve kilometres to the north west, and the whole length can be walked without too much hardship. Rock-cut dwellings and tombs are scattered along the entire route, but you'll see the most impressive set at the other, north western, end of it. If you're mobile and want to head directly to these, they're roughly halfway between Módica and Íspica, six kilometres up a minor road signposted off the main SS115. There's a half-hearted **information office** at the bar here, and whoever's around will be glad to guide you to the more notable of the caves in the vicinity. A torch would be useful.

Cómiso, Vittória and the southern coast

CÓMISO and VITTÓRIA, situated to the west of Ragusa, are strictly for passing through, only of interest to lovers of Baroque or students of small-town life. Both are on the main railway line from Ragusa to Gela, and could be seen in half a morning each.

That said, the journey to **CÓMISO** is worth making by bus or car if you can, crossing a barren 600m-high plateau that looks away to the distant sea and down to the massive domes dominating the town's skyline. Cómiso is better-known these days as the scene of violent confrontations between Italian police and demonstrators, following the contentious siting of **American cruise missiles**, just five kilometres to the north at MAGLIOCCO, in 1984. A women's peace camp was set up here, and elicited far rougher treatment from the police than was the case at similar camps in Britain: broken bones and deportations for foreign protesters were the norm. The missiles, the last to be installed in western Europe, are not due for removal until at least 1990.

Such matters seem a million miles from the parochial atmosphere in town. Although the Chiaramonte and other noble families filled Cómiso with a wealth of architecture during the Middle Ages, it is the Baroque spirit which infuses the place, most prominent in the two major churches, the **Chiesa Matrice** and the nearby **Santíssima Anunziata**. Both are post-1693 products and overwhelm everything else within reach of their ponderous shadows. A relief, then, to wander up via Virgilio (or, from the Anunziata, via degli Studi) to gaze on a much more modest affair, the 13C church of **San Francesco**, to which a rich Renaissance chapel was added in 1517 to house the tombs of the powerful Naselli family. You can see their restored **castello** near the centre of town, at the end of via San Biagio.

Another ten minutes by train, **VITTÓRIA** lies at the centre of a rich wine district. Founded in 1607 by Vittoria della Colonna, daughter of the Spanish viceroy and wife of the Count of Módica, it differs from other hillside towns in the region in its location on the plain west of the Iblean mountains – a setting reflected in its flat and regular street-plan. You can confine your visit here to the two principal squares, piazza del Pópolo and piazza Ricca, the first graced by the curved facade of the church of **Madonna della Grazia** and the later neoclassical Teatro Comunale. The smaller piazza Ricca lies in the lee of the church of **San Giovanni Battista**, its interior dripping with gilt.

Along the coast: archaeology and beaches

The coast – and the start of the so-called 'riviera' which extends as far as GELA (p.228) – is only ten kilometres south west of Vittória, at SCOGLITTI. Three kilometres south of here, just beyond the mouth of the river Íppari, lie the desolate remains of ancient **Camarina**, a Syracusan colony founded in 599 BC, several times devastated in the conflicts with nearby Gela, and eventually destroyed by Rome in 258 BC. Only reachable **by bus** from Ragusa, this dispersed area lies on a headland overlooking beaches on either side, though an **Antiquario** (Mon–Sat 9am–2pm, Sun 9am–1pm; free) marks the site's centre, containing everything that hasn't already been appropriated by Ragusa's museum. Behind the antiquario is all that's left of a 5C BC **Tempio di Atena**, surrounded by the rubble of city walls. West of it lie the various ruins of the Hellenistic-Roman city, accessible from separate entrances along the road, each keeping the same hours as the antiquario.

At the bottom of steep cliffs south of here is a swish *Club Med* complex, while five kilometres further down the coast, at **PUNTO BRACCETTO**, are a clutch of **campsites**, most open only in the summer, though the *Baia dei Coralli* (☎0932-918.192) stays open all year round. Carry on down to the next point, **PUNTA SECCA**, to see another minor archaeological site, Byzantine **Caucana**. There are traces of a 4–6C harbour here, and the remains of a basilica, though nothing very thrilling. You might be more engaged by the nearby sandy **beach**, one of the area's most fashionable. The coast stretches further east dotted by a series of minor resorts and attendant bars and hotels. None of it is overdeveloped, and some of the small towns – **MARINA DI RAGUSA** and **DONNALUCATA** – are quite appealing, if rather dismal out of season. (There are campsites at Marina di Ragusa, see *Ragusa practicalities*)

Without your own wheels, the only way to reach the coast is **by bus**, from Ragusa to Marina di Ragusa or Camarina, or from Scicli to Donnalucata. There's a coastal road that connects them all, though little or no transport service between.

festivals

April
Last Sunday St George's Day celebrations in RAGUSA IBLA: statues paraded through the streets and a costumed procession.

May
1 Procession in SIRACUSA, with the statue of Santa Lucia carried around town.

May and June
Classical drama festival at SIRACUSA, even-numbered years only, events taking place in the Greek theatre.

August
First Sunday Boat-race (*Palio*) round Ortygia island in SIRACUSA, in which the five traditional

quarters of the city compete with raucous enthusiasm.

27–29 Festivities in RAGUSA to mark the city's patron St John the Baptist; more processions and statues.

29 Start of Madonna delle Lacrime festival

(devoted to the 'weeping' Madonna) in SIRACUSA; runs until September 3.

Last Sunday Festival of San Corrado in NOTO.

December

13 Festival of Santa Lucia in SIRACUSA: a procession to the church of Santa Lucia.

travel details

Trains

From Siracusa to Augusta/Lentini/Catania (18 daily; 30min/50min/1½hr); Taormina/Messina (14; 2½hr/3hr); Noto (11; 40min); Noto/Módica/Ragusa (6; 30min/2hr/2hr 20min); Gela (3; 4hr).

From Ragusa to Cómiso/Vittória/Gela/Licata (7 daily; 30min/40min/1hr 20min/1hr 40min); Módica (12; 25min); Módica/Scicli/Pozzallo/Íspica/Noto/Siracusa (9; 25min/35min/1hr/1hr 10min/1½hr/2hr 20min).

Buses

From Siracusa to Catania (Mon–Sat 7 daily, Sun 1; 1¼hr); Catania airport (6–9; 1hr); Ragusa (Mon–Sat 8, Sun 1; 1½hr); Augusta (hourly, Sun 4; 40min); Lentini (Mon–Sat 10 daily, Sun 1; 50min/55min); Palazzolo Acréide (Mon–Sat roughly hourly, Sun 1; 50min); Sortino (Mon–Sat 7 daily; 30min); Ferla (Mon–Sat 3; 40min); Palermo (Mon–Sat 4; 4hr 10min); Noto (half-hourly; 40min); Ávola/Noto/Pachino (Mon–Sat 12 daily, Sun 3; 40min/55min/1½hr); Eloro (3; 1hr); Caltagirone/Piazza Armerina (Mon–Sat 1 daily; 2hr/2½hr); Rome (1; 12hr).

From Ragusa to Módica (half-hourly, Sun 6; 20min); Scicli (Mon–Sat 8 daily; 40min); Íspica (hourly, Sun 4; 40min); Pozzallo (3–7 daily; 1hr); Marina di Ragusa (Mon–Sat hourly; 30min); Camarina (Mon–Sat 2 daily; 40min); Noto/Siracusa (Mon–Sat 6, Sun 1; 1hr/1½hr); Gela/Agrigento (Mon–Sat 2; 1hr/2½hr); Palermo (1–2 daily; 4hr).

From Módica to Ragusa (half-hourly, Sun 6; 20min); Scicli (Mon–Sat 9 daily; 20min); Pozzallo (Mon–Sat 11, Sun 5; 40min); Íspica (Mon–Sat 13, Sun 5; 20min); Pachino (Mon–Sat 2; 1hr); Siracusa (5–10 daily; 1hr 20min).

From Pachino to Portopalo di Capo Pássero (Mon–Sat 9 daily; 15min); Marzamemi (Mon–Sat 4; 10min); Ragusa (2; 1½hr).

Ferries

From Siracusa to Catania/Réggio di Calabria (3 weekly; 2¼hr/6½hr); Naples (1 weekly; 18hr); Malta (3 weekly; 5hr).

Hydrofoils

From Siracusa to Malta (June to Sept Wed 2 daily & Fri 2 daily; 1hr 50min).

CHAPTER SIX

THE INTERIOR

. . . for the last five hours all they had set eyes on were bare hillsides flaming yellow under the sun . . . They had passed through crazed-looking villages washed in palest blue; crossed dry beds of torrents over fantastic bridges; skirted sheer precipices which no sage and broom could temper. Never a tree, never a drop of water; just sun and dust.

Giuseppe di Lampedusa, *The Leopard.*

Sicily's slow cross-country trains and the limited-exit motorway (the A19) do little to encourage stops in the island's vast and mountainous **interior**, but it's only here that you really begin to get off the tourist trail. Intensely rural, there are just two or three decent-sized towns, bunched together almost in the dead centre of the island: outside these, much of the land is burned dry during the long summer months, the cracked fields and shrivelled plantations affording a meagre living to the sparse population. Unlike other parts of Italy, those who cultivated the land here (if it was cultivable) actually travelled to work from their towns and villages rather than living on site. Now thoroughly depleted by mass emigration, the countryside is empty and you're unlikely to see many signs of life outside the small hilltop towns. But these towns, though often moribund, occasionally possess an exuberance and vitality that's in startling contrast with the stillness of the interior's rolling hills.

Travelling in the interior can get monotonous, as much of the land is given over to extensive cornfields – a feature of the Sicilian landscape since Greek times. But there are compensations for coming this far off the beaten track. Some of the minor inland routes give fascinating glimpses of a life that's all but disappeared in the rest of Sicily (indeed Italy), and there are some of the finest routes and views on the island, as well as some of its most curious towns. **Enna** is as central as you can get, a blustery mountain settlement dominating the dry hills below, and making a good starting-point for trips to the untouched towns and villages of the **north eastern interior**, of which **Nicosia** is the main attraction. The biggest town in the region, **Caltanissetta**, is also the most disappointing, largely modern and devoid of life. But with your own transport, the region beyond it – the little-visited **western interior** – makes an absorbing journey, stretching to **Corleone**: an agricultural centre that, like so many in the neighbourhood, is tainted by its Mafia associations.

Although the Arabs settled the centre of the island, leaving their mark in a number of place-names and warren-like towns, the Greeks and Romans tended to leave Sicily's interior alone. Nevertheless, the **southern interior** boasts some unexpected ancient gems, not least **Piazza Armerina** and its fabulous Roman mosaics, and the nearby excavations at **Morgantina**. And

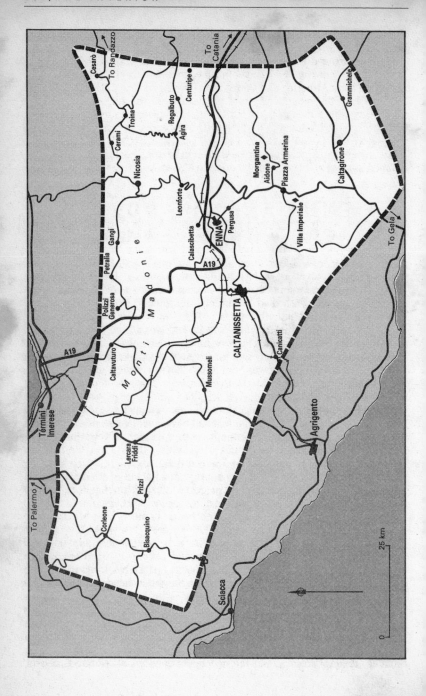

there's interest, too, in ceramic-studded **Caltagirone**, a handy departure point for the Baroque towns of the south east (for which, see p.194).

Getting around the interior can be tricky. Public transport is patchy at best, though you can easily reach all the important centres – Enna, Caltanissetta, Piazza Armerina and Caltagirone – by bus or train. It's more difficult to travel into the mountains: most accessible are the hilltop towns of the north east, with **buses** running out of Enna and along the two major routes. Virtually impossible to reach without your **own transport**, are the towns and villages west of Caltanissetta. You should plan ahead if you want to stay the night anywhere, as good **accommodation** is scarce; most of the options are detailed in the text, but it's worth noting that there are *no* official **campsites**.

ENNA AND THE NORTH EASTERN INTERIOR

Despite its stranded mountaintop position and the frontier feel of the town, there's no great effort involved in getting to **Enna** these days: there are regular buses and trains from Catania and Palermo. But without your own transport you'll usually have to be prepared to spend the night, certainly if you intend to move further into the **north eastern interior** to some of the least-developed parts of the island. Fairly frequent **buses** leave Enna for towns along the eastbound **SS121**, which eventually runs right the way to Catania. From **Leonforte**, first stop on this route, there are buses north to **Nicosia**: like Enna, a good place to base yourself. Nicosia sits in the middle of a second route, the **SS120**: east to **Cesarò** and on into the foothills of Etna, though this is fairly hard to travel by public transport; or west to **Polizzi Generosa**, an easier choice, as all the towns on this stretch are connected by bus. A few places along the SS120 (east and west) can also be reached from towns on the Tyrrhenian coast, cutting across dramatic tracts of the Nébrodi and Madonie mountains.

You may be able to help matters by **hitching** some of the way between towns in the north east, but don't count on it: traffic is scarce and strangers are viewed with suspicion. If you do get stuck, it's of some comfort to know that some towns at least have good, cheap **hotels**.

Enna

From a bulging V-shaped ridge almost 1000m up, **ENNA** lords it over the surrounding hills of central Sicily. One of the most ancient towns on the island, Enna has only ever had one function: Livy described it as 'inexpugnabilis' and, for obvious strategic reasons, Enna was a magnet for successive hostile armies, who in turn besieged and fortified it. The approach to this mountain stronghold is still formidable, the bus climbing slowly out of the valley and looping across the solid crag to the summit and the town. Enna remains medieval at heart, as any foray into its densely packed streets shows, and even the modern development echoes the town's defensive past, its office blocks rising like so many watchtowers from a distance.

The very distinct hill-town atmosphere here is worth staying overnight for. Summer evenings in Enna are among the most enjoyable in Sicily, watching the sun set from some of the finest vantage-points imaginable. Come in winter and you should expect snow, the wind blowing hard through the streets, white slopes blending with the anaemic stone buildings.

Arriving and getting around

All long-distance and most local buses use the **bus terminal** on viale Diaz in the new town – turn right out of the terminal and right again down Corso Sicilia, around a ten-minute walk to piazza Vittorio Emanuele. If you possibly can, arrive by bus: Enna's **railway station** is five kilometres below town, a long and dauntingly steep walk, though a local bus runs roughly hourly to the town centre (but only at 9.10am, 4.10pm, 7.10pm, 8.10pm and 9.15pm on Sunday). You can reach everywhere in Enna itself very easily on foot, though **buses for Pergusa**, #4, leave from outside San Francesco church; you'll need a ticket (L500) before you get on, bought from *tabacchi* and valid for one hour. Information, as well as a good free **map** of Enna, is available from the **EPT** in piazza Garibaldi (Mon–Sat 8.30am–1.30pm; ☎0935-21.184); there's a smaller **AAST** in piazza Colaianni (Mon–Fri 9am–1pm & 4–6.30pm, Sat 9am–1pm; ☎0935-26.119), next to the *Grande Albergo Sicilia*.

The town

Despite the numerous wars that have touched the town over the years, most of Enna's remains are medieval and in good nick, prize exhibit being the 13C **Castello di Lombardia** (daily 9am–1pm & 3–7pm; free) dominating the easternmost spur of town. Built by the Swabian Frederick II, it's a mighty construction with its strong walls complete, guarding the steep slopes on either side of town. Six surviving towers (out of an original twenty) provide lookouts and the tallest, the Torre Pisana, takes in magnificent views of Enna itself, some rugged countryside in all directions and, if you're lucky, Mount Etna. The main courtyard is used as an open-air theatre in the summer, and there's plenty of room elsewhere to lounge about with a picnic.

A road to the side of the castle climbs a little way further to the **Rocca di Cerere**, an exposed outcrop where some scattered foundations are presumed to be the remnants of a temple erected by Gelon in 480 BC. Enna was the centre of the Greek cult of Demeter, the fertility goddess (her Roman counterpart was Ceres, hence the rock's name), and the most famous of the myths associated with the goddess – the carrying off of her daughter, Persephone, to the underworld – is supposed to have taken place just a few kilometres away, at Lago di Pergusa (see p.209).

Attractive chunks of the **old town** survive intact too, though much worn by the brisk winds that scurry across the squares and streets, even in summer. Tightly packed houses hug the two ridges that divide Enna, occasional gaps revealing swirling drops down into the valleys. Though it's fun to wander through the crumbly southern and eastern sections of Enna, virtually all the

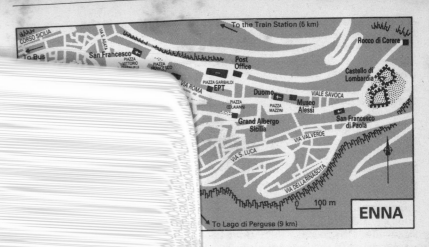

along and around the better-preserved **via**
...astle. It's a narrow street, interrupted by
...s the hemmed-in **Duomo** (usually open
...307. Rebuilt several times since, its long
medieval wall, which has ...touches, is hardly complemented by the
Duomo's thin Baroque facade, while the spacious 16C interior features huge
supporting alabaster columns, the bases and capitals of which are covered
with an amorphous, writhing mass – manic heads with human hands and
snake bodies, snarling mouths and dome-like pates. Outside, the **Museo
Alessi** (Mon–Sat 9am–1pm; free) fields the impressive contents of the
cathedral's own treasury, including a tall 18C wooden cabinet which opens to
reveal a silver throne. Some of the handiwork on display is remarkable: a 17C
gold and crystal crown is decorated with minute scenes from the life of
Christ, picked out with studded jewels. There's a rich collection of local
church art too, downstairs, and cases of old coins on the floor above. A
second museum, equally good, lies just over the way in piazza Mazzini – the
Museo Archeologico (Mon–Sat 9am–1.30pm, Sun 9.30am–1pm; free),
which covers Neolithic to Roman times, all the exhibits dug up in the locality,
including a fine series of painted Greek vases.

Via Roma continues down past the Catalan-Gothic **Palazzo Pollicarini**,
just around the corner from which, in piazza Coppola, the tower of the church
of **San Giovanni** is crowned by a little cupola. It's one of the few surviving
relics of the Arab occupation of Enna, though the winding central streets
suggest an eastern influence, too. The Arabs spent twenty years trying to
gain entrance to the town and eventually resorted to crawling in through the
sewers in 859.

The eastern extremity of via Roma is marked by the sloping, rectangular
piazza Vittorio Emanuele, focal point of the evening *passeggiata*. Off here, a
long cliff-edge promenade looks out to the little rust-coloured village of
CALASCIBETTA (p.209) over the valley, and there's a good bar (with outside

tables) at the top of the square if you want a drink. The plain, high wall of the church of **San Francesco**, which flanks the piazza, has a massive 16C tower, previously part of the old town's system of watchtowers, which linked the castle with all Enna's churches. One of the watchtowers, the **Torre di Federico II**, still stands in isolation in the **Giardino Pubblico** (summer daily 8am–8pm, winter daily until sunset), in the largely modern south of the town. An octagonal tower, 24m high, it's a survivor of the alterations to the city made by Frederick of Aragon, who added a (now hidden) underground passage connecting the tower to the castle. There should be someone around to let you in for more views from the top of the tower.

Sleeping and eating

There isn't a great choice of **accommodation** in Enna, its two hotels both fairly swish, and you could always take a bus to nearby Pergusa instead, where there are several cheaper possibilities. (If you're coming to Enna from PIAZZA ARMERINA, you'll pass through Pergusa first.) Best choice, if it's open after restoration, is the *Belvedere*, piazza Francesco Crispi (☎0935-21.020; L31,000), magnificently sited, as its name suggests, on the terraced promenade off the main piazza Vittorio Emanuele. Otherwise, there's the *Grande Albergo Sicilia* in piazza Colaianni (☎0935-21.127; L43,000 with bath). There is also a very cheap and slightly dubious *Allogio* at via Trieste 95 in the southern part of town, but I've never yet found it open.

As for **eating**, there are several places not entirely given over to the passing tourist trade. Most basic, and perfectly adequate, is the *Ristorante Familiare*, via Sant'Agata 123 (near San Francesco church); the *Grotta Azzurra*, close by on via Colaianni (between piazza Matteotti and piazza Vittorio Emanuele), is more adventurous but still reasonably priced. Considerably more expensive, but worth every lira, is the *Ristorante Ariston*, via Roma 365 (closed Sun), which specialises in fresh pasta, good Sicilian dishes and the local *vino Pergusino*; expect to pay around L25,000 a head for a full meal with wine. The **market** in Enna is held on Tuesday at the end of viale Diaz, below the Torre di Federico II. For a good **bar**, try the chrome-trimmed *Extra Bar*, via Roma 391, which deals in tasty snacks as well as drinks.

Listings

Car problems *ACI*, via Roma 200 (☎0935-26.365)

Chemist *Librizzi*, piazza Vittorio Emanuele.

Cinema *Supercinema Grivi*, piazza Ghisleri, near piazza Umberto.

Hospital *Ospedale Umberto I*, via Trieste (☎0935-21.913).

Police *Questura* at via San Giuseppe 2 (☎0935-21.081).

Post Office via Volta, off piazza Garibaldi.

Taxis Ranks along viale Diaz, near the bus terminal, and on via Pergusa.

Telephone office *SIP*, piazza Umberto (daily 8am–8pm).

Train information Timetables at the EPT; and at *Agenzia Viaggi FF.SS*, via Sant'Agata 28.

Around Enna: Calascibetta and the Lago di Pergusa

Closest to Enna, on a lower hill to the north across the valley, the small town of **CALASCIBETTA** hints at what Enna would be like without the tower blocks. Once a Saracen town, it was fortified by Count Roger in his successful attempt to take Enna in 1087, and the brooding atmosphere in its tangled streets seems straight from that age. Tightly packed red-stone buildings are perched above a sheer drop on the eastern side, rising to the restored Chiesa Madre at the very top. There are frequent buses to Calascibetta from Enna's bus terminal (or two-hourly from Enna's railway station); if you're driving, the trattoria halfway up the steep road there is said to be very good.

Nine kilometres south of Enna, the **Lago di Pergusa** is the legendary site of Hades' abduction of Persephone to the underworld. The story has it that Persephone, surrounded by nymphs, was gathering flowers on the lush banks of the lake, when Hades emerged from a chasm beneath the water and spirited her away. Demeter searched in vain for her daughter, and her grief at the loss of Persephone prevented the corn from growing. To settle the matter, Zeus ruled that Persephone should spend half the year as Queen of the Underworld, living for the other six months in Sicily with her mother as one of the island's goddesses. In her gratitude, Demeter, as goddess of grain and agriculture, made the corn grow again – a powerful symbol in a traditionally fertile land.

Today, the lake is encircled by a motor-racing track, and despite the wooded banks beyond the water, it's difficult now to imagine a less romantic spot. Mary Taylor Simeti's journal, *On Persephone's Island*, labels the lake 'a brilliant example of the Sicilians' best efforts to ruin their landscape'; and certainly, it's not worth coming here for any glimpse of the truth behind the legend, though it is a possible base near Enna. Alongside the lake there are several new **hotels**, the two cheapest on the Enna road: the *Miralago* (☎0935-36.272; L30,000 with bath) or *La Pergola* (☎0935-36.017; L26,000 with bath) further up. There's a **campsite** too, just off the race track, and a swimming pool. If you don't want to go back into Enna you can **eat** pizza in the evenings at the *Miralago*, or try the *Trattoria Al Carretino* on the main road, whose local pasta speciality (*Cavatelle al Carretino*) is excellent. (The last bus from Enna to Pergusa is at 8.30pm; from Pergusa to Enna at 9pm.)

The SS121: Enna to Centúripe

Out of Enna, and beyond Calascibetta, it's around forty minutes by bus to **LEONFORTE**, typical of the many small towns you'll come across east of Enna, with its roots firmly in the 17C. The most notable sight here is **La Granfonte**: a fountain built in in 1651 with 24 separate jets. It's about 300m on foot down from the Chiesa Matrice (or follow the signs at the western end of the village if you're driving), overlooking the hills on the edge of town.

Stick with the bus from Enna. It steers a course further east through **AGIRA**, again well-sited on the brow of a hill. If you're mobile, you could pause here for **lunch** at the excellent *Trattoria di Sanariti Maria*, via Vittorio Emanuele 343, the main road through town. Agira's also the only place for an

overnight stop on this route, at the tidy *Albergo Aurora*, via Annunziata 6 (☎0935-691.547; L20,000). There's a disturbingly early 6am bus north, to TROINA – useful if you want to get to the SS120 (see below).

The SS121 bus route continues through tiny REGALBUTO, and eventually to Catania, a journey that strikes through land fiercely contested during the short Sicilian campaign of World War II. The hills between Agira and the western slopes of Etna saw most of the heaviest fighting. Just out of Agira, close to the Lago di Pozzillo, there's a poignant **war cemetery** sited on a gentle hillside, the resting-place of 490 Canadian soldiers killed in July 1943.

Some twenty kilometres on, a minor road leads south for eight kilometres through orange and olive groves to **CENTÚRIPE**, which faces Etna across the Simeto river valley, giving it a strategic importance that accounts for the struggles for control of this isolated outpost over the centuries. Various medieval campaigns destroyed the town, while the last great battle in August 1943 dislodged Hermann Goering and his forces. Most of the damage has since been made good, rather to the detriment of Centúripe, which is an uneasy mix of new building and an untouched central piazza. A terrace not far from here is the best vantage-point for the outstanding views that earned for Centúripe the tag 'balcony of Sicily'.

The towns beyond Centúripe, on and off the SS121, are covered in the section on the Cirumetnea railway; see p160.

Across the mountains: the SS120

Before the Palermo-Messina coastal road was built, traffic between the two cities passed inland, on a long mountainous route that took in some of the island's most impressive scenery. Today, free of the traffic that clogs the coast, **the SS120** makes an attractive trans-island alternative, across some of the remoter stretches of the Madonie and Nébrodi mountains. Make sure you book accommodation in advance, though, as the few hotels there are tend to fill up quickly.

Nicosia

The biggest town on this stretch, and best base for excursions east and west, is **NICOSIA** (reachable by buses from Leonforte, Palermo, Términi Imerese and Santo Stéfano/Mistretta), a basically medieval, convoluted mass of cracked palazzi topped by the remains of a Norman castle. In the cramped centre, the chatter-filled piazza Garibaldi is the site of Nicosia's lovely old cathedral, **San Nicola** (daily 8–10.30am), a stately construction with a 14C facade and bell-tower, and a sculpted Gothic portal. Sadly, it's still encumbered by scaffolding, in place since an earthquake all but wrecked the building in 1967, but you'll be able to get in for a look around in the morning.

Behind the cathedral, via Salomone rises steeply to the former Saracen district of the town, a jumble of streets occupying one of the four hills on which Nicosia is built. At the top, **Santa Maria Maggiore**, founded in 1267 but rebuilt after an 18C landslide, has the bells from its campanile piled up outside – they fell down after another earthquake and the sound of them is now electrically produced. Inside, amid 'No Spitting' notices, there's an impressive marble polyptych by Antonello Gagini and a throne used by Charles V when he passed through here in 1535, on the way back from his Tunisian crusade. The views from outside encompass the town's other three promontories, on the highest of which sits the ruined **castello**.

Of the two or three cheap **hotels** here, try *La Greca*, via della Pace 6 (☎0935-648.258; L16,000), one hundred metres down the main street from piazza Garibaldi, with its own good **trattoria**. Otherwise, there's the *Albergo Patria*, via Vittorio Emanuele 11 (☎0935-646.103; L25,000), back up the main drag. **Buses** leave Nicosia from piazza Marconi, at the bottom of the street.

East to Cesarò

The towns to the **east of Nicosia** are set in a bare landscape astride the Nébrodi mountains, dominated ever more dramatically by the giant silhouette of Etna. There's no public transport to the first stop, **CERAMI**, 21km away, which lies at the foot of a massive rock topped by the remains of a castle. But you can reach the next town east, **TROINA**, by bus from Agira, a tortuous thirty-kilometre ride to what, from a distance, appears like a silver thimble perched on a hill, 1120m high. Troina played a prominent role in the reconquest of Sicily from the Arabs, when it became one of the first cities to be taken by the Normans. Count Roger withstood a siege here for four months in 1064 that nearly put paid to his Sicilian adventures, a victory which he commemorated by founding the convent of **San Basilio**, now in ruins near the present Capuchin convent. But it's the journey to this wind-blown village that's the real event.

CESARÒ, twenty kilometres further east, stands at the crossroads with the SS289, which runs north to the coast. Well within the lee of Etna, it's endowed with some remarkable views over to the volcano. Climb up to the cemetery above town, and from behind the battered castle fragments, Etna is framed between gentle hills. It's difficult to reach Cesarò from the west by public transport, only possible if the early morning bus from Nicosia still runs. However, there are buses from Sant'Agata on the Tyrrhenian coast and from Giardini-Naxos on the Ionian, the latter route taking' you through Randazzo (p.162) and the volcano's foothills. If you're stuck for a **bed**, Cesarò has a couple of hotels, cheapest the *Nébrodi*, via Margherita 30 (☎095-696.107; L21,000 with bath).

West to Polizzi Generosa

The towns and villages on the western stretch of the SS120 are easier to see by bus, linked up by several daily services from Nicosia. **SPERLINGA**, only fifteen minutes away, is one of the most interesting. The name derives from the Latin *spelonca* or 'grotto' a reference to the numerous cave-dwellings, some hundreds of years old, that pit the sandstone slopes on which the town stands. Sprouting above is a formidable battlemented **castello**, its store-rooms, cellars and stables hewn out of the rock. The lookouts above give onto a ruckled brown landscape that's typical of this part of Sicily, described by Giuseppe di Lampedusa as 'a sea suddenly petrified at the instant when a change of wind had flung the waves into a frenzy'. On a wall in the castle, you can make out an old Latin inscription referring to the time when Sperlinga was the only town in Sicily to open its doors to the Angevins, bloodily expelled from other Sicilian towns during the 13C Wars of the Vespers: barricading themselves inside the castle, the French held out for a year before surrendering. If the castle's closed, ask at the Pro Loco on the main street, or at the Municipio.

Half an hour on, **GANGI** forms a symmetrical mound on its hilltop, the shape of a tortoise-shell. The town produced two 17C artists, each known as Zoppo di Gangi ('the cripple of Gangi'), one of whom has an excellent *Last Judgement* in the church of **San Nicola** – identifiable by its incomplete 14C campanile. From Gangi you can take a bus along the minor SS286, north to Castelbuono and down to the coast at Cefalù, though if you're going to do this it'll probably necessitate a night in Gangi as the bus leaves early. The only **hotel** is the modern *Miramonti*, via Nazionale 13 (☎0921-44.424; L36,000), on the main road below town.

A better target than Gangi, if you want to combine some exploring with an overnight stop, is fourteen kilometres on. The two towns of PETRALIA are actually quite separate, on opposite sides of a hill. It's the lower town, **PETRALIA SOTTANA**, that holds more of interest, and the only accommodation. There are several weathered medieval churches here, strung along the lively main street, via Agliata. Particularly evocative is the **Chiesa Matrice** whose crumbling bell-tower looks down upon an elegant piazza. The sacristy holds a 10C or 11C Islamic bronze candelabra unique in Sicily – which is kept locked away: short of bribing the sacristan, your only chance to see it will be at a religious ceremony. If you're **staying** here, the *Madonie*, via Agliata 81 (☎0921-41.106; L28,000) is excellent value, and if you want to **eat**, the *Petra Leius* on the same street features a generous L10,000 tourist menu.

It's a three-kilometre hike across to the upper town, **PETRALIA SOPRANA**, quieter and older than its neighbour, at an altitude of nearly 1150m. This was the birthplace of Fra Úmile da Petralia (1580–1639), whose wooden crosses are to be found in churches all over southern Italy. From the edge of the village you get a long view over the Madonie and Nébrodi mountains, and, if you're westward bound, a last dim sight of Etna.

Minor roads connect the Petralias with a lovely mountain region to the north centred on Piano Battáglia (p.88), though there's no bus this way. The service along the SS120 branches off for **POLIZZI GENEROSA**, half an hour west and right in the heart of the Madonie mountains. Stop here to see the grand old **Chiesa Matrice**, containing the area's greatest work of art: a tryptych of the Madonna and Child flanked by saints; attributed to a mysterious 15C Fleming known only as the 'Maître au Feuillage brodé', it's reckoned to be his best work.

From Polizzi, two buses a day cross the autostrada and head to **CALTAVUTURO**, a predominantly Baroque town despite its Saracen castle and Arabic name. Nearby, smaller **SCLÁFANI BAGNI** also attests to its former importance as a feud of the Scláfani family by notching up two 14C castles and a cathedral. These, though, are minor diversions, and you might as well sit tight in Polizzi Generosa and await the onward bus to the Tyrrhenian coast, or to Palermo, an hour-and-a-quarter away.

CALTANISSETTA AND THE WESTERN INTERIOR

With twice as many inhabitants as Enna, **Caltanissetta** is easily the largest town in the interior, though there's little else that's remarkable about it. Beyond lie the rolling expanses of Sicily's **western interior**, the rural heart of the island. The towns and villages you'll pass through are uniformly poor and raddled; at times, positively ghost-like. Many, like **Corleone**, have names that have become familiar through their Mafia associations, but few are worth even a coffee-stop. The only place that merits more than a cursory glance is the village of **Sant'Ángelo Muxaro**, whose 3000-year-old tombs dot the hill below.

Access **by public transport** is very awkward: you can get to Caltanissetta easily enough, but otherwise you're unlikely to be able to see much more of the region than what you can glean from a bus window on the fast route between Agrigento and Palermo. From Caltanissetta, the railway line meanders north west (ultimately to Palermo), past a series of empty upland plains occasionally pocked by unexpected crags and gullies, one of the most desert-like of Sicilian journeys.

Caltanissetta

CALTANISSETTA, capital of its province, is a brisk modern town, near enough to PIAZZA ARMERINA (p.217) to make it a convenient base for day-trips there; the bus timetables, for once, are kindly disposed. If you're heading for Enna by train from the south coast, you might also be changing transport here as it's better to arrive in Enna by bus. But there's little else to entice you: Caltanissetta's one worthy attraction is the **Museo Cívico** (Mon–Fri 9am–1.30pm, Sat 9am–noon), on via Napoleone Colajanni, close to the railway station, which contains some of the earliest of Sicilian finds, including vases and Bronze Age sculpted figures. Otherwise, with time to kill, you could strike out to one of Sicily's stranger castle-sites. The **Castello di Pietrarossa** lies at the town's western extremity, though within easy walking distance from Caltanissetta's centre, piazza Garibaldi. Ridiculously balanced on an outcrop of rock, the castle – of Arab or Norman origin – looks like it should have fallen down years ago, and you get the feeling that no one would notice if it did.

Back in the centre of town, take a spin round the sagging walls of the 17C **Palazzo Moncada**, off Corso Umberto. An aristocratic mansion, belonging to one of Sicily's great feudal dynasties, it's undergoing belated restoration. For some views and fresh air in this traffic-drowned town, it's best to stroll down viale Regina Margherita (a continuation of Corso Umberto), where there's a park and belvedere.

If you're **staying** in Caltanissetta, the realistic choice is the *Hotel Europa*, via Gaetani 5 (☎0934-21.051; L25,000), off Corso Vittorio Emanuele and cheap for its three-star rating. The only alternative is the much dearer *Hotel*

Diprima, via Kennedy 16 (☎0934-26.088; L56,000). The **EPT** (☎0934-21.731), just round the corner from here, keeps arbitrary hours, but should be open in the morning. There's also a *SIP* **telephone** office (daily 8am–7.30pm) two doors down; when closed, phone from the *Hotel Diprima*.

Train travellers **heading to Enna** would be advised to take a bus instead from Caltanissetta as Enna's railway station is a long way out of town (see p.206). To get to Caltanissetta's **bus station**, head up via Rosso di San Secondo from the EPT: the bus station is past the second set of lights, on your right in piazza Trento.

CALTANISSETTA

By train to Canicattì

Buses run south west down the SS640 from Caltanissetta, reaching Agrigento in around an hour-and-a-quarter. It's more fun to do the same journey by **train**, though, steering out of Caltanissetta through wooded hills and up through almond- and olive-planted slopes into higher, craggy country. At **CANICATTÌ**, the line splits, trains running south to LICATA (p.231) on the coast, or continuing for another hour south west to AGRIGENTO (p.232).

Canicattì itself is intriguingly referred to by Italians as their equivalent of Timbuktu, a reference to the town's supposed remoteness. It's actually just a dull market town, not all that remote and barely worth venturing off the train for.

Into the western interior

Unless you're driving, the only part of the **western interior** you'll see much of is along the train or bus route between Agrigento and Palermo. The quickest route between the two places – and the way that the direct Agrigento-Palermo bus runs – is the **SS189**. But if you've the time, you might consider driving along the less-used **SS118**, which passes through some of the remoter inland towns and villages. Either way, there are several short detours you can make that are worth doing. Both the routes below are described heading north from Agrigento.

The SS189

Around forty kilometres north of Agrigento, a side-road off the main **SS189** turns east up to **MUSSOMELI**. On the other side of the town is the extraordinary crag-perched castle of **Castello Manfredónico**, erected in the 14C by the powerful Chiaramonte family. It makes a vivid impression on the unsuspecting traveller, tilting over its tall rocky base as if lashed by a strong wind.

About ten kilometres west of the SS189, **Monte Cammarata** (1578m) was a key-point of the Axis defences in World War II, an impregnable redoubt that was expected to seriously delay the American advance to Palermo in 1943. In the event it was taken without a shot being fired, apparently due to pressure exerted on the Italian soldiers by Calógero Vizzini ('Don Calò'), head of the island's Mafia. As a reward for his services, Vizzini was appointed mayor of his home town of **VILLALBA**, twenty kilometres north east of Mussomeli. It's a shabby place, little more than a village really, typical of the area in its poverty and long-standing subjection by absentee landlords; indeed, the sole function of the countless obscure villages that dot this landscape has always been to house the labour for the great feudal estates, watched over by complacent, self-interested priests.

Back on the main road, halfway between Agrigento and Palermo, **LERCARA FRIDDI**'s claim to fame is as the birthplace of the Sicilian-American gangster Lucky Luciano, freed from a thirty- to fifty-year prison sentence (convicted on 62 counts of 'compulsory prostitution') in the US, to be sent to Sicily. Like Don Calò, Luciano was enlisted by the Americans in their Sicilian campaign, which was fully backed by the Mafia in its anxiety to end the Fascist rule.

A few kilometres north of Lercara, you pick up the SS121 which winds across the entire length of Sicily from Catania, and finishes its run in Palermo. Twenty-five kilometres north of the junction at **BAGNI DI CEFALÀ** – signposted just off the SS121 – are some 11C Arab baths, flowing with thermal waters, which the locals use for washing clothes, though you can swim here too. There are few other examples of Arab architecture in such good condition in Sicily.

The SS118

Taking the alternative **SS118**, a minor road that wriggles all the way to Palermo, turn off thirty kilometres north of Agrigento at RAFFADALI for **SANT'ÁNGELO MUXARO**. This small agricultural centre in the middle of the steeply sloping Plátani river valley boasts a number of local tombs (or *tholos*) hollowed out of the rock in dome-shaped caves. The earliest date from the 11C BC, but most are from around the 8C to 5C BC, and in design recall Minoan and Mycenean examples. You'll spot them as you approach the bare hillside on which the village stands: the road leads up past a ramshackle brick wall, beyond which a path heads along the sheer rock to the 'beehive' caves. At the bottom, the largest is known locally as the **tomba del Príncipe**: later converted into a Byzantine chapel, it's half-hidden by over-hanging trees, and you may have to backtrack to get inside. Like all the others, it's empty now, the finds scattered in various museums around Europe.

You can get to Sant'Ángelo by **bus** from Agrigento with the *Lattuca* line, leaving from outside Agrigento's *Astor* cinema on piazza Vittorio Emanuele (daily at 9am and 2pm); the last bus back leaves at 4pm. The route takes you through depressed villages, in a landscape given over to grain cultivation and the almonds for which the region is famous.

The best countryside begins past ALESSANDRIA DELLA ROCCA, the road climbing up to 1000m at PRIZZI, from where there are occasional bus services down to **CORLEONE**. A fairly large town for these parts, squeezed between a couple of rocks with a craggy column at its centre, the only tourists who pass this way come on the scent of the Mafia. Especially in the immediate post-war years, statistics showed the town to have one of the highest murder rates in the world, with 153 violent deaths (out of a population of 18,000) in the four years between 1944 and 1948. One of the men who met a violent end in this period was the trade union leader, **Plácido Rizzoto**, who took advantage of the Mafia's internal preoccupations to do the unthinkable and manoeuvre into power a left-wing town council. Two years after his disappearance in 1948, the fire brigade hauled out his dismembered corpse from a ninety-foot crevice near Corleone, along with sackfuls of other bodies of Mafia victims. His killers were acquitted for lack of evidence, the most usual end to murder charges brought against *mafiosi*. More recently, the town's notoriety has been fuelled since it lent Mario Puzo's fictional Godfather, Don Corleone, his adopted family name. There's little to see here though, just some rather old-fashioned bars clustered around a small town centre, and there's nowhere to stay either. But there is a **trattoria**, *La Giara*, on the southern approach road to the town.

From Corleone, regular buses run through the hills to Palermo, sixty kilometres away. If you're driving, though, you could make a stop at **FICUZZA**, around 25km north, backed by the wooded heights of Rocca Busambra (1613m), which is criss-crossed by a network of mountain paths. The tiny hamlet was once a hunting centre and it's still dominated by Ferdinand III's hunting lodge, the stately **Palazzina Reale**: if the custodian's about, you should be able to get inside to have a look. In any case, take time for **lunch** in one of the trattorias in the piazza, before heading on to the hills around Piana degli Albanesi, 25km from Palermo.

THE SOUTHERN INTERIOR

The **southern interior** has a tamer feel than any of the other inland areas. Journeys here are easy on the eye, through intensely cultivated slopes to a succession of small country towns, which hold most of the region's population. Sights are confined to the area's lively main towns of **Piazza Armerina** and **Caltagirone** and their surroundings – aside from Enna, the only two places in the whole interior that you might pick as specific destinations. Close to the first is easily the region's biggest draw, the lavish Roman mosaics at the **Villa Imperiale**, which features high on any list of Sicily's top attractions. Caltagirone, on the other hand, is one of the unsung towns of the region, plastered with assertive Baroque buildings and emblazoned with the ceramics for which it is renowned. Other brief diversions might take in the extensive Greek ruins of **Morgantina** and the planned 18C settlement of **Grammichele**.

The southern interior, is also well-served by **public transport**. Regular buses run to Piazza Armerina from Enna and Caltanissetta, and Caltagirone and Grammichele are accessible by train and bus from Gela or Catania.

Piazza Armerina

Less than an hour from Enna, **PIAZZA ARMERINA** lies amid thickly forested hills: a quiet, unassuming place, mainly 17C and 18C in appearance, with a skyline pierced by towers and houses huddled together under the joint protection of castle and cathedral. It's a thoroughly pleasant place to idle around, though few who come to Piazza Armerina bother to do so, given the enticement of an Imperial **Roman villa**, which stands in rugged countryside at CASALE, five kilometres south west of town. Hidden under mud for 700 years, the excavations reveal a rich villa, probably a hunting lodge and summer home, decorated with multicoloured mosaic floors that are unique throughout the Roman world in their quality and extent.

Arriving and surviving

Most **buses** will drop you in or around piazza Generale Cascino in the lower, modern town; those from Caltagirone stop in piazza Marescalchi, further back up the main road (viale Generale Muscara). The old town is further up the hill, centred around piazza Garibaldi, off which is the **AAST**, via Cavour 15 (Mon & Sat 8am–2pm, Tues–Fri 8am–2pm & 4.30-7.30pm; ☎0935-680.201), who can provide a map and endless brochures and information about the

mosaics. For **bus information and tickets** to Aidone, Caltagirone and Dittaino (the nearest railway station to Piazza Armerina, 35km north), ask in the *Bar della Stazione* in piazza Marescalchi, or the *AST* office next door.

There are only two places to **sleep**, and neither are cheap. The *Selene*, viale Generale Gaeta 30 (☎0935-80.254; L45,000), in the lower town, is friendlier and more central than the *Hotel Park Paradiso* (☎0935-680.841/85.700; L45,000), one kilometre beyond the church of Sant'Andrea. If you can time the buses right, it's cheaper to stay at Lago di Pergusa (p.209) or Caltanissetta (p.213) and see the mosaics on a day-trip – though you'll have to allow time to get from Piazza Armerina to the villa (see below).

As for **eating**, there are a good few trattorias and restaurants around the old town. *La Tavernetta* (closed Sun) in via Cavour isn't bad value, or try the L13,000 tourist menu at *Da Pepito* (closed Tues) in via Roma, opposite the park. In the lower town, you won't do better (or cheaper) for pizza than the tavola calda/pizzeria *La Rústica 2001*, viale Generale Muscara (near where the bus stops), which has a couple of sit-down tables. And the *Ristorante Europa* across from here, in piazza Generale Cascino, is soft on the wallet too.

The town

Given that seeing the villa and the mosaics might well entail spending the night in Piazza Armerina, you're going to have at least some time to spare for the town, one of the prettiest in the interior. Small enough to cover in a morning's stroll, a score of dilapidated but graceful churches and palazzi line the narrow streets and squares of the hilltop old-town area, which centres around sloping piazza Garibaldi. From here, via Cavour winds up to piazza del Duomo and the elegant 17C **Duomo** itself, built at the town's highest point: an earlier (15C) campanile sports blind Catalan-Gothic windows, a nice contrast to the Baroque antics of the rest of the church. But what really sets off this handsome, view-laden square is the simple facade of the 18C **Palazzo Trigona** adjacent, its spruced exterior crowned by a spread-eagle plaque.

Narrow alleys lead down from the terrace of piazza del Duomo into the older parts of town: an endearing jumble of cobbled flights of steps and faded grandeur, oddly adapted to the modern age. Just behind the cathedral, on a spur off via Cavour, the 17C church and former convent of **San Francesco** is now in use as a hospital; at the bottom of a steep street nearby, via Castellina, the surviving medieval town wall has had a rough arch hacked through it for traffic access; and there's someone living in the adjacent watchtower. The other way, down via Floresta (to the side of Palazzo Trigona), leads to the closed and tumbledown **castello**, built at the end of the 14C and surrounded by once-rich palaces in a similar state of decay. Best route, though, is down the steep **via Monte**, once the medieval town's main street.

The town's compact enough for you to get out fairly easily into the fields and slopes beyond. It's only a kilometre's walk to the 12C Norman church of **Sant'Andrea**, north of town, and still impressive despite its simple proportions. Another kilometre or so down the same road, through orchards and gardens, is the 16C church and convent of **Santa Maria di Gesù**, a low building, gently set amid green hills.

Casale: the Villa Imperiale

Built on terraces in the rolling countryside that surrounds Piazza Armerina, the **Villa Imperiale** at the otherwise virtually uninhabited hamlet of **CASALE** is a confusing swatch of rooms and corridors, built and decorated with pictorial mosaics on a sumptuous scale. There are conflicting theories about its function, though the most convincing explanation of its siting in the middle of deserted slopes and woods is that the villa was an occasional retreat and hunting lodge: a theory supported by the many mosaics of animals and birds, including two specific hunting scenes. Dating from the early 4C (though built over an earlier structure), it was used right up until the 12C when a mudslide largely covered it until comprehensive excavations began in the 1950s. It's been covered again, more recently, to protect the mosaics, a new roof and walls added to indicate the original size and shape, while walkways lead visitors through the rooms.

Getting there

The **minibus** service from piazza Marescalchi to MAZZARINO (daily at 1.30pm, except Sun) passes the turn-off for the villa, one kilometre beyond. Otherwise you'll have to **walk** or hitch, usually an easy enough proposition: head down via Matteotti or via Principato and follow the signs – it takes around an hour on foot. Note that the return bus from Mazzarino passes the turn-off at around 3.30pm on its way back to Piazza Armerina. If you're pushed for time, or there's a group of you, it's probably worth hiring a **taxi**, from piazza Generale Cascino, which costs around L25,000 to take you to the site, wait for an hour and bring you back. As for food, you can either take your own or there's a bar-restaurant at the site.

Coming **from Caltanissetta**, currently the 8.30am bus gets to Piazza Armerina at 9.50am, returning at 4.05pm. **From Enna**, there's a bus at

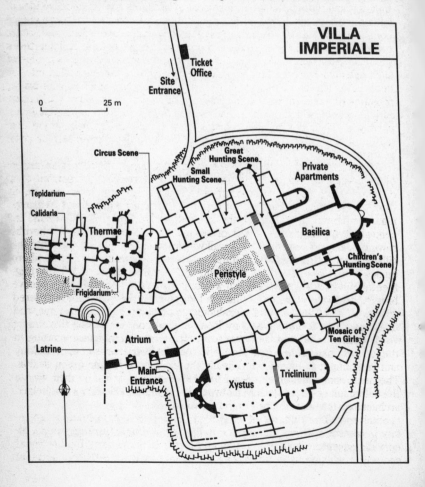

VILLA IMPERIALE

0   25 m

Site Entrance
Ticket Office
Circus Scene
Great Hunting Scene
Small Hunting Scene
Private Apartments
Tepidarium
Calidaria
Thermae
Basilica
Children's Hunting Scene
Peristyle
Frigidarium
Mosaic of Ten Girls
Latrine
Atrium
Main Entrance
Triclinium
Xystus

8.15am, arriving 9am, or 10.30am, arriving at noon; the return bus leaves from Piazza Armerina at 5.10pm. Bear in mind that you'll still have to get from Piazza Armerina itself to the site.

The Villa Imperiale

Open daily, 9am–1hr before sunset; L2000

It's immediately clear from the extent of the uncovered remains that the villa belonged to an important owner, possibly Maximianus Herculeus, co-Emperor with Diocletian between 286 and 305 AD. There's considerable evidence to support this view, not least what's left of the villa's palatial structure. It's made up of four separate groups of buildings, built on different levels of the hillside and connected by passageways, doors and courtyards. Nearly all of what you see would have been occupied by the family it was built for, and though the modern structural additions give an effective idea of what the villa actually looked like when in use, the remains are by no means complete: the slaves' housing, presumably fairly extensive, and other outbuildings are still to be excavated properly. Yet it's not the building that's the main attraction – although there are few enough surviving examples of such splendid Imperial Roman wealth – so much as the unrivalled interior decoration. The floors of almost the entire building are covered with bright **mosaics** of excellent quality, stylistically belonging to an early 4C Roman-African school, which explains many of the more exotic scenes and animals portrayed. Their design also contains several hints as to their period and patron, though given their extent they're likely to have taken fifty or sixty years to complete.

What's left of the villa's **main entrance** gives one of the best impressions of its former grandeur, the approach leading through the remains of a columned arch into a wide courtyard. Today's site entrance, though, is through the adjacent **thermae** (or baths): a typical arrangement of dressing/massage-rooms and plunge-baths around an octagonal **frigidarium**, its central mosaic a marine scene of sea-nymphs, tritons and little cherubs rowing boats and spearing fish. A walkway leads out of the baths and into the villa proper, to the massive central courtyard or **peristyle**: this is where guests would have been received and the vestibule displays a badly fragmented mosaic depicting a formal welcome by an attendant holding an olive branch, while the corridor around the four sides of the courtyard is covered with a series of animal-head medallions, snarling tigers, yapping dogs, and unicorns. Just off here, a balcony looks down upon one of the villa's most vivid pictures, a boisterous circus scene showing a chariot race: starting in the top right-hand corner, the variously coloured chariots rush off, overtaking and crashing at the turns, until finally there's victory for the green faction. The next room's mosaic shows a family, attended by slaves, on their way to the baths: full of period detail – footwear, hairstyles and clothes – that helped archaeologists to date the rest of the mosaics.

Small rooms beyond, on either side of the peristyle, reveal only fragmentary geometric patterns, although one displays a **small hunting scene**, an episodic adventure ending in a peaceful picnic in the centre. Another room contains what is probably the villa's most famous image, a two-tiered scene of

ten girls – realistically muscular figures in Roman 'bikinis' taking part in various gymnastic and athletic activities. One of the girls is clearly the winner of the competition, sporting a laurel wreath and a palm frond.

The peristyle is separated from the private apartments and public halls beyond by a long, covered corridor which contains the best of the villa's mosaic works: the **great hunting scene**, which sets armed and shield-bearing hunters against a panoply of wild animals, on sea and land. Along the entire sixty-metre length of the mosaic are tigers, ostriches, elephants – even a rhino – being trapped, bundled up and down gangplanks and into cages, destined for the games back in Rome. The caped figure overseeing the operation, impassive, square-hatted, with his retinue behind, is probably Maximianus himself: much of the scene is set in Africa, Maximianus' main responsibility in the Imperial Tetrarchy of which he was a member, while an ivy-leaf symbol on the costume of the attendant to his right is that of his personal legion, the *Herculiani*.

Other rooms beyond – family apartments and public halls – are nearly all on a grand scale. A large courtyard, the **xystus**, gives onto the **triclinium**, a dining-room with three apses, whose mosaics feature the labours of Hercules. One bloody scene portrays his fight against the giants, who writhe and wail with contorted faces, all stuck by arrows. A path leads around the back to the **private apartments**, based around a large basilica, with mosaics which echo the spectacular scenes of the main building: a **children's circus**, where the small chariots are drawn by colourful birds, and a **children's hunt**, the tiny tots being chased and pecked by the hares and peacocks they're supposed to snare.

Aidone and the site of Morgantina

Fifteen kilometres north west of Piazza Armerina, there's more classical interest in the extensive remains of the Greek city of **Morgantina**, at its height in the 4C BC. The site's hard to reach without your own transport, though there are hourly **buses** from Piazza Armerina (from piazza Marescalchi) to AIDONE, a twenty-minute ride. The site is another five kilometres beyond the village, along the minor SS288, an easy enough walk or hitch.

You'll want to stop in **AIDONE** for at least as long as it takes to see the **Museo Archeologico** (Mon–Sat 9am–1.30pm & 4–7pm, Sun 9.30am–1pm; free), an indispensable preliminary to seeing the site itself. Housed in an ex-Capuchin monastery on a rise near the centre of town (signposted, above piazza Municipio), the museum gathers together all the removable bits and pieces from the ancient city: ceramics, statuettes and 3C BC busts, as well as some domestic artefacts, all imaginatively displayed, while aerial photos and plans of the excavations provide a useful idea of Morgantina's layout.

The **site** itself (daily 9am–1hr before sunset; free) occupies a dusty hillside, the only life here the tapping of the archaeologists and the occasional jangle of a herd of goats. If you're spending any time at the site you'll probably appreciate the **bar and restaurant** close by.

After its demise, the city became buried and forgotten for almost two thousand years, and even after the site's discovery it wasn't identified as Morgantina until 1957. To date, only a fifth of the city has been excavated, but the finds have shed much light on the island's pre-Hellenic Sikel population, who inhabited central Sicily from the 9C BC. In the 6C BC Chalcidinian Greeks settled here, and lived in harmony alongside the Sikels until the city became the centre of a revolt led by the Sikel leader Ducetius, who destroyed it in the late 5C BC. Swiftly rebuilt on a grid plan with walled and towered defences, Morgantina reached its apogee in the 4–3C BC under the protection of Syracuse, and many of the surviving buildings date from this period. A couple of hundred years later the city was in decline and soon after was abandoned altogether: 'Once Morgantina was a city; now it no longer exists,' the historian Strabo wistfully recorded at the end of the 1C BC.

From the site entrance, a path leads directly onto Morgantina's most distinctive ruin, the **agora**, bounded by the three stepped sides of an uncompleted polygon, the steps used as seats for public meetings. The small **teatro** to its right was built in the 3C BC but reconstructed in Roman times. There's an inscription to Dionysos on a seat in the fifth row from the top, third wedge from the right. Immediately in front is a Roman building, behind which (next to the *agora*) is a 4C BC **santuario** of Demeter and Kore. Many votive objects were found here, including lanterns and cups, most buried in two sacred trenches or *bothroi*, and produced in a small furnace, since excavated at the bottom end of the sanctuary area. On the level ground behind the *agora* is a square slaughter-house, beyond which stretches the long **stoa**, the stumps of its columns running all the way down its 100m length. Above it stand the ruins of some Hellenic **houses**, with two mosaic-laid floors, one of which, the so-called 'House of Ganymede', has a damaged illustration of the youth Ganymede being carried away to Olympus by Zeus's eagle to become the cup-bearer of the gods.

South to Caltagirone

The bus from Piazza Armerina follows a good road across the valleys, through MIRABELLA IMBACCARI and SAN MICHELE DI GANZERIA, up into the heights of **CALTAGIRONE**, an hour's ride away.

There were settlers here well before the Greeks, making it one of the most ancient of Sicilian towns, but the present name derives from the Arabic (*kalat*, castle and *gerun*, caves). Nothing from these periods survives, and the dominant impression of the town is Baroque, its central swathe of monumental buildings dating from the rebuilding after the 1693 earthquake which flattened the area. Its old **upper town** has great public edifices, decorative churches and public gardens spread across three hills, the effect lightened by tiled decoration found in nooks and crannies everywhere, for which Caltagirone is noted. Most effective are the ceramic flowers and emblems flanking both sides of a bridge (the Ponte San Francesco) on the way into the centre from the railway station. The grandest statement, though, is made by the 142 steps of **La Scala**, which cut right up one of Caltagirone's hills to the church of Santa Maria del Monte at the top: the 'risers' in between each step are covered with a ceramic pattern, no two the same. If you're interested, there's a **Museo della Cerámica** (Tues–Sun 9am–2pm) stuffed full of ceramic-ware, in the large public garden off via Roma.

The upper town also holds the most striking buildings. Beyond piazza Umberto and the re-styled Duomo is the length of the 17C **Corte Capitaniale**, a sturdy, low building decorated by the Gagini family. Back below piazza Umberto, the solid square-built block with grilled windows and

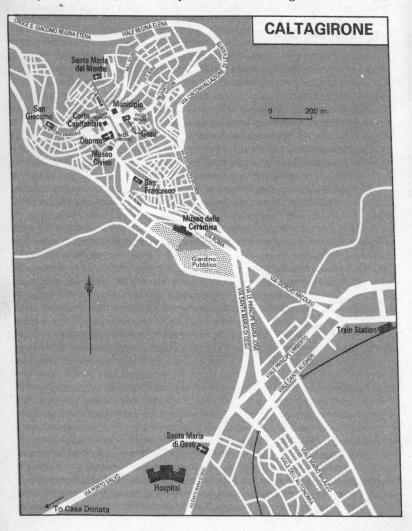

spike-studded metal doors was once an 18C Bourbon prison, and now houses the **Museo Cívico** (Mon, Tues & Sat 9.30am–1.30pm, Wed & Fri 4–7pm, Sun 10am–noon; free). This has a small but rather good display of modern ceramics, though the rest of the collection is the usual load of local junk – architectural fragments, barrowloads of paintings by the Vaccaro family who renovated the cathedral in the 19C, and a decrepit processional cart.

Practicalities

Buses nearly all stop first in piazza Municipio in the upper town, where you should get off if you're only looking around for the day. If you're planning on staying, travel on to the new town, a couple of kilometres below, which is home to the **railway station** and Caltagirone's only accommodation. When **leaving town**, *Pitrelli* buses to Ragusa (6am, 8am, 1pm and 2.30pm) depart from viale Príncipe Umberto 215, and *AST* services leave from outside the *Metropol* cinema further up the road – though again they should all call at piazza Municipio in the upper town on the way.

The only reasonable **place to stay** is the excellent *Casa Donata*, at via Portosalvo 22b (☎0933-25.684; L30,000 with bath), beyond the hospital in the new town: it's a country house with immaculate, large rooms and sweeping views over the hills to Caltagirone, about a kilometre up the road past the monstrously expensive and ugly *Villa San Mauro* hotel. The *Casa Donata* is also the best **place to eat** in town, with tasty home cooking and good local wine. You don't need to stay at the hotel to eat there, and if you're just passing through there's also a pizzeria on the way in from the railway station; a good tavola calda/bar at via Duomo 2, opposite the cathedral; and a daily **market** in the back-streets behind and below the Municipio.

Around Caltagirone: Grammichele and Monte San Mauro

Just ten minutes **east** of Caltagirone by train, **GRAMMICHELE** is worth an expedition to view one of the most ambitious of the new towns built after the 1693 earthquake. The best place to appreciate Grammichele's hexagonal design would be from the air – failing that, position yourself at the dead centre of the town's imposing central piazza to see the six radial streets reaching out, each bisected by secondary piazzas. The shape's no longer entirely perfect, due to a surfeit of new streets around the station at the southern edges of town, but it makes for an intriguing couple of hours' stroll, with more chances than you might think for getting lost, since all the streets in each segment correspond exactly to their neighbours in dimension and appearance. Despite the grand design, Grammichele still manages to look a mite tatty: it's a predominantly rural-looking town and the impressions are all countryish ones – a donkey tethered in the main square, chickens cooped in the basement of someone's house, and farms near the railway station. Best **place to eat** – and not a bad reason in itself for a trip from Caltagirone – is *La Tavernetta*, a barn-like trattoria at via Garibaldi 100: walk straight up from the railway station, along Corso Vittorio Emanuele, over the piazza and it's down the first street on the right.

If you're driving or travelling by train **south** of Caltagirone, you might ask someone to point out the hill of **Monte San Mauro**, halfway to NISCEMI, which was the scene of the one battle that could be called a separatist uprising in Sicily. At the end of 1945, Concetto Gallo, lawyer, landowner, and commander-in-chief of the Separatist army (*E.V.I.S.*), much reduced by desertion, led 58 men in a last stand against a force of 5000 Italian troops commanded by three generals. Gallo's inevitable defeat signalled the effective end of the Separatist movement in Sicily (see *Historical Framework*, p.288).

festivals

March/April

Easter Holy Week celebrations in ENNA including processions, special Masses and the parade of saintly relics. Running all week from Palm Sunday to Easter Sunday, the best day is Good Friday, when thousands march in silent procession, dressed in the white-hooded costumes of the medieval fraternities. More costumed processions can be seen at TROINA, and at CALTANISSETTA (best days Maundy Thursday and Good Friday), with processional carts (the *misteri*) and monks. PRIZZI, in the western interior, is a good place to be on Easter Sunday, when giant statues of Christ and the Virgin Mary are taunted by masked figures representing Death and the Devil, to whom onlookers are forced to give money.

Motor racing The season starts at the *Autodromo di Pergusa*, around the LAGO DI PERGUSA, running until September.

May

Sagra del Lago Throughout the month at LAGO DI PERGUSA, with folk events and fireworks, singing competitions and games.

Penultimate Sunday *Festa dei Rami* at TROINA, in which laurel branches are carried to the tomb of Saint Silvester.

July

Estate Ennese Beginning of a series of concerts and opera in the open-air theatre at the castle in ENNA. Runs until end of August.

23 Festival of San Giácomo in CALTAGIRONE, when the La Scala steps are illuminated.

August

13–14 *Il Palio dei Normanni* in PIAZZA ARMERINA, a medieval pageant commemorating Count Roger's taking of the town in the 11C. Processional entry into town on the thirteenth, ceremonial joust on the fourteenth, along with costumed parades and other festive events.

September

Festival of *Madonna dell'Alto* in PETRALIA SOTTANA with a nocturnal procession on horseback and a maypole dance known as the *Ballo della Cordella*.

travel details

Trains

From Enna to Catania (9 daily; 1hr 20min); Caltanissetta (9; 1hr); Palermo (3; 2hr 20min).

From Caltanissetta to Canicattì/Agrigento (9 daily; 30min/1hr 20min); Licata/Gela (8; 1hr 20min/2hr).

From Caltagirone to Gela (hourly; 40min); Grammichele (11 daily; 15min); Catania (11; 1hr 50min).

Buses

From Enna to Calascibetta (hourly; 25min); Pergusa (Mon–Sat 12 daily; 30min); Caltanissetta (Mon–Sat 5; 1hr); Catania (3–7 daily; 1hr 20min);

Piazza Armerina/Gela (1–2; 45min/1hr 40min); Piazza Armerina (local bus 1–4; 1½hr); Palermo (3–4; 1hr 50min); Leonforte (11; 40min); Leonforte/Agira/Regalbuto/Catania (2–3; 40min/1hr 5min/1½hr/2½hr).

From Leonforte to Nicosia and vice versa (2–4 daily; 45min).

From Agira to Troina and vice versa (1–3 daily; 55min).

From Nicosia to Leonforte/Agira/Catania (2–5 daily; 45min/1hr 10min/2hr 35min); Sperlinga/Gangi (2–6; 15min/45min); Petralia Soprana/Sottana (2–5; 1hr 20min/1½hr); Polizzi Generosa

(3–5; 2hr); Palermo (2–4; 3¼hr); Mistretta (Mon–Sat 2 daily; 55min, continuing 1hr 20min later to Santo Stéfano di Camastra).

From Cesarò to Nicosia (1 daily at 7am; 1½hr); Sant'Agata (1 daily at 4.30pm; 1½hr); Randazzo (Mon–Sat 3; 1hr 10min); Randazzo/Giardini-Naxos/Messina (Mon–Sat 2; 1hr 10min/2½hr/3½hr).

From Polizzi Generosa to Caltavuturo (Mon–Sat 2 daily; 35min); Términi Imerese (Mon–Sat 3; 1½hr); Cefalù (Mon–Sat 1 at 6.30am; 1hr);

Palermo (3–5; 1¼hr).

From Caltanissetta to Enna (Mon–Sat 5 daily; 1hr); Piazza Armerina (1; 1hr 20min); Caltagirone (2; 2hr 10min); Canicattì/Agrigento (3–4; 35min/1¼hr); Catania (3–5; 1hr 35min).

From Piazza Armerina to Caltagirone (1–4 daily; 1hr); Gela (2; 1hr); Enna (3–5; 1hr); Aidone (hourly; 20min); Palermo (2–3 daily; 3hr).

From Caltagirone to Piazza Armerina (1–4 daily; 1hr); Catania Mon–Sat 2; 1hr 10min); Ragusa (4; 1½hr).

CHAPTER SEVEN

THE SOUTH COAST

T he long **south coast**, from Gela to Sciacca, should be one of the most attractive parts of Sicily. Sparsely developed, there are good beaches and some low-key Mediterranean ports and resorts which are barely known to Italians, let alone other tourists. Nevertheless, sporadic but spectacularly ugly industrial development along the coast conspires to put off many people. The sea is heavily polluted in some areas, particularly around **Gela**, a large port and petrochemical town. But to give this coast a miss would be to ignore some of the most important sights on the island. Gela itself retains its extensive Greek fortifications, while further west the hill-top town of **Agrigento** overlooks a series of splendid ancient temples, unrivalled in extent and preservation outside Greece. North west of Agrigento, isolated sandy **beaches** pan out, and with a car you can reach some of the better stretches, at the end of several minor roads and tracks which branch off from the main SS115. One of the best lies just below another Hellenic site, **Eraclea Minoa**. **Sciacca** is more accessible, a fishing port and summer resort, and from here you can make a couple of diversions into the tall and craggy mountains that back this part of the coast. Or you might consider heading out to the **Pelágie Islands**: barren spots in the Mediterranean, closer to Africa than Europe, but connected by regular ferry with **Porto Empédocle**, near Agrigento.

Regular **train** and **bus** services link the coastal towns and villages, while there are less frequent services to the inland towns, these detailed in the text. **Hotel** accommodation is limited outside the major towns, but there are plenty of opportunities to **camp**, either in sites or freelance among the dunes.

Gela

GELA couldn't present a worse aspect as the train edges into town, through a mess of futuristic steel bubbles and pipes. There are fine dune-backed beaches in the vicinity but there must be serious doubts about the cleanliness of the water, and there's often a chemical tang to the air. It was not always so. Gela was one of the most important of Sicily's Greek cities, founded in 688 BC, and under Hippocrates in the 5C BC rivalled even ancient Syracuse as the island's political hub. Its artistic eminence attracted literary stars, most notably the dramatist Aeschylus, who left his mark on the city (literally) when felled by a tortoise dropped by an eagle, which – the tale

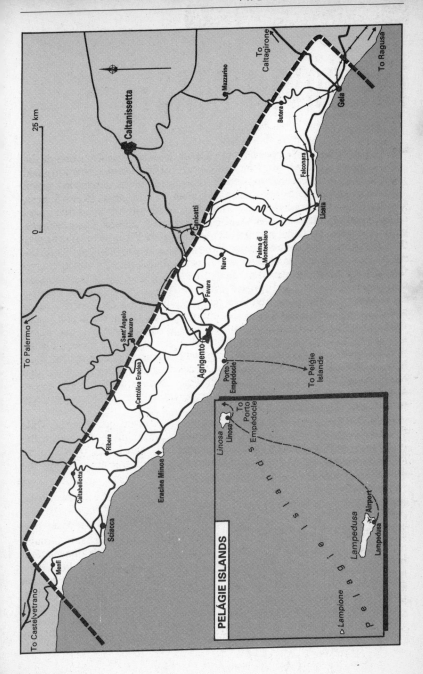

To Castelvetrano
To Palermo
To Caltagirone
To Ragusa

25 km

0

Caltanissetta

Mazzarino

Butera

Gela

Falconara

Canicatti

Licata

Palma di
Montechiaro

Naro

Favara

Sant'Angelo
Muxaro

Cattolica Eraclea

Agrigento

Porto
Empedocle

To Pelgie
Islands

Ribera

Eraclea Minoa

Caltabellotta

Sciacca

Menfi

PELAGIE ISLANDS

Linosa
Linosa

To
Porto
Empedocle

Lampione

Lampedusa

Airport

Lampedusa

P e l a g i e   I s l a n d s

relates – mistook his bald head for a stone on which to dash its prey. However, Gela's heyday was short-lived. Hippocrates' successor, Gelon, transferred his power and half the city's population east to Syracuse in 485 BC, the deep-water harbour there more to the tyrant's liking. Gela was subsequently smashed by the Carthaginians and the Mamertines, its walls razed to the ground in the 3C BC and abandoned to the encroaching sands. Modern Gela was the first Sicilian town to be liberated by the Allies in 1943, but otherwise – beyond an excellent archaeological museum and a fine set of Greek defensive walls – is almost entirely without interest.

If you want to see these, best leave your bags at the **railway station** left-luggage office: there's really no need to stay longer than half a day. Outside the station (also where **buses** pull up) turn right down the main road and, at the junction, bear right for the town centre and the main Corso Vittorio Emanuele, at either end of which are Gela's two sights. To the left, a twenty-minute walk, Gela's **Museo Archeologico** (daily 9am–1.30pm; free) is notable largely for its important collection of painted vases upstairs. Mainly 7–5C BC, the black and red jugs and beakers were Greek Gela's speciality: most major world museums tend to feature one or two, but the bulk are here. Other impressive finds include an animated sculpture of a horse's head (6C BC) and the remains of necropoli from Geloan dependencies. Outside the museum a small **acropolis** has been uncovered, consisting of a few walls and a single temple column from the 5C BC, though the small site loses all its romance to the brooding, dirty industrial plant which dominates the beach below.

There are more archaeological remains at **Capo Soprano**, at the other end of town. Head along the Corso and take a left fork (via Manzoni), which runs parallel to the sea as far as the red gates of the site, a three- to four-kilometre walk. The **Greek fortifications** here (daily 9am–1hr before sunset; free) date from the 4C BC. Preserved by the sand dunes under which they were discovered, the walls stand nearly eight metres high in parts, made up of perfectly fitted stone blocks topped by a layer of brick, and now covered in protective glass panels. It's a beautiful site and you're free to wander around the line of the walls: in some places you can make out the remains of watchtowers and gateways, while waves crash onto a duned stretch of beach below. If you've come this far out of town, you may as well nip around the corner (back towards the centre and left, by the hospital), to via Europa, to see the remains of Gela's 4C BC **public baths**, the only ones from Greek times discovered in Sicily and still equipped with their original seats.

Although you won't need (or want) to stay in Gela, a few **practical details** may be useful. The **AAST** is at via Palazzi 66 (Mon–Sat 9am–1pm & 4–7pm; ☎0933-935.805), further up via Europa and then right. There are regular **bus departures** from outside the railway station to nearby towns, including Licata and Agrigento, Vittória, Caltanissetta and Siracusa. All the timetables are posted up in the railway-station bar.

Along the coast to Agrigento ... and some inland diversions

The long empty coastline to the west of Gela is dotted by pillboxes left behind after the war. Following the SS115 from Gela, there's a decent sand **beach** at **MANFRIA**, just off the main road, although you won't get to stop here if you're travelling by train, which loops inland soon after Gela and doesn't stop until **FALCONARA**, a few kilometres beyond. There's little at either place apart from their respective beaches, though Falconara does have a 14C castle – the private property of Palermitan aristocrats – and a couple of **campsites**: the *Dallas* (☎0934-946.3038), and the *Due Rocche* (☎0934-946.964), both open all year, the latter with cabins to rent and a **hotel** attached, the *Lido degli Angeli* (☎0934-946.693; L31,000).

Ten kilometres further along the coast, the port of **LICATA** is worth pushing on to, a bustling blend of old and new, with a decent hotel and a selection of fish restaurants. Climb up the hill to the top of the town for a view over the lively harbour, and you can work your way round the hill to reach an imposing 16C **castello**. The town below has some good palazzi on show, the most prominent the gargoyle-studded **Palazzo Canarelli** on via Roma, while the **Museo Cívico** in piazza Linares, off the main Corso Umberto (Mon–Sat 9am–1.30pm; free), displays a good deal of local prehistoric material. You can also get **maps and information** from the museum; when it's closed, try the travel agency next door. You might well want to stay overnight, given Licata's nearby **beach** (and its proximity to the one at Falconara), and there's a **hotel** just over the street from the museum: the *Roma*, Corso Serrovira 54 (☎0922-861.075; L30,000). Evenings get pretty busy in Licata, and there are plenty of **bars and restaurants** – two of the best the *White Horse* in via Gabriele d'Annunzio (off Corso Umberto) and *Il Gabbiano*, further down the same road behind the cathedral.

If you're heading straight for Agrigento, it's quicker to pick up a direct bus at Licata than stick with the train, which swoops inland to Canicattì before doubling back to the coast. If you're driving, though, there are a couple of stops you could make along the way. From Licata, it's twenty kilometres to **PALMA DI MONTECHIARO**, which lies just off the SS115. This was once the seat of the Lampedusa family, the last of whom – Giuseppe Tomasi di Lampedusa – wrote the acclaimed novel, *The Leopard*. He died in 1957 (*The Leopard* was published a year later), though the palace in Palma had lain derelict for a long time before that. Today, the only echoes of the great feudal family recorded in the novel are to be found in Palma's 17C **Chiesa Matrice**, built by one of Lampedusa's ancestors, and the ruined site of the **Castello di Palma**, a few kilometres east of town at the end of a small track.

North of here, the road climbs seventeen kilometres up to medieval **NARO**, whose 13C and 14C buildings may merit a look if you're mobile and have time on your hands. The best of these are the Chiaramonte **castello** at Naro's highest point, and the nearby ruins of the old cathedral; other churches in this walled and battlemented town are emphatically Baroque.

Agrigento

No one comes to **AGRIGENTO** for the town, though its worn medieval streets and buildings soak up thousands of tourists every year. The interest instead focuses on the substantial remains of Akragas, Pindar's 'most beautiful city of mortals', a couple of kilometres below. Strung out along a ridge facing the sea, its series of Doric temples are the most captivating of Sicilian Greek remains, and are unique outside Greece.

In 581 BC colonists from nearby Gela and Rhodes founded the city of Akragas between the rivers of Hypsas and Akragas. They surrounded it with a mighty wall, formed in part by a higher ridge where they placed the acropolis (and where, today, the modern town stands). The southern limit of the ancient city was a second, lower ridge and it was here, in the so-called 'Valley of the Temples' (*Valle dei Templi*), that the city architects erected their sacred buildings during the 5C BC. They were – and are – stunning in their effect, reflecting the wealth and luxury of ancient Agrigento: 'Athens with improvements', as Henry Adams had it in 1899.

Come by public transport, and you'll **arrive** in the centre of town. While you could easily jump a bus straight down to the archaeological park, it's a long day's sightseeing: given the good accommodation possibilities in Agrigento, you may as well track down a room first and give yourself time to see the town as well – no mean attraction itself.

The town and around

It would be a mistake not to scout around the modern **town of Agrigento**. Modern only in comparison with the temples, it's thoroughly medieval at its heart, the main street, **via Atenea**, starting at the eastern edge of town, above the railway station. The streets off both sides harbour ramshackle palazzi and minuscule *cortili* or courtyards, and while just ambling around here is entertainment enough, there are a couple of specific buildings worth seeking out. Close to the station, **Santo Spírito** was built for Cistercian nuns in 1290: although the attached convent is currently under restoration, someone should appear with the keys to show you the chapter house, with its vaulted ceiling, and the old dormitory upstairs – from where there are marvellous views of the temples across the fields. Via Atenea cuts right through the oldest part of town, at its most grand around the **Municipio**, housed inside a 17C convent. The narrowest and steepest of the streets spread up the hill from here, passing the church of **Santa Maria dei Greci**, built over a Greek temple of the 5C BC: the flattened columns are visible in the nave, and outside, viewable from an underground tunnel in the courtyard, the stylobate and column stumps are incorporated into the church's foundations. Just up from here, via Duomo leads past a line of decrepit palazzi to the massive **Duomo**, set on a terrace at the top of the hill and fronting a spacious piazza below.

Just **out of Agrigento** (at the end of the flyover leading out towards PORTO EMPÉDOCLE; bus #11 hourly from the railway station) the suburb of **CAOS** was the birthplace of **Luigi Pirandello**, and the inspiration for the

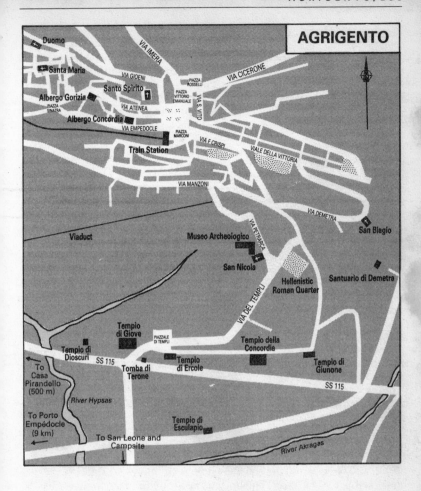

Taviani brothers' film, *Kaos*, which was based on four of his short stories. One of the greats of 20C Italian literature, Pirandello is best known for his dramatic works, such as *Six Characters in Search of an Author* and *Henry IV* – though his 1934 Nobel Prize was awarded as much for his novels and short stories. He had a rather tragic life: his wife was committed to an asylum having lapsed into insanity following the ruin of her family and the birth of their third son, and for much of his life Pirandello was forced to write to supplement his frugal living as a teacher. His drama combines elements of tragedy and comedy with keenly observed dialogue: the nature of identity and personality, reality, illusion and the absurd are all recurring themes, and Pirandello's ideas – and innovations – formed the blueprint for much subsequent 20C drama. His house, signposted *Casa Natale di Luigi Pirandello*, has been converted into a **museum** (summer 9am–1pm & 3–7pm, winter

9am–1pm & 3–5pm; free, but tip). Although Pirandello left while still quite young – to study in Berlin and later live in Rome – he spent time here every summer, and you can see the study where he wrote, crammed with foreign editions of his works. As well as a couple of murals painted by him, there are stacks of photographs, including one sent by George Bernard Shaw. After seeing the house, wander down through the grounds to a windswept pine, at the base of which lie the writer's ashes, though the views he once enjoyed over the sea are now ruined by a patch of industrial horror.

All the practicalities

Trains arrive at the railway station (Agrigento Centrale) at the edge of the old town; don't make the mistake of getting out at Agrigento Bassa, three kilometres north of town. **City buses** leave from outside the station in piazza Marconi for the temples, the campsite and Porto Empédocle (for ferries to the Pelágie islands). **Buses** from elsewhere in Sicily will drop you at the terminal in piazza Roselli, near the post office. The **AAST** (Mon–Sat 8am–2pm & 5-7pm; ☎0922-20.391) is in the *Banco di Sicilia* building on piazza Marconi and has hotel listings and free maps. The **post office** is the circular building in piazza Vittorio Emanuele, near the bus terminal; make **telephone calls** (8am–8pm) from the office at the top of the steps which lead up from piazza Vittorio Emanuele.

Sleeping

Finding **somewhere to stay** in Agrigento shouldn't be a problem, except perhaps in peak season. There are a few basic **rooms** for rent (marked *cámere*) at via di Vela 6, off via Atenea; L10,000 per person. Cheapest and grottiest of the **hotels** is the *Albergo Gorizia*, via Boccerie 39 (☎0922-20.105; L18,000), off via Atenea, but if funds permit it's probably worth moving up a class. The *Concordia*, behind the railway station at piazza San Francesco 11 (☎0922-56.266; L30,000), has some smart rooms, and there are two others similarly priced and worth a try: the *Bella Napoli*, piazza Lena 6, off via Bic Bac (☎0922-20.435; L30,000), and the *Belvedere*, via San Vito 20 (☎0922-20.051; L30,000), across the square and up from the AAST. (Incidentally, the only hotel in the Valle dei Templi – you pass it on the way down by bus – is well-sited but extremely expensive: the *Villa Athena*, ☎0922-56.288; L97,000 with bath.)

The nearest **campsite** is five kilometres away at the coastal resort of SAN LEONE, the *Internazionale San Leone* (☎0922-77.625/24.140; April to Sept); bus #10 from outside the railway station, and a one-kilometre hike along the coast at the other end.

Eating and drinking

For **eating**, the food and local wine are excellent at *La Forchetta* (closed Sun), next door to the *Concordia* hotel, but it's not particularly cheap – though there is an L11,000 *pranzo turístico*. Best of the budget restaurant options is the *Trattoria Atenea*, via Ficani 32 (just off via Atenea), while you can't beat the L10,000 pasta, pizza and drink combination at *La Corte degli*

Sfizzi, a trendy little eatery on Cortile Contarini, an alleyway above via Atenea. The crowded *Trattoria Impero*, just off via Atenea at via Eugenio Bertoni (closed Mon), has a good set menu, at L9000. For cheaper food and **snacks**, there's a self-service restaurant, *Self-Service Taglialavoro*, on via Pirandello, on the way to piazza San Francesco. And if you want a late **drink**, hit the *Paninoteca Manhattan*, up the steps to the right at the beginning of via Atenea: good sandwiches, draught beer and taped music until midnight.

The Valle dei Templi: the archaeological zone

A road winds down from the modern city to the **VALLE DEI TEMPLI**, buses (#8, #9 or #10) from outside the railway station dropping you at a car park between the two separate sections of archaeological remains, the eastern and western zones. You'll pass Agrigento's archaeological museum on the way, and if you're intent upon doing the ancient site amd museum in one go, you'll need a full day here: take a picnic, as the bar-tavola calda at the car park is expensive.

The main site

The **eastern zone** is unenclosed and is at its crowd-free best in the early morning or late evening, when there's often a spectacular sunset. A path climbs up to the oldest of Akragas's temples, the **Tempio di Ércole** (Herakles). Probably begun in the last decades of the 6C BC, it's a long structure, nine of the original 38 columns re-erected, everything else scattered around like a half-finished jigsaw puzzle. Retrace your steps, back over what remains of a deep wheel-rutted Greek street, and the main path continues up past the site of the city's ancient necropolis to the **Tempio della Concordia** (Temple of Concord), dated to around 430 BC: perfectly preserved and beautifully sited, with fine views to the city and the sea, the tawny stone lending the structure warmth and strength. It's the most complete of the temples, and has required less renovation than the others, mainly due its conversion in the 6C AD to a Christian church. Restored to its (more or less) original layout in the 18C, the temple has kept its simple lines and slightly tapering columns, although sadly it's fenced off to keep the crowds at bay. Circle the temple at least once to get a decent view, and stand well back to admire its elegant proportions. The path continues, following the line of the ancient city walls which hug the ridge, to the **Tempio di Giunone** (Temple of Juno, or Hera), an engaging structure, half in ruins, standing at the very edge of the spur on which the temples were built. A long altar has been reconstructed at the far end of the temple; the patches of red visible here and there on the masonry denote fire damage, probably from the sack of Akragas by the Carthaginians in 406 BC.

All the temples in the eastern zone are **illuminated at night** to great effect, something well worth trudging down to see. You'll catch them floodlit from January to March and October to December between 9pm and 11pm; April to September between 9.30pm and 11.30pm.

The **western zone** (daily 9am–1hr before sunset; free), back along the path and beyond the car park, is less impressive, though still archaeologically engaging – a vast tangle of stone and fallen masonry from a variety of temples. Most notable is the mammoth pile of rubble that was the **Tempio di Giove**, or Temple of Olympian Zeus. The largest Doric temple ever known, it was never completed, left in ruins by the Carthaginians and further damaged by earthquakes and the removal of stone to build the port of Porto Empédocle to the south. Still, the stereobate remains, unnaturally huge in scale, while on the ground, face to the sky, lies an eight-metre-high *telamone*: a supporting column sculpted as a male figure, arms raised and bent to bear the temple's weight. **Other scattered remains** litter the area, not least piles of great column drums marked with a U-shaped groove, which enabled them to be lifted with ropes. Beyond, behind the excavated gates and walls of the Greek city, is the earliest sacred site, the Sanctuary of the Chthonic Deities, marked by two altars (one square and fire-reddened, the other round), dating from the 7C BC, before the official foundation of the colony. This is also the site of the so-called **Tempio dei Dioscuri** (Temple of Castor and Pollux), rebuilt in 1832, its columns and corner-work actually made up of unrelated pieces from the confused debris on the ground.

The Museo Nazionale Archeologico . . . and more ruins

The road that leads back to town from the car park, via dei Templi, runs past the excellent **Museo Nazionale Archeologico** (Tues–Fri 9am–1.30pm & 3–5pm, weekends 9am–12.30pm; free). Since the bus passes by outside, you could always start here first before the temples, though it's better to make a separate visit if you can: it's an extraordinarily varied collection, devoted to finds from the temples, the ancient city and the surrounding area, and can occupy a good couple of hours when you combine it with seeing the remains of the residential area of the old city, just over the road.

Unusually for an archaeological museum, there's much here that's of artistic merit as well as historical interest, and it's probably best to skip the initial local prehistoric and Bronze Age finds and head straight to the crucial sections of the museum. **Room 3** features an outstanding vase collection, beguiling 6–3C BC pieces, one of which depicts the burial of a warrior. Among the other objects here there's a tiny candlestick holder engraved with a galloping horse. But it's the finds from the temples themselves that make this collection come alive: in **room 4** there's a series of sculpted lion's-head water-spouts, a common device for draining the water from the roofs of the city's temples, while **room 6** is given over to exhibits relating to the Temple of Olympian Zeus. Some useful model reconstructions help to make sense of the disjointed wreckage on the ground, although the prime exhibit is a re-assembled *telamone*, stacked against one wall: all the weather damage can't hide the strength implicit in this huge sculpture. Rooms beyond hold coins, inscriptions and finds from local necropoli; typical is a child's sarcophagus in **room 11** showing poignant scenes from his life, which was cut short by illness and early death. The last couple of rooms contain finds from the rest of the province, one of which, in **room 15**, is the equal of anything that's gone before: a 5C BC *krater* displays graphic red figures in the Battle of the Amazons, hacking and slicing away, amply demonstrating the famed Geloan (from Gela) skill as masters of vase-ware.

In the grounds of the museum, take time to look at the Gothic doorway of the adjacent church of **San Nicola**. There's an invigorating view from the terrace outside over the temple valley, while just beyond is a small *odeion* (3C BC) used for public meetings, during which the participants stood rather than sat in the narrow rows. Nip over the road on the way out of the museum too: the **Hellenistic-Roman quarter** opposite (daily 9am–1hr before sunset; free) contains rows of houses, inhabited (on and off) until the 5C AD, many with mosaic designs still discernible.

Other archaeological remains

You could see everything already described in four or five hours, but without your own transport the archaeological park's remaining sights mean a lot of extra walking. The quickest way to reach the most distant is to climb over the wall to the side of the Tempio di Concordia and scramble down through the field to the road. Here, at the end of a dusty track, stands the undersized **Tempio di Esculapio** (Temple of Asclepius), with solid walls instead of a colonnade. Nearby, back along the main road and close to the crossroads, is a large two-storeyed Roman tomb (75 BC), the **Tomba di Terone**, mistakenly named by historians after the Greek tyrant Theron. The road then heads up, past the car park and museum, where a right fork followed by another right turn (via Demetra) leads to the tiny **chiesa di San Biagio**, a three-kilometre walk. A Norman chapel, this was built over the visible remains of a temple, contemporary with the ones below on the ridge. It's currently closed for restoration, but hang around and a custodian will lead you down the cliff behind the chapel to the eerie **Santuario di Demetra** (be prepared to tip). A stone-built chambered shrine hides two dingy caves which stretch twenty metres into the hillside: the thin corridor between building and caves was a sort of vestibule with niches for water so that worshippers could wash themselves. It's the most ancient of Agrigento's sacred sites, once devoted to the cult of Demeter and Persephone and in use even before Akragas was founded. It's at its best as the sun sets, with shadows flitting across the dark and silent caves, a mysterious and evocative place.

The Pelágie Islands

The remote **PELÁGIE ISLANDS** (Isole Pelágie) are little more than dry rocks, even further south than Malta and bang in the middle of the Mediterranean. Throughout history they've been neglected, often abandoned or uninhabited, and only occasionally has their strategic importance been recognised. In 1943 the Allies bombed the main island, Lampedusa, prior to springing into Sicily; and Colonel Qadhafi of Libya nearly gave a repeat performance in 1987 when he retaliated against the American bombing of Tripoli by targeting missiles at the US base on Lampedusa. Italian troops were mobilised, and Sicily was on a virtual war-footing for three days, though in the event the missiles dropped into the sea short of the island. That said, the only danger you're likely to face now – trigger-happy US foreign policy aside – is a rough sea-crossing. You're going to have to be a pretty dedicated island-fanatic (or a Trappist monk) to want to make the trip anyway: only Lampedusa has any semblance of life.

Most travellers get to the islands by ferry from **Porto Empédocle**, the boats calling at **Linosa** (6hr) and larger **Lampedusa** (8hr): one-way tickets to Linosa cost around L27,000, to Lampedusa around L34,000, returns twice these amounts. The tiniest islet, **Lampione**, is uninhabited and not on the ferry route. The only way to cut this time would be to **fly from Palermo** direct to Lampedusa, an hour's flight, for a normal one-way fare of about L70,000 (but see p.13 for special deals). For full ferry and plane schedules see *Travel Details*.

Catching the ferry: Porto Empédocle

PORTO EMPÉDOCLE, just six kilometres south west of Agrigento, is as ugly, depressing and dirty a town as you could ever wish to visit, a large oily port dominated by its enormous cement works. The only reason to come is to catch the daily summer ferry (six weekly in winter) to the islands: this doesn't leave until midnight, so those with tickets don't have to come to Porto Empédocle until the evening. **Buses** (L1150) leave for the port from Agrigento every half an hour or so from outside the railway station, dropping you in piazza Italia, one block from the waterfront; the last bus from Agrigento leaves at 8.30pm. Get **ferry tickets** either from travel agencies in Agrigento or from the *Siremar* office (☎0922-66.683/5) in Porto Empédocle, right on the quayside. If you've got a car, there's no point in taking it across: use the **garage** down at the port, *Stagno*, at one end of via Roma, which charges L4000 a day. If it's full, you should be able to leave your vehicle inside the port itself, preferably near the *Dogana* (customs) or anywhere else where it's likely to be watched over by official eyes; enter by the eastern entrance, and drive through.

Linosa

Northernmost of the islands, **LINOSA** is the tip of a submerged volcano, with four extinct craters to poke around, some lavial beaches and not much else in the way of sights. A haven for pirates in the 16C, the small island (five square kilometres) wasn't really settled properly until the mid-19C, though even now the only village has just a few hundred inhabitants, rather fewer cars and a minimal road system. There are tracks, though, which lead away from the port if you want to clamber around the cliffs and coves, and reach the couple of black sand beaches. About the only exciting events to disturb this quiet island were when the government in Rome sent their latest star Mafia prisoner to be detained on the island pending trial – a practice which seems to have been suspended recently since the tourist trade picked up.

There is one **hotel** in Linosa village, the *Algusa* (☎0922-972.052; L67,000 with bath), at which you should really make a reservation in advance if you want to stay, and an unofficial **campsite** near the port.

Lampedusa

The other ferry stop is **LAMPEDUSA**, fifty kilometres south and much bigger than Linosa. Around 5000 people live here, mostly in the town of the same name, the majority making their living from fishing, though more tourists are arriving every year. Historically, Lampedusa has been as neglected as the other Mediterranean islands off Sicily: in 1667 it passed into the hands of the Tomasi family (as in Giuseppe Tomasi di Lampedusa, of *The Leopard* fame), one of whose descendants attempted to sell the island to Queen Victoria in 1840 when it still had only twenty or so inhabitants. The queen lost out on the sale to Ferdinand II, the Neapolitan king, no doubt aghast at the prospect of losing such a scraggy but strategically important island.

Lampedusa is flat and dry, the main attraction for visitors the beaches and the sea around the island. For years the bitingly clean water offered some of the best swimming and skin-diving in the Mediterranean, though recently the port has become the repository of much of the island's filth, a situation that won't change until a new sewage purifier comes into operation. The same myopic attitude has meant the complete deforestation of Lampedusa over the years – the resulting soil erosion accounting for the arid, uncultivable state of the land. But you'll have no trouble in finding uncontaminated spots to swim, away from the port, and while tourism can often be blamed for destroying local communities, on Lampedusa the increasing number of visitors is gradually forcing the *comune* to clean up its act.

Points of **arrival** – plane or ferry – are very close to Lampedusa town, and easily walkable. From town it's another short walk across to the other side of the port to the beach, and most of the hotels. Surprisingly, perhaps, there's no shortage of accommodation and there'll be no problem finding somewhere to stay. Most of the many **hotels** have double rooms for under L30,000 with shower. There's an official **campsite**, too, *La Roccia* (☎0922-970.055), open all year, at Cala Greca.

You can cover the island easily enough on foot. There's a few **beaches** strung out along the length of its coastline, a **sanctuary** in the middle of the island to which there's a pilgrimage every September and some nice cliff-walks – though the land's all barren and stripped dry by the wind. If you can, it's well worth circling the island **by boat**: this way, you'll get better views of the cliffs and grottoes of the western end of Lampedusa. Ask in Lampedusa town about boat-hire.

Lampedusa is also the starting-point for trips to the third island, **LAMPIONE**, a mere speck of land to the west. Starkly vegetated and uninhabited, the offshore fishing here is wonderful – you should be able to persuade someone to take you in their boat from Lampedusa town, around a two-hour crossing.

Eraclea Minoa

Back on the Sicilian mainland, frequent buses travel to SCIACCA from Agrigento in around two-and-a-half hours. With your own transport, you could branch off towards Palermo along a couple of inland routes (see p.215). Keeping to the coast, and with the time and energy to do some walking, you can drop in on the other important Greek site on this stretch, **ERACLEA MINOA**. According to the historian Diodorus, this was originally named

Minoa after the Cretan King Minos, who chased Daedalus from Crete to Sicily and founded a city where he landed. The Greeks settled here in the 6C BC, later adding the tag *Heraklea*. A buffer between the two great cities of Akragas, forty kilometres to the east, and Selinus (Selinunte), sixty kilometres west, Eraclea was dragged into endless border disputes, but flourished nonetheless: most of what's left dates from the 4C BC, the city's most important period, three hundred years or so before it fell into decline.

It's a bit of an effort to **reach the site** without wheels of some description. Best advice is to catch any **bus** running between Agrigento and Sciacca, and ask the driver to put you off at the turning, five kilometres west of MONTALLEGRO, on the SS115; the site is another four kilometres from there. **Heading on** west, from the site turn-off you should be able to flag down a bus *en route* to Sciacca.

The **site** (daily 9am–1hr before sunset; free) sits on a ridge high above a beautiful arc of sand, with the mouth of the river Plátani on the other side. Apart from the city **walls**, once six kilometres long and with a good part still standing, the most impressive remains are of the sandstone **theatre**, disconcertingly wrapped in a protective plastic covering. Above the theatre, excavations have also revealed tombs and traces of a Greco-Roman temple, while below are the ruins of a grand house, with fragments of Roman mosaics. Many of the finds are held in a small on-site **antiquario** (Mon–Sat 9am–3pm, Sun 9am–1pm; free).

While you're here, you'll be hard put to resist a trip down to the **beach**, one of the best on Sicily's southern coast, backed by trees and chalky cliffs, and with a **campsite** with cabins within easy walking distance: *Camping Eraclea* (☎0922-847.310; May to Oct).

Sciacca

If you're fed up with archaeology and the ugly industry around the southern coast's other towns, **SCIACCA** could be just the thing; a working fishing port with a good-looking upper town that's virtually untouched by tourism. In ancient times a spa-town for nearby Selinus, it enjoyed great prosperity under the Arabs, from whom its modern name is thought to derive (the Arabic *xacca* meaning 'from the water'). The town was at the centre of a long feud between Catalan and Norman families that simmered on for a century, resulting in the deaths of a good half of the local population. Despite the destruction, Sciacca preserves some notable buildings, which infuse its agreeable Mediterranean air with more than a passing historical interest, and make for some pleasant strolling through the weaving streets.

The upper town is still walled, entered through one of five grand gates, the westernmost of which, Porta San Salvatore, leads onto the **chiesa del Cármine**, whose facade is lent a skew-whiff air by an off-centre Gothic rose window. Past the church, up via Gerardi, the 15C **Palazzo Steripinto** is even more ungainly, its embossed exterior only partially offset by some slender arched windows. From here, Sciacca's main street, **Corso Vittorio**

Emanuele runs right the way down to the lovely piazza Scandaliato, enhanced by wide views over the port and distant bays. The most enduring Arab legacy in town is the street layout, and back from the piazza, above the Duomo, a Moorish knot of passages and steep alleys leads up to the rather feeble remains of the 14C **Castello Conti Luna**, which belonged to one of the feuding families that disrupted medieval Sciacca. A little way down from here, the 12C church of **San Nicolò** (open Sat evening) is a tiny construction with three apses and some elegant blind arcading.

Practicalities

Buses arrive at piazza Rossi, just up from piazza Scandaliato, or at the Villa Comunale at the eastern end of town: both places are linked by Corso Vittorio Emanuele, home to the **AAST** at no.84 (Mon–Sat 8am–1.30pm & 3–7.30pm; ☎0925-22.744).

There are two **places to stay**: the welcoming *Pensione Buenos Aires*, via Triolo (☎0925-21.837; L20,000), inconspicuously tucked-away off via Licata, parallel to the Corso; and the *Paloma Bianca* (☎0925-25.7; L36,000), past piazza Friscia at the end of the Corso. There are also a couple of **campsites**, four kilometres to the west of town at CONTRADA FOGGIA, best of which is the *Mimose* (June to Sept), right on the sea and with a trattoria-bar at its entrance; close by is *Camping della Gioventù* (☎0925-91.167; open all year). Direct buses run to these between June and September only, though outside these months you can get to the turn-off for the sites from the SS115 on the bus to MENFI (three daily), from piazza Friscia – the sites another ten minutes' walk from there.

Best place to **eat** is in the fish restaurants at the port, down the steps from the main piazza. Of these, the cosiest is the *Ardizzone Trattoria*, known locally as 'Zia Maria', though the sign outside proclaims something entirely different; whatever it's called, it's not difficult to find, just to the left of the lower town's most distinctive feature, a steepled modern church.

Inland . . . and the route west to Menfi

Inland from Sciacca, you can sweat off a few kilos in the vaporous caves at **Monte San Calógero**, eight kilometres out of town. Recent finds have shown that the site has been used since antiquity, and bus #5 runs here in 25 minutes, every hour-and-a-half from Sciacca. The other expedition inland is to the cloud-swathed village of **CALTABELLOTTA**, magnificently perched on three jutting fangs of rock, from which tremendous views stretch out on all sides. On the highest of these pinnacles, you can pass through the solitary surviving entrance of the Norman castle that once stood here, and climb up some rock-cut steps to the very top, from which the village below appears as a patchwork of grey roofs. The castle itself, ruined by an earthquake, was where the peace treaty was signed between the Angevins and Aragonese ending the Wars of the Vespers. Immediately below sit the Norman **Chiesa Madre** and the Gothic **chiesa di San Salvatore**, both wonderfully sited against a rocky backdrop. *SAIS* buses to Caltabellotta run from Sciacca three times a day, the last one back leaving at 2.25pm – an impressive ride, past sparkling fresh streams and jagged outcrops of rock.

Along the coast from Sciacca, the road carries on north west to SELINUNTE and CASTELVETRANO (see chapter 8), a journey you can make by *FS* bus from RIBERA, east of Sciacca, several times daily (including Sun). The service calls at Sciacca's abandoned railway station (beyond the port), and at **MENFI**, planned in the 18C but devastated by an earthquake in 1968. Today it presents a very mean aspect: lacerated churches on derelict central streets, a jumble of untidy prefab housing – still being used – and bland rebuilding on the outskirts.

festivals

February
1st/2nd week Almond blossom festival, the *Sagra del Mandorlo in Fiore*, at AGRIGENTO: events take place in the Valle dei Templi – costumes, music and processions.

February/March
Carnevale at SCIACCA, with participation of the entire town in parades and competitions.

March/April
Easter Holy Week processions in AGRIGENTO.

June
27–29 *Festa del Mare* at SCIACCA: three days of games and competitions.

July
1st/2nd Sunday Festival at AGRIGENTO in honour of San Calógero.
Pirandello week Plays and concerts held at Pirandello's house at CAOS, near Agrigento; check with EPT for dates.

September
22 Pilgrimage and religious procession at LAMPEDUSA, in honour of *La Madonna di Porto Salvo*.

travel details

Trains
From Gela to Licata/Canicattì (10 daily; 30min/1½hr, change at Canicattì for the 10 daily service to Agrigento; Caltagirone (11; 1hr); Vittória/Ragusa (8; 40min/1hr 20min).
From Agrigento to Canicattì/Caltanissetta (8 daily; 1hr/1½hr); Palermo (11; 2½hr).

Buses
From Gela to Licata/Agrigento (Mon–Sat 4 daily; 45min/1½hr); Piazza Armerina/Caltanissetta (2–4 daily; 1hr/2hr); Enna/Palermo (2; 1hr 40min/3hr 40min); Vittória (Mon–Sat 6 daily; 50min); Siracusa (1–2 daily; 2hr); Catania (Mon–Sat 2; 2hr).
From Agrigento to Canicattì/Caltanissetta/Catania (3–4 daily; 40min/1¼hr/2hr 50min); Palermo (4; 2hr); Montallegro/Ribera (for Eraclea Minoa, Mon–Sat hourly, Sun 2; 30min/1hr); Sciacca (9 daily, Sun 2; 2hr); Licata (hourly;

45min); Gela (3 daily; 1½hr); Porto Empédocle (half-hourly until 8.30pm; 20min); Trápani (Mon–Sat 2 daily; 3½hr).
From Sciacca to Caltabellotta (3 daily; 25min); to Menfi/Selinunte/Castelvetrano (6; 35min/65min/1½hr).

Ferries
From Porto Empédocle to Linosa/Lampedusa (June to Sept 1 daily at midnight; 6hr/8¼hr; rest of the year 1 daily Mon–Sat at midnight).
From Lampedusa to Linosa/Porto Empédocle (same schedule as above, departing at 10.15am from Lampedusa, 12.15pm from Linosa); Pantelleria (1 weekly on Thurs at 8am; 6hr); Trápani (2 weekly, on Tues at noon, Sun at 8am; 10hr).

Planes
From Palermo to Lampedusa (2 daily; 45min).
From Lampedusa to Palermo (2 daily; 45min); Rome (1 daily; 1½hr).

CHAPTER EIGHT

TRAPANI AND THE WEST

Thanks to the A29 motorway heading out from Palermo, Sicily's **west** is now more integrated with the rest of the island than it has ever been. Traditionally poor and remote, its economy dependent on fishing and small-scale farming, there's still much here that's different from the rest of the island. Historically, the region has always been distinct, influenced by a strong **Phoenician** and **Arab** culture rather than the prevailing Greek and Norman tradition elsewhere in Sicily. Visually too, the flat

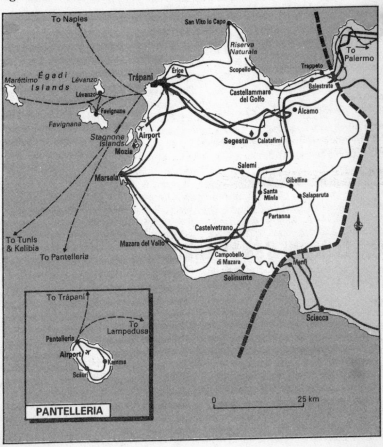

land, dotted by white cubic houses, is strongly reminiscent of North Africa, itself only 150km across the Mediterranean, and considerably closer than the Italian mainland.

On the northern coast, the **Golfo di Castellammare** is only an hour's train ride from Palermo, and though there are patches of industrial development along the gulf, it still manages to offer some empty beaches and a couple of unspoiled villages at its western end. **Trápani**, capital of the province that embraces almost this entire area, has a stronger identity: a port town within sight of the flat salt-pans on which its wealth was based. You could make the city a base for visiting the small, offshore **Égadi** archipelago and, inland, the mountain town of **Érice** – originally a centre of Punic influence, though diverging from the region's dominant trend in its uniform Norman and medieval character. The pattern re-establishes itself a little way down the coast at **Mózia**, Sicily's best example of a Phoenician site, while further south, the Moorish imprint is discernible in the secretive alleys and courtyards of **Marsala** and **Mazara del Vallo**.

Although the Greeks never wielded much influence in the area, the Hellenic remains at **Segesta** and **Selinunte** (Selinus) count among the island's most stunning. Between the two, the Valle del Belice delineates the region struck by an earthquake in 1968, which left a trail of destruction still visible in many of the towns and villages, notably at **Gibellina**, left in its ruined state as a powerful reminder. There could be no greater contrast to this disorder than the peaceful island of **Pantelleria**, a distant outpost, much nearer to Africa than Europe, mountainous and wind-blown, and visited mainly by birds as a stop on their long migrations.

You'll find **getting around** the coast a simple matter as regular buses and trains cover the short distances between all the towns and villages. There's much less public transport, though, if you strike off **inland**: what interior bus services there are depart from Castelvetrano, while if you're driving, apart from the two arms of the A29 motorway, there's only one other main road, the SS188 between Marsala and Salemi.

The Golfo di Castellammare

Backed by a forbidding wall of jagged mountains, the wide bowl of the **Golfo di Castellammare** is almost entirely made up of small holiday towns, sometimes uncomfortably close to industrial plants, though these disappear as you progress west. The main railway line from Palermo skirts the bay, but despite the ease of access and the consequent development, the resorts have not entirely shrugged off their original role as fishing villages – though they have completely lost the mean look they had when fishing was the only source of income. If you're after a beach, some would make a reasonable morning's halt. Otherwise, the train ride is as fair an entertainment, hugging the coast at the base of massive wedges of rock, often of a raw red colour, echoed by smaller, weathered nuggets poking out of the sea.

TERRASINI, forty minutes out of Palermo, is typical of the small ports along the gulf, with a sandy beach, several trattorias and a clutch of expensive tourist hotels. An extra diversion is the private collection of Sicilian painted carts in the **Museo del Carretto Siciliano**, on the seafront in the Palazzo d'Aumale (daily 9am–1pm & 3–5pm; free). If you're looking to stay on the coast, the only **campsite** for thirty kilometres or so is within walking distance of Terrasini, to the north, at **MARINA DI CINISI**: *Club Zeta* (☎091-869.3217; May to Sept), with a few cabins for rent.

The next two villages, **TRAPPETO** and **BALESTRATE**, five minutes apart on the train, offer more of the same, their tidy sense of well-being in sharp contrast to the poverty that Danilo Dolci found when he came to the region in 1952. His *Sicilian Lives* records his first impressions of Trappeto: 'Coming from the North, I knew I was totally ignorant. Looking all around me, I saw no streets, just mud and dust. Not a single chemist – or sewer. The dialect didn't have a word for sewer.' Nowadays, the villages are regularly visited by Palermitan holidaymakers, and things have dramatically improved; there is a **hotel** in each place, cheapest the *Del Golfo* in Balestrate, via Madonna del Ponte 109 (☎091-878.6328; L25,000).

Inland from here, and just inside the Trápani provincial boundary, **ÁLCAMO** is the only large town hereabouts, founded by Frederick II in the 13C and spread across a low hill overlooking the sea. It'll only be of interest to fans of ecclesiastical architecture, its churches all found around the old town's narrow main street, Corso VI Aprile, though there's an impressive 14C castle too, just up from the central piazza Ciullo. To get here at all, though, you really need to be mobile as the railway station (ÁLCAMO DIRAMAZIONE) lies five kilometres below town, off the main SS113. If you get stuck, Álcamo has a reasonable **hotel**, the *Miramare*, Corso Médici 72 (☎0923-21.197; L25,000).

Castellammare del Golfo and Scopello

Back on the gulf, **CASTELLAMMARE DEL GOLFO** is the last coastal stop before the railway line winds inland to Trápani. It's the biggest of the fishing ports on the gulf, built on and around a hefty rocky promontory, though there's little to warrant a stop here. The town's incredible pedigree of bloodshed once gave it one of the worst reputations in Sicily for Mafia violence. It's been asserted that in the late 1950s eighty per cent of the town's adult males had served prison sentences, and one in three had committed murder: coupled with this are the official statistics for the same period, that classify one family in six as destitute.

There are a couple of hotels here, and a **campsite**, *Nausicaa*, four kilometres east of town (☎0923-31.518; April to Sept), but if you're looking for a place to stay you could do much better by moving a little further west up the coast, to **SCOPELLO**, nothing more than an old tuna fishery (*tonnara*) and its associated outhouses, where the writer Gavin Maxwell lived and worked in the 1950s, basing his *Ten Pains of Death* on his experiences there. It's almost too picturesque to be true – not least the *tonnara*, its row of buildings and ruined old watchtowers tottering on jagged pinnacles of rock above the sea. The whole area is regulated by building restrictions and although the public are not officially allowed into the *tonnara* itself, there should be no objections if you ring at the gate and ask permission to look around.

Otherwise, there's no shortage of other equally unspoiled coves and gravelly beaches in the area, connected by paths to the road above, and there are two **campsites** back down the road. The nearest is *Baia di Guidaloca* (☎0924-596.022; April to Sept), three kilometres south and a stone's throw from the lovely bay of **Cala Bianca** where there's good swimming.

The road itself stops three kilometres beyond Scopello *tonnara*, at a **nature reserve**, the *Riserva Naturale dello Zíngaro*, where you can proceed on foot through pristine country. There's no building, hunting, camping or motor-boating allowed here, but lots of clean swimming and guaranteed privacy for a good five kilometres before the road starts again, leading up to the point at Capo San Vito (see p.255).

Apart from the campsites further back down the road, the area's only accomodation is three kilometres inland at the tiny village that once serviced the *tonnara*, **SCOPELLO DI SOPRA** – little more than a paved square and a fountain, but rather an exclusive retreat these days given the building restrictions which limit the hotel space. If you've come on the bus from Castellammare to Scopello (two daily at 6am and 2pm), this is where you'll be dropped, and you should make haste and track down a **room**. There are a few expensive *pensioni*, three on via A. Diaz including the *La Tranchina* (☎0924-596.063; L40,000 with breakfast), and *La Tavernetta* (☎0924-596.007; L38,000 half-board only): between July and September you're unlikely to find space without booking ahead; out of season you might be able to negotiate a lower price. *La Tavernetta*, incidentally, is the only place for miles around where you'll find **something to eat** outside the summer season, with a reasonable tourist menu at L13,000.

Trápani

TRÁPANI is the first of three major towns on Sicily's western edge, and although predominantly modern, has an elegant old centre squeezed into a narrow arm of land pointing out to sea. Lent an end-of-the-line feel by its port, the town's inconspicuous monuments give no great impression of its long history. Nonetheless, Trápani flourished as a Phoenician trading centre and as the port for Eryx, modern Érice, profiting from its position looking out towards Africa. Later, as an important stopover on the sea-routes linking Tunis, Naples, Anjou and Aragon, the town was ensured an enduring role throughout the Middle Ages, when Europe's crowned heads virtually passed each other on the quayside: the Navarrese king Theobald died here of typhoid in 1270; two years later Edward I of England touched down after a Crusade to learn he'd inherited the throne; while Peter of Aragon arrived in 1282 to claim the Sicilian throne following the expulsion of the Angevin French. The city's growth over the last century has been founded on the development of salt, fishing and wine industries, though severe bombardment in World War II has given rise to miles of dull post-war building around Trápani's outskirts.

Still, as a **touring base** for the rest of the west, Trápani can't be beaten. There are a good few accommodation possibilities, all in the old-town area,

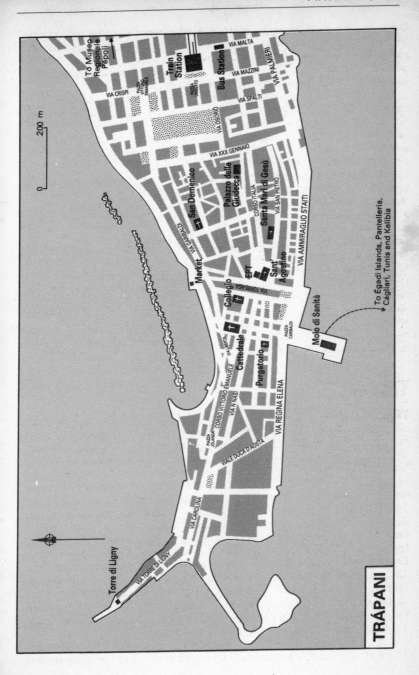

TRÁPANI

To Museo Regionale Pepoli

Train Station
Bus Station
VIA MALTA
VIA MAZZINI
VIA PALMIERI
VIA SPÁLTI
VIA CRISPI
PIAZZA VITTORIO EMANUELE
VIA OSORIO
VIA XXX GENNAIO
San Domenico
Palazzo della Giudecca
Santa Maria di Gesù
CORSO ITALIA
VIA SAN PIETRO
VIA GARIBALDI
Market
EPT
Sant' Agostino
VIA AMMIRAGLIO STAITI
Collegio
VIA TORREARSA
Cattedrale
VIA TRAPANI
Purgatorio
PIAZZA GARIBALDI
CORSO VITTORIO EMANUELE
VIA NASI
Molo di Sanità
VIA REGINA ELENA
PIAZZA JOLANDA
VIALE DUCA D'AOSTA
VIA CAROLINA
Torre di Ligny
VIA TORRE DI LIGNY

To Égadi Islands, Pantelleria, Cágliari, Tunis and Kelibia

200 m
0

regular trains south to nearby Marsala and Mazara del Vallo, buses to Érice and the more distant site of Segesta . . . and the nearest of the Égadi Islands is only half an hour away by hydrofoil.

The best time to visit Trápani itself is at **Easter**, to see the famous procession of the **Misteri** – 18C wooden images arranged in scenes representing the last days of Christ's life. If you're aiming to be here then, make sure of a hotel room in advance, though you should have no problem finding space at any other time.

Arriving, getting around and finding a place to stay

The **railway station** and main **bus station** (for buses from elsewhere in Trápani province) are at the edge of the modern part of town, in piazza Umberto and the adjacent piazza Malta respectively. **Buses from Palermo and Agrigento** drop you in piazza Garibaldi, further up the scimitar of land that holds the old town, and just across the road from here are the docks (Molo di Sanità) for the **ferries and hydrofoils** to the Égadi Islands, Pantelleria, Ústica, Naples, Cágliari (Sardinia) and Tunis and Kelibia in Tunisia; see *Listings* and *Travel Details* for ticket office addresses and full schedules. Trápani's **airport**, incidentally, has connecting flights to the major Italian cities and Pantelleria, and is fifteen kilometres south of the city, at BIRGI, from which there are connecting *AST* buses into the centre.

The **old town**'s narrow and irregular layout occupies around a square kilometre at Trápani's western end, centred on the main **Corso Vittorio Emanuele**, which is around a fifteen-minute walk from the railway station. Everything in the old town is easily reachable on foot, though you'll need to catch a **city bus** (#1, #10 or #11) to visit Trápani's museum in the new part of the city: all routes start and finish their journeys at piazza Generale Scio, at the western end of Corso Vittorio Emanuele.

For information, accommodation listings and free maps, the **EPT** is at piazzetta Saturno (Mon–Sat 9am–1pm & 2–8pm, Sun 9am–1pm; ☎0923-29.000), though there are smaller offices in the railway station (Mon–Sat 8am–8pm) and at the docks (Molo di Sanità; Mon–Sat 8–9am & 6–8pm).

Sleeping

Outside the Easter period, finding **somewhere to stay** is no problem. Best of the cheaper hotels is the *Messina*, Corso Vittorio Emanuele 71 (☎0923-21.198; L20,000), though it's often full, followed closely by the *Maccotta*, via degli Argentieri 4 (☎0923-28.418; L24,000), visible off piazza Sant'Agostino. One block north of the Corso, the *Moderno*, via Genovese 20 (☎0923-21.247; L27,000) has more character than the others, but the plumbing's on the primitive side; or for roughly the same price you could go for the *Sole* (☎0923-22.035; L26,500), piazza Umberto 3, outside the railway station. The nearest **campsite** is a twenty-minute bus-ride away at LIDO VALDÉRICE (☎0923-73.086; April to Sept) – five to seven buses daily from the bus terminal – or there's another at FAVIGNANA, on the Égadi Islands.

Around the city

Old Trápani

Corso Vittorio Emanuele, the **old town**'s pedestrianised main street, is dominated at its eastern end by the pinkish marble front of the **palazzo del Municipio**, the 17C town hall. It adds a touch of grandeur to the thin promenading strip, otherwise hemmed in by balconied palazzi and a couple of dowdy and neglected Baroque churches. The Corso runs to the very tip of the curving promontory from which the town took its Phoenician name (*Drepanon* or 'sickle'), ending at the **Torre di Ligny**, an old Spanish fortification whose squat tower has recently been reconditioned to hold Trápani's collection of prehistoric finds, the **Museo Cívico di Preistoria** (daily 9.30am–12.30pm & 3.30–6.30pm; L1000). This holds a quantity of bones, fossils, elephant tusks, animal and mineral fragments, as well as photographs of the drawings from the *Grotta del Genovese* on the island of Lévanzo (see p.258).

Other sights in Trápani's old town are scattered around the maze of streets on the far side of via Torrearsa, back towards the railway station. Most interesting is the 17C **chiesa di San Domenico** (daily 9–11am & 4–5.30pm), up a flight of steps off via Garibaldi, primarily because it has become the home, albeit temporarily, of the **Misteri**, life-size wooden statues depicting scenes from the Passion. Sculpted in the 18C, each of the twenty groups of chocolate-brown figures is associated with one of the town's trades – the fishermen, or the salt-workers, etc – whose representatives undertake to maintain them, and, draped in cowls and purple robes, carry them shoulder-high every Good Friday through Trápani's streets, in one of Sicily's most evocative religious processions. There's usually a priest around to explain which of the trades are responsible for each of the sculpted groups, and what the particular figures represent – though most of the scenes are familiar enough. (The *Misteri* are to be returned to the chiesa del Purgatorio, their original quarters, as soon as restoration work is complete: typically, no one knows when that might be.)

Architecturally more appealing is the 16C **chiesa di Santa Maria di Gesù**, in via San Pietro, whose two doors display a diversity characteristic of the town, the right-hand one Gothic, the other defiantly Renaissance, with a good relief in the architrave. Step inside, and at the end of the nave there's a terracotta *Madonna degli Ángeli* by Andrea della Robbia, sheltered beneath a graceful marble canopy, the work of Antonello Gagini. There's little more to see in this part of town apart from a few unusual facades, one of them buried in the wedge of hairline streets and alleys north of Corso Italia, at via della Giudecca 43, where the 16C **Palazzo della Giudecca** sports a plaque-studded front and some Spanish-style Plateresque windows. The building lies at the heart of Trápani's old **Jewish quarter**, an area dating from Trápani's medieval role at the centre of Mediterranean trade.

The Santuario dell'Anunziata and the Museo Pépoli

The only incentive to set foot in the **modern city** is to visit Trápani's most lavishly decorated monument, the **Santuario dell'Anunziata** (8.30am–noon

& 4–6pm; free), a 14C convent and church whose cloisters also incorporate the town's main museum. It's a long walk – a good three kilometres – so you might as well take a bus: #1, #10 or #11 from piazza Scio, Corso Vittorio Emanuele, via Libertà or via Garibaldi; get off at the park, Villa Pépoli, which is just in front of the building.

The sanctuary was rebuilt in 1760 and only the facade, with its Gothic portal and magnificent rose window, is original. Inside (entrance on via Pépoli), there are a series of sumptuous **chapels**, two dedicated to Trápani's fishermen and seamen – one echoing the facade's shell motif around the sides of the room – and best of all, the **Cappella della Madonna**, containing Trápani's sacred idol: the beautiful smiling *Madonna and Child*, attributed to Nino Pisano in the 14C. Responsible for a host of miracles, the statue is housed under a grandiose marble canopy sculpted by Antonello Gagini, and surrounded by polychrome marble . . . and generally by a crowd of hushed worshippers.

The **Museo Regionale Pépoli** (Mon–Sat 9am–1pm & Sun 9am-12.30pm, also Tues & Thurs 4–6.30pm; L2000) is adjacent, entered through the Villa Pépoli. Although the museum was designed by one of Italy's foremost architects in the field, it's equipped with abysmal lighting, since it was intended that the exhibits should be seen in full daylight, so come early to get your money's worth, preferably in the morning. The wide-ranging collection takes in everything from exemplary Gagini statuary and 17C coral craftwork to a grim wooden guillotine from 1789, and there's a good medieval art section, too – including a powerful *Pietà* by Roberto Oderisio, and a couple of good 15C tryptychs by the anonymous *Maestro del Políttico di Trápani*. There's also a coin collection, with Greek, Roman, Arab and later Italian examples, and in the next room a 17C map of Trápani showing the harbour to the left, salt-pans to the right, and now mostly disappeared buildings in the middle.

Eating and drinking

Eating out in Trápani is one of the city's better attractions. You can get fresh fish along the harbour front (though you pay for the location), and couscous almost everywhere. If you're really hungry, the *Trattoria Safina*, piazza Umberto I (closed Sun), opposite the railway station, serves abundant portions – the best bargain in town. For something a bit classier, the *Casablanca*, via San Francesco d'Assisi 69 (closed Mon), is popular, with crepes, couscous, fish dishes and more – a bright and cheerful (if pricey) environment. Much earthier is the *La Bettolaccia*, just around the corner: a good floor show but appalling service. If you just want a **pizza**, seek out *Pizzeria Mediterranea*, Corso Vittorio Emanuele 195, opposite piazza Jolanda – a take-away joint with a couple of tables at the back (sitting down you'll pay an extra 15%, a bit steep). Ask for the *Riniata*, made with fresh oregano, tomato, garlic, anchovies and pecorino cheese – a local speciality. There's the same kind of set-up at another excellent back-street pizzeria, *Calvino*, via N. Nasi 79, parallel to the Corso.

If you're desperate for an **ice-cream**, make a bee-line for *Gino's* in piazza Garibaldi (closed Wed) – invariably bulging with customers; if you want to sit and sample a **granita**, there's *Colicchia*, at the corner of via delle Belle Arti and via Carosio, behind via Torrearsa. There are quite a few lively **bars** around this street, while at the northern end of via Torrearsa itself, you could always drop in on the daily **market**: fish, fruit and veg sold from the arcaded piazza Mercato di Pesce – though it's all over by the early afternoon.

Listings

Airport At Birgi (☎0923-841.124/130), twenty minutes' drive from the city; or *AST* buses from the bus station.

Air tickets For flights to Pantelleria and the mainland from *Agenzia Salvo* (☎0923-27.480), Corso Italia 52; note that they offer their customers a free bus service to the airport.

Buses *Autoservizi Segesta*, from piazza Garibaldi (for Palermo); *AST*, from piazza Malta (for destinations within the province, including Érice, Marsala, Mazara del Vallo, Castelvetrano, Gibellina, San Vito Lo Capo, Salemi, Valderice, and the airport); *S. Lumia*, from piazza Garibaldi (for Agrigento and Sciacca).

Car problems *ACI* at via Virgilio 75 (☎0923-22.618).

Chemist *Bianchi*, via Torrearsa 30.

Ferries *Siremar*, via Ammiraglio Staiti 63 (☎0923-40.515), for the Égadi Islands and Pantelleria; *Tirrenia*, at *Agenzia Salvo* Corso Italia 52 (☎0923-27.480), for Tunis.

Garages *Bulgarella*, via Mazzini 17; *Berretta*, via La Bassi 93, in the new town; *Serse*, via Passo Enea 30.

Hospital At via Cosenza, ☎0923-62.944.

Hydrofoils *SNAV* at Molo Sanità (☎0923-24.014) for Pantelleria, Naples, Capri, Ústica and Kelibia (Tunisia); *Siremar* (see *Ferries* above) for the Égadi Islands.

Left Luggage At the railway station; open 24hr.

Police *Questura* at via Virgilio (☎0923-22.333).

Post office At piazza Vittorio Véneto, at the bottom of via Garibaldi; open Mon–Sat 8.30am–7pm.

Taxis Ranks at piazza Umberto (☎0923-22.808) and via Ammiraglio Staiti, at the hydrofoil dock (☎0923-23.233).

Telephones *SIP* office on via Marino Torre 65, near the railway station; open daily 8am–7.30pm.

Travel agent *Traghetti delle Isole*, via Ammiraglio Staiti 23; tickets for ferries to the Égadi Islands and Pantelleria.

Out from Trápani

Aside from the Égadi Islands themselves (see p.256), there are three easy day-trips possible from Trápani. Frequent daily buses leave for **Érice**, forty minutes away in the hills and, at 750m, offering some of the most seductive views in Sicily. The unenclosed Greek ruins of **Segesta** are slightly further afield, around thirty kilometres inland; and it's further again to western Sicily's best beach, at **Capo San Vito**, both places also accessible by bus (Segesta by train too).

Érice

Although only a short ride away from Trápani, **ÉRICE** couldn't be further away in spirit. It's a walled mountain town with powerful associations, thoroughly medieval with its creeping hillside alleys, grey stone buildings and silent charm. Founded by Elymians, who claimed descent from the Trojans, the original city was known to the ancient world as Eryx, and a magnificent temple, dedicated to Aphrodite Erycina, Mediterranean goddess of fertility, once topped the mountain, and was big enough to act as a landmark to sailors. According to legend, Daedalus, fleeing from Minos, brought a golden

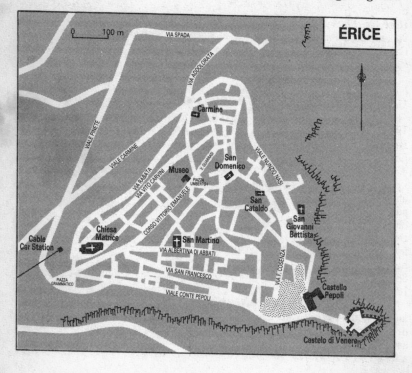

honeycomb to the temple as his gift to the goddess. Although the city was considered impregnable, Carthaginian, Roman, Arab and Norman forces all forced entry over the centuries, but all respected the town's sanctity, the Romans rebuilding the temple and setting two hundred soldiers to serve as guardians of the shrine. Later, the Arabs renamed the town Gebel-Hamed, or Mohammed's mountain, while Count Roger called it Monte San Giuliano, a name which stuck until Mussolini gave it back its ancient moniker in 1934.

The only blots in the town's otherwise homogeneous aspect are 20C ones: the pylons towering above the grey walls and the coach-loads of tourists that regularly call here during the summer – though as people have always come to Érice to sightsee and worship, it seems churlish to resent these. In any case, there's little specific to see in town, and enough cobbled alleys and quiet spots to enable you to avoid the tour groups; and as long as the mist keeps off, the **views** from Érice's terraces are superb, taking in Trápani, the slumbering whales of the Égadi Islands and even (allegedly) distant Cape Bon in Tunisia. Scout around the town at random: the most convoluted of routes is only going to take a couple of hours and every street and piazza is a delight.

You enter through the Norman **Porta Trápani**: just inside is the battlemented 14C campanile of the **Chiesa Matrice** which did service as a lookout tower for Frederick III of Aragon. From here the main Corso Vittorio Emanuele leads up to the pretty **piazza Umberto** with its couple of outdoor bars. Here you'll find the small **Museo Comunale** (Mon–Sat 8.30am–1.30pm, Sun 9am–noon; free), whose main piece is a good *Annunciation* by Antonello Gagini on the ground floor. Sooner or later you'll come to the ivy-clad 12C **Castello di Vénere** (Sat–Thurs 10am–1pm & 3–5pm; free), built on the site of the famed ancient temple of Aphrodite, chunks of which are incorporated into the walls. Stuck in the middle of the public garden below is a restored 15C tower, the **Torretta Pepoli**, lived in until the turn of this century.

The practical details

Buses from Trápani pull up on viale Conte Pepoli: walk a few metres further up and you'll find the helpful **AAST** (summer daily 8.30am–2pm & 4.30–7pm, winter same times but closed Sun; ☎0923-869.388).

If you want to **stay** in Érice you're going to have to pay through the nose, and – in summer, or at Easter and Christmas – you'd do well to book in advance. The cheapest **hotel** is the *Edelweiss*, Cortile Padre Vincenzo (☎0923-869.158; L42,000 with bath), tucked up a cobbled alley off piazzetta San Domenico; or you can **rent rooms**, either at via A. Palma 7, or from the friendly Famiglia Móttola, via Generale Salerno 31 (☎0923-869.502; L15,000 a head). There's also an unofficial **youth hostel**, viale delle Pinete (☎0923-869.144), outside the town walls, though this is generally only open during July and August; check with the AAST before heading out there.

If you want to **eat**, Érice's vastly inflated prices mean that you could do a lot worse than bring your own picnic and sit in the woods beyond the town; or there's a *panineria* on Corso Vittorio Emanuele, if you wanted to buy a sandwich. Some of the restaurants do have tourist menus for around L13,000 a head: try *La Pentolaccia* in via Guarnotti (closed Fri), or *La Vetta* – also called *Da Mario* – in via G. Fontana (closed Thurs), which does a good couscous. Slightly more expensive, but worth it, is *Ulisse* in via Chiaramonte (down vico San Rocco off the main square).

Segesta

Around thirty kilometres east of Trápani, in deserted green countryside, the remains of the ancient city of **Segesta** are among the most inspiring on the island. All that still stands is a Doric temple and a brilliantly sited theatre, relics of a city whose roots – like Érice – lay back in the 12C BC. Unlike Érice, though, ancient Segesta was eventually Hellenised and spent most of the later period disputing its border with Selinus (see p.267). The temple dates from a time of prosperous alliance with Athens, but it was never finished – work on it being abandoned when a new dispute broke out with Selinus in 416 BC.

The site is unenclosed, steps rising past a café and car park to the **temple** itself, crowning a low hill. Started in 424 BC, from a distance you could be forgiven for thinking that it's complete: the 36 regular white stone columns, entablature and pediment are all intact, and all it lacks is a roof. However, get closer (and for once you're allowed to roam right inside) and you see just how unfinished the building is: stone studs, always removed on completion, still line the stylobate, the tall columns are unfluted and the *cella* walls are missing. In a way, this only adds to the natural grandeur of the site, and it's not too fanciful to imagine that the temple simply grew here – a feeling bolstered by the birds nesting in the unfinished capitals, the lizards scampering over the stone, and the pitted and sun-bleached interior.

Below the car park, a road (open to cars, daily 9am–1hr before sunset) winds up through slopes of wild fennel and marigolds to a small **theatre** on a higher hill beyond. The view from the top is justly lauded, across green slopes and the plain to the sea, the deep blue of the bay a lovely contrast to the theatre's white stone – the panorama not much damaged by the stilted motorway snaking away below.

Some travel information . . . and Calatafimi

Coming from Trápani, if you've got a car, the easiest way to Segesta is along the A29 (dir) motorway. Otherwise, it's most convenient to take the direct **bus** organised by Trápani's EPT, leaving daily (Mon–Sat) at 8.30am from piazza Garibaldi and costing L4,500 for a return ticket; more information from the EPT. Other options all require some walking, though nothing off-putting: the **train** from Trápani to Álcamo/Palermo makes an early morning stop at SEGESTA-TEMPIO (current dep. 8.15am, arr. 8.43am) and another at lunchtime (dep.12.50pm, arr.1.18pm), from where it's a twenty-minute walk uphill, the temple up on the right. To return, unless you make the 11.57am from Segesta-Tempio, you'll have to walk from the site car park to the small town of **CALATAFIMI**, a signposted four kilometres away. This was the site of the first of Garibaldi's victories against the Bourbon forces in 1860, which opened the way to Palermo and hence the rest of Sicily. The battle took place on the Salemi road, 4½km south of Calatafimi, on a hilltop marked by a monument. There are a couple of cheap **hotels** in Calatafimi (most central the *Mille Pini*, piazza F. Vivona 2 (☎0924-951.260; L27,000) – handy if you fancy a night in these quiet surroundings – and trains back to Trápani, at 2.31pm, 3.23pm, 5.41pm and 8.41pm.*

North to Capo San Vito

The coastline **north of Trápani** is mainly a rugged, sparsely populated strip, not really suitable for swimming until you reach Capo San Vito. The road weaves under some of the gigantic outcrops of rock characteristic of Sicily's west, most spectacular of which is **Monte Cófano** (859m). The village of **CUSTONACI** nestles under here, slightly inland, famous as a marble-cutting centre and with a smart seaside area lower down on the coast, sprinkled with resort facilities.

The road plunges east and inland here, to re-emerge beside sparkling clear water and more rocky beaches leading up to the resort of **SAN VITO LO CAPO**: a small town clustered around one of Sicily's finest sand **beaches**, wide and clean, and overlooked by more jagged slabs of rock. With its dense ranks of trattorias, hotels and bars, the place is geared to consumers, yet its remoteness has helped to stave off the worst pressures of the tourist industry, even in high season; in winter you won't find a soul. Nor, very likely, will you find many of the **hotels** open, though there should be some possibility for staying, even if it means renting a room.

In summer you'll be spoiled for choice, most options on the main via Savoia or the parallel roads, via Mulino and via Arimondi. Good choices are the *Pensione Costagaia*, via Savoia 123 (☎0923-972.268; L27,000), or *La Ruota*, via Cavour 88 (☎0923-972.629; LL26,000). The *Vecchio Mulino*, via Mulino 49 (☎0923-972.518; 41,000) is a more expensive alternative. Among the **rooms to rent**, the *Bougainvillea*, via Mulino 51 (☎0923-972.207) is worth a look. If you're thinking of **camping**, there are three sites in the area: one of these is very plush, *El Bahira* (☎0923-972.577; May to Sept), four kilometres south of town, and charges accordingly; the others are more modest and more central *La Fata* (☎0923-972.133; June to Sept) and *Soleado* (☎0923-972.166; May to Sept). There are 'No Camping' signs on the beach.

The road climbs beyond the point of **Capo San Vito**, to skirt the high cliffs looking down over the Golfo di Castellammare. It's a secluded and dramatic landscape, with few opportunities for descending to the alluringly deserted coves below. After a few kilometres, the road finishes altogether at the *Reserva dello Zíngaro*, a nature reserve (see p.246).

Regular daily **buses** run up from Trápani's bus terminal to San Vito Lo Capo. The last bus back to Trápani leaves at 7.45pm; or you can move on to **Palermo** on the *Russo* line, buses leaving from San Vito twice a day (not Sun), last one at midday.

---

* You can also reach Segesta **from Palermo**. One **train** (the 10.20am) stops at Segesta-Tempio, a ninety-minute ride, returning at 1.18pm; or there are three daily **buses** from Palermo to Calatafimi (*Autoservizi Verga* company from piazza Marina), which pass the site.

The Égadi Islands

Moored off the western coast, the three **Égadi Islands** (Isole Égadi) are the easiest of Sicily's offshore islands to visit – something that accounts for the summer crowds swarming over Favignana, the nearest of the Égadis to the Sicilian mainland. The other islands are much less affected, however, and if you come out of season things are noticeably quieter everywhere.

Before the advent of tourism, the economic success of the islands was largely based on a historical relationship with the North Italian city of Genova, whose sailors plied the trading routes on which the Égadis stood throughout the Middle Ages; the seal was formalised in the middle of the 17C, when the Bourbon king Philip IV sold all the islands, in lieu of a debt, to Genovese businessmen. Then, as now, the major element in the local economy was the tuna fish, which congregate here to breed at the end of spring. Channeled through the straits between the two main islands during their migrations around the Sicilian coast, they are systematically slaughtered in an age-old rite known as **La Mattanza**, which has been transformed into a rather obscene tourist attraction.

Favignana, the biggest island and site of the main fishery is only 25 minutes away from Trápani by hydrofoil. The Genovese link is most apparent in the island of **Lévanzo**, across the strait, which is named after a quarter in the city of Genova, and shelters the **Grotta del Genovese**, a cave in which a rich bounty of prehistoric cave-paintings was discovered. These days, with the annual tourist influx, the greatest hope for peace and quiet lies in the furthest island, **Maréttimo**, whose rugged coasts are indented with a succession of coves, ideal for clean and secluded swimming. The island also offers a choice of easy **hikes** across its interior and along the rocky coasts.

You could easily see any of the islands as a day-trip from Trápani; seeing two on the same day is fairly simple, too. If you want to stay longer, be warned that **accommodation** is extremely limited, and in summer you should phone ahead to reserve a room. **Prices** are generally high: if you're intending to stay, bring with you as much food as you can manage to carry.

Ferries and hydrofoils depart several times daily from Trápani, and are more frequent between June and September. They generally call at Favignana, Lévanzo and Maréttimo in that order; the return journey is in reverse, though there are occasional exceptions, and sometimes services don't run as far as Maréttimo. Ferries and hydrofoils **depart** from the terminal in Trápani at Molo di Sanità; buy **tickets** from the agencies mentioned in Trápani's *Listings*, along via Ammiraglio Staiti, or else (for hydrofoils) at a booth on the dockside. Ferries are less frequent and take around twice as long as the hydrofoils, but they're roughly half the price: one-way ferry tickets to Favignana and Lévanzo cost L2700, L6000 to Maréttimo; one-way hydrofoil tickets are L5500 and L12,600 respectively; all return tickets cost exactly twice as much. See *Travel Details* for frequencies and journey-times.

Favignana

The main island, **FAVIGNANA** has progressed over the years from prison to tuna centre, and now tourist resort. Looking like a lop-sided butterfly, the island is almost split in two, its narrow 'waist' holding the port and most of the island's population. To the east are Favignana's best swimming spots, the water accessible from a succession of rocks and inlets, while the western half of the island is only reachable along the southern coastal road, and consists mainly of the island's one hill, Monte Santa Caterina (300m). Its peak is occupied by the deserted, fortified prison, while Favignana's main tuna fishery is at its base, looking across to the port on the other side of the bay.

The port, **FAVIGNANA TOWN**, is the first stop for ferries and hydrofoils from Trápani, and, as the archipelago's only town, the focus of most of the tourist traffic. It holds the island's one reasonably priced hotel and various bars and trattorias, but otherwise there's no particular reason to hang around. The town's only distinctive feature is the imposing building near the port, the **Palazzo Florio**. Now the town hall, this was built by Ignazio Florio, an entrepreneur who took over the islands in 1874 and revitalised the fisheries; there's a statue of him in nearby piazza Europa. The **hotel** lies off the main piazza Madrice to the right of the church, the small and unremarkable *Égadi*, via Cristóforo Colombo 17 (☎0923-921.232; L25,000). You'd be advised to book well in advance here if you're coming in summer, when they're likely to raise the prices and slap an obligatory breakfast-charge on your bill. **Campsites** lie out of town to the east, an easy walk and well-signposted; the *Quattro Rose* (☎0923-921.223; May to Sept), or, slightly more expensive, the *Camping Egad* (☎0923-921.555; June to Sept), both with cabins available.

The best way to **get around the island** is by bike. There's a **bicycle-hire shop**, *Isidoro*, at via Mozzini 40, and a couple of others in nearby streets: expect to pay about L5000 a day. The flat terrain and good road surfaces enable you to see the whole island in an afternoon. It's tidily cultivated, pitted with square white houses built from *tufa* quarried from curious pits all over the island – an export that has historically provided Favignana with a second source of cash (after fishing).

The only sand **beach** on Favignana is at **Cala Burrone** on the island's south side; otherwise just follow the roads and plunge in off the rocks. Call in at **Cala Azzurra**, below the lighthouse at the island's eastern end, or, just north of here, **Cala Rossa**, whose name – 'Red Cove' – is said to derive from the blood washed ashore after the Roman defeat of the Carthaginians in a fierce sea-battle in 241 BC.

If you're here in May or June you may want to watch the bloody spectacle of the **Mattanza**, the slaughter of the local tuna catch. The killings take place two or three times a week, presided over by a *Rais* – a title handed down from the Arabs to indicate the fisherman in charge of the operation. The huge fish are surrounded, netted, impaled, dragged aboard and bludgeoned to death. Most of the meat is sold to the huge Japanese vessels that call in at fishing ports all over the Mediterranean; they transport the cargo back to Japan, where it's put into cans and re-exported back to Europe. For more details ask at the town's **Pro Loco**, piazza Madrice 7 (☎0923-921.647; Mon–Sat 9am–1pm), or else the fishermen at the port will tell you if a slaughter is scheduled for the next morning.

Lévanzo

The other Égadi Islands are remote and primitive after Favignana. **LÉVANZO**, four kilometres north, is the smallest of the three main islands, most of it used to pasture sheep and goats and, with its turquoise seas and white houses, having very much the feel of a Greek island. Its population is concentrated in **LÉVANZO TOWN**, little more than a cluster of houses around a tiny port, where you'll find the island's one **hotel**, the *Paradiso*, via Calvario (☎0923-924.080; L30,000), with marvellous views over the sea. In summer, they'll only take you if you're prepared to pay half-board (L45,000) or full-board (L58,000). Alternatively, you can usually find someone who'll rent you a **room**, if you ask around the port.

You don't need to stay, though, to see Lévanzo's main attraction, its prehistoric cave-paintings in the Grotta del Genovese. The coastline is rocky and largely inaccessible, but you can get around on foot by following the dirt paths along the shore. Twenty minutes west of the port, you'll come to a rocky spire sticking out of the sea, beyond which you can continue north up the coast to the **Grotta del Genovese** itself. The cave is best approached, though, by following an inland route, shorter and prettier, along a path through the valley in the centre of the island. It's difficult to find on your own, and unless you can persuade one of the local kids in the port to guide you, you'll have to ask the official custodian, Signor Giuseppe Castiglione, who lives at via Calvario 11 (☎0923-921.704), near the hydrofoil quay. His rates are highly negotiable, depending on how many you are, and whether you go on foot or by mule, but you shouldn't have to pay more than L15–20,000 each; the round-trip is roughly ten kilometres and takes about three hours.

Discovered in 1949, the cave's walls display some remarkable Palaeolithic **incised drawings**, mostly of animals, between 6000 and 10,000 years old, as well as later Neolithic pictures. Despite their age, the evocative drawings retain their impact, drawn by prehistoric man in an attempt to harness and influence the power of nature: one lovely picture of a deer, kept behind glass near the entrance, dates from when the island was still connected to the Sicilian mainland. The later Neolithic sketches are easy to pick out, too; less well-drawn, more stylised representations of men, and even of tuna fish.

Many of the other grottoes on the island were once used by locals to hide from the corsairs who regularly called on raiding missions. To see the caves, you might bargain for a **boat-hire** at the port; again, prices are very flexible.

Maréttimo

Wildest and furthest out from Trápani, **MARÉTTIMO** was claimed by Samuel Butler, in his *The Authoress of the Odyssey*, to be the original Ithaca, home of Odysseus; more far-fetched, Butler also thought that Homer himself was the princess Nausicaa of ancient Trápani. The theories aside, there are compelling reasons to come to Maréttimo. Its spectacular fragmented coastline is pitted with rocky coves sheltering hideaway **beaches**, and there are numerous gentle **walks** to be done which will take you all over the island. Even in high season, you're likely to have much of Maréttimo to yourself, as few tourists can be bothered to visit a place without any hotel and no more than three trattorias.

Nobody advertises rooms in **MARÉTTIMO TOWN**, though they do exist, and if you want **to stay** your best bet is to make for the port's main square and ask at the café there. Otherwise, the people at the *Siremar* agency opposite will point you in the right direction, or you could try the *Pirata* restaurant, via Scalo Vecchio 27 (☎0923-923.159) two minutes away, which has some rooms. Expect to pay from around L30,000 for a double room, though if there's a crowd of you (four or five), it might be better to **rent a flat**, usually an empty holiday home, which can be as cheap as L10,000 per person a night: contact Tomasso Torrente (☎0923-923.145). If you're desperate, there's some level ground in a small pine-thicket, five minutes north from the main square, where you could throw down a sleeping bag. The only place **to eat** that's open all year is on the main street, around L10,000 for a plate of fish; otherwise there's a summer pizzeria above the town, and a bakery near the main.

There's little on Maréttimo to distract you from the natural beauty of the place, though you'll have to get out of the port to see the best of it. Two of the island's **beaches** are conveniently close, one on either side of the town, but you'll find other bathing spots on the way to destinations further afield; at Cala Sarde and Cala Nera on the south coast, or at the Saracen castle at the north eastern point of the island. The two main footpaths are rarely used, so you'll find the hiking details below helpful: none of the walks are particularly onerous, though you might have to scramble at times – and you should take water with you in the summer if you're planning to stay away from the village for any length of time; around three litres a day per person minimum. Alternatively, you could splash out (around L50,000) for a three-hour **boat-tour** of the island from the port, letting you see Maréttimo's entire rocky coastline, and dive into otherwise inaccessible waters, clean and clear and a joy for snorkellers.

Maréttimo Hikes

1. To the Case Romane

The simplest walk takes you to some old Roman defensive works, still in quite good condition. Follow directions in the port to *Pizzeria Flli Pipitone*, turning left up a track on reaching a water-tap. Keep to the right over a small iron bridge twenty minutes on, and turn right again after another five minutes. The remains are half an hour on, sitting next to a small and dilapidated church that shows marked Arab characteristics, but is thought to have been built by Byzantine monks in the 12C.

2. To Cala Sarde and Cala Nera

Follow the stony vehicle track south of Maréttimo port, turning inland after about a kilometre where the path divides. There's a steep climb, with the town's cemetery below you, rising to about 300m. After about half an hour, you'll pass a pine forest and a small outhouse, looking out on views towards Tunisia; below is the **Cala Sarde**, a small bay reachable along a smaller path to the left in another half an hour.

Instead of descending to the bay, continue for about an hour on the main path along the island's rocky west coast. You'll pass a lighthouse and a route down to **Cala Nera**, where you can swim off the rocks in perfect isolation. Continuing along this path on the other side of the inlet, you could meet up with the path across the island's back, taking you up to nearly 500m at Punta Ansini, and down to the other side via the Roman remains detailed in walk 1.

/continues overleaf

Maréttimo Hikes (continued)

3. To the castle at Punta Troia

This walk follows the footpath all the way to the north eastern tip of the island, a hike that should take you around three hours. Go past the post office with the sea on your right, and keep to the coast along the path for about ten minutes, until the terrace wall on your left stops. *Don't continue along the path*, but cut up about ten metres to find the main path on a small spur above you. This stretches along the whole length of the island about 100m above the sea, ending at some concrete steps that descend to a lovely secluded beach and the foot of the **castle**. This precipitous fortification was originally built by the Saracens, enlarged by Roger II, and further extended by the Spanish in the 17C, under whom it became a prison, acquiring a dire reputation for cruelty.

Mózia

Fifteen kilometres down the coast from Trápani lies another, much smaller group of islands, the **Stagnone Islands** (Isole dello Stagnone), uninhabited and mostly given over to salt extraction since the 15C. The long, thin Isola Grande shelters the only one of the Stagnone group that's visitable: **San Pantaleo**, just offshore in the middle of a shallow lagoon, holding the site of the ancient Phoenician settlement of Motya, or **MÓZIA**. Along with Palermo and Solus (Solunto), Motya was one of the three main Phoenician bases in Sicily, settled some time in the 8C BC, and completely razed to the ground by Dionysius I in 397 BC. It's the only one of the three sites that wasn't subsequently built over, though it remained undiscovered until the 17C, and wasn't properly excavated until the English Whitaker family (one of the *marsala* wine dynasties) bought the island in the last century and began digging it up.

Getting there is easiest **from Trápani**'s bus station, from where there are daily (not Sun) organised coach **excursions** to Mózia, leaving at 8.35am, returning at 12.20pm (L8000 return plus the ferry; more information from the AAST); or **from Marsala**, from where there's a thrice-daily **bus** (#4, not Sun) to the landing-stage for the ferry across to San Pantaleo. Otherwise take any bus running between Trápani and Marsala and get off at RAGATTISI – location also of the nearest **railway station** – from where it's a kilometre's walk to the jetty. In summer, a steady flow of visitors to the island means that there's usually a **ferry** waiting or on its way. If there isn't, you'll have to ring the museum custodian (☎0923-959.598; 9am–1hr before sunset) to arrange to be picked up (the nearest phone is at the *alimentari* back on the main road), something you should do anyway during the winter, before setting out; tickets are L2500 return.

Once there, you could circle the island's perimeter in three quarters of an hour, but it's more enjoyable to make a day of it and bring a **picnic**: the site encompasses the whole island, and as long as you can get a ferry there, it's always open. Don't bother bringing your swimming costume though: the linguistic link between the islands' name, *Stagnone*, and our 'stagnant' is not entirely coincidental.

The island: the remains of Motya

Only 2½ kilometres in circumference, flat and cultivated San Pantaleo is one of the most manageable of Sicily's ancient sites, the unique Phoenician ruins spread across the whole island and easily reached by some gentle strolling. The ferry – little more than a dinghy – leaves you close to the small **Museo Whitaker** (daily 9am–1.30pm; L2000), its outside adorned by an aristocratic bust of its founder, 'Giuseppe' Whitaker. You might as well call in here first to see the finds from the island, two rooms packed with a random collection of jewellery, arrowheads and domestic artefacts, the earliest pieces from the 8C BC. Pride of place goes to the magnificent 5C BC marble sculpture of a youth, *L'Auriga*: posing proudly – almost camply – the subject's identity is unknown, but he was likely to have been a high-ranking official, suggested by the subtle indentations round his head, indicating some kind of crown or elaborate headwear.

The remains on the ground start immediately outside the museum: in front and a hundred metres to the left is the **Casa dei Mosaici**, two houses containing some faded black-and-white mosaics. One, probably belonging to a patrician, shows animal scenes, the other, thought to be a craftsman's, yielded numerous shards of pottery. Further along the path you come to the **cothon**, a small artificial boat-dock built within the ancient town's walls, and similar in style to a much larger one at Carthage itself.

The other way, back past the museum and café, leads along the rough tracks that were once the city's main thoroughfares, most of which end at one of the gates on Motya's formerly well-fortified shore. The once strong **north gate**, now a ragged collection of steps and ruined walls – up beyond the museum and right – lies at the head of a causeway built by the Phoenicians in the 6C BC connecting the island with the mainland (and a necropolis) at Birgi, seven kilometres to the north: the road is still there, although these days it's submerged under the water. Just inland of the gate, the **Cappiddazzu** site shows the foundations of a large building, probably a temple, while left along the shore from the gate is the **Tophet** burial ground. Most of the information about day-to-day life in Motya has come from here, the sanctuary revealing a number of vases containing the ashes of animals and people – mainly children – sacrificed to the Phoenician gods, chiefly *Baal Hammon*.

Marsala

When the island-city of Motya had been put to the sword by the Syracusans, the survivors founded Lilybaeum, modern **MARSALA**, ten kilometres to the south. The main city of the Phoenicians in Sicily, and the only one to resist the Greek push westwards, Lilybaeum finally succumbed to Rome in 241 BC, and not long after was used as a springboard for an attack against the Carthaginian heartland itself. The town's position at Sicily's western tip later made it the main Saracenic base on the island, and it was re-named in Arabic *Marsah Ali*, the port of Ali, son-in-law of the Prophet, from which its modern name derives.

More recently, the town has scored a place in modern Italian history for its role in the saga of the *Risorgimento*, the struggle for Italian unity in the 19C. It was here that Garibaldi kicked off his campaign to drive out the Bourbons, in the company of his red-shirted 'Thousand'. Until a planned Garibaldi museum on Marsala's eastern seafront (on via Scipione Africano) gets round to opening, memorials to the swashbuckling freedom-fighter are confined to a few statues and street-names, and the nearby Porta Garibaldi, at the end of via Garibaldi, which recalls the hero's entry into the town.

The town

The town centre is a mainly Baroque assortment of buildings, though there are hints of the older town's layout in the narrow, largely traffic-free streets around the central **piazza della Repubblica**. The square's elegance is due to its two 18C buildings: the arcaded **Palazzo Comunale** and the **Duomo** – 'San Tomasso di Canterbury', patron saint of Marsala – from which four statues peer loftily down. In the large but rather disappointing interior, there's a number of Gagini sculptures, and a plaque near the door commemorating a returned emigrant's donation of funds in 1956 for the completion of the cathedral facade. The most central of Marsala's two museums lies behind the d4uomo, at via Garraffa 57. The sole display at the **Museo degli Arazzi** (daily 9am–1pm & 4–6pm; L1000) is a series of eight enormous hand-stitched wool and silk tapestries depicting the capture of Jerusalem. Made in Brussels in the 16C, they were the gift of the Spanish Ambassador, who doubled as the Archbishop of Messina, and are beautifully rich, in burnished red, gold and green.

Threading up from piazza della Repubblica, via XI Maggio has some pretty courtyards and leads on to piazza della Vittória at its far end, where there are a couple of good bars. Beyond the piazza lies **Cape Boeo**, the westernmost point of Sicily that was the first settlement of the survivors of annihilated Motya. All the town's major antiquities are concentrated here, including the old **Insula Romana** (daily 9am–noon, 2pm–1hr before sunset; free), accessible from via Vittorio Véneto. The site contains all that's been excavated so far of the city of Lilybaeum, though most of it is 3C BC Roman, as you might guess from the presence of a *vomitarium*, lodged in the most complete section of the site – the **edificio termale**, or bath-house. There's some good mosaic-work here: a chained dog at the entrance, and, much better, a richly coloured **hunting scene** in the *atrium*, showing a stag being savaged by a wild beast. If the site's closed, ask at the museum round the corner (see below).

From piazza della Vittória, viale Sauro leads to the church of **San Giovanni**, under which is a grotto reputed to have been inhabited by the sibyl Lilibetana, endowed with paranormal gifts. There's another slice of mosaic here, and a well whose water is meant to impart the gift of second sight.

Beyond the church, in one of the stone-vaulted warehouses that line the promenade, is the **Museo Marsala** (Mon–Sat 9am–2pm; also Wed, Sat and Sun 3–6pm; free), most of whose space is given over to what was, until recently, the only example of a warship from the classical period. Surprisingly well-preserved, and displayed under a heat- and humidity-regulated plastic tent, it still ranks as the only extant *liburnian*, a specifically Phoenician or **Punic warship**, probably sunk during the First Punic War in the great sea-battle off the Egadi Islands that ended Carthage's rule of the waves. Brought here in 1977 after eight years of underwater surveying by an English team working under the archaeologist Honor Frost, the vessel – originally 35m long and rowed by 68 oarsmen – has been the source of much detailed information on the period, including what the crew ate and the stimulants they chewed to keep awake. Scattered about the museum is a medley of items found in or around the ship: heaped amphorae and anchors, and various photographs and explanations of the ship's retrieval from the sea. Other rooms have a variety of more mundane finds from Motya and ancient necropoli in the neighbourhood, as well as some colourful examples of Italian and North African pottery.

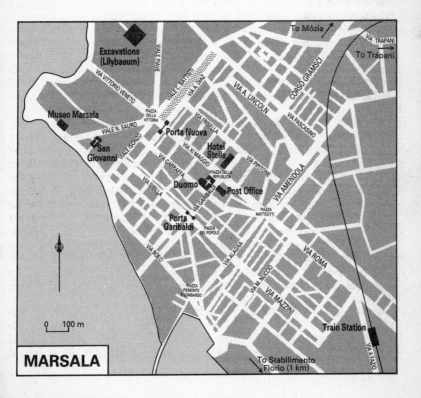

The *Baglio Anselmi*, in which Marsala's archaeological museum is housed, is one of a number of old *bagli*, or warehouses, conspicuous throughout this wine-making region. Many are still used in the making of the famous dessert wine that carries the town's name. It was an Englishman, John Woodhouse, who first exploited the commercial potential of **marsala wine**, when he visited the town in 1770. Woodhouse soon realised that, like port, the local wine could travel for long periods without going off, when fortified with alcohol. Others followed: Ingham, Whitaker, Hopps and many more whose names can still be seen on some of the warehouse doors. Interestingly, it was the English presence in Marsala that persuaded Garibaldi to launch his campaign here rather than Sciacca (his first choice), judging that the Bourbon fleet wouldn't dare to interfere so close to Her Majesty's commercial concerns.

Marsala owes much of its current prosperity to the marketing of its wine, still a thriving industry, though no longer in British hands. You can visit some of the *bagli* and **sample** the stuff for free: try the *Stabilimento Florio* (daily 10.30am–1pm & 3.30–6pm), on lungomare Mediterraneo, beyond the port to the south of town. For enthusiasts, there's also a wine museum, the **Enoteca** (daily 9am–1pm; free) on via Circonvallazione on the south eastern outskirts of town, and an **Enomuseum** (daily 9am–1pm; free) at Contrada Berbaro (three kilometres along the road to MAZARA DEL VALLO), where you can look over the old apparatus and techniques for wine-making. Otherwise, you'll find *marsala* or the sweeter *marsala all'uovo* (mixed with egg-yolks) in every bar and restaurant in town.

Practicalities

You'll arrive in Marsala **by bus** at piazza del Pópolo (also known as piazza Marconi), near Porta Garibaldi, or **by train** at the railway station at the bottom of via Mazzini, which runs off from the piazza. If you're planning to visit Mózia, bus #4 leaves from piazza del Pópolo for the ferry to the island-site. The **Pro Loco** (Mon–Sat 8am–8pm, Sun 9am–noon; ☎0923-958.097) is at via Garibaldi 45. There's a **post office** opposite the Duomo on the same road; and you can **telephone** from via Alagna 68 (Mon–Sat 8am–1pm & 3–8pm, Sun 8am–1pm) or at night from the *Motel Agip* on the Mazara road.

There's an extremely limited choice of **accommodation** in Marsala. The cheapest hotel is behind the railway station, right over the level crossing and right again: the *Garden*, via Gambino 36 (☎0923-982.320; L36,500), what you'd expect for the price, clean and modern. The only feasible alternative is the *Stella d'Italia*, via Rapisardi 7 (☎0923-953.003; L47,000), behind piazza della Repubblica, also tidy and rather dull. Whether you're staying here or not, though, the *Stella d'Italia*'s restaurant is an excellent place to **eat**; otherwise there are a couple of pizzerias up from the Museo Marsala, and the cosier *Kalos* pizzeria in via Armando Diaz, at the end of via XI Maggio (closed Wed).

Mazara del Vallo

The North African element in the island's cultural mélange is stronger than ever at the major fishing port of **MAZARA DEL VALLO**, a half-hour's train- or bus-ride down the coast from Marsala. Under the Muslims, Mazara was one of Sicily's most flourishing towns, and capital of the biggest of the three administrative districts, or *walis*, into which the island was divided, hence the 'del Vallo' tag. The first Sicilian city to be taken by the Arabs, and the last they surrendered, Mazara's prosperity lasted for 250 years, coinciding with the height of Arab power in the Mediterranean. Count Roger's anxiety to establish a strong Norman presence in this Muslim power-base ensured that Mazara's importance lasted long after his conquest of the city in 1087, and it didn't give up its rank as provincial capital until Trápani took over in 1817.

There's little left of Mazara's past glory today, though the Arab links have revived since the lively port became the prime Sicilian destination for Tunisian immigrants flocking across the sea to work in the vast fishing fleet – one of Italy's biggest. Indeed, wandering through the town's *casbah*-like back-streets there are moments when you could imagine yourself to be in North Africa, passing Tunisian shops, a *hammam*, and a café plastered with pictures of the Tunisian president and crowded with French-speaking men smoking hubble-bubbles. There's also a mosque planned for the families who have decided to stay and make their home here.

The town

Mazara's main street, **Corso Umberto**, ends at the spacious piazza Mokarta, and the ruins of Count Roger's **castello**: magnificently floodlit at night, when the square is the focus of Mazara's youthful crowds. Fronting the garden to one side of the piazza is the **Duomo**, originally Norman but completely remodelled in the late 17C – though the relief over the main door showing a mounted Count Roger trampling a Saracen underfoot was carved in 1584. Inside there's an almost indigestible profusion of stuccoed and sculptured ornamentation, though it's worth persevering and seeking out the presbytery, where a group of seven marble statues depicts the *Transfiguration*, carved by Antonello Gagini. To the right, a niche reveals a newly discovered fragment of Byzantine fresco, dating from the end of the 13C, and there's some excellently chiselled Roman sarcophagi, through the marble doorway on the right side of the nave, with reliefs of a lively hunting scene and a battle, rich with confusion.

Outside the duomo, **piazza della Repubblica** heralds a harmonious set of Baroque buildings: the square itself is flanked by the double-storey porticoed facade of the **Seminario** and the **Palazzo Vescovile**, both 18C, while in nearby piazza del Plebiscito, the earlier **Collegio dei Gesuiti** houses the tiny **Museo Cívico** (Mon–Sat 9am–2pm; free) – two rooms off the impressive courtyard, displaying a smattering of minor, mainly Roman, finds from the area. You'll find many other Baroque constructions in the intricate network of streets and squares that makes up Mazara's old town, many best seen at night, and most built after its teeming Arab population had dwindled to nothing. But it's also around here, especially in the old Pilazza quarter, that their descendants have returned, congregating around via Porta Palermo and nearby via Bagno. In this **Tunisian quarter**, you'll come across an authentic Tunisian café and shop in via Goti, and the *hammam* in the aptly named piazza Bagno. The steam room and massage parlour here (open daily 7am–9pm; women 2–5pm Mon–Fri) is modern and presumably much smaller than the earlier baths that occupied this site.

The area is bordered by the **Mázaro** river, its waters hidden by the hulls of the 200 or so trawlers that clog Mazara's brisk **port**. Heavy over-fishing and the use of illegal explosives (dropped into the sea to stun the fish) have greatly decreased the catch in recent years, but the rich waters above the continental shelf have ensured that there are enough fish left to make it worthwhile for the fishermen to pursue their trade – at least given the reduced wages that the Tunisians are prepared to accept.

Crossing over the bridge further down the river, you can walk past the docks to Mazara's seafront, mostly sandy **beach**, though a good part of it is choked by seaweed. It gets better the further up you go, but bathers might bear in mind that the stretch between Mazara and the Stagnone Islands was recently found to be one of Sicily's most polluted coastlines. If you're looking for a **swim** you'd be better advised to jump on a bus from Mazara's railway station to TONNARELLA LIDO, seven kilometres south.

There's one more easy **excursion out from the centre** of Mazara – walkable this time – a couple of kilometres away on the outskirts of town, though drivers could see it on their way in or out by following via Circonvallazione, the main SS115 running to Marsala. Signposted *Madonna del Alto*, the chapel of **Santa Maria della Giummare** sits on a slight elevation on the right-hand side of the road (looking north). Built as a Basilian convent by a daughter of Count Roger's in 1103, its portal shows a strong Saracen strain, too.

All the practicalities

Buses stop either outside the **railway station** or a hundred metres up at piazza Matteotti. The **Pro Loco** is in the old part of town, past the cathedral in piazza della Repubblica (Mon–Sat 8am–8pm, Sun 9am–noon).

As usual in this part of Sicily, there's not a lot of choice as far as **accommodation** goes. The cheapest hotel, the *Mediterraneo*, via Valeria 36 (☎0923-932.688; L37,000), is not far from the station off Corso Armando Diaz, and the only other possibility is the posh *Hopps Hotel*, via G. Hopps 29 (☎0923-946.133; L70,000 with bath), at the eastern end of the lungomare Mazzini.

As you might expect in a Sicilian/Tunisian fishing port, you can **eat** well in Mazara. A good place for **breakfast** is the *Odeon* bar (closed Thurs), at the junction of via Francesco Crispi and Corso Umberto, where you'll find pastries and fresh juices. Via Tortorici, leading up from the Duomo, has a string of popular **pizzerias and trattorias**, or try the *Pizzeria Sicilia* in via Cármine (closed Wed). But the lowest prices are on the other side of the old quarter, at via Mattarella 9, where *La Chela* (closed Sat) does a fish couscous for L5000. If you've got time and want to explore some of Mazara's southern seafront, head a couple of kilometres down the lungomare Mazzini, turning up at a roundabout. *La Barchessa* (closed Mon) is an old *baglio*, or ware-house, where you can sit outside and devour pizzas for L5000. If you want to sample some of the **local wine**, take a bottle along to *Vini Típici Siciliani*, via Carmine 9 (Mon–Sat 9am–1pm & 4.30–8pm; also accessible from the public garden) – fill-ups from a selection of brews cost between L700 and L1500 a litre.

Selinunte and around

SELINUNTE, the site of the Greek city of Selinus, lies around thirty kilo-metres east of Mazara del Vallo, stranded on a remote corner of the coast in splendid isolation. It's a crucial sight if you're travelling through the west of Sicily, its series of mighty temples lying in great heaps, where they were felled by earthquakes. The only drawback if you're not mobile is one of access, though even then seeing the site requires only a little forethought. By **public transport**, you'll have to come from Castelvetrano (see p.269), which is a twenty-minute ride from Mazara del Vallo by road or rail; Selinunte is another twenty minutes south from there by regular bus from outside Castelvetrano's railway station.

Most westerly of the Hellenic colonies, Selinus reached its peak in the 5C BC. A bitter rival of Segesta, whose lands lay adjacent to the north (see p.254), the powerful city and its fertile plain attracted enemies hand over fist, and it was only a matter of time before Selinus caught the eye of Segesta's ally, Carthage. Geographically vulnerable, the city was sacked by Carthaginians, any attempts at recovery forestalled by earthquakes which later razed the city. Despite the destruction, which left the site completely abandoned until it was rediscovered in the 16C, the city ruins have exerted a romantic hold over people ever since.

Marinella . . . and the site

The site is situated just to the west of the tiny village of **MARINELLA**, a better base than Castelvetrano, and where the buses stop. The only road winds down to a small harbour, where the fishing-boats are hauled up onto the sands by pulleys, and though it's slightly top-heavy with trattorias these days, Marinella remains otherwise untouched by the influx of tourists. There are several **hotels**: the ones overlooking the excellent sandy beach are expensive, but the *Pensione Costa D'Avorio* at via Stazione 5 (☎0924-46.011; L26,000), next to the disused railway station, is also good. There are also two **campsites** virtually next to each other on the main Castelvetrano road (the bus passes them both; one has a decent restaurant), though no one minds if you camp out in the pinewoods backing the **beach** to the east of the village: turn left out of the station (where the buses turn around) and follow the signs (*Mare Pineta*) to the beach. The beach-bar here will watch your tent during the day, and it has a trattoria at the back serving wonderfully generous fresh fish meals: a real find.

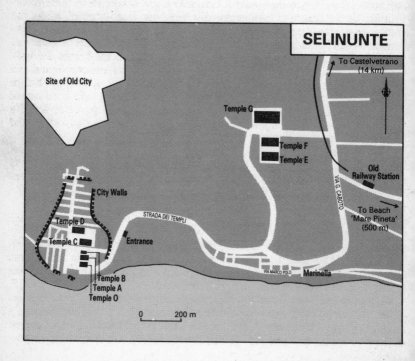

The **site** of Selinus is back behind the main part of the village, split into two parts, with temples in each, known only as Temples A–G. The first stop is at the **East Group**, just over the railway line, the entrance through a car park and open all the time. Shrouded in the wild celery which gave the ancient city its name, the temples are in various stages of reconstructed ruin: the most complete the one nearest the sea (Temple E), re-erected in the 1950s, the northernmost (Temple G) an immense tangle of columned wreckage six metres high in places and criss-crossed by rough footpaths.

The road leads down from here, across the (now buried) site of the old harbour, to the second part of excavated Selinus, the **acropolis** (daily 9am– 1hr before sunset; L2000), which contains what remains of the other temples (five in all), as well as the well-preserved city streets and massive stepped walls which rise above the duned beach below. Temple C stands on the highest point of the acropolis, giving glorious views out over the sparkling sea: it was from here that the best of the metopes (decorative panels) were removed, now on show in Palermo's archaeological museum (see p.56). The buildings immediately behind the temple were shops, split into two rooms and with a courtyard each; while at the end of the main street beyond is the **north gate** to the city – the high blocks of stone marking a gateway that was seven metres high.

The Rocche di Cusa and Tre Fontane

If you're travelling by car from Mazara del Vallo, it makes some sense to call in first at the quarries, the **Rocche di Cusa** (always open; free), where the stone for the building of Selinus was extracted in the 5C BC. They're 3½ kilometres south of the town of CAMPOBELLO DI MAZARA, a stop on the railway line between Mazara and Castelvetrano – so if you don't mind the walk you could come by train, too. You can see the massive column drums and stumps lying randomly about, quarried and chiselled into shape here before being dragged to the ancient city on wooden carts, where they formed part of the great temple complex. There are examples of all the various stages of the process, with unfinished pieces poignantly abandoned, the work interrupted when Selinus was devastated in 409 BC.

If you're looking for a place to spend the night, it's only another five kilometres or so south from here to the coast at **TRE FONTANE**. The small resort has bars and trattorias open during the summer season, and a **campsite** a kilometre before the village; *Il Sombrero* (☎0924-80.300; open all year).

Castelvetrano

You might be passing through **CASTELVETRANO**, fifteen kilometres inland, on your way to Selinunte, or you might be staying overnight in its one cheap hotel, but they're about the only reasons to bring you here. A depressed town, it's saved by an elegant centre, where the *Teatro Selinus* boasts a proud plaque commemorating Goethe's visit in 1787, and, nearby, a good-looking **Chiesa Madre** from the 16C. The church's finely-engraved doorway leads into an interior warmly illuminated by stained-glass windows –

a rare thing in Sicily – and ornamented by a number of stuccoes by Serpotta and Ferraro.

From behind the church, via Vittorio Emanuele leads down towards piazza Matteotti and the railway station. Piazza Matteotti marks the end of via Serafino Mannone, where aficionados of banditry can visit the courtyard in which the body of the island's most notorious outlaw, **Salvatore Giuliano**, was found on 5 July 1950. The courtyard is between 92 and 100 via Mannone, though it's a rather less appealing spot than its legend might suggest.

Three-and-a-half kilometres west **out of Castelvetrano** is a 12C Norman church that makes a pleasant rural excursion for anyone not in a blazing hurry. Head down via R. Séttimo from piazza Umberto, along a country lane fringed by vineyards, keeping left where the road forks. The cupola-ed church, **Santíssima Trinità di Delia**, is signposted before you arrive at the artificial lake of Lago Trinità: ring the bell to the right of the church for the key. The small, square building, its four slender columns and triple apse reminiscent of Saracenic styles, was meticulously restored by two brothers whose mausoleum the church has become. Their tombs, dominating the small interior, rival those of the Norman kings in Palermo for splendour.

Some practicalities

Buses stop at piazza Regina Margherita (below the central piazza Garibaldi), and piazza Matteotti, but if you're moving on, or stopping for the night, wait until the bus finishes its run at piazza Amendola, site of the **railway station**. Castelvetrano's budget **hotel** is nearby, the *Hotel Ideal*, via Partanna 26 (☎0924-44.299; L25,000), left out of the square and under the tracks. There's a **Pro Loco** in the centre of town, in piazza Garibaldi (Mon–Sat 8am–8pm). To **get to Selinunte**, take the bus for Marinella from outside the railway station.

Inland: Salemi and Gibellina

The interior north west of Castelvetrano is intensely rural, its few small towns little changed by the coming of the A29 motorway which cuts across the region. The whole area is green and highly fertile, mainly given over to vine-growing; indeed, the wine around the Salemi district is among Sicily's best. But it still hasn't recovered from the 1968 **earthquake**, which briefly spot-lighted western Sicily, sadly more for the reaction to it than for the actual loss of life. Four hundred died and a thousand were injured, no great number by Sicilian standards, but it was the 50,000 left homeless that had the most lingering impact on this already depressed part of the island, its effects still evident everywhere. Ruined buildings and ugly temporary dwellings being used twenty years on testify to the chronic dilatory response to the disaster, aggravated by private interests and particularly by Mafia contractors capitalis-ing on the catastrophe.

There are, though, a couple of places worth venturing out from Castelvetrano to see, linked by local bus. The town of **SALEMI**, thirty kilometres north of Castelvetrano, oddly enjoyed the privilege of being the first capital of a united Italy in 1860, albeit for only three days, as a plaque in front of its 13C **castello** records. Another plaque marks Garibaldi's declaration of a dictatorship, asserting that 'in times of war, it's necessary for the civilian powers to be concentrated in the hands of one man' – namely, himself, though King Vittorio Emanuele still gets a mention. The castle contains a **Museo del Risorgimento** (daily 9am–1pm; free) filled with war memorabilia. In the square outside, at the town's highest point, the debris of bricks and broken pillars that litter the place provide copious – and shaming – evidence of the 1968 earthquake. A third of Salemi's population had to abandon their shattered homes, and the castle tower, the town's main monument, is still literally strapped together.

But Salemi escaped lightly. Other towns were completely flattened. One of them, GIBELLINA, on the other side of the A29 autostrada, has been left in its decimated state, a distressing monument to the force of the 'quake. Gibellina's population was moved *en masse* to a site close to SANTA NINFA: **GIBELLINA NUOVA**, a modern town – so new that it doesn't even appear on most maps of the area – which has become a symbol of progress in the region, with innovative buildings that deliberately diverge from old styles: weird shapes and forms abound, designed by a handful of modern architects with big budgets. There's a vast petal astride the main SS119, huge white spheres, and giant ploughs, snails and much besides – plenty still under construction. Many buildings are apparently crumbling already, and the designs themselves are embarrassingly frozen in the images of what appeared modern ten or fifteen years ago. You'll see some of it from the road: those with an aversion to such places won't want to get any closer.

Eighteen kilometres along the SS119 towards SALAPARUTA, the old town, **RÚDERI DI GIBELLINA**, complements the new: a frightening mountain of rubble from which smashed and mutilated houses poke out, strewn over a green hillside. It's only really a practical destination if you're driving, and it's a macabre stop-off. On the way into town, you'll pass what is ironically its best-preserved fragment: a shady cemetery stretching down the valley side. Further down, modernism has left its mark here too, in the form of a wide white mantle of concrete poured over one slope, etched by grooves that recall the previous layout of streets. But everything else is as it was: only a church has been restored, and a jumble of scaffolding on a hummock cradles a stage where the new town's inhabitants are supposed to return every year to remember the catastrophe. In reality, though, the event has become an opportunity to entice tourists to a very remote spot of the Sicilian countryside to watch a series of **classical dramas**, or *Orestiadi*. As well as Euripides, Sophocles and others, there are modern interpretations by the likes of Jean Cocteau, Stravinski and John Cage. Performances take place from July to September at 9pm (not Sun); for more information phone ☎0924-67.884, or call in at the **EPT** at Gibellina Nuova, at the Museo Cívico, viale Segesta (☎0924-67.123; Mon–Sat 9am-1pm).

Pantelleria

With the exception of Malta, **PANTELLERIA** is the biggest of the islands surrounding Sicily. Forty kilometres nearer to Tunisia than to Sicily, the island has been occupied since early times by whichever power currently controlled the central Mediterranean. By the Phoenicians, who colonised the island in the 7C BC, it was called *Hiranin*, island of the birds, after the birds who still stop over here on their migratory routes; for the Greeks, it was *Kossyra*, or 'small'. But its present name probably derived from the Arabic *bint al-rion*, ('daughter of the winds'), after the restless breezes that blow around the island's rocky shores.

There are no beaches of any kind in Pantelleria, its rough black coastline mainly jagged rocks, but the swimming is still pretty good in some exceptionally scenic spots. Inland, the largely mountainous country offers plenty of rambling opportunities, all an easy moped-ride from the dull port, where most of the accommodation options are. If you're spending any length of time on Pantelleria, one novel accommodation option is to stay in one of the local *dammuso* houses: their strong walls and domed roofs keep the temperature down indoors and many are available for rent.

The main drawback to spending time on Pantelleria is the **cost of living**: food is mostly imported, and therefore expensive, and there are no hotels charging less than L36,000 for a double (and these are often full). As far as the home-grown food is concerned, the island offers some unique **gastronomic experiences**, as well as some more staple foodstuffs, like lentils, and what are boasted to be the best capers in the Mediterranean. You ought at some point to sample the locally-produced ricotta-type cheese known as *tumma*, which is one of the ingredients of *ravioli con menta e ricotta*, a slightly bitter but fresh-tasting dish for which Pantelleria is famous. The local wine is well-thought-of too, made from the *zibbibo* grapes that grow well in this volcanic soil: best-known is *Tanit*, a raisin wine with a rich golden colour and a dry and heady flavour.

Despite the expense, a weekend spent here will probably leave you wanting more. Best times are May/June or September/October, to avoid the summer's ferocious heat.

Getting there

Trápani is the only mainland port for Pantelleria if you want to arrive **by sea**. Daily **ferries** (not Sun Jan to May & Oct to Dec) do the journey in just over five hours for L22,700 one-way, and **hydrofoils** (thrice-weekly in summer) take 2½ hours, for L30,000. There's also a leisurely ferry service between Lampedusa and Pantelleria; more information from *Egatour Viaggi*, via Ammiraglio Staiti 3, Trápani (☎0923-21.754). If you're pushed for time, it's worth considering coming **by plane**: Pantelleria is a half-hour's flight from Trápani (at least two flights daily), or from Palermo (one daily). The normal return fare from Trápani is L60,000, but there are special offers at weekends: a third off if you leave on Saturday and come back Sunday, or fifty per cent off if you leave and come back on Sunday. Contact *Agenzia Salvo* in Trápani, Corso Italia 52 (☎0923-27.480), and see *Travel Details*.

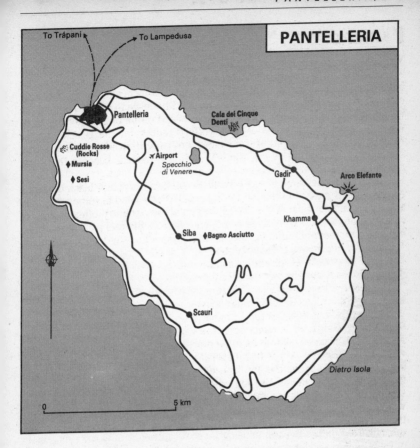

Arriving . . . and the practicalities

If you **arrive by plane**, take advantage of the free connecting airport bus service for PANTELLERIA TOWN, five kilometres north west, though it's a short hitch or easy downhill walk if you miss it. Otherwise, **arriving by sea**, you'll disembark close to the centre of town, where you'll find most of the bars, restaurants and hotels (see below).

Your first call might be at the town's helpful **Pro Loco**, via San Nicola (☎0923-911.838; Mon–Sat 9am–12.30pm, July & Aug 5–8pm too); it's not very clearly marked – it's inside the first block on the left on the airport road, on the port side of town. If there are no **mopeds to rent** on the quayside, call directly at Gianni Gabriele's house in the block just up from here on the other side of the road, or telephone ☎0923-911.741. He charges L15,000 a day. It's the best way to see the island, though there's a strong wind outside the summer months, so take a woolly out with you. **Car rental** is from *Errera-Consolo* (☎0923-911.213), at L35,000 a day. The town has a **post office** and a **bank** with exchange facilities, both in the main piazza Cavour.

Pantelleria town: where to stay, where to eat

PANTELLERIA TOWN is not your idyllic island port: most of it was flattened during the last war when Allied bombers pulverised what had become one of the main German bases in the Mediterranean. The scars are still evident, and the numbered blocks of concrete destined for the rebuilding of the harbour are still waiting outside the port. The only building here that predates the war is the morose, black (and closed) **Castello Barabacane** in the centre of town, a legacy of the Spaniards.

The town has most of the island's **accommodation**, cheapest hotel the comfortable *Miryam*, Corso Umberto I (☎0923-911.374; L36,500) with the *Agadir*, via Catania (☎0923-911.100; L48,000 with bath) a good second. There's no **campsite** on the island and camping rough is impractical given the terrain and the lack of water. If there are two or three of you, a stay in the idiosyncratic *dammuso* houses dotted around the island might be a good idea: try the agency, *Dammuso*, Contrada San Vito (☎0923-911.827), or else ask at the Pro Loco.

Most of Pantelleria's **restaurants** are around piazza Cavour. The *Trattoria Paladino* (closed Mon) in via Roma, behind the piazza, is fairly reasonably priced. If you want a **snack** or just a beer, there's a pretty lively birreria off the square in via Cágliari. It's usually packed with soldiers from one of the island's garrisons, and the pace rarely slackens.

Around the island

Surprisingly, most of Pantelleria's population of 8000 are **farmers** rather than fishermen: with a soil nourished by frequent past eruptions (the last in 1831), the islanders traditionally preferred tilling to risking life and limb in a sea swarming with pirates on the prowl. There are, however, problems relating to farming in Pantelleria, not least the numerous chunks of lava and basalt in the earth that preclude mechanical ploughing, not to mention the incessant wind, scorching sun and almost complete lack of water. But the islanders have evolved methods of minimising these disadvantages by some ingenious devices that would bring a gleam to an ecologist's eye. The prolific *zibbibo* vines are individually planted in little ridges designed to capture the precious rainwater; and the famous *giardini arabi* – walls of stone built round orange trees and other plants – give protection from the wind and the salt it carries with it.

Otherwise, it's a blackened landscape, thick with volcanic debris, in which the local **dammusi** houses, when whitewashed, provide some visual relief. Unembellished, these sombre cubic dwellings, unique to the island, blend in perfectly with their environment. These too are examples of technological adaptation, the thick walls and shallow-domed roofs designed to maintain a cool internal temperature, while their roofs are ridged to catch the rain.

There are a number of points you could make for on your travels on Pantelleria, though few of them get so much as a signpost: you'll have to make do with the very approximate map provided by the Pro Loco and ask directions – the islanders are generally friendly and helpful. Immediately south of the town (on the left, opposite and above the island's flashiest hotel, the *Cossyra*) are the **Cuddie Rosse**, volcanic red rocks that mark the site of a prehistoric cave settlement. A little further on – still to the left, about 300m up at the bottom of a rough track – is the first of the island's strange **Sesi**, massive black Neolithic funeral mounds of piled rock, with low passages leading inside; a second one lies further up to the left. They're thought to be products of Pantelleria's first settlers, possibly from Tunisia.

The coastal road leads down past **SATARIA**, little more than a a couple of rocks where hot springs gush into the sea, reputed to be good for curing rheumatism and skin diseases. From the rocks at **SCAURI**, three or four kilometres further on, you're supposed to be able to see Cape Mustafa in Tunisia on a clear day. From here the extensive south eastern segment of the island, the *Dietro Isola*, curves round – its most deserted stretch, with the road mostly riding high above the sea with few opportunities for access. The island's best **bathing spot** is further still, below the hamlets of **KAMMA** and **TRACINO**: a path leads down from the road, past the half-submerged wreck of a ship, to the **Arco dell'Elefante**, or 'Elephant Arch', named after the lovely hooped formation of rock that resembles an elephant stooping to drink. Again there's no beach, but it's a good place to swim anyway.

A couple of kilometres from here, **GADIR** has more thermal pools and a pretty quay. The bay that stretches away to the north, the **Cala dei Cinque Denti**, has some fantastic-shaped rocks that jut out of the sea like monstrous black teeth, hence its name, 'Bay of the Five Teeth', though these rocks are best seen from the sea. Inland from here is the island's small lake, **Specchio di Vénere** ('Venus Mirror'), set in a former crater. Half of it is clear blue, half muddy-brown – it has a pleasantly warm temperature and is great for a paddle.

The other inland destination is up to Pantelleria's main volcano, the **Montagna Grande** (836m), whose summit is the island's most distinctive feature seen from out at sea. The best route up is from the port, turning sharp left past the airport for the crumbly old village of **SIBA**. Keep left at the telephone box here, and strike off the main road. The mountain's slopes afford the best views on the island, and are pitted by numerous volcanic vents, the *Stufe de Khazen*, marked by the escaping threads of vapour. From Siba, you could take another path that brings you in around twenty minutes (signposted) to a natural sauna, **Sauna Naturale** (or *Bagno Asciutto*), where you can sweat it out for as long as you can stand. It's little more than a slit in the rock-face, where you can crouch in absolute darkness, breaking out into a heavy sweat as soon as you enter. They say ten minutes is the most you should attempt the first time; emerging into the midday sun is like being wafted by a cool breeze. Bring a towel.

festivals

February
3 Festival of San Biagio in SALEMI, with pasta figures given to children and a slippery-pole competition.

March
19 Festival of San Giuseppe at SALEMI, with poetry recitals and sculptures of Jesus, Mary and Joseph made out of bread.

March/April
Good Friday Procession of the *Misteri* in TRÁPANI and ÉRICE.
Easter Thursday Enactment of the Passion in MARSALA, in brightly jewelled processions with gorgeous finery.
Easter Sunday Symbolic meeting of statues of Christ and Mary in MAZARA DEL VALLO.

May/June
La Mattanza tuna slaughter in FAVIGNANA.

June
19–21 Festival of Santa Maria dei Mirácoli at ÁLCAMO, with a pilgrimage to Monte Bonifato.
29 Feast of Saints Peter and Paul in PANTELLERIA.

July
Music festival in TRÁPANI at the Villa Margherita.
10–13 Feast of the Three Maries in PANTELLERIA.

August
Festival of modern Italian art in MARSALA.
15 Horse race around Specchio di Vénere lake in PANTELLERIA.
Last Sunday *Sagra di San Vito* in MAZARA DEL VALLO, with costumed land- and sea-processions.

December
24 Procession of characters from the Nativity story in SALEMI.

travel details

Trains
From Trápani to Álcamo/Palermo (10 daily; 40min/2hr); to Segesta-Tempio (3; 30min); to Ragattisi (6; 20min); Marsala/Mazara del Vallo/Castelvetrano (10; 25min/50min/1hr 10min).
From Marsala to Ragattisi (12 daily; 20min); to Trápani (10; 25min); to Mazara del Vallo/Castelvetrano (11; 25min/45min).
From Mazara del Vallo to Marsala/Trápani (12 daily; 25min/50min); to Campobello di Mazara/Castelvetrano (10; 15min/20min).
From Castelvetrano to Mazara del Vallo/Marsala/Trápani (10 daily; 20min/45min/1hr 10min); to Álcamo/Palermo (8; 45min/2¼hr).

Buses
From Castellammare to Scopello (2 daily; 30min).
From Trápani to Érice (Mon–Sat 11 daily, Sun 5; 40min); San Vito Lo Capo (7 daily; 45min); Marsala/Mazara del Vallo (6; 45min/1¼hr); Castelvetrano (7; 1½hr); Castellammare del Golfo (2; 1hr); Álcamo (6; 40min); Palermo (hourly; 2hr); Marsala/Agrigento (Mon–Sat 2; 45min/3hr).
From Érice to Trápani (Mon–Sat 11 daily, Sun 5; 40min).
From San Vito Lo Capo to Trápani (Mon–Sat 7 daily; 45min); Palermo (Mon–Sat 2; 1hr).
From Marsala to Mózia (3 daily, not Sun; 30min); Trápani (6; 45min); Mazara del Vallo (6; 30min); Palermo (Mon–Sat 8, Sun 2; 2½hr).
From Mazara del Vallo to Trápani 6 daily; 1hr);

Marsala (6; 30min); Palermo (Mon–Sat 8, Sun 2; 2½hr).
From Castelvetrano to Marinella (for Selinunte, Mon–Sat 7 daily; 20min); Mazara del Vallo/Marsala/Trápani (7; 20min/40min/1½hr); Salemi (4 Mon–Sat; 30min); Gibellina (4 Mon–Sat; 30min); Sciacca (6; 1½hr); Palermo (4; 2hr).
From Marinella/Selinunte to Menfi/Sciacca (6 daily; 30min/1hr).

Ferries
From Trápani to Favignana/Lévanzo/Maréttimo (6–7 weekly; 55min/1hr 40min/2hr 50min); Pantelleria (6–7 weekly; 5hr); Lampedusa (2 weekly; 10½hr); Cágliari (1 weekly; 11hr); Civitavecchia (north of Rome, 1 weekly; 17hr); Tunis (1 weekly; 7½hr).
From Pantelleria to Trápani (6–7 weekly; 5hr); Lampedusa (1 weekly; 11hr)

Hydrofoils
From Trápani to Favignana/Lévanzo/Maréttimo (10 daily; 20min/35min/1hr 5min); Pantelleria (3 weekly; 2¼hr); Ústica (June to Sept 3 weekly; 2½hr); Naples (June to Sept 3 weekly; 6hr 45min); Kelibia (Tunisia, June to Sept 3 weekly; 3hr 40min).
From Pantelleria to Trápani (3 weekly; 2¼hr).

Planes
From Trápani to Pantelleria (2–3 daily; 30min); Rome (2; 1hr 40min).
From Pantelleria to Trápani (2 daily; 30min); Palermo (1; 35min); Rome (1; 2½hr–3hr 45min).

PART THREE

THE

CONTEXTS

sicilia

THE HISTORICAL FRAMEWORK

Sicily has a richer and more eventful past than any of the other islands dotted around the Mediterranean. Its strategic importance made it the constant prey of conquerors, many of whom, while contributing a rich artistic heritage, also turned Sicily into one of the most desolate war zones in Europe, their greed utterly transforming its ecology and heaping misery onto the vast majority of its inhabitants.

EARLY TIMES

There are numerous remains of the **earliest human settlements** in Sicily, left mainly along the coast by people originally from mainland Europe. The most interesting of these are the cave-paintings in Addaura, on the northern face of Monte Pellegrino, and those in the Grotta del Genovese, on Lévanzo in the Égadi Islands, which give a graphic insight into late Ice Age **Palaeolithic** culture, from between 10,000 and 20,000 BC.

In the later **Neolithic period**, between 4000 and 3000 BC, there was a new wave of settlers from the eastern Mediterranean, landing on Sicily's east coast and in the Aeolian Islands. Examples of their relatively advanced *Stentinello* culture – incised and patterned pottery and simple tools – are displayed in the

museum on Lípari in the Aeolians. Agricultural advances, the use of ceramics and the domestication of animals, as well as the new techniques of metal-working imported by later waves of Aegean immigrants in the **Copper Age** (3000–2000 BC), permitted the establishment of fixed farms and villages and an expansion of trade, promoting greater contact with far-flung Mediterranean cultures. The presence of Mycenaean ware, from the Greek mainland, became more noticeable in the **Bronze Age** (2000–1000 BC), a period to which the sites of Capo Graziano and Punta Milazzese on the Aeolian islands belong. In about 1250 BC there were further population movements, this time from the Italian mainland: the Ausonians settled in the Aeolians, and the **Sikels** in eastern Sicily, pushing the indigenous tribes inland. It was the Sikels, from whom Sicily takes its name, who are thought to have first excavated the vast necropolis of Pantálica, near Siracusa. At about the same time, the Sicans occupied the western half of the island, a people thought to have originated in North Africa. Not much more is known about another tribe in western Sicily, the **Elymians**, who claimed descent from Trojan refugees: their chief city, Segesta, was alleged to have been founded by Aeneas' companion, Acestes.

THE CARTHAGINIANS AND THE GREEKS

After about 900 BC, Mycenaean and Aegean trading contacts began to be replaced by **Carthaginian** ones from North Africa, particularly in the west of the island. The Carthaginians – originally Phoenicians from the eastern Mediterranean – first settled at Panormus (modern Palermo), Solus (Solunto) and Motya (Mózia), during the 8C and 7C BC, their arrival coinciding with the establishment of **Greek colonies** in the east of Sicily. As was the case in previous migrations, the Aegean Greeks who colonised Sicily's eastern coast were driven by a shortage of cultivable land back home. The first Greek settlements had already been made on the Italian mainland in Tuscany and around the bay of Naples, and the colonisation of **Naxos** in 734 BC was undertaken primarily for strategic reasons. The possibilities for expansion soon became apparent and the Chalcidinians and Naxians who founded this colony were quickly followed by Megarians at **Megara Hyblaea**, north of Siracusa, Corinthians at **Ortygia** in Siracusa itself, and Rhodians, Cnidians and Cretans in **Gela**. These cities, while continuing to have close links with their original homes, became independent city-states and founded sub-colonies of their own, most important of which were **Selinus** (Selinunte), and **Akragas** (Agrigento). Along with the Greek colonies on the Italian mainland, these scattered communities came to be known as *Magna Graecia*, 'Greater Greece', whose wealth eventually overtook that of Greece itself.

The settlers found themselves with huge resources at their disposal, not least the island's fertility, which they quickly exploited through the widespread cultivation of corn – so much so that Demeter, the Greek goddess of grain and fecundity, became the chief deity on the island: the lake at Pergusa, near Enna, was claimed to be the site of the abduction of her daughter, Persephone. The olive and the vine were introduced from Greece, and commercial activity across the Ionian Sea was intense and profitable, reflected in the magnificence of the temples at Syracuse and Akragas that often surpassed those at the major shrines in Greece. But the settlers also imported their native rivalries, and the history of Hellenic Sicily is one of almost uninterrupted warfare between the cities, though they generally joined forces in the face of common foes such as the Carthaginians. It was the alliance against Carthage of Gela, Akragas and Syracuse, and the resulting Greek victory at **Himera** in 480 BC, that determined the ascendancy of **Syracuse** in Sicily for the next 270 years. The defeat in about 450 BC of a rebellion led by **Ducetius**, a Hellenised Sikel, extinguished the remnants of any native resistance to Greek hegemony, and the following century has been hailed as the 'Golden Age' of Greek Sicily.

The accumulation of power by Syracusan **tyrants** attracted the attention of the mainland Greek states, Athens in particular worried by the rapid spread of Corinthian influence in Sicily. Eventually, in response to a call for help from its ally, Segesta, at war with Syracuse-supported Selinus, Athens despatched in 415 BC the greatest armada ever to have sailed from its port, later known as the **Great Expedition**. By 413 BC Syracuse itself was under siege, but the disorganisation of the attacking forces, who were further hampered by disease, led to their total defeat, the execution of their generals and the imprisonment of 7000 soldiers in Syracuse's limestone quarries, many destined for slavery. This victory represented the apogee of Syracusan power. Civil wars continued throughout the rest of the island, attracting the attention of the Carthaginian **Hannibal**, who responded to attacks on his territory by sacking in turn Selinus, Himera, Akragas and Gela. A massive counter-attack was launched by the Syracusan tyrant **Dionysius I**, or 'the Elder' (405–367 BC), which culminated in the complete destruction of the Phoenician base at Motya, its survivors founding a new centre on the western tip of the island at Lilybaeum – modern Marsala.

The general devastation in Sicily caused by these wars was to some extent reversed by **Timoleon** (345–336 BC), who rebuilt many of the cities and re-established democratic institutions with new injections of settlers from Italy and Greece. But the carnage continued under the tyrant **Agathocles** (315–289 BC), who was unrivalled in his sheer brutality. Battles were fought on the Italian mainland and North Africa, and the strife he engendered back in Sicily didn't end until **Hieron II** (265–215 BC) opted for a policy of peace-keeping, and even alliance, with the new power of the day, Rome. The **First Punic War** that broke out in 264 BC when the mercenary army in control of Messina, the **Mamertines**, appealed to Rome for help against their erstwhile Carthaginian protectors, left Syracuse untouched, though again it led to the ruin of much of the island, before the final surrender of the Carthaginian base at Lilybaeum in 241. For Syracuse and its territories, though, this was a period of relative peace, and Hieron used the breathing space to construct some of the city's most impressive monuments.

ROMAN SICILY

Roman rule in Sicily can be said to have begun with **the fall of Syracuse**, a momentous event that became inevitable when the city, whose territory was by now the only part of Sicily still independent of Rome, chose to side with Carthage in the **Second Punic War**, provoking a two-year siege that ended with the sack of Syracuse in 211 BC. For the next 700 years, Sicily was a province of Rome, though in effect a subject colony, since few Sicilians were granted citizenship until the 3C AD, when all inhabitants of the Empire were classified as Romans. Much of the island's present appearance was determined during this period. Large parts of the remaining forests were cut down to make way for the grain cultivation that was to become Sicily's major function. Sicily was Rome's granary, as Cato had it, 'the nurse at whose breast the Roman people is fed'. The land was apportioned into large units or *latifondia*, which became the basis for the vast agricultural estates into which Sicily is still to a certain extent divided. Conditions on these estates were so harsh that the 2C BC saw two **slave revolts**, in 135–132 BC and 104–101 BC, involving tens of thousands of men; women and children, most of whom had been Greek-speaking citizens from all over Rome's newly won Mediterranean and Asian empire. Far more damaging to the island, however, was the **civil war** between Octavian, the future emperor Augustus, and Sextus Pompey, who seized Sicily in 44 BC. For eight years the island's crucial grain exports were interrupted, and the final defeat of Sextus – in a sea-battle off Mylae, or Milazzo – was followed by harsh retribution against the island.

These were isolated incidents however, and on the whole Sicily benefited from the relative calm bestowed by the Romans. But little of the heavy tribute exacted by Rome was expended on the island itself, and though a degree of local administration existed, all important decisions were taken by the Roman Senate. It was represented on the island by two tax-collectors, or *quaestors*, stationed in Syracuse and Lilybaeum, and a governor (*praetor*), who normally spent his year-long term extracting as much personal profit from the island as he could. The *praetor* **Verres** used his three terms of office, from 73 to 71 BC, to strip the countryside and despoil a large part of the treasure still held in the island's lavish temples. **Cicero**'s prosecution of Verres, though undoubtedly exaggerated, constitutes our main source of information on Sicily under the Roman Republic. It gives some idea of the extent of the ruination wreaked by the unscrupulous *praetor*. 'When I arrived in Sicily after an absence of four years, it seemed to me a

land in which there had been fought a prolonged and cruel war. Those fields and hills which I had seen bright and green I now saw devastated and deserted, and it seemed as if the land itself wept for its ancient farmers.'

With Octavian instated as emperor in 27 BC, Sicily entered a more peaceful period of Roman rule, with isolated instances of imperial splendour, notably the extravagant Villa Casale, near Piazza Armerina. The island benefited especially from its important role in Mediterranean trade, and Syracuse, which handled much of the passing traffic, became a prominent centre of **early Christianity**, supposedly visited by Saints Peter and Paul on their way to Rome. Here, and further inland, at Akrai, catacombs were burrowed from the 3C AD onwards – and in caves throughout Sicily, Christian sanctuaries took their place alongside the shrines of the dozens of other cults prevalent on the island.

BARBARIANS, BYZANTINES AND ARABS

Rome fell to the Visigoths in 410 AD, though Sicily became prey to another Germanic tribe, the **Vandals**, who launched their invasion from the North African coast. The island was soon reunited with Italy under the Ostrogoth Theodoric, though the barbarian presence in Sicily was only a brief interlude, terminated in 535 AD when the **Byzantine** general Belisarius occupied the island, encountering a minimum of resistance. Although a part of the population had been Latinized, Greek remained the dominant culture and language of the majority, and the island willingly joined the Byzantine fold. In 663 Syracuse even became briefly the centre of the eastern empire, possibly for political reasons but no doubt partly with an eye to the reconquest of barbarian lands and the ultimate revival of the Roman Empire.

But Constantinople was never able to give much attention to Sicily, and the island was perpetually harried by piratical attacks, particularly from North Africa, where the Moors had become the most dynamic force in the Mediterranean. In around 700, the island of **Pantelleria** was taken, and it was only discord among the Arabs that prevented Sicily itself from being next. In the event, trading agreements were signed, Arab merchants settled in Sicilian ports, and it was not until 827 that a fully-fledged **Arab invasion** took place, when a Byzantine admiral rebelled against the emperor and invited in the Aghlabid Emir of Tunisia. Ten thousand Arabs, Berbers and Spanish Muslims (known collectively as **Saracens**) landed at Mazara del Vallo, and four years later Palermo fell, though it wasn't until 965 that the invading forces reached the Straits of Messina. As with the Roman invasion, however, the turning-point came with the fall of Syracuse in 878, its population massacred and the city plundered of its legendary wealth.

Palermo became the capital of the **Arabs in Sicily**, under whom it grew to become one of the world's greatest cities, wholly cosmopolitan in outlook, furnished with gardens, mosques (more than anywhere the traveller Ibn Hauqal had seen barring Cordoba) and luxurious palaces. The Arabs brought great benefits to the rest of the island, too, resettling rural areas, renovating and extending the irrigation works, breaking down many of the unwieldy *latifondia* and introducing new crops, including citrus trees, sugar-cane, flax, cotton, silk, melons and date palms. Mining was developed, the salt industry greatly expanded, and commerce improved, with Sicily once more at the centre of a flourishing trade network. Many Sicilian place-names testify to the extent of the Arab settlement of the island, with prefixes such as *calta-* (castle) and *gibil-* (mountain) plentiful; while other terms still in use indicate an impact on fishing, such as the name of the swordfish boats prowling the Straits of Messina (*felucca*), or the tuna fishing terminology of the Égadi Islands. Taxation was rationalised and reduced, and religious tolerance was greater than under the Byzantines, though non-Muslims were subject to a degree of social discrimination – a factor which probably helped to persuade a large number of Christians to adopt the Muslim faith.

But the Arabs were prone to divisive feuding, and when in the 10C the Aghlabid dynasty was toppled in Tunisia, and their Fatimid successors shifted their capital to Egypt, Sicily lost its central position in the Arab Mediterranean empire and was left vulnerable to external attack. In 1038 the Byzantine general **George Maniakes** attempted to draw the island back under Byzantine sway, but he was unable to extend his occupation much beyond Syracuse. The real threat came from western Europe, particularly from the **Normans**, some of whom had accompanied Maniakes and seen for themselves the rewards to be gained. One of these, William 'Bras de Fer', who had earned his nickname ('Iron-arm') by his slaying of the Emir of Syracuse with one blow, was the eldest of the Hauteville brothers whose exploits were soon to change the map of southern Europe.

THE NORMANS

The **Hauteville brothers** had long been active in southern Italy by the time the youngest of them, Roger, seized Messina in 1061 in response to a call by one of the warring Arab factions. It took another thirty years to take control of the whole island, in a series of bloody and destructive campaigns that often involved the enlistment of Arabs on the Norman side, but in 1072 Palermo was captured and adopted as the capital of **Norman Sicily**, and was subsequently adorned with palaces and churches that count among their most brilliant achievements.

The most striking thing about the Norman period in Sicily is its brief span. In little more than a century, five kings bequeathed an enormous legacy of art and architecture that is still one of the most conspicuous features of the island. When compared with the surviving remains of the Byzantines, who reigned for three centuries, or the Arabs, whose occupation lasted roughly two, the Norman contribution stands out, principally due to its absorption of previous styles: the best examples of Arab art to be seen in Sicily are elements incorporated into the great Norman churches. It was this fusion of talent that accounted for the great success of Norman Sicily, not just in the arts but in administration, justice and religious tolerance.

The policy of acceptance and integration was largely determined by force of circumstances: the Normans could not count on having adequate numbers of their own settlers, or bureaucrats to form a governmental class, and instead were compelled to rely on the existing framework. They did, however, considerably streamline and centralise administration, and gradually introduced a Latinised aristocracy and clerical hierarchy from Northern Italy and France, so that the Arabic language was largely superseded by Italian and French by 1200.

The first Sicilian ruler, **Count Roger** or Roger I, sustained his power in accordance with Byzantine notions of absolutism and through his retention of a permanent mercenary army and strong fleet. He was a strong and successful ruler, marrying his daughters into two of the most powerful European dynasties, one of them to the son of the western emperor Henry IV; his death in 1101, followed soon after by the death of his eldest son, left Sicily governed by his widow Adelaide, as regent for his younger son, who in 1130 was crowned **Roger II**. This first Norman king of Sicily was also one of medieval Europe's most gifted and charismatic rulers, who consolidated his father's gains by making the island a great melting-pot of the most vigorous and creative elements in the Mediterranean world. He spoke Greek, kept a harem, and surrounded himself with a medley of advisers, notably **George of Antioch**, his chief minister, or *Emir of emirs*. As well as being a patron of the arts, Roger extended his kingdom to encompass all of southern Italy, Malta and parts of North Africa, and more enduringly drew up the first written code of law in the island.

His son, William I (1154–1166) – '**William the Bad**' – dissipated these achievements by his enthusiasm for pleasure-seeking and his failure to control the barons, who exploited racial tensions to undermine the king's authority. During the regency that followed, the Englishman Walter of the Mill had himself elected Archbishop of Palermo and dominated the scene for some twenty years, along with two other Englishmen: his brother Bartholomew and Bishop Palmer. This triumvirate preserved a degree of stability, but also encouraged the new king William II (1166–1189), or '**William the Good**', to establish a second archbishopric and construct a cathedral at **Monreale** to rival that of Palermo, just ten kilometres away. The period saw a general consolidation of Christianity and a shift away from Muslim influence, though Arabs still constituted the bulk of the rural population, and William himself resembled an oriental sultan in his style and habits, building a number of Arab-type palaces.

The death of William, aged only thirty-six, and with no obvious successor, signalled a crisis in Norman Sicily. The barons were divided between **Tancred**, William's illegitimate nephew, and **Constance**, Roger II's aunt who had married the Hohenstaufen (or Swabian) Henry, later to become the Emperor Henry VI. Tancred's election by an assembly was the first sign of a serious erosion of the king's authority: others followed, notably a campaign in 1189 against Muslims living on the island, which caused many of them to flee; and a year later the sacking of **Messina** by the English Richard I, on his way to join the Third Crusade. Tancred's death in 1194 and the succession of his young son, **William III**, coincided with the arrival in the Straits of Messina of the Hohenstaufen fleet. Opposition was minimal, and on Christmas Day of the same year Henry crowned himself King of Sicily. William and his mother were imprisoned in the castle at **Caltabellotta**, never to be seen again.

HOHENSTAUFEN AND ANGEVINS

Inevitably, Henry's imperial concerns led him away from Sicily, which represented only a source of revenue for him on the very outer limits of his domain. A revolt broke out against his authoritarian rule, which he repressed with extreme severity, but in the middle of it, he went down with dysentery, died, and the throne passed to his 3½-year-old son, who became the Emperor Frederick II, **Frederick I** of Sicily.

At first the running of the kingdom was entrusted to Frederick's mother Constance, but there was little stability, with the barons in revolt and a rash of race riots in 1197. Frederick's assumption of the government in 1220 marked a return to decisive leadership, with an immediate campaign to bring the barons to heel and eliminate a Muslim rebellion in Sicily's interior. The twin aims of his rule in Sicily were to restore the broad framework of the Norman state, and to impose a more authoritarian and imperial stamp on society, indicated by his fondness for classical Roman allusions in his promulgations and coinage. He allowed himself rights and privileges in Sicily that were impossible in his other possessions, emphasising his own authority at the expense of the independence of the clergy and the autonomy of the cities. As elsewhere in southern Italy, strong **castles** were built, such as those at Milazzo, Catania, Siracusa and Augusta, to keep the municipalities in check. When the most progressive of these, Messina, rebelled in 1232, the port was ruthlessly punished.

A unified legal system was drawn up, embodied in his *Liber Augustales*, while his attempts to homogenise Sicilian society involved the harsh treatment of what had now become minority communities, such as the Muslims. He encouraged the arts, too, championing Sicilian vernacular poetry, whose preeminence was admitted by Petrarch and Dante. A multi-talented ruler, Frederick acquired the name, ***Stupor Mundi*** ('Wonder of the World'), reflecting his promotion of science, law and medicine, and the peace that Sicily enjoyed during the half-century of his rule.

However, Frederick's mounting preoccupation with his other territories was to the detriment of the island, and the balance of power he achieved within Sicily laid the foundations for many of the island's future woes — for example, the weakening of the municipalities at a time when most European towns were increasing their autonomy. His centralised government worked so long as there was a powerful hand guiding it, but when Frederick died in 1250, decline set in, despite the efforts of his son **Manfred**, who strove to defend his crown from the encroachments of the barons and the acquisitiveness of foreign monarchs. New claimants to the throne were egged on by Sicily's nominal suzerain, the Pope, anxious to deprive the Hohenstaufen of their southern possession, and he eventually auctioned it, selling it to the king of England who accepted it on behalf of his eight-year-old son, Edmund of Lancaster. For ten years Edmund was styled 'King of Sicily'.

But a new French Pope deposed Edmund, who had never set foot in Sicily, and gave the title instead to **Charles of Anjou**, brother of the French king, 'Saint' Louis IX. In 1266 the Angevin forces beat the Hohenstaufen army in a battle on the Italian mainland in which Manfred was slain, and in 1268 another battle resulted in Manfred's fourteen-year-old nephew, his heir Conradin, being publicly beheaded. Backed by the papacy and with a degree of popular support, Charles of Anjou embarked on a punitive campaign against the majority of the Sicilian population who had supported the Hohenstaufen, plundering land to give to his followers and imposing a high level of taxation to recoup the cost of the recent war. The nobility too were affected by Charles' draconian measures and some began negotiating with the Ghibelline, anti-papal faction in Aragon, where the king, Peter, had become the champion of the Hohenstaufen cause by marrying Manfred's daughter. But in the end it was a grass-roots revolt that sparked off the **Sicilian Vespers**, an uprising against the French that began on Easter Monday 1282, traditionally held to have started after the bell for evening services, or 'Vespers', had rung at Palermo's church of Santo Spirito. The incident which sparked it all off was an insult to a woman by a French soldier, which led to a general slaughter in Palermo, soon growing into an island-wide rebellion against the French. It was the one moment in Sicilian history when the people rose up as one against foreign oppression — though in reality it was more an opportunity for horrific butchery and the settlement of old scores, than a glorious expression of patriotic fervour.

The movement was given some direction when a group of nobles enlisted the support of Peter of Aragon, who landed at Trápani five months after the initial outbreak of hostilities and was acclaimed king at Palermo a few days later. The ensuing **Wars of the Vespers**, fought between Aragon and the Angevin forces based in Naples, lasted for another 21 years, mainly waged in Spain and at sea, while in Aragonese Sicily, people settled down to over five centuries of Spanish domination.

THE SPANISH IN SICILY

Sicily's new orientation towards Spain and its severance from mainland Italy meant that it was largely excluded from all the great European developments of the fourteenth and fifteenth centuries. There was no liberation from feudalism, and little impact was made by the Renaissance. Rather, the feudal bonds were reinforced at the expense of social mobility, with the granting of large portions of land to a Spanish aristocracy in return for military service, while intellectual life on the island was suffocated by the strictures of the Spanish Inquisition.

Although Peter of Aragon insisted that the two kingdoms of Aragon and Sicily should be ruled by separate kings after his death, his successor James ignored this and even re-opened negotiations with the Angevins to sell the island back to them. But his younger brother Frederick, appointed by James as Lieutenant of Palermo, convened a 'parliament' which elected him king of an independent Sicily as **Frederick II** (1296–1337). As a result of the barons' support for him, Frederick was obliged to increase their feudal privileges, at the expense of his own. Factions arose, growing out of the friction between Angevin and Aragonese supporters and fuelled by Angevin Naples, and open warfare followed, not ending until 1372 when the independence of Sicily, or *Trinacria* – 'three-cornered' – as it was known under the terms of the treaty (possibly because the kingdom of Naples wanted to retain the name *Regnum Siciliae*), was guaranteed by Naples in return for an annual tribute and the recognition of the suzerainty of the Pope.

It was the populace that suffered most from this feuding, since the policy of both sides was to avoid pitched battles and strike instead at the food sources in the country. Combined with the effects of the **Black Death** during the 14C, the interior of Sicily became depopulated and unproductive. The feudal nobility spent time mainly in the **towns**, and here at least there is some evidence of wealth in the mansions constructed during this period, in the **Chiaramonte** or the later, richly ornate **Catalan-Gothic** styles. A tradition of artistic patronage grew up, though most of the artists operating in Sicily came from elsewhere – for example Francesco Laurana and the Gagini family were originally from northern Italy. A notable exception was **Antonello da Messina** (1430–1479), who soaked up the latest Flemish techniques on his continental travels. With the closing off of the eastern Mediterranean by the Ottoman Turks in the 15C, Sicily was isolated from everywhere except Spain – from which, after 1410, it was ruled directly. The ports of Palermo and Messina continued to do a certain amount of business, but most of the merchants were from Genova, Pisa and Lucca. Sicily found itself on the very fringes of Europe, an Aragonese outpost in the firing line from

Turkish incursions and raids from North Africa. The unification of Castile and Aragon in 1479, followed soon after by the reconquest of the whole Spanish peninsula from the Moors, meant that Sicily's importance to its Spanish monarchs declined even more, and the island soon became of most use as a source of cash, crucial for the financing of the *Riconquista* and the wars against the Turks.

Athough **Alfonso II** (1416–1458) made the island the base for his expansion to Naples, the two territories were separated again after his death, and Sicily came under the rule of a succession of **viceroys**, who were to wield power for the next 400 years. Few of these were Sicilian (none at all after the first fifty years), while the only Spanish king to visit the island during the whole viceregal period was Charles V in 1535, on his way back from a Tunisian crusade.

Little else of note happened in the **16C**, though the curse of piracy was partially removed by the victory of the combined fleets of Spain, Venice and the Vatican against the Ottomans in 1571, at the Battle of Lepanto. But with the Spanish centres of power removed from the Mediterranean, and mercantile and imperial interest focused instead on the Atlantic, the period saw the utter **stagnation** of Sicily. The island's close bond to Spain meant that its degeneration deepened with Spain's decline in the **17C and 18C**. The aristocracy maintained their power and privileges whilst they were being eroded everywhere else in Europe, and corruption thrived in the viceroy's court, with offices being bought and sold and political patronage the order of the day. Throughout this period, Sicily still had a parliament, though it was largely symbolic. More far-reaching was the influence of **the Church**, one of the main pillars of the state and mainly non-Sicilian at its highest levels. This was bolstered by the wide powers of **the Inquisition**, both institutions playing a great part in creating and enforcing a sense of loyalty and even veneration to the Spanish Crown, though the overall effect was a docile acceptance of the status quo on the part of Sicilians. Certainly there were few serious attempts at rebellion during this period, apart from a couple of isolated and short-lived uprisings in Sicily's two major towns, Palermo and Messina. There were, too, occasional revolts against the excesses of the zealous Inquisition, though on the whole discontent manifested itself in a resort to **brigandage**, for which the forest and wild *maquis* of Sicily's interior provided an ideal environment. The mixed fear and respect that the brigand bands generated played a large part in the future formation of an organized criminal class in Sicily.

Already burdened by the ever-increasing taxes demanded by Spain to finance its remote religious conflicts (principally, the Thirty Years' War, 1618–1648), the misery of the Sicilians was compounded by sporadic outbreaks of **plague**, and at the end of the 17C two appalling natural disasters. The **eruption of Etna** in 1669 devastated a large part of the area around Catania, while the **earthquake of 1693** – also in the east of the island – flattened whole cities, killing around five per cent of the island's population. These disasters did at least provide an opportunity for Sicilian craftsmen to show off the latest **Baroque building** techniques when called upon to repair the damage. With the death of Charles II of Spain in 1700 and the subsequent Wars of the Spanish Succession, the island once more took a back seat to mainland European interests, was bartered in the **Treaty of Utrecht** that negotiated the peace, and given to the northern Italian House of Savoy, only to be swapped for Sardinia and given to Austria seven years later.

The **Austrian government** of the island – as usual administered through viceroys – lasted only four years, cut short by the arrival of another Spaniard, Charles of Bourbon, who claimed the throne of the Two Sicilies for himself. Though he never visited Sicily again after his first landing, **Charles III** (1734–1759) brought a refreshingly constructive air to the island's administration, showing a more benevolent attitude towards his new subjects, to whom he granted significant tax concessions. But with his succession to the Spanish throne in 1759 and the inheritance of the Neapolitan Crown by his son, **Ferdinand IV**, it was back to the bad old days. Whatever meagre attempts at reform were made by his viceroys were opposed at every turn by the reactionary aristocracy, who were closing ranks in response to the progress of the Enlightenment and the ideas unleashed by the French Revolution. In the ensuing **Napoleonic Wars** which wracked Europe, Sicily, along with

Sardinia, was the only part of Italy unconquered by Napoleon, while the Neapolitan *ancien régime* was further buttressed by the decision of Ferdinand (brother-in-law of Marie Antoinette) to wage war against the revolutionary French. He was supported in this by the British, who sustained the Bourbon state, so that when Ferdinand and his court were forced to flee Naples in 1799, it was **Nelson**'s flagship they sailed in, accompanied by the British Ambassador to Naples, Sir William Hamilton, and his wife Lady Emma. Nelson was rewarded for his services by the endowment of a large estate at Bronte, just west of Etna.

Four years later, Ferdinand was able to return to Naples, though he had to escape again in 1806 when Napoleon gave the Neapolitan crown to his brother Joseph. This time he had to stay longer, remaining in Palermo until after the defeat of Napoleon in 1815 – a stay which was accompanied by a larger contingent of British troops and a heavy involvement of British capital and commerce. **Liberalism** became a banner of revolt against the king's continuing tax demands, to which Ferdinand's autocratic reaction provoked the British commander **Bentinck** to intervene. Manoeuvring himself into a position where he was the virtual governor of Sicily, Bentinck persuaded the king to summon a new parliament and adopt a **Constitution** whereby the independence of Sicily was guaranteed and feudalism was abolished.

Although the reforms had little direct effect on the peasantry, it was nonetheless a drastic break with the past, and, following the departure of the British, the Constitution was dropped soon after Ferdinand's return to the mainland. He now styled himself 'Ferdinand I, King of the Two Sicilies' and repealed all the reforms previously introduced. Renewed talk of independence in Sicily spilled over into action in 1820, when a rebellion was put down with the help of Austrian mercenaries. The **repression** intensified after Ferdinand I's death in 1825, and the island's fortunes reached a new low under Ferdinand II (1830–1859), nicknamed *Re Bomba* for his five-day **bombardment of Messina** following major insurrections there and in Palermo in 1848–1849. Another uprising in Palermo in 1860 proved a spur for Garibaldi to pick Sicily as the starting point for his unification of Italy.

UNIFICATION, AND TWO WORLD WARS

On May 11 1860, five weeks after the Palermo revolt, **Giuseppe Garibaldi**, a professional soldier and one of the leading lights of the movement for Italian unification – **Il Risorgimento** – landed at Marsala with a thousand men, with whom he intended to liberate the island from Bourbon rule, in the name of the Piedmont House of Savoy. His skill in guerrilla warfare, backed by an increasingly co-operative peasantry, ensured that the campaign progressed with astonishing speed. Four days after disembarking, he defeated 15,000 Bourbon troops at **Calatafimi**, closely followed by an almost effortless occupation of Palermo. A battle at **Milazzo** in July decided the issue: apart from Messina (which held out for another year), Sicily was free of Spain for the first time since Peter of Aragon acquired the crown in 1282.

A **Plebiscite** was held in October which returned a 99.5 per cent majority in favour of union with the new kingdom of Italy under Vittorio Emanuele II. The result, greeted by general euphoria, marked the end of Garibaldi's five-month dictatorship, and the official **annexation** of the island to the Kingdom of Savoy. Later, however, many began to question whether anything had been achieved by this change of ruler: the new **parliamentary system**, in which only one per cent of the island's population were eligible to vote, made few improvements for the majority of people, with political patronage, as ever, determining voting tendencies. Attempts at opposition – and local uprisings such as that at Palermo in 1866 – were met with ruthless force, sanctioned by a distant and misinformed government convinced that the island's problems were fundamentally ones of law and order. Sicilians responded with their traditional defence of *omertà*, or silent noncooperation, along with a growing **resentment** of the new Turin government (transferred to Rome in 1870) that was even stronger than their distrust of the more familiar Bourbons.

A series of reports made in response to criticism of the Italian government's failure to solve what was becoming known as **'the southern problem'** found that the lot of the Sicilian peasant was, if anything, worse after unification than it had been under the Bourbons. Power had shifted away from the landed gentry to the middlemen to whom they leased the land, the *gabellotti*. These men became increasingly linked with the **Mafia**, a shadowy, loosely knit criminal association that found it easy to manipulate voting procedures, while simultaneously posing as defenders of the people. Everywhere, liberal programmes of reform were similarly subverted by the deep-rooted power-relationships of the rural society onto which they had been superimposed. But at the end of the 19C a new, more organised opposition appeared on the scene in the form of *fasci* – embryonic trade-union groups demanding legislation to protect peasants' interests. Violence erupted, and when land-owners called for repressive measures, the Italian Prime Minister, **Francesco Crispi** – a native Sicilian who had been one of the pioneers of the *Risorgimento* – despatched a fleet and 30,000 soldiers to put down the 'revolt', making use of an armoury of autocratic measures in the process, such as closing newspapers, censoring postal services and detaining suspects without trial. But, just as rashly, he soon followed repression by a radical series of reforms designed to effect a fairer and more efficient distribution of the land. These proposals, and others to grant partial autonomy to the region, were rejected by conservative Sicilians who complained of interference in their affairs.

Although there were some signs of progress by the **end of the 19C**, in the formation of worker co-operatives and in the enlightened land-reform programmes of individuals such as **Don Sturzo**, mayor of Caltagirone, the overwhelming despair of the peasantry was expressed in **mass emigration**. Despite their intimate attachment to the land and their close-knit family structure, one-and-a-half million Sicilians decided to leave in the years leading up to 1914, most to North and South America. Many of these were people who had been left homeless in the wake of the great **Messina earthquake** of 1908, in which upwards of 80,000 lost their lives. The high rate of emigration was a crushing indictment of the state of affairs on the island, though it had many positive effects for those left behind, who became the beneficiaries of huge remittances sent back from abroad, and of the wage increases that resulted from labour shortages.

But any advantages were offset by Italy's military adventures, the **conquest of Libya** in 1912 closely followed by World War I, both heavy blows to the Sicilian economy. In 1922 **Mussolini** gained power in Rome – largely without Sicilian support – and despatched **Cesare Mori** to solve 'the southern problem' by putting an end to the Mafia. Free of constitutional and legal restrictions, Mori was able to imprison thousands of suspected *mafiosi*. But the effect was only to drive the criminal class deeper underground, while the alliance he forged with the landed classes to help bring this about dissolved all the gains that had been made against the ruling élite, setting back the cause of agrarian reform. In the **1930s** Mussolini's African concerns and his drive for economic and agricultural self-sufficiency gave Sicily a new importance for Fascist Italy, the island now vaunted as 'the geographic centre of the empire'. In the much-publicised '**Battle for Grain**', wheat production increased, though at the cost of the diversity of crops that Sicily required, resulting in soil exhaustion and erosion. Mussolini's popularity on the island is best illustrated by his order that all Sicilian-born officials be transferred to the mainland in 1941, on account of their possible disloyalty.

In **World War II**, Sicily was the first part of Europe to be invaded by the Allied forces, when in July 1943 Patton's American Seventh Army landed at Gela, and Montgomery's British Eighth Army came ashore between Pachino and Pozzallo further east. This combined army of 160,000 men was the biggest ever seen in Sicily, but the campaign was longer and harder than had been anticipated, with the Germans mainly concerned with delaying the advance until they had moved most of their men and equipment over the Straits of Messina. Few Sicilian towns escaped **aerial bombardment**, with Messina itself the most heavily bombed of all Italian cities, before it was taken on 18 August.

MODERN TIMES

The **aftermath** of the war saw the most radical changes in Sicily since unification, and a series of intense and convoluted struggles between competing interests. With anarchy and hunger widespread, a wave of banditry and crime was unleashed, while the **Mafia** were reinstated in their behind-the-scenes role as adjudicators and power-brokers, now allied to the land-owners in the face of large-scale land occupations by a desperate peasantry. **Separatism** became a potent rallying cry for protestors of all persuasions, who believed that Sicily's ills could best be solved by permanently cutting its links with the mainland, and a Separatist army was formed, financed by some of the gentry, though lacking the organisation or resources to make any great impact. It was largely in response to this call for independence that, in 1946, the island was granted **regional autonomy**, with its own assembly and president – its status comparable to that of Northern Ireland in the UK before the dissolution of Stormont. The same year saw the declaration of a republic in Italy, the result of a popular mandate.

Autonomy failed to heal the island's divisions however, and brute force was used by the Mafia and the old gentry against what they perceived as the major threat to their position – **communism**, already strong in the north of the country. The most famous bandit of the time, **Salvatore Giuliano**, who had previously been associated with the Separatists, was enlisted for the cause, organising a campaign of bombings and assassinations, most notoriously at the 1947 May Day celebrations at **Portella della Ginestra**, a mountain pass near Palermo. Giuliano's betrayal and murder in 1950 was widely rumoured to have been carried out to prevent him revealing who his paymasters were, though it all helped to glorify his reputation in the popular imagination.

By the **1950s**, many saw the **Christian Democrat** party, *Democrazia Cristiana*, as the best hope to defend their interests. Along with the emotional hold it exerted by virtue of its close association with the Church, the *DC* could draw on many of the Sicilians' deepest fears of change. It became especially important after **Fanfani**'s revitalisation of the party after 1954, with Sicily holding about a third of his supporters country-wide. But the party was too closely involved with business and the landowning classes to have any real enthusiasm for reform. All attempts at enterprise were channeled through the party's offices, and favours were bought or bartered. Cutting across party lines, political patronage, or *clientelismo*, grew to be stronger than ever, still today affecting people's lives on all levels, especially in the field of work – from finding a job to landing a contract. The favours system was also evident in the workings of the island's sluggish **bureaucracy**, considered even more contorted than the mainland's, so that the smallest reforms proved cumbersome and complicated to put into practice, often taking years to effect. In 1971 a law was passed to improve the functioning of the bureaucracy, and though progress has been made, the essential problem is unchanged, with the elaborate machinery of the civil service often exploited to accumulate and dispense personal power.

One area that managed to avoid bureaucratic control or planning of any sort was **construction**, one of Sicily's greatest growth industries, the physical evidence of which is one of the visitor's most enduring impressions of the island. The building boom was inextricably connected with the Mafia's involvement in land speculation, and boosted by the phenomenal rate of **urban growth** all over Sicily. But both in the towns and the rural areas, the minimum safety standards were rarely met, as highlighted by the **1968 earthquake**, in which 50,000 were made homeless along the Valle di Belice, although the 'quake was seismically quite small. But, while large expanses of the countryside were blighted by rapid and often unsafe development, other areas were badly neglected, for instance Palermo, where, in some parts, bomb damage has still not been made good after 45 years.

Industry, too, has been subject to mismanagement, and, apart from isolated cases, has rarely shown the potential it promised after the discovery of oil near Ragusa and Gela in the 1950s, and the development of refineries and petrochemical plants on the Golfo di Augusta: other projects have failed miserably, despite the huge resources allocated to them. **Agriculture**, on the other hand, has been deprived of both funds and attention, though investment and the better use of land can produce outstanding results, as shown by the success of citrus cultivation in the north and east of the island, and the draining of the Piana di Catania. Substantial subsidies have helped in these and other programmes, mainly through a financial agency called the *Cassa del Mezzogiorno*, set up in 1950 but discontinued

in 1983, and from the **EEC**, which Italy joined in 1958. But membership of the European Community, in which Sicily – a 'problem region' – is more marginalised than ever, also poses problems for the local economy, with more competition for farmers predicted following the accessions of Spain, Greece and Portugal.

Subsidy and support, meanwhile, has not prevented Sicilians from complaining of being left out of Italy's great 'economic miracle' of the Fifties and Sixties, complaints repeated in the Eighties. While Italy claims to be the eighth most industrialised nation in the West, it is the great urban centres of the north of Italy that flaunt their prosperity, while the south of Italy, *Il Mezzogiorno*, is left far behind. The other side of the coin is that the huge financial concessions made to the island have provoked resentment from Italy's more self-sufficient regions, for whom the failure of land-reform programmes and industrial development is chiefly due to corruption and incompetence in the island itself. Few Sicilians would wholly deny this; a longer view, however, points to Sicily's disadvantages being derived principally from the past misuse of resources, coupled with a culture and mentality that have never given much credence to collectivist ideals. But **progress** has been made, and the threefold increase of *per capita* income in the thirty years since 1951 is reflected in greater numbers of newer and bigger cars jamming the island's roads every year, while laws passed relating to land distribution and reform of the bureaucracy show a greater commitment to change. There is more awareness, too, on the part of the state that the fight against **organised crime** (see below) requires more than moralistic speeches and the despatch of a new Chief of Police.

But beneath the superficial improvements, the deep problems that have always bedevilled Sicily still exist in some form. Unemployment, still high at 15–20 per cent, is not helped by the fewer outlets available for **emigration**, though a million still managed to escape the island between 1951 and 1971, along with the majority of Sicily's most outstanding artists and writers. Perhaps the greatest hope for the island lies in the exploitation of **tourism**: the island is subject to an annual deluge of mainly French, Swiss and Germans, but again its concentration in specific areas means that most Sicilians are missing out.

THE 1980s: THE OFFENSIVE AGAINST THE MAFIA

In Sicily, there is 'mafia' and there is the 'Mafia'. Mafia refers to a criminal mentality, the Mafia to a specific criminal organisation. In Italy's deep south, where a man can look *mafioso*, or talk like a *mafioso*, meaning he has the aura, or stench, of criminality about him, mafia is enmeshed in the very fabric of society. The Mafia, on the other hand, operates outside society, and even transcends state boundaries. And while notions of family solidarity and the moral stature of the outlaw mean that mafia can never be completely extirpated from Sicilian society, the Mafia is an entity whose members can be eliminated and its power emasculated. What has always prevented this from happening is the shadowy nature of the organisation, protected by the long-standing code of silence, or *omertà*, that invariably led to accusations being retracted at the last moment, or to crucial witnesses being found dead with a stone, cork, or a fistful of banknotes stuffed into their mouths, or else simply having disappeared off the face of the earth. As a result, many have doubted the very existence of the Mafia, claiming that it's nothing more than the creation of pulp-thriller writers, the invention of a sensationalist press, and the fabrication of an Italian government embarrassed by its inability to control an unusually high level of crime in Sicily.

But in 1982 proof of the innermost workings of the Mafia's organisation emerged when a high-ranking member, **Tommaso Buscetta**, was arrested in Brazil, and – after a failed suicide attempt – agreed to prise open the can of worms. His reason for daring this sacrilege, he claimed, was to destroy the Mafia. In its stampede to grab the huge profits to be made from the international heroin industry, the 'Honoured Society' (*La Società Onorata*) had abandoned its original ideals: 'it's necessary to destroy this band of criminals', he declared, 'who have perverted the principles of *Cosa Nostra* and dragged them through the mud'. But he was doubtless motivated, too, by a less noble passion, revenge: all of those he incriminated – Michele Greco, Pippo Calò, Benedetto Santapaola, Salvatore Riina and many others – were leaders of, or allied to, the powerful Corleonese family who had recently embarked on a campaign of terror to monopolise the drugs industry, in the process eliminating seven of Buscetta's closest relatives in the space of four months, including his two sons.

THE BACKGROUND

Buscetta's statements to Giovanni Falcone, head of Sicily's anti-Mafia 'pool' of judges, and later to the Federal Court in Manhattan, were the most important revelations about the **structure** of *Cosa Nostra* since Jo Valachi – a prominent member of the New York Genovese family – provided the first inside view in 1962. Mafia 'families' are centred on areas, he revealed: villages or quarters of cities from which they take their name. The boss (*capo*) of each group is chosen by election, and appoints a lieutenant (*sottocapo*) and one or more *consiglieri*, or counsellors. Larger groups also have officers known as *capodecini*, each in command of ten men. Above the families is the **Commission**, a governing body that includes representatives from all the major groupings. Democracy and collective interest, Buscetta claimed, had been replaced in the Commission by the greed and self-interest of the individuals who had gained control. Trials of strength alone now decided the leadership, often in the form of bitter feuds between rival factions – or *cosche* (literally, artichokes, their form symbolising solidarity).

The existence of the Commission sets the Mafia apart from the normal run of underworld gangs, for without a high level of organisation, the international trafficking in heroin which they engage in would be inconceivable. The route is a circuitous one, starting in the Middle and Far East, moving on to the processing plants in Sicily, and ending up in New York, where American Mafia channels are said to control sixty per cent of the heroin market. This multi-million-dollar racket – known in the US as the '**Pizza Connection**', because Sicilian pizza parlours were used as covers for the operation – was blown apart chiefly as a result of Buscetta's evidence, and led to the trial and conviction of the leading members of New York's Mafia Commission in September 1986. The trial introduced a significant new note in Mafia cases when the defence lawyers stated at the outset that their clients were self-confessed members of *Cosa Nostra* – making the issue more one of whether the Mafia was necessarily a *criminal* organisation; with most of the American drug profits safely invested in legitimate gambling, construction and high finance, there was little to distinguish it from any other business cartel.

THE HISTORY

The Mafia has certainly come a long way since its rustic beginnings in feudal Sicily. Although Buscetta denied that the word 'Mafia' is used to describe the organisation – the term preferred by its members is *Cosa Nostra* – the word has been in currency for centuries, and is thought to derive from the Arabic, *mu'afah*, meaning 'protection'. In 1863 a play entitled *I Mafiusi della Vicaria*, based on life in a Palermo prison, was a roaring success among the high-society of the island's capital, giving the word its first extensive usage: when the city rose against its new Italian rulers three years later, the British consul described a situation where secret societies were all-powerful: '*Camorre* and *maffie*, self-elected *juntas* share the earnings of the workmen, keep up intercourse with outcasts, and take malefactors under their wing and protection.'

Previously, *mafiosi* had been able to pose as defenders of the poor against the tyranny of Sicily's rulers, but in the years immediately following the toppling of the Bourbon state in Italy, *mafiosi* were able to entrench themselves in Sicily's new power-structure, acting as intermediaries in the gradual redistribution of land and establishing a *modus vivendi* with the new democratic representatives. There is little or no documentary proof of the rise to power of the 'Honoured Society', but most writers agree that between the 1890s and the 1920s its undisputed boss was **Don Vito Cascio Ferro**, who had close links with the American 'Black Hand', a Mafia-type amalgam of southern Italian emigrants. Despite numerous homicide charges brought against him, the only man whom Ferro admitted to shooting was an American detective, Jack Petrosino, killed on the same day he docked at Palermo to investigate links between the Sicilian and American organisations.

Ferro's career ended with Mussolini's anti-Mafia purges, instigated to clear the ground for the establishment of a vigorous Fascist structure in Sicily. **Cesare Mori**, the *Duce*'s newly appointed Prefect of Palermo, arrived in the city in 1925 with the declared aim of 'clearing the ground of the nightmares, threats and dangers which are paralysing, perverting and corrupting every kind of social activity'. This might have worked, but the clean sweep that Mori made of the Mafia leaders (in all, 11,000 cattle-rustlers, thieves and 'conspirators' were gaoled in this period, often on the basis of flimsy hearsay) was annulled after World War II when the prisons were opened and Mafia leaders, seen as unjustly gaoled by the Fascist regime, returned to their regular operations. In the confusion that reigned during Italy's reconstruction, illegal crime flourished throughout the south, and criminal leagues regrouped in Naples (the *Camorra*) and Calabria ('*ndrángeta*), controlling the black market and smuggling rackets. In Sicily, men such as **Don Calógero Vizzini** were the new leaders, confirmed in their power by the brief Anglo-American post-war administration, in return for their contribution towards the smooth progress of the Allied landings and occupation. One of them, **Lucky Luciano**, one of the founder-members of the American Commission, was even flown out from prison in America to facilitate the invasion. Later he was alleged to be responsible for setting up the Sicilian-American narcotics empire, taken over at his death in 1962 by **Luciano Liggio**, who subsequently manoeuvred himself into the leadership of the Corleone family (though he has been in gaol since 1974).

THE NEW MAFIA

The cycle by now was complete: the Mafia had lost its original role as a predominantly rural organisation, and had transformed itself by its post-war 'Americanisation' – transferring its operations to the cities and moving into entrepreneurial activities like construction, real estate and ultimately drugs smuggling. With the growth of the heroin industry, the stakes were raised immensely, as shown by the vicious civil wars fought over the division of the spoils. The Italian state responded with an anti-Mafia Parliamentary Commission that sat from 1963 to 1976, which posed enough of a threat to the underworld to provoke a change of tactics by the Mafia, who began to target important state officials in a sustained campaign of terror that continues to this day. In

1971 Palermo's chief public prosecutor, Pietro Scaglione, became the first in a long line of '**illustrious corpses**' – *cadáveri eccellenti* – which have included journalists, judges, lawyers, police chiefs and left-wing politicians. A new peak of violence was reached in 1982 with the ambush and murder in Palermo's city centre of **Pio La Torre**, Regional Secretary of the Communist Party in Sicily, who had proposed a special government dispensation to allow lawyers access to private bank accounts.

One of the people attending La Torre's funeral was the new Sicilian prefect of police, **General Dalla Chiesa**, a veteran in the state's fight against the *Brigate Rosse*, or Red Brigades, and whose despatch promised new action against the Mafia. The prefect began investigating Sicily's lucrative construction industry, which provided an efficient means of investing drugs profits. His scrutiny of public records and business dealings threatened to expose one of the most enigmatic issues in the Mafia's organisation: the extent of corruption and protection in high-ranking political circles, the so-called '**Third Level**'. But exactly one hundred days after La Torre's death, Dalla Chiesa himself was gunned down, together with his wife, in Palermo's via Carini. The whole country was shocked, and the murder revived questions about the depth of government commitment to the fight. In his engagement with the Mafia, Dalla Chiesa had met with little local co-operation, and had received next to no support from Rome, to the extent that Dalla Chiesa's son had accused the mandarins of the Christian Democrat party – former prime minister Andreotti among them – of isolating his father. Nando Dalla Chiesa refused to allow many local officials to his father's funeral, including Vito Ciancimino, former mayor of Palermo and a Christian Democrat. Later, Ciancimino was accused not just of handling huge sums of drugs money, but of actually being a sworn-in member of the Corleonese family. Those who were present at the funeral included the Italian President and senior cabinet ministers, all of them jeered at by an angry Sicilian crowd, and pelted with coins – an expression of disgust that has since been repeated at the funerals of other prominent anti-Mafia fighters.

To ward off accusations of government inertia or complicity, the law that La Torre had demanded was rushed through parliament soon afterwards, and was used in the the **super-trials**, or *maxiprocessi*, arising from the confessions of Buscetta and the other *pentiti* ('penitents') who had followed his lead. The biggest of these trials, lasting eighteen months, started in February 1986, when five hundred *mafiosi* appeared in a specially built maximum-security bunker adjoining the Ucciardone prison in the heart of Palermo. The insecurity felt by the Mafia was reflected in continuing bloodshed in Sicily throughout the proceedings, but the worst was to come after the trial closed in December 1986, starting right on the steps of the courthouse with the murder of one of the accused *mafiosi* – many of whom were freed after they had squealed on their accomplices.

THE OUTLOOK

The violence continues to the present day, but whether it consists of reprisals against informers or represents a new power-struggle is still unclear. After all the publicity of the show-trials has died down, the Mafia's vigour appears undiminished, suggesting that those behind bars today are the 'old guard', their places taken by a younger and largely unknown generation of gangsters. Nonetheless, an important breakthrough has been achieved. Many convictions were made, and, more importantly, many of the accused turned on their 'friends' (*amici*) in the organisation, to an extent that would have been unthinkable a decade ago. There is a new openness in talking about the Mafia, and an example of courage has been given by the wife of one 'illustrious' victim, Judge Cesare Terranova (killed in 1979). She has led a women's movement against the Mafia, and her initiative has been followed by student organisations. 'If you manage to change the mentality,' she said, 'to change the consent, to change the fear in which the Mafia can live – if you can change that, you can beat them.'

The strongest weapon in the Mafia's armoury is precisely that element of 'consent' among ordinary Sicilians. The product of fear, it is the foundation of the Mafia's existence, an attitude which sees the *mafioso* stance as a revolt against the state, justified by centuries of oppression by successive regimes. The corrupt government of foreigners and their acolytes has forfeited any deep respect for the law in Sicily, in place of which the *mafioso* relies on self-assertion and intimidation, from which it's a small step to bombs and bullets. But despite the continuing assassinations, it may be that the Mafia is indeed dead, its original altruistic ideals, if they ever existed, long forgotten. And the hierarchical power-structure which is the prerequisite for an organisation such as the Mafia, or *Cosa Nostra*, is rent with divisions, as shown by two decades of feuding and self-destructive wars to preserve its markets. But the greatest inroad that has been made against its hold on Sicily is a psychological one: the myth of its invincibility has been irreparably dented.

SICILIAN BAROQUE

Most of the church and civic architecture you'll come across in Sicily is Baroque in style, certainly in the east of the island. More particularly, it's of a type known as Sicilian Baroque, and this is a brief introduction to the subject, designed to serve as a handy reference for some of the more important aspects of the style mentioned in the text. It will at least explain the hows and whys of Baroque architecture in Sicily with respect to some of the major towns and sights. For more academic studies, check the recommendations in the Books listings, p.305; and for more information about the specific places detailed below, follow up the page references given.

ORIGINS

The qualities which attract art historians to the Sicilian Baroque – the 'warmth and ebullience', 'gaiety', 'energy', 'freedom and fantasy' – to some extent typify all **Baroque** architecture. The style grew out of the excesses of Mannerism, a distorted, 16C mode of painting and architecture which had flourished in Italy in reaction against the restraint of the Renaissance. The development of a full-blown, ornate Baroque style followed in the late 16C, again originating in Italy, and it quickly found a niche in other countries touched by the Counter-Reformation. The Jesuits saw in Baroque art and architecture an expression of a revitalised Catholicism, its particular theatrical forms involving the congregation by portraying spiritual ecstasy in terms of physical passion.

The origin of the word 'Baroque' is uncertain: the two most popular theories are that it comes either from the 17C Portugese 'barroco' meaning a misshapen pearl, or the term 'barocco' used by philosophers in the Middle Ages to mean a contorted idea. Whatever its origins, it was used by contemporary critics in a derogatory sense, implying odd or extravagant shapes, as opposed to the much-vaunted classical forms of the Renaissance.

Although Baroque was born in Rome, the vogue quickly spread throughout Europe. Everywhere, the emphasis was firmly on elaborate ornamentation and spectacle, something that reflected the growing power of the aristocracy, who had begun to challenge the established wealth and tradition of the church. Civic architecture gained in importance, at the expense of formerly preeminent religious buildings, the motivating force behind the decoration of the buildings was primarily the need to impress the neighbouring gentry: building to the glory of God came a poor second.

Some of the finest (though least-known) examples of Baroque architecture are to be found in Sicily, although there's some debate as to the specific origins of the **Sicilian Baroque** style. During the 18C alone, Sicily was conquered and ruled in turn by the Spanish Hapsburgs, the Spanish Bourbons, the House of Savoy, the Austrian Hapsburgs and the Bourbons from Naples, lending a particularly exuberant flavour to its Baroque creations – which some say was borrowed from Spain. Others argue that the dominant influence was Italian: Sicilian architects tended to train and to travel in Italy, rather than Spain, and brought home what they learned on the mainland, adapting prevalent Roman Baroque ideas to complement peculiarly Sicilian architectural traditions. Both theories contain an element of the truth, though perhaps more pertinent is Sicily's unique long-term history: two-and-a-half millenia of invasion and domination has produced a very distinct culture and society – one that is bound to have influenced, or even produced, an equally distinct architectural form.

BAROQUE TOWNS

Sicily's seismic instability has profoundly affected its architectural history. The huge **earthquake of 1693** which almost flattened Catania, and completely destroyed Noto, Ragusa, Ávola and Módica, provided a fantastic opportunity for local architects, who began massive rebuilding programmes in the south east corner of Sicily. To them, as to all contemporary Baroque planners, a **Baroque town** aspired to be, and should have been seen to be, a centre of taste and sophistication:

they designed their new towns to please and delight their citizens, to encourage the participation of passers-by and to impress outsiders, with long vistas contriving to focus on the facade of a church or a palace, or an unexpected view of the sea. To enhance the visual effect even more, a building was designed to have multiple, changing views from different angles of approach. This way, a completed plan might include all the buildings in a square, or series of squares, and the experience of walking from place to place through varied but harmonious spaces was considered as important as the need to arrive at a destination. Moreover, as much of 18C Sicilian town-life took place outside, the facade of a building became synonymous with the wealth and standing of its occupant: external features became increasingly elaborate and specialised, and some parts of buildings – windows and staircases for example – were often merely there for show. Invariably, what seem to be regular stone facades have been cosmetically touched-up with plaster to conceal an asymmetry or an angle of less than 90°; a self-conscious approach to town planning that can sometimes give the impression of walking around a stage set. Interestingly, this approach remained confined to the south and east of Sicily: outside the earthquake zone, in the west of the island, local architectural traditions continued to dominate in towns which hadn't had the dubious benefit of being levelled and left for the planners.

Ideally, where there was scope for large-scale planning, an entire city could be constructed as an aesthetic whole. As early as 1615 the Venetian architect and theorist **Vincento Scamozzi** published a treatise called *Dell'Idea dell'architettura universale*, in which he stated that the architectural harmony of the ideal city should reflect the perfect relationship between the prince, the judiciary, the Church, the market place and the populace.

Noto (p.191) is an almost perfect example of Scamozzi's ideal city. After the 1693 earthquake, the old town was so devastated that it was decided to move its site and rebuild from scratch. The plan which was eventually accepted was nearly an exact replica of Scamozzi's: Noto is constructed on a grid plan, traversed from east to west by a wide Corso crossing a main piazza, which is itself balanced by four smaller piazzas. The buildings along the Corso show remarkable balance and grace, while the attention of the Baroque planners to every harmonious detail is illustrated by the use of a warm, golden stone for the churches and palazzi.

Neighbouring towns in the south east were also destroyed by the earthquake, and rebuilt along similar lines, utilising wide squares and thoroughfares, designed with the possibility of future tremors in mind. **Ávola** (p.191) and **Grammichele** (p.225) were both moved from their hilltop positions to the coastal plain, and their polygonal plans were similarly influenced by Scamozzi. Grammichele, particularly, retains an extraordinary hexagonal layout, unique in Sicily. **Ragusa** (p.195) is more complex, surviving today as two towns, the medieval Ragusa Ibla, which the inhabitants rebuilt after the earthquake, and the Baroque upper town of Ragusa, which is built on a sloping grid plan, rather similar to Noto. Although Ibla isn't built to any kind of Baroque pattern, it does lay claim to one of the most spectacular of Sicilian Baroque churches (see below).

Catania (p.144), unlike the other south eastern towns, was not completely destroyed by the earthquake, and was rebuilt over its old site. New, broad streets were built to link existing monuments and to facilitate rescue operations in case of another earthquake. The city is divided into four quarters by wide streets meeting in piazza del Duomo, and wherever possible these spaces are used to maximise the visual impact of a facade or monument. The main piazza was conceived as a uniform set-piece, and although several different architects collaborated, their intention was to produce a homogenous ensemble. They also went a step further in utilising the city's natural assets: the main street, via Etnea, cuts a swathe due north from piazza del Duomo, always drawing the eyes to the volcano, Mount Etna, smoking in the distance.

Over on the other side of the island, Baroque **Palermo** (p.36) evolved differently, without the impetus of any one great natural disaster. There's no comparable city plan, Palermo's intricate central layout owing more to the Arabs than to 17C and 18C designers; what Baroque character the city possesses is almost entirely to do with its highly individual churches and palaces. They were constructed in a climate of apparent opulence but encroaching bankruptcy: as the Sicilian aristocrats were attracted to Palermo to pay court to the Spanish viceroy, they left the management of their lands to pragmatic agents, whose short-sighted polices allowed the estates to fall into neglect. This ate away at the wealth of the gentry, who responded by mortgaging their lands in order to maintain their living standards. The grandiose palaces and churches they built in the city still stand, but following the damage caused during World War II many are in a state of terrible neglect and near collapse; wild flowers grow out of the facades and chunks of masonry frequently fall into the street below. Renovation work is hampered by the local Mafia, and minor earthquake tremors always ensure that the need for repair is one step ahead of the builders.

SPECIFIC FEATURES

Eighteenth-century aristocrats in Palermo felt the need for **summer villas** outside the city, to which they could escape in the hottest weather, and many of these still survive around Bagheria (p.76). The villas tend to be quite small, simply designed, but are bedecked with balconies and terraces for afternoon strolling, and were approached by long, impressive driveways. Above all, they are notable for their **external staircases**, leading to the main entrance on the first floor (the ground floor usually contained the kitchen and servants' quarters). It's typical of the Baroque era that an external feature should take on such significance in a building – and that they should show such a remarkable diversity, each reflecting the wealth of the individual owners. Beyond the fact that they were nearly always double staircases, symmetrical to the middle axis of the facade, each one was completely different, and though external staircases can be found elsewhere on mainland Europe, they're rarely of such imaginative construction as in Sicily.

Balconies had always been a prominent feature of Sicilian domestic architecture, but during the 18C they became prolific. The balcony supports, or buttresses, were elabo-

rately carved: manic heads, griffins, horses, monsters and mythical figures all featured as decoration, fine examples of which survive at Noto's **Palazzo Villadorata** (p.193), as well as in Módica (p.198) and Scicli (p.199). The wrought-iron balustrades curved outwards, almost like theatre boxes, to allow room for women's billowing skirts; they still afford the best views of street processions and other festivities at *Carnevale*.

Church building, too, flourished during this period. Baroque architects could let their imaginations run wild: the facade of the **Duomo** at Siracusa (p.175) was begun in 1728, based on designs by Andrea Palma of Palermo, and the result is highly sophisticated and exciting. Other designs adapted and modified accepted forms for church architecture, as well as inventing new ones. In Palermo especially, typically Sicilian elements – like central circular windows – were used to great effect.

It was in the church **interiors**, however, that Sicilian Baroque came into its own, with tomb sculpture ever more ostentatious and stucco decoration abundant. Inlaid marble, a technique introduced from Naples at the beginning of the 17C, became *de rigueur* for any self-respecting church. It reached its prime in the second half of the century, when whole walls or chapels would be decorated in this way. Palermo fields some of the best examples of all these techniques, most impressive the church of **San Guiseppe dei Teatini** (p.46), designed by Giacomo Besio, a *genovese* who lived most of his life in Sicily. For real over-the-top detail, though, the churches of **Santa Caterina** (p.47) and **Il Gesù** (p.50), also in Palermo, conceal a riot of inlaid-marble decoration.

Palermo is also distinguished by a series of highly decorative **oratories**, built in the late 17C and early 18C when the Spanish viceroys placed much of the city's power in the hands of the local aristocrats, who could afford to endow monasteries with new funds. Much was spent on small private chapels, where local sculptors had the chance to shine. The master of the genre was Giacomo Serpotta (see below), and his best works are in the oratories of Santa Zita (see below), **San Domenico** (p.55) and **San Lorenzo** (p.58), though he left his mark over much of the west of the island.

ARCHITECTS AND SCULPTORS

Rosario Gagliardi was responsible for much of the rebuilding of Noto and Ragusa, and became known as one of the most important architects in south east Sicily. Born in Siracusa in 1698, he worked in Noto as a carpenter from the age of ten, and was first acknowledged as an architect in 1726. Between 1760 and 1784 he was chief architect for the city of Noto, and during this time also worked on many different projects in Ragusa and Módica. As far as is known, he never travelled outside Sicily, let alone to Rome, yet he absorbed contemporary architectural trends from the study of books and treatises, and reproduced the ideas with some flair.

Gagliardi's prime interest was in facades and his work achieved a sophisticated fusion of Renaissance poise, Baroque grandeur and local Sicilian ornamentation. He had no interest, however, in spatial relationships or structural innovation and the interiors of his buildings are disappointing, when compared to the elaborate nature of their exteriors. Perhaps his most significant contribution was his development of the belfry as a feature. Sicilian churches traditionally didn't have a separate bell-tower, but incorporated the bells into the main facade, revealed through a series of two or three arches – an idea handed down from Byzantine building. Gagliardi extended the central bay of the facade into a tower, a highly original compromise satisfying both the local style and the more conventional notions of design from the mainland. The belfry on the church of **San Giorgio** in Ragusa Ibla (p.197) is an excellent example of this, and is Gagliardi's masterpiece.

Giovanni Battista Vaccarini was the principal architect working on the design and rebuilding of Catania after the 1693 earthquake. He was born in Palermo in 1702 but trained in Rome and embraced the current idiom, working with such illustrious figures as Alessandro Specchi (who built the Papal stables) and Francesco de Sanctis (designer of the Spanish Steps). In 1730 he arrived in Catania, having been appointed as city architect by the Senate, and at once began work on finishing the Municipio (p.149): the lower two floors had been designed by a local architect, but Vaccarini completely ignored the original plan and transformed the building by redesigning the *piano nobile* in the Roman style. Outside it he placed a fountain whose main feature is an obelisk supported by an elephant, the symbol of Catania – reminiscent of Bernini's elephant-fountain in Rome.

Giacomo Serpotta, master of the Palermitan oratories, was born in Palermo in 1656. He cashed in on the opulence of the Church, and specialised in decorating oratories with moulded plasterwork in ornamental frames. He would include life-size figures of Saints and Virtues, surrounded by plaster draperies, trophies, swags of fruit, bouquets of flowers and other extravagances much beloved of the Baroque. One of the most remarkable of his works is the Oratory of the Rosary in the church of **Santa Zita** (p.57), where the end wall is a reconstruction of the Battle of Lépanto. Here three-dimensional representation is taken to an extreme and actual wires are used as rigging.

Other Baroque architects are less well known, but influential in Sicily all the same. **Giacomo Amato** (1643–1732) was a monk, sent to Rome in 1671 to represent his Order, where he came into contact with the works of Bernini and Borromini. Dazzled by what he'd seen, after his return to Palermo he neglected his religious duties in order to design some of the city's most characteristic churches, **Sant'Ignazio all'Olivella** and **San Domenico** (p.55) among them. **Vincenzo Sinatra** had a more traditional career, starting as a stone-cutter before working with Gagliardi in the 1730s as his foreman. In 1745 he married Gagliardi's niece, a move which did him no harm at all, since by 1761, when Gagliardi had a stroke, Sinatra was managing all his affairs. For ten years he directed the construction of Noto's Municipio, and during the rest of his life Sinatra worked in collaboration with the other city architects on a variety of projects – a respectable career, but one which makes it difficult to trace any personal architectural method. More important, and certainly with an identifiable style, was **Giovanni Verméxio** who was working in Siracusa at around the same time. His work graces the city's piazza del Duomo, notably the **Palazzo Arcivescovile**, while he gets a couple of ornate-interior credits, too, in the shape of one of the Duomo's chapels, and the octagonal **Cappella di San Sepolcro** in the church of Santa Lucia in the Achradina quarter of Siracusa.

SICILY IN FICTION

Some of the most respected modern Italian authors are Sicilian. Extracts from the work of just three – Lampedusa, Vittorini and Sciascia – are reprinted below, and although each author has his own particular viewpoint and style, there's a similarity apparent too: each of the extracts touches upon a different aspect of the same theme, namely the intricacies of Sicilian life and the unique problems of the island.

THE LEOPARD

*Perhaps the best-known of Sicilian novels, The Leopard is a towering record of a 19C aristocrat's reactions to the old order crumbling around him as the Bourbon state of Naples and Sicily draws to a close, to be replaced by a new unified Italy. It was the posthumously published masterpiece of **Giuseppe Tomasi di Lampedusa** (1896–1957), himself from a Sicilian aristocratic family that claimed descent from a commander of the Imperial guard of the 6C Byzantine emperor Tiberius. Certainly Lampedusa would have had some considerable understanding of the emotions felt by the Prince, Don Fabrizio, as he contemplates the destruction of the traditional values he cherishes. The Leopard appeared in 1958 to immediate critical acclaim, although Lampedusa wrote little else of note. In the extract below, the Prince is out hunting at his country estate with his retainer, Don Ciccio, shortly after the Plebiscite on unification.*

"And you, Don Ciccio, how did you vote on the twenty-first?"

The poor man started; taken by surprise at a moment when he was outside the stockade of precautions in which, like each of his fellow townsmen he usually moved, he hesitated, not knowing what to reply.

The Prince mistook for alarm what was really only surprise, and felt irritated. "Well, what are you afraid of? There's no one here but us, the wind and the dogs."

The list of reassuring witnesses was not really happily chosen; wind is a gossip by definition, the Prince was half Sicilian. Only the dogs were absolutely trustworthy and that only because they lacked articulate speech. But Don Ciccio had now recovered; his peasant astuteness had suggested the right reply -nothing at all. "Excuse me, Excellency, but there's no point in your question. You know that everyone in Donnafugata voted 'yes'."

Don Fabrizio did not know this; and that was why this reply merely changed a small enigma into an enigma of history. Before this voting many had come to him for advice; all of them had been exhorted, sincerely, to vote "yes." Don Fabrizio, in fact, could not see what else there was to do: whether treating it as a *fait accompli* or as an act merely theatrical and banal, whether taking it as a historical necessity or considering the trouble these humble folk might get into if their negative attitude were known. He had noticed, though, that not all had been convinced by his words; into play had come the abstract Machiavellianism of Sicilians, which so often induced these people, with all their generosity, to erect complex barricades on the most fragile foundations. Like clinics adept at treatment based on fundamentally false analyses of blood and urine which they are too lazy to rectify, the Sicilians (of that time) ended by killing off the patient, that is themselves, by a niggling and hair-splitting rarely connected with any real understanding of the problems involved, or even of their interlocuters. Some of these who had made a visit *ad limina leopardorum* considered it impossible for a Prince of Salina to vote in favour of the Revolution (as the recent changes were still called in these remote parts), and they interpreted his advice as ironical, intended to effect a result in practice opposite to his words. These pilgrims (and they were the best) had come out of his study winking at each other – as far as their respect for him would allow – proud at having penetrated the meaning of the princely words, and rubbing their hands in self-congratulation at their own perspicacity just when this was most completely in eclipse.

Others, on the other hand, after having listened to him, went off looking sad and convinced that he was a turncoat or half-wit, more than ever determined to take no notice of what he said but to follow instead the age-old proverb about preferring a known evil to an untried good. These were reluctant to ratify the new national reality for personal reasons too; either from religious faith, or from having received favours from the former regime and not being sharp enough to insert themselves into the new one, or finally because during the upsets of the liberation period they had lost a few capons and sacks of beans, and had been cuckolded either freely like Garibaldini volunteers or forcibly like Bourbon levies. He had, in fact, the disagreeable but distinct impression that about fifteen of them would vote "no", a tiny minority certainly, but noticeable in the small electorate of Donnafugata. Taking into consideration that the people who came to him represented the flowers of the inhabitants, and that there must also be some unconvinced among the hundreds of electors who had not dreamt of setting foot inside the palace, the Prince had calculated that Donnafugata's compact affirmative would be varied by about forty negative votes.

The day of the Plebiscite was windy and grey, and tired groups of youths had been seen going through the streets of the town with bits of paper covered with "yes" stuck in the ribbons of their hats. Amid waste paper and refuse swirled by the wind they sang a few verses of *La Bella Gigugin* transformed into a kind of Arab wail, a fate to which any gay tune in Sicily is bound to succumb. There had also been seen two or three "foreigners" (that is from Girgenti) installed in *Zzu* Menico's tavern where they were declaiming Leopardi's lines on the "magnificent and progressive destiny" of a renovated Sicily united to resurgent Italy. A few peasants were standing listening mutely, stunned by overwork or starved by unemployment. These cleared their throats and spat continuously, but kept silent; so silent that it must have been then (as Don Fabrizio said afterwards) that the foreigners decided to give Arithmetic precedence over Rhetoric in the Quadrivium arts.

The Prince went to vote about four in the afternoon, flanked on the right by Father Pirrone, on the left by Don Onofrio Rotolo; frowning and fair-skinned, he proceeded slowly toward the Town Hall, frequently putting up a hand to protect his eyes lest the breeze loaded with all the filth collected on its way should bring on the conjunctivitis to which he was subject; and he remarked to Father Pirrone that though the health-giving gusts did seem to drag up a lot of dirt with them. He was wearing the same black frock coat in which two years before he had gone to pay his respects at Caserta to poor King Ferdinand, who had been lucky enough to die in time to avoid this day of dirty wind when the seal would be set on his own incapacity. But had it really been incapacity? One might as well say that a person succumbing to typhus dies of incapacity. He remembered the king busy putting up dykes against the flood of useless documents: and suddenly he realised how much unconscious appeal to pity there was in these unattractive features. Such thoughts were disagreeable, as are all those which make us understand things too late, and the Prince's face went solemn and dark as if he were following an invisible funeral car. Only the violent impact of his feet on loose stones in the street showed his internal conflict. It is superfluous to mention that the ribbon on his top hat was innocent of any piece of paper; but in the eyes of those who knew him a "yes" and "no" alternated on the glistening felt.

On reaching a little room in the Town Hall used as the voting booth he was surprised to see all the members of the committee get up as his great height filled the doorway; a few peasants who had arrived before were put aside, and so without having to wait Don Fabrizio handed his "yes" into the patriotic hands of Don Calogero Sedàra. Father Pirrone, though, did not vote at all, as he had been careful not to get listed as a resident of the town. Don 'Nofrio, obeying the express desires of the Prince, gave his own monosyllabic opinion about the complicated Italian question; a masterpiece of concision carried through with the good grace of a child drinking castor oil. After which all were invited for a "little glass" upstairs in the mayor's study; but Father Pirrone and Don 'Nofrio put forward good reasons, one of abstinence, the other of stomach-ache, and remained below. Don Fabrizio had to face the party alone.

Behind the Mayor's writing desk gleamed a brand new portrait of Garibaldi and (already) one of King Victor Emmanuel hung, luckily, to the right: the first handsome, the second ugly;

both, however, made brethren by prodigious growths of hair which nearly hid their faces altogether. On a small low table was a plate with some ancient biscuits blackened by fly droppings and a dozen little squat glasses brimming with *rosolio* wine: four red, four green, four white, the last in the centre: an ingenious symbol of the new national flag which tempered the Prince's remorse with a smile. He chose the white liquor for himself, presumably because the least indigestible and not, as some thought, in tardy homage to the Bourbon standard. Anyway, all three varieties of the *rosolio* were equally sugary, sticky and revolting. His host had the good taste not to give toasts. But, as Don Calogero said, great joys are silent. Don Fabrizio was shown a letter from the authorities of Girgenti announcing to the industrious citizens of Donnafugata the concession of 2,000 lire towards sewage, a work which would be completed before the end of 1961 so the Mayor assured them, stumbling into one of those *lapsus* whose mechanism Freud was to explain many decades later; and the meeting broke up.

Before dusk the three or four easy girls of Donnafugata (there were some others there too, not grouped but each hard at work on her own) appeared on the square with tricolour ribbons in their manes as protest against the exclusion of women in the vote; the poor creatures were jeered at even by the most advanced liberals and forced back to their lairs. This did not prevent the *Giornale di Trinacria* telling the people of Palermo four days later that at Donnafugata "some gentle representatives of the fair sex wished to show their faith in the new and brilliant destinies of their beloved Country, and demonstrated in the main square amid great acclamation from the patriotic population".

After this the electoral booths were closed and the scrutators got to work; late that night the shutters on the balcony of the Town Hall were flung open and Don Calogero appeared with a tricolour sash over his middle, flanked by two ushers with lighted candelabra which the wind snuffed at once. To the invisible crowd in the shadows below he announced that the Plebiscite at Donnafugata had had the following results:

Voters, 515; Voting, 512; Yes, 512; No, zero.

From the dark end of the square rose applause and hurrahs; on her little balcony Angelica, with her funereal maid, clapped lovely rapacious hands; speeches were made; adjectives loaded with superlatives and double consonants reverberated and echoed in the dark from one wall to another; amid thundering of fireworks messages were sent off to the King (the new one) and to the General; a tricolour rocket or two climbed up from the village into the blackness towards the starless sky. By eight o'clock all was over, and nothing remained except darkness as on any other night, always.

Reprinted from The Leopard *by Giuseppe di Lampedusa, translated by Archibald Colquhoun, published by Collins.*

CONVERSATION IN SICILY

Elio Vittorini *(1908–1966) was born in Siracusa, a staunch anti-Fascist whose first novel was censored under Mussolini. His best work,* Conversation in Sicily, *written in 1937, initially managed to escape the same fate, as Vittorini wrapped his simple, taut story of a man's visit to his mother in an abstract, almost poetic style. The book deals with the return to Sicily, after fifteen years, of an emigrant who now lives in the industrial – and comparatively wealthy – north of Italy. The 'conversations' are the emigrant's encounters with fellow travellers and villagers in Sicily – encounters which lead him to rediscover a humanity in their otherwise downtrodden, despairing existence. The extract reprinted below follows his approach to his former home, a route that today is still redolent with the flavours that Vittorini records.*

Toward midnight I changed train at Florence, then again about six in the morning at the Termini station in Rome, and about midday I reached Naples. There it was not raining, and I sent off a telegraphic money-order of fifty lire to my wife. I wired to her: 'Returning Thursday.'

Then I took the train for Calabria. It began raining again, and night came on. It all came back to me, the journey, and I as a child on my ten flights from home and Sicily, travelling back and forth through a countryside of smoke and tunnels, the rending whistles of the train halted by night in the jaws of a mountain or by the sea, and the names — Amantea, Maratea, Gioia Tauro — evoking dreams of ancient times. And so, suddenly, the mouse within me was no longer a mouse, but scent, savour, and the heavens, and the pipe no longer played mournfully, but merrily. I fell asleep, awoke, fell asleep again, and awoke once more, until at last I found myself on board the ferry-boat for Sicily.

The sea was black and wintry. Standing on that high plateau of the top deck, I saw myself once again as a boy breathing the air, gazing hungrily at the sea, facing towards the one coast or the other, and gazing hungrily at the sea, with all that garbage of coastal town and village heaped at my feet in the rain-swept morning. It was cold, and I remembered myself as a boy feeling cold yet remaining obstinately on that elevated windy platform, with the sea speeding swiftly by below.

We were a tight fit. The boat was full of little Sicilians travelling third-class, hungry, frozen, without overcoats, yet mild-looking, jacket lapels turned up and hands dug into trouser pockets. I had bought some food at Villa San Giovanni, some bread and cheese, and I was munching away on deck at the bread, raw air, and cheese, with zest and appetite, because I recognized the old tang of my mountains, and even their odours — herds of goats and wormwood — in that cheese. The little Sicilians, bowed with backs to the wind and hands in pockets, watched me eat. They had dark, but mild faces, with beards four days old. They were workers, labourers from the orange groves, and railwaymen wearing grey caps with the thin red piping of the labour gangs. Munching, I smiled at them, and they looked back at me unsmiling.

"There's no cheese like our own," I said.

No one replied. They all stared at me, the women in their voluminous femininity seated on their great bags of belongings, the men standing, small and as if scalded by the wind, hands in pockets.

Again I said: "There's no cheese like our own."

Because I felt suddenly enthusiastic about something — that cheese, its savour in my mouth, with the bread and the sharp air, its flavour clear but acrid, and ancient, its grains of pepper like sudden embers on the tongue:

"There's no cheese like our own," I said for the third time.

Then one of the Sicilians, the smallest and gentlest and darkest of the lot, and the most scalded by the wind, asked me:

"But are you a Sicilian?"

"Why not?" I replied.

The man shrugged his shoulders and said no more. He had what looked like a little girl with him, sitting on a bag at his feet. He bent over her, and taking a great red hand out of his pocket, he seemed to touch her caressingly while he adjusted her shawl to keep her warm.

Somehow this gesture made it clear that she was not his daughter but his wife. Meanwhile Messina drew near, and it was not a heap of garbage on the sea's edge, but houses and moles, white tramcars and rows of dark-hued wagons in the railway sidings. The morning seemed wet, though it was not raining. Everything on the top of the deck was moist, the wind blew moist, the sirens from the ships sounded moist, and the railway engines ashore whistled with a moist note; but it was not raining. And suddenly we saw the lighthouse sailing by in the wintry sea, very high, heading for Villa San Giovanni.

"There's no cheese like our own," I said.

All the men, who were standing, pressed toward the deck rail to gaze at the city, and the women too, seated on their bags, turned their heads. But no one made a move towards the lower deck to be ready to disembark. There was still time. From the lighthouse to the jetty I remembered, took fifteen minutes or more.

"There's no cheese like our own," I said.

Meanwhile I finished eating. The man with the wife who looked like a child bent down once again: in fact, he knelt; he had a basket at his feet and, watched by her, he began to busy himself with it. It was covered by a piece of wax-cloth sewn with string at the edges. Very slowly he undid a bit of the string, dug his hand under the wax-cloth, and produced an orange.

It wasn't big or very luscious or highly tinted, but it was an orange, and without a word, without rising from his knees, he offered it to his baby wife. The baby looked at me; I could discern her eyes inside the hood of the shawl; and then I saw her shake her head.

The little Sicilian seemed desperate, and remained on his knees, one hand in his pocket, the other holding the orange. Then he rose again to his feet and stood with the wind flapping the soft peak of his cap against his nose, the orange in his hand, his coatless diminutive body scalded by the cold, and frantic, while immediately below us the sea and the city floated by in the wet morning.

"Messina," said a woman mournfully. It was a word uttered without reason, merely as a kind of complaint. I observed the little Sicilian with the baby-wife desperately peel his orange, and desperately eat it, with rage and frenzy, without the least desire; then without chewing he gulped it down and seemed to curse, his fingers dripping with the orange juice in the cold, a little bowed in the wind, the peak of his cap flapping against his nose.

"A Sicilian never eats in the morning," he said suddenly. "Are you American?" he added.

He spoke with desperation, yet gently, just as he had always been gentle while desperately peeling the orange and desperately eating it. He spoke the last three words excitedly, in a strident tense voice, as if it were somehow essential to the peace of his soul to know if I were American.

I observed this, and said: "Yes, I am American. For the last fifteen years."

Reprinted from Conversation in Sicily *by Elio Vittorini, translated by Wilfrid David (Quartet Books).*

THE DAY OF THE OWL

*Widely regarded as one of Italy's finest contemporary writers, **Leonardo Sciascia**, born in 1912 in Racalmuto in south western Sicily, uses the island as a backdrop in all his work. Both the novels and short stories provide keen insights into the world of the Mafia, the church in Sicily, the mores of the people and the island's tortuous history – all touched by the same wit and sharp, perceptive characterisation. The Day of the Owl is at heart a crime story: a Carabinieri inspector arrives from the mainland to investigate a Mafia murder, described below in the book's opening pages.*

The bus was just about to leave, amid rumbles and sudden hiccups and rattles. The square was silent in the grey dawn; wisps of cloud swirled round the belfry of the church. The only sound, apart from the rumbling of the bus, was a voice, wheedling, ironic, of a fritter-seller; fritters, hot fritters. The conductor slammed the door, and with a clank of scrap-metal the bus moved off. His last glance round the square caught sight of a man in a dark suit running towards the bus.

'Hold it a minute,' said the conductor to the driver, opening the door with the bus still in motion. Two ear-splitting shots rang out. For a second the man in the dark suit, who was just about to jump on the running-board, hung suspended in mid-air as if some invisible hand were hauling him up by the hair. Then his briefcase dropped from his hand and very slowly he slumped down on top of it.

The conductor swore; his face was the colour of sulphur; he was shaking. The fritter-seller, who was only three yards from the fallen man, sidled off with a crab-like motion towards the door of the church. In the bus no one moved; the driver sat, as if turned to stone, his right hand on the brake, his left on the steering wheel. The conductor looked round the passengers' faces, which were blank as the blinds.

'They've killed him,' he said; he took off his cap, swore again, and began frantically running his fingers through his hair.

'The *carabinieri*,' said the driver, 'we must get the *carabinieri*.'

He got up and opened the other door. 'I'll go,' he said to the conductor.

The conductor looked at the dead man and then at the passengers. These included some women, old women who brought heavy sacks of white cloth and baskets full of eggs every morning; their clothes smelled of forage, manure and wood smoke; usually they grumbled and swore, now they sat mute, their faces as if disinterred from the silence of centuries.

'Who is it?' asked the conductor, pointing at the body.

No one answered. The conductor cursed. Among the passengers of that route he was famous for his highly skilled blaspheming. The company had already threatened to fire him since he never bothered to control himself even when there were nuns or priests on the bus. He was from the province of Syracuse and had had little to do with violent death: a soft province, Syracuse. So now he swore all the more furiously.

The *carabinieri* arrived; the sergeant-major, with a black stubble and in a black temper from being woken, stirred the passengers' apathy like an alarm-clock: in the wake of the conductor they began to get out through the door left open by the driver.

With seeming nonchalance, looking around as if they were trying to gauge the proper distance from which to admire the belfry, they drifted off towards the sides of the square and, after a last look around, scuttled into alleyways.

The sergeant-major and his men did not notice this gradual exodus. Now about fifty people were around the dead man: men from a public works training centre who were only too delighted to have found such an absorbing topic of conversation to while away their eight hours of idleness. The sergeant-major ordered his men to clear the square and get the passengers back onto the bus. The carabinieri began pushing sightseers back towards the streets leading off the square, asking passengers to take their seats on the bus again. When the square was empty, so was the bus. Only the driver and the conductor remained.

'What?' said the sergeant-major to the driver. 'No passengers today?'

'Yes, some,' replied the driver with an absent-minded look.

'Some,' said the sergeant-major, 'means four, five or six . . . I've never seen this bus leave with an empty seat.'

'How should I know?' said the driver, exhausted from straining his memory. 'How should I know? I said "some" just like that. More than five or six though. Maybe more; maybe the bus was full. I never look to see who's there. I just get into my seat and off we go. The road's the only thing I look at; that's what I'm paid for . . . to look at the road.'

The sergeant-major rubbed his chin with a hand taut with irritation. 'I get it,' he said, 'you just look at the road.' He rounded savagely on the conductor. 'But you, you tear off the tickets, take money, give change. You count the people and look at their faces . . . and if you don't want me to make you remember 'em in the guardroom, you're going to tell me now who was on that bus! At least ten names . . . You've been on this run for the last three years, and for the last three years I've seen you every evening in the Café Italia. You know this town better than I do . . . '

'Nobody would know the town better than you do' said the conductor with a smile, as though shrugging off a compliment.

'All right, then,' said the sergeant-major, sneering, 'first me, then you . . . But I wasn't on the bus or I'd remember every passenger one by one. So it's up to you. Ten names at least.'

'I can't remember,' said the conductor, by my mother's soul I can't remember, Just now I can't remember a thing. It all seems a dream.'

'I'll wake you up,' raged the sergeant-major, 'I'll wake you up with a couple of years inside . . . ' He broke off to go and meet the police magistrate who had just arrived. While making his report on the identity of the dead man and the flight of the passengers, the sergeant-major looked at the bus. As he looked, he had an impression that something was not quite right or was missing, as when something in our daily routine is unexpectedly missing, which the senses perceive from force of habit but the mind does not quite apprehend; even so its absence provokes an empty feeling of discomfort, a vague exasperation as from a flickering light-bulb. Then, suddenly, what we are looking for dawns on us.

'There's something missing,' said the sergeant-major to *Carabiniere* Sposito, who being a qualified accountant was the pillar of the *Carabinieri* Station of S., 'there's something or someone missing.'

'The fritter-seller,' said *Carabiniere* Sposito.

'The fritter-seller, by God!' The sergeant-major exulted, thinking: 'An accountant's diploma means something.'

A *carabiniere* was sent off at the double to pick up the fritter-seller. He knew where to find the man, who after the departure of the first bus, usually went to sell his wares at the entrance of the elementary schools. Ten minutes later the sergeant-major had the vendor of fritters in front of him. The man's expression was that of a man roused from innocent slumber.

'Was he there?' the sergeant-major asked the conductor.

'He was,' answered the conductor gazing at his shoe.

'Well now,' said the sergeant-major with paternal kindness, 'this morning, as usual, you came to sell your fritters here ... As usual, at the first bus for Palermo ...'

'I've my licence,' said the fritter-seller.

'I know,' said the sergeant-major, raising his eyes to heaven, imploring patience. 'I know and I'm not thinking about your licence. I want to know only one thing, and, if you tell me, you can go off at once and sell your fritters to the kids: who fired the shots?'

'Why,' asked the fritter-seller, astonished and inquisitive, 'has there been shooting?'

Reprinted from The Day of the Owl *by Leonardo Sciascia, translated by Archibald Colquhoun and Arthur Oliver (Carcanet Press Ltd).*

BOOKS

There are only a few modern writers who have travelled in and written about Sicily, though the island has provided the inspiration for some great literature, by both Sicilians and European visitors. Most of the books listed below are in print and easy to come by, though for the more specialised works and a handful of obscure 18C and 19C travelogues, visit *The Travel Bookshop*, 13 Blenheim Crescent, London W11.

TRAVEL AND GENERAL

Hans Christian Andersen *A Visit to Germany, Italy and Malta, 1840-1841* (Peter Owen £12.50). Andersen steams down the Ionian coast of the island on his way to Malta, making flowery asides about the towns as he passes them.

Stefano Ardito *Backpacking and Walking in Italy* (Bradt £6.95). The only thing there is on serious hiking in Sicily, with a very short eleven-page chapter on the island; walks in the Madonie, Etna region and on Mare'ttimo.

Anthony Blunt *Sicilian Baroque* (o/p). The only book specifically on the subject, contains everything you ever wanted to know about Sicilian Baroque, very readable and anecdotal, with pages of black-and-white photos. Out of print, but should be available in large public libraries.

Vincent Cronin *The Golden Honeycomb* (Grafton £6.95). Disguised as a quest for the mythical golden honeycomb of Daedalus, this is a searching account of a sojourn in Sicily in the 1950s. Although overwritten in parts, it manages to combine colourful descriptions of Sicily's art, architecture and folklore, mixed with a knowing and erudite commentary.

Francis M. Guercio *Sicily: the Garden of the Mediterranean* (Faber o/p). Fairly comprehensive but dated (pre-war) introduction to the island, and with more than a passing sympathy for Mussolini. Interesting as a period-piece, though, and the history and archaeological site accounts are sound.

Russell King *Sicily* (David & Charles o/p). One of the Islands Series, this is an informed and comprehensive read, with chapters on archaeology, industry, bandits, the Mafia, and volcanoes and earthquakes. If you can't track down a copy you'll usually find it in public libraries.

Maria Concetta di Natale *Conoscere Palermo* (Edizioni Guida L10,000). Best available guide on Palermo in Italian, packed with historical accounts of the city and its monuments, and with full practical listings. Available from Palermo's main EPT or from piazzale Ungheria 73, Palermo.

Fiona Pitt-Kethley *Journeys to the Underworld* (Chatto & Windus £10). English poet searches Italy for the sibylline sites, a good third of her time spent in Sicily – though Pitt-Kethley's salacious appetite for sexual adventure often distracts from the real interest.

Mary Taylor Simeti *On Persephone's Island* (Penguin £4.95). Sympathetic record of a typical year in Sicily by an American who married a Sicilian professor and has lived in the west of the island since the early 1960s. Full of keenly observed detail about flora and fauna, customs, the harvests, festivals and – above all – the Sicilians themselves.

Stephen Tobriner *The Genesis of Noto* (Univ. of California Press o/p). A rather weighty tome, which contains a mass of detail about the rebuilding of Noto, with fascinating facsimiles of medieval and Baroque plans and maps, and some old photos of 19C Noto.

Philip Ward *The Aeolian Islands* (The Oleander Press £4.50). Short historical account of the islands off Sicily's northern coast, together with Ward's travelling and ethnographical digressions.

HISTORY, POLITICS, AND ARCHAEOLOGY

David Abulafia *Frederick II: A Medieval Emperor* (Viking £17.95). Definitive new account of the Hohenstaufen king, greatest of the medieval European rulers, with much on his rule in Sicily as well as elsewhere in Europe. It's a reinterpretation of the usual view of Frederick, revealing a less formidable king than the omnipotent and supreme ruler usually portrayed.

M.I. Finlay, D. Mack Smith & C.J.H. Duggan *A History of Sicily* (Chatto & Windus £14.95). A recent and updated abridgement of the trilogy first published in 1968, this is the best available history of the island, from the Stone Age to the early 1980s.

Margaret Guido *Sicily: An Archaeological Guide* (Faber £3.95). Indispensable and approachable account of Sicily's prehistoric and Roman remains and the island's Greek sites, comprehensive and with good site-plans. One reservation is that it's not been revised since 1977 – which means there are a few gaps and the practical information is out of date.

John Haycraft *Italian Labyrinth: Italy in the 1980s* (Secker & Warburg £12.50). Fine, rambling study of modern Italy, its customs, politics, social problems, economy and arts. There's much on Sicily, with interesting insights into the Church, Mafia and corruption in Palermo. A good, chatty read.

Christopher Hibbert *Garibaldi and his Enemies* (Penguin £5.99). A popular treatment of the life and revolutionary works of Giuseppe Garibaldi, thrillingly detailing the exploits of 'The Thousand' in their lightning campaign from Marsala to Milazzo.

John Julius Norwich *The Normans in the South* (Solitaire Books £4,50). Accessible, well-researched story of the Normans' explosive entry into the south of Italy. His *Kingdom in the Sun* (Faber o/p) deals with their creation in Sicily of one of the most brilliant medieval European civilisations. Both are full of fascinating anecdotes and background to Sicily's glittering 11C and 12C.

Giuliano Procacci *History of the Italian People* (Penguin £5.99). A comprehensive history of the peninsula, charting the development of Italy as a nation-state; there isn't much specifically on Sicily but it puts the island's relationship with the mainland after 1000 AD into perspective.

Steven Runciman *The Sicilian Vespers* (CUP £12.95). The classic account of Sicily's large-scale popular uprising in the 13C. Dense with information covering the whole Mediterranean region. More entertaining is Runciman's *A History of the Crusades: 1, 2 & 3* (Penguin £7.95 each), complete with full details of the Norman kings of Sicily, as well as to the crusading Frederick II himself. An essential read if you want to unravel all the intricacies of the period.

CRIME AND SOCIETY

Pino Arlacchi *Mafia Business* (OUP £4.95). Dry and academic account of how the Mafia moved into big business, legal and illegal, its argument summarised by the book's subtitle *The Mafia Ethic and the Spirit of Capitalism*. The author has served on the Italian government's Anti-Mafia Commission, which makes him supremely qualified to judge accurately the Mafia's cutting-edge.

Daniel Dolci *Sicilian Lives* (Writers and Readers £4.95). Dolci's formidable record of the lives of the Sicilians he met when he moved to Trappeto in the early 1950s. Short accounts told in their own words, it's at once a moving and depressing document.

Christopher Duggan *Fascism and the Mafia* (Yale £19.95). Well-researched study of how Mussolini put the Mafia in their place. Duggan uses this account to expound his theory that there's no such thing as the Mafia, that it was simply dreamed up by Italians seeking a scapegoat for their inability to contol the delinquent society. A shame it's so expensive.

Norman Lewis *The Honoured Society* (Eland Books £4.95). Famous account of the Mafia, its origins, personalities and customs. Certainly the most enjoyable introduction to the subject available, though much of it is taken up with banditry – really a separate issue – and his lack of accredited sources leaves you wondering how much is conjecture.

Gavin Maxwell *The Ten Pains of Death* (Alan Sutton £5.95). Maxwell went to live in Scopello in 1953, and (like Dolci) records the lives of his neighbours in their own words: there's much on Sicilian small-town life and poverty, and sympathetic portraits of traditional festivals and characters. His *God Protect Me From My Friends* (o/p) is a good and sympathetic biography of the notorious bandit Salvatore Giuliano, ripe with intrigue and double-dealing, though its evasiveness about his bloody death begs more questions than it answers.

Tim Shawcross and Martin Young *Mafia Wars* (Fontana £4.50). An account of the Sicilian and American Mafia's move into the international narcotics trade, based around the evidence of a former 'Godfather', Tommaso Buscetta. The various relationships and feuds are contorted enough to require a family tree (which the book lacks) but it's a good, penetrating yarn, if sometimes carelessly constructed.

Carl Sifakis *The Mafia File* (Equation £9.95). An A–Z of organised crime in the United States. All the big Sicilian names are here, alongside intriguing entries for Frank Sinatra, George Raft and a host of other hangers-on.

LITERATURE AND BIOGRAPHY

Ilen Andrews *Impossible Loyalties* (André Deutsch £8.95) Fast-moving, if unevenly paced, narrative of an Anglo-Sicilian family caught up in the turmoil of World War II, containing an authentic portrait of pre-war *messinese* society.

Charles Carmello *La Mattanza* (Grafton £3.50). Pulp fiction about a Sicilian crime 'family' in New York. Read it on the plane – and then read *The Godfather* (see below) to see how it should be done.

David Gilmour *The Last Leopard: A Life of Giuseppe di Lampedusa* (Quartet £15.95). First biography in English of Lampedusa, though frankly no more than a readable account of the life of rather a dull man – to whom nothing very much happened except the publication (after his death) of one remarkable novel.

Giuseppe di Lampedusa *The Leopard* (Collins £4.95). The most famous Sicilian novel, written after World War II but recounting the dramatic 19C years of transition from Bourbon to Piedmontese rule from an aristocrat's point of view. A good character-study and rich with incidental detail, including some nice description of the Sicilian landscape, which was put to great effect in Visconti's epic 1963 film – a Sicilian *Gone With the Wind*. There's an extract from the novel on p.298.

Norman Lewis *The March of the Long Shadows* (Secker & Warburg £10.95). An affectionate novel set in post-war Sicily, dealing with the Separatist movement, the bandit Giuliano and a whole cast of endearing characters. Good location writing too, detailing the countryside around Palermo.

Luigi Pirandello *Six Characters in Search of an Author* (Methuen £4.50), *Henry IV* (Methuen £4.50), *Collected Plays* (J. Calder £6.95), *The Late Mattia Pascal* (Dedalus £4.95), *Short Stories* (Quartet £5.95). His most famous and accomplished work, *Six Characters . . .* , written in 1921, and his *Henry IV*, written a year later, contain many of the themes that dogged Pirandello throughout his writing career – the idea of a multiple personality and the quality of reality. *The Late Mattia Pascal* is an early novel (1904), entertainingly written despite its stylistic shortcomings; while the collection of short stories is perhaps the best introduction to Pirandello's work you can buy: abrasive stuff, the dialogue possessing an assured comic touch.

Mario Puzo *The Godfather* (Pan £3.50). The New York Godfather – Don Corleone – was born in Sicily (see p.216) and the book touches on all things Sicilian. Filmed in two parts in the early 1970s by Francis Ford Coppola, Marlon Brando played an old Don Corleone, the film the first to rehabilitate the Mafia in American eyes. The book's a great read, even if you've seen the film (which is pretty faithful to Puzo's novel). Also by Puzo is *The Sicilian* (Bantam £3.95), a novelised life of the bandit Salvatore Giuliano, and now the basis of an uninspiring 1988 film starring Christopher Lambert. Better, if you're interested, is to try and catch Francesco Rossi's 1960s film, *Salvatore Giuliano*.

Leonardo Sciascia *Sicilian Uncles* (Carcanet £8.95), *The Wine-Dark Sea* (Paladin £3.95), *Candido* (Carcanet £3.95), *The Day of the Owl & Equal Danger* (Paladin £3.95). Sciascia is the best writer working in Sicily today.

Economically written, his short stories are packed with incisive insights into the island's quirky ways, and infused with the author's humane and sympathetic view of its people. The best-known is *Day of the Owl*, an extract from which appears on p.302.

Giovanni Verga *Short Sicilian Novels* (Dedalus £3.95), *Cavalleria Rusticana* (Dedalus £4.95) and *I Malavoglia* or 'The House by the Medlar Tree' (Dedalus £4.95). Verga, born in the 19C in Catania, spent several years in various European salons before coming home to write his best work. Much of it is a reaction against the pseudo-sophistication of society circles, stressing the simple lives of ordinary people, though they're occasionally bestowed with a heavy smattering of 'peasant passion', with much emotion, wounded honour and feuds to the death. D.H. Lawrence's translations are suitably vibrant, with excellent introductions.

Elio Vittorini *Conversation in Sicily* (Quartet £5.95). A Sicilian emigrant returns from the north of Italy after fifteen years to see his mother on her birthday. The conversations of the title are with the people he meets on the way, local villagers and his mother, and reveal a pre-war Sicily that is poverty- and disease-ridden – though affectionately drawn. An extract is printed on p.300.

ONWARDS FROM SICILY: MALTA AND TUNISIA

If you're using Sicily as a springboard for travel on to the Italian mainland, all the information you'll need is covered in the comprehensive new *Rough Guide to Italy* (£6.95). Otherwise, the most obvious onward moves from Sicily are all south across the Mediterranean to Malta and Tunisia, both reachable on regular ferry or hydrofoil crossings. Malta is nearest and would make a good weekend break from Sicily; Tunisia really demands more time, and from there you're well poised to embark on the overland North African loop, known as the trans-Maghreb route – crossing into Algeria and Morocco, before heading up through Spain; a route that can be extended to cover virtually the whole of the Mediterranean shore.

MALTA

The small island of **MALTA** is just 95km away, accessible year-round by ferry, or by catamaran from June to September. Ferry departures are from Catania and Siracusa, by catamaran from the same cities as well as Naxos/Taormina; full schedules and journey times given in *Travel Details*, chapters 3, 4 and 5. The **ferries** are operated by *Tirrenia* and deck-class ticket prices are currently between L59,000 and L71,000 per person one-way, depending on season; the **catamaran** service (run by *Virtu Rapid Ferries*) takes around half the time, but is more expensive.

A FEW NOTES

Malta has much that will seem familiar if you've spent any time in Sicily: a similar history of domination (by the same powers, Phoenicians to Aragonese), little rainfall and long, hot summers. Annexed by Britain in 1814 (though independent since 1964), English-speakers will find it easy to get by – one of the reasons it's been a popular package-tour destination for years. Don't let that put you off, though, as the island combines its beaches with sights that retain a strong sense of Malta's history: Easter is a good time to visit, with island-wide celebrations and processions.

Passports and visas: British and Irish citizens, Australians and New Zealanders can stay for up to three months on a valid passport. British Consulate, 7 St Anne's Street, Valletta (☎356-221285).

Transport: Getting around the mainly flat island is easy, either on frequent buses (which all start and finish in Valletta and run up to about 11pm), or by bike, which you can hire once you're there.

Costs and curency: It's most expensive to visit Malta in summer (August especially), though even then prices compare well with Sicily. Between November and April, hotels should give discounts. Distances are very small so transport costs are cheap; eating, as in Sicily, remains good value. Currency is the Maltese Lira, the current rate around 0.6 to the £ sterling. Most banks are open Mon–Fri until noon, Sat until 11.30am.

Where to go: Valletta, the capital, is a grid-plan fortified city, built on Renaissance lines in the 16C by the Knights of St John, and full of interest. Although the island itself is fairly compact, most of the tourists congregate on the same few beaches, and it's a simple matter to reach a variety of more interesting spots: deep, natural caves and grottoes, ancient temples and archaeological remains going back nearly 6000 years, tiny fishing villages, and a preserved medieval city or two. Malta is also the largest island in a small archipelago, and regular ferries run across to Malta's sister island, **GOZO**, more fertile and much less frequented, though still with a fair selection of places to stay and some good beaches. Or you can potter around tiny **COMINO**, between the other two islands, uninhabited and largely unspoiled by the development that's prevalent elsewhere.

Sleeping: Although there's plenty of accommodation about (budget pensions and self-catering apartments to luxury hotels), especially in and around Valletta, booking in advance is recommended in summer – get a list from the Malta National Tourist Office, 207 College House, Wrights Lane, London W8; there's no office in Sicily. Count on paying between LM3–4 for the cheapest rooms. There is also a couple of *IYHF* youth hostels on the island, but camping is strictly forbidden – though you'll be able to get away with it on some of the more remote beaches.

Eating: The food is often very similar to that of Sicily: seafood, not surprisingly, is common; stuffed vegetables are always good; and other basics are pasta dishes and soups. There are restaurants in all the resort areas, Valletta is fairly well endowed too, and there's always at least one in the other towns: look for fixed-price menus, generally a bargain.

Language: The official languages are Maltese and English and nearly everyone is bilingual.

TUNISIA

If you've got the time, it's more rewarding to head for **TUNISIA**, also directly connected by sea from Sicily: either by ferry from Trápani to Tunis, or jetfoil to Kelibia. *Tirrenia* **ferries** depart all year (one weekly, currently Wed; mid-June to Sept Sun service too), an eight- to ten-hour journey, a deck-class **ticket** costs between L62,000 and L74,000 per person one-way, depending on season. If you're going in mid-summer try and buy tickets in advance, especially if you're returning from Tunis, as the boats can get packed. You'll arrive at La Goulette, port for Tunis: to get into the centre either take a taxi or ask for the TGM railway station. Get out at Ave Bourguiba, the capital's central thoroughfare, halfway down which (beyond Ave Carthage) is the source of most of the city's hotels. The **alternative crossing**, if you don't want to arrive in the capital, is to take the **jetfoil** from Trápani, via the island of Pantelleria, to Kelibia, on Cape Bon, one of the nicest and quietest resorts in Tunisia. This service, operated by *SNAV*, runs three times a week, takes around four hours, and costs from L55,000 one-way – though in rough weather the service is often cancelled.

A FEW NOTES

Whichever route you take, if you're staying for any length of time you'd do well to pick up the new edition of the *Rough Guide to Tunisia*

(£5.95) – not available in Sicily itself but in Rome from the *Lion Bookshop*, via del Babuino 181. If you're reading this on the way there, though, these few notes should help smooth the way. Tunisia is the most accessible of the Arab countries: fairly westernised in the north (where most of the package holidays concentrate), small enough to get around easily and with a history that has left some sparkling ancient remains. The people are hospitable to a degree that will seem extreme if you've become used to suspicious Sicilian ways; and there's little of the hassle associated with travelling in, say, Morocco.

Passports and visas: British citizens can stay for up to three months on a valid passport; Australians and most EC nationals need a visa and can get one at the border; New Zealanders have to get one before entering the country (apply at the Tunisian Consulate, via Asmara 7, Rome; ☎06-839 0748).

Transport: Buses are common, with *SNT* (the state company) connecting Tunis to most towns in the country fairly regularly. Or you can travel by *louage* – large, shared taxis – which charge slightly more but are much quicker. Trains cost around the same as a *louage*, but the system isn't very comprehensive and they're often delayed and crowded. Hitching's no problem, though you often have to pay a small contribution; otherwise the best way to go is by bike – you'll need to bring your own.

Costs and currency: Most things – hotels, basic meals and transport – are very cheap in Tunisia and you'll live fairly well on £70 a week, though you could get by on a lot less. Currency is the Tunisian Dinar (TD), the rate around 1 to the £ sterling; confusingly it's often written as 1500TD, instead of 15TD. Travellers' cheques can be exchanged at most banks or hotels, though bank opening hours are fairly limited.

Where to go: Carthage, obviously, just outside Tunis, is a major draw, while the capital itself is no mean attraction: its Medina, the old Arab town, is choc-full of mosques, palaces and markets, and there's a stunning museum of Roman mosaics, the Bardo. The north of the country holds some of the best Roman sites in the world, as well as some spectacular white sand beaches. Kairouan in the east is Tunisia's oldest Arab city, a holy Islamic centre visited for its splendid Great Mosque. Much further south of here, the cave-villages around Matmata are a strange sight; and the oases in the south west, on the edge of the vast Chott salt lake, give an intriguing view of modern Tunisian life.

Eating: Every town has at least one cheap restaurant, serving simple cooked food which is kept warm all day: basic meals are of couscous or pasta with a little meat or fish, and a spicy sauce on top. In bigger cities and tourist resorts there are good-value French restaurants. You'll drink sweet and strong coffee and tea, though home-produced wine is available in some places and is generally excellent.

Sleeping: The cheapest places to stay are always the basic hotels in the Medina area of a town; other options include camping (at sites or on the beaches outside the main tourist areas) and a few youth hostels. Many people also find themselves befriended and asked to spend at least one night with a Tunisian family, an ideal way to meet the people.

Language: French is widely spoken and should get you by without too many problems. Arabic is the main language, but is very difficult to learn.

LANGUAGE

The ability to speak English confers enormous prestige in Sicily, but though there's no shortage of people willing to show off their knowledge, particularly returned *emigrati*, few outside the tourist resorts actually know more than some simple words and phrases – those more often than not culled from pop songs or films.

SOME TIPS

You'd do well to master at least a little **Italian**, a task made more enjoyable by the fact that your halting efforts will often be rewarded by smiles and genuine surprise that an English-speaker should stoop to learn Italian. In any case, it's one of the easiest European languages to learn, especially if you already have a smattering of French or Spanish, both extremely similar grammatically.

Easiest of all is the **pronunciation**, since every word is spoken exactly as it's written, and usually enunciated with exaggerated, open-mouthed clarity. The only difficulties you're likely to encounter are the few **consonants** that are different from English:

c before e or i is pronounced as in **ch**urch, while **ch** before the same vowels is hard, as in **c**at.
sci or **sce** are pronounced as in **sh**eet and **sh**elter respectively. The same goes with **g** – soft before **e** and **i**, as in **g**eranium; hard when followed by h, as in **g**arlic.
gn has the ni sound of our 'o**ni**on'.

gl in Italian is softened to something like li in English, as in sta**lli**on.
h is not aspirated, as in **h**onour.

When **speaking** to strangers, the third person is the polite form (ie *Lei* instead of *Tu* for 'you'); using the second person is a mark of disrespect or stupidity. It's also worth remembering that Italians don't use 'please' and 'thank you' half as much as we do: it's all implied in the tone, though if you're in any doubt, err on the polite side.

All Italian words are **stressed** on the penultimate syllable unless an **accent** (´´ or ``) denotes otherwise, although accents are often left out in practice. Note that the ending **-ia** or **-ie** counts as two syllables, hence *trattoria* is stressed on the i. We've put accents in, throughout the text and below, wherever it isn't immediately obvious how a word should be pronounced: for example, in *Maríttima*, the accent is on the first **i**; conversely *Catania* should theoretically have an accent on the first **a**; other words where we've omitted accents are common ones (like *Isola*, stressed on the I), some names (*Domenico*, *Vittorio*) ,and words that are stressed similarly in English, such as *archeologico* and *Repubblica*.

None of this will help very much if you're confronted with a particularly harsh specimen of the **Sicilian dialect**, which virtually qualifies as a separate language. However, television has made a huge difference and almost every Sicilian can now communicate in something approximating standard Italian.

BASICS

Good morning	*Buon giorno*
Good afternoon/ evening	*Buona sera*
Good night	*Buona notte*
Hello/goodbye	*Ciao* (informal; when speaking to strangers use the phrases above)
Goodbye	*Arrivederci* (formal)
Yes	*Sì*
No	*No*
Please	*Per favore*
Thank you (very much)	*Grázie (molte/mille grazie)*
You're welcome	*Prego*
Alright/that's OK	*Va bene*
How are you?	*Come stai/sta?* (informal/formal)

I'm fine	*Bene*
Do you speak English?	*Parla inglese?*
I don't understand	*Non capisco*
I haven't understood	*Non ho capito*
I don't know	*Non lo so*
Excuse me/sorry (informal)	*Scusa*
Excuse me/sorry (formal)	*Mi scusi/Prego*
Excuse me (in a crowd)	*Permesso*
I'm sorry	*Mi dispiace*
I'm here on holiday	*Sono qui in vacanza*
I'm English/Scottish/ Welsh/Irish	*Sono inglese/scozzese/ gallese/irlandese*
I live in…	*Abito a…*
Today	*Oggi*
Tomorrow	*Domani*
Day after tomorrow	*Dopodomani*
Yesterday	*Ieri*
Now	*Adesso*
Later	*Più tardi*
Wait a minute!	*Aspetta!*
In the morning	*di mattina*
In the afternoon	*nel pomeriggio*
In the evening	*di sera*
Here (there)	*Qui/Là*
Good/bad	*Buono/Cattivo*
Big/small	*Grande/Píccolo*
Cheap/expensive	*Económico/Caro*
Early/late	*Presto/Ritardo*
Hot/cold	*Caldo/Freddo*
Near/far	*Vicino/Lontano*
Vacant/occupied	*Líbero/Occupato*
Quickly/slowly	*Velocemente/ Lentamente*
Slowly/quietly	*Piano*
With/without	*Con/Senza*
More/less	*Più/Meno*
Enough, no more	*Basta*
Mr…	*Signor…*
Mrs…	*Signora…*
Miss…	*Signorina…*

(*il Signor, la Signora, la Signorina* when speaking about someone else)

QUESTIONS AND DIRECTIONS

Where? (where is/ are…?)	*Dove? (Dov'è/Dove sono)*
When?	*Quando?*
What? (what is it?)	*Cosa? (Cos'è?)*
How much/many?	*Quanto/Quanti?*
Why?	*Perché?*

It is/there is (is it/is there…?)	*È/C'è (È/C'è…?)*
What time is it?	*Che ora è/Che ore sono?*
How do I get to…?	*Come arrivo a…?*
How far is it to…?	*Cuant'è lontano a…?*
Can you give me a lift to…?	*Mi può dare un passaggio a…?*
Can you tell me when to get off?	*Mi può dire scendere alla fermata giusta?*
What time does it open?	*A che ora apre?*
What time does it close?	*A che ora chiude?*
How much does it cost (…do they cost?)	*Quanto costa? (Quanto costano?)*
What's it called in Italian?	*Come si chiama in italiano?*
Left/right	*Sinistra/Destra*
Go straight ahead	*Sempre diritto*
Turn to the right/left	*Gira a destra/sinistra*

ACCOMMODATION

Hotel	*Albergo*
Is there a hotel nearby?	*C'è un albergo qui vicino?*
Do you have a room…	*Ha una cámera…*
for one/two/three people	*per una/due/tre person(a/ e)*
for one/two/three nights	*per una/due/tre nott(e/i)*
for one/two weeks	*per una/due settiman(a/e)*
with a double bed	*con un letto matrimoniale*
with a shower/bath	*con una doccia/un bagno*
with a balcony	*con una terrazza*
hot/cold water	*acqua calda/fredda*
How much is it?	*Quanto costa?*
It's expensive	*È caro*
Is breakfast included?	*È compresa la prima colazione?*
Do you have anything cheaper?	*Ha niente che costa di meno?*
Full/half board	*Pensione completa/mezza pensione*
Can I see the room?	*Posso vedere la cámera?*
I'll take it	*La prendo*
I'd like to book a room	*Vorrei prenotare una cámera*
I have a booking	*Ho una prenotazione*
Can we camp here?	*Possiamo fare il campeggio qui?*

Is there a campsite nearby?	C'è un camping qui vicino?
Tent	Tenda
Cabin	Cabina
Youth hostel	Ostello per la gioventù

FINDING THE WAY

Aeroplane	Aeroplano
Bus	Autobus/pullman
Train	Treno
Car	Mácchina
Taxi	Taxi
Bicycle	Bicicletta
Ferry	Traghetto
Ship	Nave
Hydrofoil	Aliscafo
Hitch-hiking	Autostop
On foot	A piedi
Bus station	Autostazione
Railway station	Stazione ferroviaria
Ferry terminal	Stazione maríttima
Port	Porto
A ticket to…	Un biglietto a…
One-way/return	Solo andata/andata e ritorno
Can I book a seat?	Posso prenotare un posto?
What time does it leave?	A che ora parte?
When is the next bus/train/ferry to…?	Quando parte il próssimo pullman/treno/ traghetto per…?
Where does it leave from?	Da dove parte?
Which platform does it leave from?	Da quale binario parte?
Do I have to change?	Devo cambiare?
How many kilometres is it?	Quanti chilómetri sono?
How long does it take?	Quanto ci vuole?
What number bus is it to…?	Que número di autobus per…?

Where's the road to…?	Dov'è la strada a…
Next stop please	La próssima fermata, per favore

SOME SIGNS

Entrance/exit	Entrata/Uscita
Free entrance	Ingresso líbero
Gentlemen/ladies	Signóri/Signore
WC	Gabinetto, bagno
Vacant/engaged	Líbero/Occupato
Open/closed	Aperto/Chiuso
Arrivals/departures	Arrivi/Partenze
Closed for restoration	Chiuso per restauro
Closed for holidays	Chiusò per ferie
Pull/push	Tirare/Spingere
Out of order	Guasto
Drinking water	Acqua potabile
To let	Affítasi
Platform	Binario
Cash desk	Cassa
Go/walk	Avanti
Stop/halt	Alt
Customs	Dogana
Do not touch	Non toccare
Danger	Perícolo
Beware	ttenzione
First aid	Pronto soccorso
Ring the bell	Suonare il campanello
No smoking	Vietato fumare

DRIVING

Parking	Parcheggio
No parking	Divieto di sosta/Sosta vietata
One way street	Senso único
No entry	Senso vietato
Slow down	Rallentare
Road closed/up	Strada chiusa/guasta
No through road	Vietato il transito
No overtaking	Vietato il sorpasso
Crossroads	Incrocio
Speed limit	Límite di Velocità
Traffic light	Semáforo

Best of the **phrasebooks** is *Italian at Your Fingertips* (Routledge £3.95), its words and phrases listed alphabetically. More conventionally, *Travellers' Italian* (Pan £1.50) is divided according to subject. If you're more serious about **learning the language**, then *Teach Yourself Italian* (Hodder & Stoughton £3.95) is a good starting point. The *Oxford English-Italian Mini-Dictionary* is a useful pocket-size **dictionary** (OUP £1.95).

A GLOSSARY OF ARTISTIC AND ARCHITECTURAL TERMS

AGORA Square or market place in an ancient Greek city.

APSE Domed recess at the altar-end of a chucrh.

ARCHITRAVE The lowest part of the entablature.

ATRIUM Forecourt, usually of a Roman house.

BOTHROS A pit which contains votive offerings.

CAMPANILE Bell-tower, sometimes detached.

CAPITAL Top of a column.

CATALAN-GOTHIC Hybrid form of architecture, mixing elements from 15C Spanish and Northern European building styles.

CAVEA The seating section in a theatre.

CELLA Sanctuary of a temple.

CUPOLA A dome.

DECUMANUS The main street in a Roman town.

ENTABLATURE The part of the building above the capital on a classical building.

EX-VOTO Decorated tablet designed as thanksgiving to a saint.

HELLENISTIC PERIOD 325-31 BC (Alexander the Great to Augustus).

HYPOGEUM Underground vault, often used as an early Christian church.

KOUROS Standing male figure of the Archaic Period (700–early 5C BC).

KRATER Ancient conical bowl with round base.

LOGGIA Roofed gallery or balcony.

METOPE A panel on the frieze of a temple.

NAUMACHIA Mock naval combat, or the deep trench in a theatre in which it took place.

NAVE Central space in a church, usually flanked by aisles.

ODEION Small theatre, usually roofed, for recitals.

ORCHESTRA Section of the main floor of a theatre, where the chorus danced.

PANTOCRATOR Usually refers to Christ, portrayed with outstretched arms.

POLYPTYCH Painting or carving on several joined wooden panels.

PORTICO The covered entrance to a building.

PUNIC Carthaginian/Phoenician.

SCENE-BUILDING Structure holding scenerey in Greek/Roman theatre.

STELAE Inscribed stone slabs.

STEREOBATE Visible base of any building, usually a temple.

STOA A detached roofed porch, or portico.

STYLOBATE Raised base of a columned building, usually a temple.

TELAMONE A supporting column in the shape of a male figure.

THERMAE Baths, usually elaborate buildings in Roman villas.

TRYPTYCH Painting or carving on three joined wooden panels.

A GLOSSARY OF ITALIAN WORDS AND ACRONYMS

ITALIAN WORDS

ALISCAFO Hydrofoil.
ANFITEATRO Amphitheatre.
AUTOSTAZIONE Bus station.
AUTOSTRADA Motorway.
BELVEDERE A look-out point.
CAPPELLA Chapel.
CASTELLO Castle.
CENTRO Centre.
CHIESA Church (Chiesa Matrice/Madre, main 'mother' church).
COMUNE An administrative area; also, the local council or the town hall.
CORSO Avenue/boulevard.
DUOMO/CATTEDRALE Cathedral.
ENTRATA Entrance.
FESTA Festival, carnival.
FIUME River.
FUMAROLA Volcanic vapour emission from the ground.
GOLFO Gulf.
LAGO Lake.
LUNGOMARE Seafront promenade or road.
MARE Sea.
MERCATO Market.
MONGIBELLO Italian name for Mount Etna.
MUNICIPIO Town Hall.
PALAZZO Palace, mansion or block (of flats).
PARCO Park.
PASSEGGIATA The customary early evening walk.
PIANO Plain.

PIAZZA Square (or largo, place).
PINETA Pinewood.
SANTUARIO Sanctuary.
SENSO ÚNICO One-way street.
SOTTOPASSAGGIO Subway.
SPIAGGIA Beach.
STAZIONE Station (Railway Station, Stazione Ferroviaria; Ferry Terminal, Stazione Maríttima).
STRADA Road/street.
TEATRO Theatre.
TEMPIO Temple.
TORRE Tower.
TRAGHETTO Ferry.
USCITA Exit.
VIA Road (always used with name; as via Roma).
ZONA Zone.

ACRONYMS

AAST Azienda Autonoma di Soggiorno e Turismo (local tourist office).
ACI Italian Automobile Club.
DC Democrazia Cristiana; the Christian Democrat party.
EPT Ente Provinciale di Turismo (provincial tourist office).
FS Italian State Railways
IVA Imposta Valore Aggiunto (VAT).
MSI Movimento Sociale d'Italia; the Italian Fascist party.
PCI Partito Comunista d'Italia; the Italian Communist Party.
PSI Partito Socialista d'Italia; the Italian Socialist Party.
RAI The Italian state TV and radio network.
SIP Italian state telephone company.
SS Strada Statale; equivalent to British 'A' road; eg SS120.

HELP US UPDATE

We've gone to a lot of effort to ensure that this first edition of the Rough Guide to Sicily is completely up-to-date and accurate. However, things do change – opening hours are notoriously fickle – and any suggestions, comments, or corrections would be much appreciated. We'll credit all contributions, and send a copy of the next edition (or any other Real Guide if you prefer) for the best letters. Send them along to: Rough Guides, 149 Kennington Lane, London SE11 4EZ.

INDEX